TIMETABLE FOR BAKING:

Bread (375°–400°), 40 to 60 minutes

Rolls (375°–400°), 10 to 20 minutes

Sponge cake (325°), 45 to 60 minutes

Plain cake (350°), 30 to 40 minutes

Fruit cake (250°–300°, with a pan of water in the bottom of the oven), 2 to 3 hours

Cookies (375°–400°), 10 to 15 minutes

Bread pudding (325°–350°, set in a pan of water), 1 hour

Rice and tapioca pudding (350°), 1 hour

Indian pudding (325°), 2 to 3 hours

Plum pudding (300°), 2 to 3 hours

Custards (325°, set in a pan of water), 20 minutes

Potatoes (350°–375°), 30 to 45 minutes

Baked beans (250°–300°), 6 to 8 hours

Braised meat (300°–325°), 3 to 4 hours

TIMETABLE FOR BOILING:

Fowl, turkey, veal, 2 to 3 hours

Corned beef, tongue, 3 to 4 hours

Ham, 4 to 5 hours

Fish, 6 to 15 minutes

TIMETABLE FOR FRYING:

Croquettes, 1 minute

Fritters and doughnuts, 3 to 5 minutes

Slices of fish, breaded chops, 4 to 6 minutes

TIMETABLE FOR ROASTING:

Beef, 12 to 15 minutes per pound for rare

   18 to 20 minutes per pound for well-done

Veal, 30 to 35 minutes per pound

Mutton, 15 to 18 minutes per pound, slightly longer for the leg

Lamb, 18 to 20 minutes per pound

Pork, 30 to 35 minutes per pound

Venison, 12 to 15 minutes per pound

Turkey, under 15 pounds, 25 minutes per pound

   over 15 pounds, 15 to 20 minutes per pound

Goose, 25 to 30 minutes per pound

Chicken, 3 to 4 pounds, 1 hour

Duck, 20 to 30 minutes per pound

Rabbit, 20 minutes per pound

Fish, 6 to 8 pounds, 1 hour; small, 20 to 30 minutes

A hot oven = 450°

A quick oven = 375°–400°

A moderate oven = 350°

A slow oven = 300°–325°

HOME MADE

HOME MADE

An Alternative to Supermarket Living

RECIPES FROM THE NINETEENTH CENTURY,

Rescued, Reinterpreted, and Commented Upon by

SANDRA ODDO

Including Also a Wealth of Wisdom Concerning
HOUSEHOLD MANAGEMENT

And a Special Section of
EFFICACIOUS HOME REMEDIES

Galahad Books • New York City

Published by arrangement with Atheneum
ISBN: 0-88365-250-1
Copyright © 1972 by Sandra Oddo
Library of Congress catalog card number 74-77016
Manufactured in the United States of America
Designed by Harry Ford

To ROBERT SCHNELLER, *butcher and friend extraordinary;*
to my sister, MARJORIE WOOD, *for cake baking*
beyond the call of duty;
to CINDY TARVER, *for her typing, thanks.*

And I dedicate HOME MADE *to my husband,* JASPER ODDO,
who ate (almost) everything that was put in front of him
during the testing of this book.

SANDRA ODDO

—◄•►—

Sandra Oddo lives in a comfortable country house rescued from dereliction and rebuilt largely by her own hands. Its root cellar bursts with her own produce, its canning shelves are loaded with her own preserves, and its cabinets are filled with her own home-made preparations for housekeeping and good health. Born in the Midwest and educated in the East, she has lived in or traveled through most of the United States, Europe, and Latin America. *Life*, *Newsweek*, *The Village Voice*, *The Christian Science Monitor*, and the Los Angeles *Times* are among the publications Mrs. Oddo has written for. She is a free-lance writer—and an incomparably good cook.

CONTENTS

—◆—

Part I. *The Cook's Education in Old and New Ways*

1. *Introduction*   3
2. *Utensils, Old and New*   9
3. *Processes*   14

Part II. *Recipes: Food According to Its Seasons*

4. *January*   45
    BREAD; YEAST; MORE OR LESS QUICK BREADS; ROLLS,
    MUFFINS, BISCUITS; CRACKERS; DOUGHNUTS AND FRIED
    CAKES; PANCAKES AND WAFFLES; PASTRY,
    NOODLES; DRIED BEANS, PEAS; DRIED FRUITS

5. *February*   86
    INVALIDS' DISHES; INFANTS' DISHES; PUDDINGS AND
    CREAMS; MAPLE SUGAR

6. *March*   102
    MILK AND CREAM; BUTTER; CHEESE AND CHEESE DISHES;
    SHAD

7. *April*   116
    VEAL; INNARDS; VEAL SOUPS; LAMB; KID; SALMON

8. *May*   142
    RHUBARB; ASPARAGUS; WATERCRESS; DANDELIONS; POKE;
    PRIMROSES; TROPICAL FRUITS; SHELLFISH; SALT-WATER FISH;
    FRESH-WATER FISH; FISH SOUPS

[vii]

Contents

9. *June* 182
WEDDING CAKES; JUNE VEGETABLES; STRAWBERRIES;
WALNUTS; ROSES; CANDIED FLOWERS; ICE CREAM; SHERBETS

10. *July* 201
BERRIES; BANANAS; JULY PICKLES; JULY VEGETABLES;
TURTLES; SALT FISH

11. *August* 228
EGGS; PICKLES; AUGUST VEGETABLES; MELONS; MUSHROOMS;
AUGUST FRUITS; ELDERBERRIES; NASTURTIUMS; FROGS

12. *September* 262
CHICKEN; OYSTERS; TOMATOES; CARROTS; CELERY; PEARS;
GRAPES

13. *October* 290
GOOSE; DUCK; RABBIT; SQUIRREL; GAME BIRDS; APPLES;
CIDER; QUINCES; POTATOES; GREEN TOMATOES; CABBAGE;
CAULIFLOWER; EARTH VEGETABLES; LEEKS AND ONIONS;
PUMPKINS; NUTS

14. *November* 337
BEEF; STOCKS, GRAVIES, SOUPS; INNARDS; PRESERVED BEEF;
MUTTON; PORK; VENISON; TURKEY; CRANBERRIES;
FRUITCAKE; THANKSGIVING DISHES

15. *December* 401
CITRUS FRUITS; CAKES; ICINGS; RAISIN, NUT, AND CITRON
CAKES; COOKIES; CANDY; CHRISTMAS DISHES; BEVERAGES

16. *Staples* 436

Part III. *The Care of House and Body*

17. *Remedies* 453
18. *Household Hints* 458
    Glossary 466
    Bibliography 472
    Index 477

PART I

The Cook's Education in Old and New Ways

[1]

Introduction

This book is a collection of recipes from the peak years of one of the world's great cooking styles: nineteenth-century American. It was an era of great eating so remote from us now that the very memory of it is gone, lost beyond the cultural shock that rattled cooks loose from their mothers' generation when the scientific revolution, somewhat belatedly, hit the kitchen. We have acquired refrigerators and gas stoves, we were introduced to bacteria by name, we discovered that the balanced diet contained fats, proteins, and carbohydrates (though what we made of the discovery can be deduced from the starch-heavy cookbooks of the twenties and thirties), and we realized, as markets converted to supermarkets, that we really didn't have to do all that work. But something valuable got misplaced: several centuries of observation and experiment and eating experience.

Nineteenth-century American cooking had personality. It was full of robust flavors and surprise associations of taste (fricasseed rabbit, for instance, in which the mushrooms are small explosions of Madeira in the middle of the sauce), but it was also capable of the finest subtleties. The meats and vegetables are generally honest and straightforward, but the gravies are as delicate as cream sauces, the puddings range from exquisite simplicity to very complex splendor, and the bread . . . ah, well, the bread.

The style was eclectic. Good nineteenth-century cooks picked up and used many tricks of French cooks—thickening sauces, for instance, with a roux made of flour and butter rubbed together—but where much fine French cooking originated under the thrifty Gallic compulsion to make odds and ends and substandard food into something edible, fine American cooks started with first-class ingredients. The results are sometimes spectacular.

But above all, nineteenth-century American cooking was practical and it was healthful. The housewife in the 1800s was running a household that was far more dependent on natural abundance, far less reliant on industrial food processing than the average kitchen today. A hundred years ago nearly *everything* was home made, and not much went to waste. The meat from the stockpot, if it wasn't eaten with the soup, made mincemeat; the stock inspired other dishes; the leftovers turned into forcemeat balls to adorn bisques or bouillabaisse; and the grease skimmed from the top of the pot, or dripped from the roast, eventually became soap or candles.

The recipes that follow are word for word as they were then. Granting, of course, the ability of the cook, most of those home products are superior in quality to much that can be bought in the stores now. The absence of a standard for comparison has perhaps allowed industrial food processers to slip.

The nineteenth century marks a turning point in cooking, as it does in art (the Impressionists), music (Schoenberg), drama (Alfred Jarry), industry (the Industrial Revolution), social thought (Karl Marx), and science (pick a name, almost any name). It was the kitchen stove that did it. The man who invented it was an American, Benjamin Thompson, born in Rumford, Massachusetts, in 1753. He fought brilliantly on the wrong side in the American Revolution, and left the country, exiled, at the end of the war. He settled in Bavaria, where the emperor Maximilian put him to work to improve the eating fare of the Bavarian peasant. There, in 1789, he constructed the first kitchen stove.

It was basically a firebox which heated water in pots set into it. Cooking was done, double-boiler fashion, in the pots of boiling water. It had obvious disadvantages—it couldn't bake or heat above the boiling point of water—but it saved tremendous amounts of fuel and space. Maximilian made Thompson a count for it and for his other culinary contributions. Thompson, whose petitions to be allowed to return to the United States were consistently refused, chose the designation "Count Rumford." He died in France, still in exile, in 1814.

For the next sixty years, kitchens around the world were in an uproar. The range of ranges was diverse and highly controversial: "A chimney fireplace or grate is preferable to a stove, which is apt to give the air a close or disagreeable smell and produce headache or stupor." True enough, when charcoal or kerosene supplied the heat—and the fumes. Most stoves did one thing well and skimped on others, and everybody had an opinion as to which was the best: "Stoves of brick or earthenware," for instance, "used in various parts of

Europe, are said to be better than iron." "Don't make a mistake in buying untried experiments," cried the Standard Lighting Company, as late as 1894. "This is the fifth year for the 'New Process' stove . . . our line is unequalled." For a while, trading in your range every couple of years was a status symbol equaled only later on by Detroit and the two-year car cycle. In 1837, "A Lady" could declaim in her *Housekeeper's Book:* "The fireplace of a kitchen is a matter of great importance. I have not, it is certain, been so circumstanced as to witness the operations of *many* of the newly invented steam kitchens and cooking apparatus which the last twenty years have produced, but those which I have seen have failed to give me satisfaction. To say the truth, the inventors of cast-iron kitchens [stoves] seem to me to have had every other object in view, but that of promoting good cooking. It is certainly desirable and proper that every *possible* saving should be made in the consumption of fuel; but I am sure it is *not possible* to have cooking to perfection without a proper degree of heat and, as far as my observation has gone, meat cannot be well roasted unless it be before a good fire." By 1898, when Mrs. Moritz and Miss Kahn wrote the *The Twentieth Century Cook-Book,* instructions universally read, "move the pot to a cooler part of the range."

Sixty years. A short time in which to undo a thousand years or so of habits in an area as important—and as universal—as eating is. Most of the other nineteenth-century revolutions we have tended to call "progress." And the kitchen revolution is, too, but perhaps not entirely. In the name of making the housewife's lot an easier one (which it has done, of course), "progress" has degraded her position as manager of a complex and difficult operation from skilled, respected labor to a job that women feel vaguely they must apologize for—"I'm just a housewife"—something less than engrossing, less than admired, and far less than satisfying.

Food, once a year-long cycle full of interesting little surprises, demanding knowledge and expertise, is now a weekly trip to the supermarket for groceries that I find it hard to imagine ever grew under a hot sun.

It is pointless, and a little silly, to cry for a return to the good old days. They weren't that good. Kitchens were once built outside the main house so that nobody but the cook had to stand the heat of the fireplace in mid-August. Clothes were washed once a winter because the process of getting the fuel, boiling the water, beating them out on washboards—which was necessary because they were so seldom washed—and trying to deal with stains and soil in non-color-fast fabrics, in unheated houses, in the midst of ice and snow, was excruciating. When it is a matter of sheer necessity, pickling the summer's supply of meat because there is no other way to keep it isn't all that much fun.

But the nineteenth century is still full of tricks that can improve the quality of our twentieth-century lives. I have tried to include the best and the most interesting or unusual recipes in the following pages, along with words of wisdom, in their own words, from some of the more charming experts. And there are a few extras.

Most of the old books had sections of home medicines and household products. So does this new one: home cures and home cleaners, waxes, polishes, paints, and hints for turning housework into . . . well, nearly . . . play. The trick is the use of common sense and a few staples like salt, baking soda, old newspapers—all things less harmful to the sewage system than the merest laundry tub full of enzyme detergent, and, some of them, equally effective.

I have included recipes that, at first thought, might seem a little pointless now—recipes for curing hams, for making molasses, for pressing cheese, for jerking beef—for three reasons. First, the processes themselves have been edited out of cookbooks year by year. No doubt the editing is sensible. Bread, which took up twenty-five pages in the front of *Fannie Farmer* as recently as 1921 (in a section that ended "aerated bread . . . is a product of the bakers' skill, but has found little favor except in a few localities") is now relegated to five pages, buried in the middle of the book by that same bakers' skill. All our bread is aerated. But the processes themselves are interesting, and often are still practical, and should not be lost. What book, for instance, will tell you how to dry apples for the winter? What will you do if you have an overflowing apple tree and a Calvinist hatred for waste?

Second, this book is not just a collection of novel recipes, but the beginning of a different approach to the whole subject of food. Bulk buying, dealing with seasonal foods, was once a necessity. It is now an economy and an aesthetic pleasure. A jar of home-canned peaches *tastes* better than store-bought ones; it costs less because you don't bother to can them unless it is the middle of peach season, when prices are down (even city-dwellers can take advantage of seasons, by buying in bulk, perhaps in cooperation with friends, at wholesale markets); and for those of us who read the small-print lists of ingredients on commercial cans with horror, there is a good deal of satisfaction in being able to pronounce the name of everything that went into those peaches.

Following this approach leads naturally to a recipe book arranged by seasons (in the Northeast) rather than by classes of cookery. It can also lead to a weekly shopping list that might consist merely of, say, 25 pounds of flour, 4 pounds of on-sale butter, some milk, lettuce, and eggs, and half a bushel of beans. The beginning of a fine laziness.

And that leads naturally to the third reason for including, for instance, lard making and rosewater and dandelion beer. People seem to be drifting back toward the land, trying to reclaim some of the responsibility they long ago delegated to anonymous bakeries and corporations of food handlers. And whether it happens by accident or in full consciousness, a rosebush, a field full of dandelions, one's own pig, and a desire for self-sufficiency do make certain connections within us. Soon we need recipes.

These are the original recipes, *verbatim*, from the old books. Although the style in which they are written is occasionally curious, the recipes are not curiosities. Every one is workable. Where usages or ingredients have changed, I have tried to put translations or comments within the recipes in italics. Translations of measurements can be found on the end papers, and unfamiliar terms are defined in the Glossary at the end.

All the "about a cup"s and "take a pinch"es are still here, because that is the way I cook, and the way most of the good cooks I know do things. Few people driven to creation in the kitchen are happy unless they can try improvements on the recipes they use, in spite of the 1920s mania for science that still has us measuring down to the ⅛ teaspoonful. And besides, the old directions and measurements are not that haphazard. A pinch, for instance, is what can be picked up between the thumb and first two fingers, an amount that does not differ much from person to person.

The nineteenth century allows for individual tastes and foibles. In fact, it demands them. The basic assumption in the minds of most cookbook writers in the 1800s was almost a mirror image of that which most twentieth-century writers seem to hold. We assume that you want to make, say, *boeuf bourguignon*, and therefore we make up a list of ingredients for you to go out and buy. The nineteenth-century writer assumes that you have some beef, and you want to decide what to do with it. Therefore, the recipe will start "Take some beef. . . ." What follows is usually logical, explicit, and adaptable to whatever amount of beef you have.

I find the old attitude far more comfortable to work with, since I usually buy what looks good, what is in season, or what is on sale, and then come home to my cookbooks. "It is well to be particular in receipts; but it is idle to put out of sight the fact that particulars vary every day, in every country, and in every household. The quantity to be used, therefore, must continually vary. Everybody knows that vegetables are not alike in flavor; some apples are comparatively tasteless, as are some carrots, and one lemon is sharper than another." (Septimus Berdmore, *The Principles of Cookery*, 1887)

I have tried to make up for what is skimped in directions with a chapter on basic processes, where you will find general rules for the production of cakes, bread, pickles, wine, etc.

[7]

Part I: The Cook's Education

Some of these recipes, perhaps, will be of no immediate use to city-dwellers. Dealing with bushels of tomatoes at a time does take a certain amount of space. But making soap takes very little, uses materials that would otherwise be thrown away, and produces a perfectly adequate, less-polluting product. Home-made bread is a beautiful sight on any table, and home-made candles are far more impressive (and cheaper) than those supplied by a store.

So this is a book for those of us who love good food, who are trying to lessen our dependence on the supermarket system and to reclaim the responsibilities we relinquished to it, for those of us with gardens or those of us who, in the city, care to take a little extra effort to have better, better-tasting food. And, quite frankly, it is for those of us who are just natural-born putterers in the kitchen.

⌈ 2 ⌉

Utensils, Old & New

Utensils necessary in the kitchen of a small family
(FROM Elisabeth S. Miller, *In the Kitchen*, 1875)

WOODENWARE: One bread board; one rolling pin; one small spoon for stirring pudding sauce; two large spoons; one potato pounder; one lemon squeezer; one wash board.

TINWARE: One boiler for clothes holding six gallons; one boiler for boiling a ham; one bread-pan holding five or six quarts; one deep pan for preserving and canning fruits; four milk pans; two dish pans; two two-quart basins; two one-pint basins; two two-quart covered pails; a fourteen-quart covered pail; two tin-lined saucepans with covers, holding four quarts each, for boiling potatoes, cabbage, etc.; two tin-lined saucepans with covers, holding two quarts each, for vegetables that do not require much room, like okra, rice, tomatoes; two cups with handles; two pint moulds for rice, blanc-mange, etc.; four half-pint moulds; one skimmer with handle; two dippers of different size; two funnels, one for jugs and one for cruets; one quart measure; one pint measure; half-pint measure; one gill measure; three scoops of different sizes; four bread-pans for baking (the smallest make the best sized loaves and will do for cake also); four jelly-cake pans; four round and two long pie-pans; one coffee pot; one colander; one large bread-grater; one small nutmeg grater; two wire sieves, one twelve inches across and one four inches; one wire cloth sieve, for sifting salt; one small hair sieve, for straining jelly; one frying basket; two egg beaters; one apple corer; one cake turner; one spice box; one pepper box; one cake cutter; one potato cutter; one dozen muffin rings; one soap shaker.

IRONWARE: One copper saucepan; one pair of scales; one pot holding two gallons, with steamer to fit; one pot holding three gallons with close-fitting covers, for soup; one preserving kettle; one tea-kettle; one fish-kettle; one large frying pan; one small frying pan; two sheet-iron dripping pans of different sizes; two sets of gem pans; two spoons with long handles; two spoons with handles of moderate length; two spoons with wooden handles; one griddle; one gridiron; one waffle iron; one toasting rack; one large meat-fork; one jagging iron; one can opener.

EARTHEN AND STONEWARE: Two crocks, holding one gallon each; two crocks holding two quarts; one bean-pot; one bowl holding six quarts; one bowl holding four quarts; one bowl holding three quarts; one bowl holding two quarts; two holding one pint each; one nest of six baking dishes of different sizes.

And that's before you get to the dishes and silverware.

It isn't that bad. Most twentieth-century kitchens are perfectly adequate for cooking in the nineteenth century, with the addition of a couple of nonstandard items.

That miracle, the kitchen stove, marks the main difference between our kitchens and those of our great-grandmothers. Most of it is in our favor. I want a quick oven? Set the dial for 375°. I want to sear, simmer, or sauté? No problem: turn the knob. A little adventure may be gone, a little chance to demonstrate nonchalant skill. But I can do without sticking my arm into the oven and counting until I can't bear the heat any longer in order to determine the temperature.

The only other major difference between a nineteenth-century kitchen and a modern one is space—and not space in the kitchen. With overhead cabinets and lazy susans, sinks that carry the water away in skinny little pipes rather than bulky tubs, and a stove instead of a fireplace or a coal range, and far fewer, more compact utensils, we probably have as much or more storage space in the kitchen as any nineteenth-century woman had.

But besides her kitchen dresser, her jam cupboard, her pie safe and corner cabinet and sideboard and china closet, even in the city, she had an entire pantry for storing dishes and drying soap and candles. She had a storeroom, always, even in the city (she needed it, of course: she also had half the year's food supply on hand at once, and maybe half a cow). In the country, she had either a cellar where the carrots and turnips and pickled pork and hams were kept, or a springhouse with earth heaped up around the walls to keep it from freezing in winter. She had an attic for dried apples and nuts and dried peas.

We have resigned most of that to the supermarket, and food procuring has become a weekly rather than a yearly cycle. Yet, with one extra cabinet, it is possible to reverse the pattern—and reversing the pattern has these satisfactions: you eat better, you pay less for it, you know what went into it, and you have in your own control more of the responsibility for your own life.

The extra cabinet is for a small canner and for jars, for a 25-pound sack of bread-making flour, for the big breadboard to knead it on, for a set of *large* mixing bowls, for an electric mixer and a blender, and for the self-indulgence of pots, those old crocks or new French enamel casseroles that aren't essential but that make the necessary job of cooking pleasant as well.

The jars you use in the canner can go just as well in the space where the store-bought cans used to be. The home-made bread goes where the plastic store-bought bread used to be kept. The dried peas will keep in a muslin bag in the cabinet—or hung overhead if you want to be showy about it.

For most of the rest of the functions of the springhouse and cellar, a large freezer is an improvement. A refrigerator freezer really will not serve. Not enough space, for one thing—and to store it a long time, meat must be kept frozen around zero degrees, lower than most refrigerator freezers can get. But there is no reason why a neat fifteen-cubic-foot freezer, with a cover over it, can't serve as a sideboard in a city apartment. Its cost will be repaid by the first winter's savings in meat alone.

A couple of pieces of modern kitchen equipment seem ordained for use in old cookery. The electric blender replaces and surpasses the colander and hair sieve in many of their uses. In some cases, it even outdoes muslin as a medium for straining, for puréing, for chopping up, and for ensuring that everything is smooth, fine, and aesthetically homogeneous.

THE ELECTRIC MIXER does away with the incredible labor that used to go into cake baking. Instead of having to "roll out the butter and sugar" with a rolling pin, again and again, we cream in a mixer. Instead of beating "the eggs an hour and a half," we whip them to soft or stiff peaks, as needed, in minutes. Instead of whisking the icing for the *entire time* it takes the cake to bake, we can flip a switch. In fact, there is very little that the old whisk (the rotary egg beater was a newfangled gadget of the late 1800s) and the well-developed housewife's arm did that can't be done as well or better with an electric mixer. Exceptions: some sauces, some custards, puddings, and icings.

A KITCHEN SCALE is almost, but not quite, an essential to a nineteenth-century kitchen (or to a really dedicated French kitchen, for that matter). Most of the recipes measure ingredients of more than a cup by the pound. But conversion isn't that difficult, should you not have a scale. See the tables on the end papers.

As far as I'm concerned, cast-iron skillets—the old "spiders"—are still the best frying pans available. They have been made in almost their present

[11]

form since the late 1600s, when the discovery of bog iron (nuggets of pure iron found free in swampy places) gave New World housewives their first alternative to woodenware or clay. Properly seasoned, they are as stick-resistant as Teflon, and their heat-distributing properties are almost as good as those of copper.

The care of cast iron: Before you use a new pan, rub it with salt and heat it in a 450° oven for half an hour, then dump out the salt and grease the pan well with lard or bacon grease and return it to the oven for another half hour. Let it cool and wipe it out with a dry rag (*not* a damp sponge). Thereafter, *never* wash it with soap or detergent or Brillo or any other solvent. After use, rinse well with *very hot* water, use a nonmetallic scratcher to remove crusts, and wipe dry or heat briefly on the stove to evaporate the water.

The seasoning improves with age and use. My favorite skillet hasn't seen soap for more than five years, wouldn't dream of allowing anything to stick, and is far easier to care for than my Teflon pan. If by accident (a helpful but unknowledgeable guest dishwasher, for instance) the seasoning is undone, repeat the original treatment.

Stone crocks are invaluable—and, unfortunately, are usually expensive. They were made in all sizes, from a pint for salt, usually kept within reach of the stove, to 15 or 16 gallons (the size is stamped in the glaze on the outside), for the year's salted meats or apples. The early Dutch ones, gray stone with blue glaze design, are now antique collectors' items. Junk/antique shops get good prices for most of the miscellaneous ones, too. Pick them up when you can.

Those with cracks are no good. Whatever you do in them, the liquid will seep into the crack and flavor whatever you do after that. Test for cracks by giving the crock a good thump. It should give you back a clear "bong." A "thunk" means it is flawed somewhere.

A caution: Do not put acids—pickles, tomatoes, fruit—into a crock unless you are absolutely sure the glaze contains no lead. Be particularly suspicious of gray glazes. Brown ones are usually okay.

Old-style crocks are still made in beige and brown (by law, with lead-free glazes). They are usually available in hardware stores or restaurant-supply places. The only difference between them and the old ones, for the cook's purpose, is the aura.

Measuring cups and measuring spoons are devices born of the early twentieth-century mania for science in all things. They're helpful. But a tablespoon, a dessertspoon (those things that are sold as soup spoons in stainless-steel sets today), and a teaspoon, a teacup and a coffee cup (more likely a mug, nowadays) will work just as well.

2: Utensils, Old & New

Wooden spoons may just be the oldest utensils in the world; flattened sticks to stir the sabertooth-tiger stew. I don't understand how any twentieth-century housewife can operate without them. They float in the boiling ragout, cool to the touch. They blend the stiffest fruitcake batter without lacerating the hand that holds them. Only the most determined stirring of bread dough can snap their handles—and then, who cares? A replacement costs a quarter.

A couple of yards of muslin, bleached or unbleached, very inexpensive, readily available in any fabric shop, is very useful. A square of muslin placed inside a sieve makes clearer soup, better jelly, finer lard. For polishing, nothing is better than a pad of wadded-up muslin. And you need it for encasing hams or fancy baked meat. It was once a standard kitchen accouterment, and many of the recipes that follow call for its use.

It is washable, reusable, has wet strength, soaks up spills like magic, costs less than what is at your grocer's, is—if you really want to dispose of it—disposable. It makes paper toweling superfluous for use in cooking, and a ridiculous expense.

That's all. Salamanders, hair sieves, gridirons, and cake hoops all have their modern equivalents, as I have tried to indicate in the recipes. Translation across a hundred years is not difficult.

[3]

Processes

Because the old books rarely bother to go into cooking details—which, of course, every woman knows—and because this book is arranged to take advantage of the seasons of food instead of the class of cooking (in September, for example, there are recipes for apple pudding, apple wine, apple pie, apple sauce, dried apples, etc.), a chapter on basic processes is necessary: the order and manner in which ingredients are combined, the normal cooking heat and length of time, the tricks, and some of the reasons behind the methods. It is a primer for the not-too-novice cook and a guide on which the cook can base a judgment of the more unusual recipes.

BASIC BREAD MAKING

Bread making is the homely art of mixing flour and liquid and yeast together and coming up with an edible loaf. All bread recipes are fairly simple variations on the theme.

3: Processes

THE INGREDIENTS

Wheat grains come in three layers, the outer bran, then the gluten, then the starch. To make flour out of wheat means getting rid of more or less of the outer layers and pulverizing the grains to the required degree of fineness. The more of the outside there is left—the gluten is highest in vitamins and minerals—the browner the flour will be. Flour is now a good deal finer than it was in the nineteenth century, when all flour was crushed or ground, not granulated as it now can be, but there is no real substitution problem. The plainer the flour or the less refined it is, the better it will work in old recipes.

Wheat flour, rye, or cornmeal, or even potatoes or oatmeal, can be substituted for a part or all of the white flour in order to vary the flavor.

"Good flour adheres to the hand, and, when pressed tightly, remains in shape and shows the imprint of the lines of the skin on the hand. It has a yellowish-white tinge, and when made into a paste with water, and well worked, is tough and elastic. Select it carefully, and use one kind for all purposes—cakes, pastry, and bread. It is a mistaken idea that the flour which makes good bread will not make good pastry." (Mrs. Rorer, *The Philadelphia Cook Book*, 1886)

The yeast is the clue to the difference between bread and glue. It is a charming little plant that lives by eating up sugar and giving off carbon dioxide and alcohol. If you want it to help make wine, you arrange to have the carbon dioxide escape; for bread, you trap the carbon dioxide and drive the alcohol off with the heat of the oven. Yeast dies in heat, and goes dormant in cold, but it basks and thrives in a pleasant warmth. In bread making, you try to fill its simple needs, to let it go joyously to work. The bread dough, with its working yeast, should be kept where the temperature is an even 75° to 80°. It can be left in a cooler place, 60° to 70°, if you intend to let it rise overnight.

Yeast was often home made, and therefore liquid, in the nineteenth century. One-half cup of home-made yeast equals 1 package of dried yeast, dissolved in ½ cup of warm water. One package is adequate to deal with 8 to 12 cups of flour. Beyond that, add another package.

The liquid for bread can be lukewarm water, milk, the whey from cheese making, the water potatoes were boiled in, or even a little stale beer (in which case the flour should be rye and it should be sponged). Milk and beer must be scalded, then cooled to lukewarm. Two cups of liquid will usually be enough for 2 pounds of flour.

Salt is necessary to flavor bread. Other variations are optional. Sugar (or honey or molasses), by feeding the yeast, will help the bread to be light as well as sweeter. Shortening—lard or butter—will give you a moister bread. Caraway or dill or poppy seeds are adornments.

THE PROCESS

There are two schools of thought on bread mixing. Either you add the flour to the liquid, or the liquid to the flour. If you add the flour to the liquid, it is done this way: Mix together the lukewarm liquid, salt, sugar, melted shortening, or whatever in a large bowl; add the yeast, dissolved in a little warm water; begin to stir in unsifted flour. If you are sponging it (see below), you will add a little more flour than there is liquid (3 cups of flour to 2 cups of liquid, say), to make a thickish batter, and let it rise for a couple of hours before you finish adding the flour. Stir with a wooden spoon—metal ones with their short handles can't take it toward the end and wreak havoc on your fingers. When it gets too stiff to stir, flour the kneading board (tabletop, counter, etc.—but a big breadboard or a marble slab is best) heavily and turn the dough out on it, sprinkling it with flour, and begin to knead.

If you add the liquid to the flour—the old way—it is done thus: Put more flour than you think you will need into a very large container. Make a hollow in it, pressing the flour against the sides. Pour the liquid, combined with the yeast and other ingredients, into the hollow. Stir the liquid round and round—do *not* stir in the flour, but blend in what adheres to the liquid (if you are sponging it, stir until the liquid acquires the consistency of heavy batter, then put the whole thing in a warm place for several hours); continue stirring with a wooden spoon until the whole lump of dough can be lifted out by the spoon; put it on the heavily-floured kneading board. It is easier to deal with very large masses of dough by this method, and your bowl at the end isn't as messy.

"Sponging" is an extra, pre-kneading step that gives the yeast a headstart on the process, by allowing it to multiply. It results in a lighter, fluffier bread, but it takes more attention. Mix a little less than a third of the flour into all the liquid, until you have a batter somewhat thicker than pancake batter. Leave it in a cool place overnight, or in a warm place for 2 or 3 hours, to work; then proceed to stir in the rest of the flour and knead. Sponged bread needs less time to double in bulk after kneading—4 or 5 hours, or less, will do it.

Kneading has this purpose: it coats every molecule of flour evenly with water, which gives bread an elastic texture and allows the yeast to work evenly, so you won't end up with leaden bread full of huge air pockets. Kneading is done by pushing and poking and pulling the dough around, meanwhile gradually adding what flour the bread wants to absorb. I find the easiest motion is to push it from me with the heels of my hands, then roll it together and toward me with the tips of my fingers, turning the mass 90° every couple of pushes. Add flour to the board, not the bread, as needed—and only as much as needed. At first that will be a half-handful every few minutes, but toward the end, just a light dusting should do it. Nobody can tell you when bread has been kneaded enough. It's a feeling your hands have to learn. Try, first, kneading a batch made with 3 to 4 pounds of flour for 10 or 15 minutes. It should be responding then. It should give with kneading instead of lying there in a lump. The surface smooths out, it needs less and less flour to keep it from sticking to the board, and finally, it will not stick when there is no flour on the board at all. By then, the surface should be slightly glossy and should feel, as all the recipe books put it, "satiny"—or as a friend describes it, "like a baby's bottom."

Wheat- and rye-bread dough will never reach that state. They should be just slightly tacky when they have been kneaded enough, but still not sticking to the board. They feel heavier than white-bread dough.

The point of kneading is to make the grain of the bread finer. I find it a soothing way to get rid of hostilities (especially in combination with good music on the stereo), but it is not everybody's idea of relaxation. To knead too much is almost impossible and the only penalty for kneading too little is a dough that is a little more difficult to handle and a somewhat tougher bread that lets the butter drip through. Knead until you feel that it has been kneaded enough, or until you're sick of it, then stop.

Put the bread to rise covered with a towel, in something big enough to allow it to double in size. A stone crock or a thick-sided bowl helps it maintain a steady temperature in rising. Set it in a warm place—though the longer you intend to leave it, the cooler the temperature can be. If you set it overnight, room temperature is warm enough. You can hurry it some by setting it over a radiator or in the open door of a 200° oven, but if you push too fast, it will be sour.

The bread rises because the yeasts are converting wheat sugar into carbon dioxide. By the time the dough has doubled in bulk, the yeasts will have used up almost all the available sugar. If it is allowed to sit too much longer, the yeasts will use it all and the dough will turn sour. (If this should happen, a little soda kneaded in with a little more flour may help—but it's easier just to deal with it at the right time.) When the dough has doubled, dump it out of the bowl and shape it into loaves, kneading it as little as possible (a fold in the dough at this point will remain in the finished bread). Put it aside (in loaf pans, if you are making loaves), covered, to double again, about an hour.

Then bake it according to the directions given.

Normal bread baking is done at 375°–400°, for about 1 hour. When bread is done, it shrinks from the sides of the pan, and if you thump it, it sounds hollow.

BASIC COOKING METHODS

ROASTING

In the old days, large meats were roasted on a spit in an open fireplace perhaps four or five feet in height and about two feet deep. The spit for roasting would go across the fire and often there was a series of notches on the wall of the fireplace to hold it at varying heights from the flame. The laborious and constant hand power needed to turn the spit in the 1700s gave way in the 1800s to a series of ingenious mechanical devices which culminated in the automatic roasting jack, which used the rising hot air of the fire to turn a fan set into the masonry of the chimney. A rod projected from the fan through the wall over the mantelpiece. On the end of the rod was a grooved spool from which hung an endless chain. There was another grooved spool in the end of the spit which, when inserted in the loop of the chain, caused the spit to turn. Simple, yes? The roasting meat would have been protected from drafts by a meat screen set before the fire.

Birds or smaller roasts were done in various prototypes of reflector ovens (called "American ovens" then). The best one for birds, apparently, was the bottle jack, which looked like a milk can cut in half. The bird was hung from a spit that dangled from the top and could be turned by a metal loop.

Of all forms of cooking, roasting has changed the most. Now, a roast is baked meat. The usual temperature for baking it is 325°, since hotter temperatures tend to dry it out (though some people start roast beef at 450° and lower the temperature to 350° after about 20 minutes, a method I have never been able to make work). Do not salt it before you put it in, as that tends to draw the juices out. Let a good roast—beef or mutton or leg of lamb—rest for 10 minutes or so after you take it out of the oven, so that when you cut it, the juice will not run out after the knife. I find timing the cooking (see end papers) and checking the looks of the meat more reliable than meat thermometers, but I suspect that is a matter of prejudice rather than wisdom.

Thinner cuts, like breast of veal, will take less time per pound than the table indicates.

BROILING

There is nothing but a rack or a grill between the fire and the broil-ee when you are broiling. Meat, fish, poultry, or cheese, it is all the same thing, and the only difference between the nineteenth and the twentieth century is that in the nineteenth the fire for broiling was usually a hardwood fire in a fireplace, under the food to be broiled, while now, unless we are cooking outside, the fire of the broiler tends to be above the food.

The point is to seal the surface of the food with intense heat, so that it cooks with all its juices inside a heat-produced crust. Chicken and white meat take longer to broil than red meat—partly because they should be rather well done—and should be broiled at a greater distance from the heat once they are seared. For dry meats and for fish, the bars of the grill should be greased to prevent sticking. Excess fat should be trimmed from fatty meat to discourage grease-flares, and once the surface is sealed, it can be basted to keep the meat from charring. It should be turned only once, and the side you want to look prettiest broiled last. Experience is the best guide to judging done-ness, since the surface does not change color much once it is sealed, but if you touch red meat quickly and it resists your finger, chances are that it is about ready.

Meat more than an inch and a half thick, or inexpensive meat, is rarely cooked this way.

BRAISING

Food cooked in a tightly covered pot, with little or no water, in a slow oven or over a very low flame, is braised. The idea is to get it to cook in its own juices, a method very effective with middle-grade cuts of meat.

Beef or mutton should be moistened with stock or marinade (or marinated first), then seared in hot fat. Put whatever else you want into the pot but do not add liquid (or, if you feel you really must, add less than a half cup). Close the pot, and if it does not close tightly, seal it with a flour and water paste. Bake it in a 300° oven, or on an asbestos pad over the lowest flame you can keep lit, for about half again as long as you would if you were stewing or roasting.

Poultry (whole) and large fish should have a very little liquid, never more than a cup, added before you braise them. Most braised dishes call for vegetables, which provide about as much liquid as is necessary. Very fresh, very young vegetables are good braised with butter, no liquid, for slightly less time than you would normally cook them.

FRYING

In nineteenth-century terminology, "frying" usually means "deep frying." Frying as we usually think of it today is sautéing or browning.

"The ordinary way of frying in a shallow pan with only a little fat, which the French call sautéing, answers very well for some purposes, but nearly everything that requires any more fat than just enough to keep it from sticking, is much better *immersed* in hot fat. Fish balls, chops, and oysters are more quickly cooked and absorb less fat when fried by immersion than when sautéed. Some people are extremely unwilling to make the change, and persist in going on in the old way of cooking with a little half-hot fat which spatters over stove and floor, soaks into the fish or meat, and is often served as the only gravy. Upon such, dyspepsia is a fell avenger." (*Mrs. Lincoln's Boston Cook Book*, 1896)

The fat should be deep enough to cover whatever is being fried—and the pan should be deep enough to keep in the splatters, at least two inches above the level of the boiling fat. When the fat is the proper temperature for the cooking to be done, it should seal the surface of the food at once, so that cooking is done with the heat of the oil without absorbing it. (You can check the temperature of the fat by putting in a small piece of bread: if it fries crisp in a little more than a minute, it is ready for shellfish, larger pieces of meat, chicken; if it takes 50–60 seconds, it is ready for watery foods, potatoes, anything with bread-crumbs; if the bread browns in 35–45 seconds, the fat is ready for croquettes, puffed potatoes, and anything that has already been cooked—and if the bread burns immediately, the fat is too hot: all this is done just as easily with a thermometer.)

Beef suet, rendered, is the best deep-frying fat, since it can be heated hotter without burning than anything save olive oil. Vegetable oils are possible substitutes though it seems to me they smoke, splatter, and soak into food more.

Deep-frying fat can be used and reused. Strain it hot through a sieve into a pan of cold water, let it harden, then scrape the dregs off the bottom of the cake. Or strain it through muslin back into the coffee can you keep it in. The taste of everything except fish can be removed from the frying fat by heating it to about 350° and frying a sliced raw potato in it.

SAUTÉING

This is what we usually call frying: anything cooked or browned in just enough fat or butter to keep it from sticking.

BOILING OR STEWING

Meat: The slower it is boiled, the more tender it will be—which doesn't really make sense, since boiling water is always 212°, but nevertheless, it is true. If you want the broth, start meat in cold water, bring it quickly to a boil, skim it, then turn down the heat to simmer it. If you want the meat, start it in boiling water to seal its surface quickly and keep the juices in.

Vegetables: Salt in boiling water hardens the water; soda softens it—but at the expense of some of the vitamins. Green vegetables should be boiled in salted water to keep their texture, color, and flavor. Dried beans, peas, and lentils should be boiled unsalted, or with a very little soda. A little vinegar in the water in which red vegetables are cooked helps them keep their color. A little milk with white vegetables helps them from acquiring a color not their own. "Potatoes and onions never taste just right unless the water in which they are cooked be salted." (*The Caloric Book of Recipes*, 1907)

As a general rule, vegetables should be cooked in no more water than necessary to keep them from burning, for no more time than it takes to make them just tender.

SOME NOTES ON BEEF

Meat has changed considerably since the nineteenth century. Beef was not bred specifically for meat production until after 1900. The housewife in the 1800s was almost always dealing with meat that was tougher and stringier than ours, even if she had raised it herself. The cheaper grades of beef now give us the best approximation for the old recipes. In some of them, it would be a crime to use modern Prime or Choice cuts. USDA Good or Standard grades will work better.

Government grading standards are useful to know in any case. Government inspection of meat for disease or contamination is obligatory. Government grading, though most of the major meat packers request it, is not. There are eight grades, which appear with the initials "USDA" (U.S. Department of Agriculture) inside a shield, stamped in purple ink on the fat of the major cuts. Without the shield or the letters, the grading is the meat packer's own, not the government's. The grading is based on the quality and flavor of the meat, not on its nutritional value, which is the same whether the meat is tender as butter or tough as nails.

Prime is the best grade. It comes from young steers or heifers of good breeding and conformation, specially corn-fattened for individual excellence, and it is a grade that is given to perhaps one beef in 500. The lean meat is pink or cherry-red, firm, and well-marbled with fat. The fat, which covers the whole body of the beef like an envelope, is white or creamy-white and fairly thick. Prime meat is the most tender, and to make it tender, the steer has produced a lot of waste fat, poundage for which the retailer must still pay. This makes it too expensive for any but the best retail or restaurant trade. It is almost never seen in supermarkets.

Choice beef lacks the finish (a term referring to the amount and distribution of fat throughout the carcass) and quality required for Prime beef. The fat is still white or cream-white and firm, but the lean has less marbling and is a darker red than Prime meat. (Color, though, is subject to change when the meat is prepackaged and put under the lights in supermarket showcases. The change, I understand, is harmless, but . . .) Choice beef usually comes from steers, heifers, and some young corn-fed cows, is tender, has good flavor, and is reasonable in price. Supermarkets, when they have it, tend to advertise Choice beef with pride.

Good beef comes mainly from grass-fed young steers and heifers. There is only a thin coating of yellowish fat over the outside of the body and the lean is dark red with little marbling. This is like the best nineteenth-century beef. It can be slow-roasted and, if not cut too thick, broiled, but the results will not be as luscious as Prime or Choice beef.

Standard beef is darker still in color, has little or no fat sheathing the body, and the lean meat has no marbling. This is perhaps the closest to most nineteenth-century beef. It is inexpensive and there is little waste, but it should be braised, pot-roasted, or stewed. If you broil or roast it, you end up with a tough, chewy hunk of meat.

Commercial beef comes from older animals. It has a good fat covering, but the fat is yellow. The meat is dark red, and usually marbled—but do not confuse the marbling with the fine white marbling of Choice beef. Commercial beef is tough and should be pot-roasted or stewed.

Utility beef is dark, soft, coarse, and stringy, with little fat, and that which it has is yellow. It is often sold for cheap boneless cuts. Stew it.

Cutter and Canner grades are the lowest grades sold for human food, and are hardly ever seen in supermarkets. They are usually cured, canned, or ground up for use in frankfurters, bologna, or sausages.

BASIC CAKE MAKING

"Tie up your hair so that none can fall, put on a long-sleeved apron, have the kitchen put in order, and then arrange all the articles and utensils you will have occasion to use." (*Miss Beecher's Domestic Receipt Book*, 1846)

Cake baking is one of the more fundamental arts, and a home-made cake takes only a little more time and bother than a package cake. Almost all cakes are variations on fairly predictable themes. There is a pattern for ingredients, a pattern for mixing, and a pattern for baking. There are certain allowable substitutions and certain tests to prevent failure. Given the list of ingredients—and most old recipes are little more than lists—the procedure follows logically.

INGREDIENTS

Every cake has shortening, sweetening, leavening, thickening, moistening, and flavoring. The shortening is usually butter, but sometimes lard is substituted or used in combination with butter. If the moistening is cream, the proportion of shortening will be lower to allow for the butterfat in cream (that can work both ways: if the recipe calls for cream and you have only milk, add a little more butter).

Sweetening can be sugar, brown sugar, molasses, or honey. If you use molasses, use baking soda instead of baking powder and you will have a lighter cake. Honey is less sweet than sugar, so in substituting, add more, and decrease the amount of liquid.

Leavening, to make the cake rise, is almost always baking soda, baking powder (which is one-third soda to two-thirds cream of tartar), or eggs, or a combination of eggs and soda. To get the most rising power out of eggs, the whites and yolks should be beaten separately, and the stiff whites folded in at the last minute. Sometimes yeast is used; then the batter must be left to rise like bread batter.

Thickening is flour. Cake flour, a finer grind than was available in the

1800s, makes a lighter but somewhat drier cake. In substituting, use 2 tablespoons less cake flour for each cup. All-purpose flour soaks up more liquid and makes a moister cake, but beware of over-beating it or the cake will be tough.

Moistening is milk, though sometimes wine or fruit juice can be used. If the milk is sour, use soda instead of baking powder.

Flavorings are spices or extracts or grated rind. From the amounts sometimes called for in old recipes, I suspect that sharp spices were less sharp in the last century, perhaps because they traveled longer. Cinnamon and cloves frequently need to be cut down in quantity. One teaspoon of cinnamon and ½ teaspoon of nutmeg, cloves, or allspice is plenty of spicing for a cake calling for 2 to 3 cups of flour. Rosewater, a frequent flavoring, is hard to get now. Vanilla or almond extract may be substituted, if you must substitute.

If any of the normal classes of ingredients is missing from the recipe, check carefully for the reason—and if you decide that it is a mistake, use your own judgment in supplying the lack.

A note on quantity: Many of the old recipes call for huge amounts, and make enormous numbers of cakes. They can and probably should be halved or quartered. *A guide:* A two-layer cake usually calls for 2 cups of flour more or less. If the cake contains more than 2 eggs, it will need less flour for an ordinary-sized cake. If a layer or loaf cake calls for a quart of flour, for instance, chances are that more than one cake is intended.

MIXING

Butter and sugar are creamed together until they look smooth and creamy. Unless the butter starts to melt, the longer the creaming, generally, the better.

Then eggs or egg yolks are added to the creamed mixture. If there are many eggs, the batter may show a tendency to curdle. This can be controlled by adding a tablespoonful or so of flour. Often flavoring is added at this point.

The flour and dry ingredients are sifted together, then flour and milk are added alternately, beginning and ending with flour. Each addition is beaten only long enough to mix it in. This should be done fairly quickly and the finished batter beaten no more than 2 minutes.

Egg whites, beaten to a stiff froth (if the recipe calls for eggs to be beaten separately), are now folded—not beaten—in.

For fruitcakes, add the fruit now. To prevent it sinking to the bottom when it is baked, soak it overnight in wine or brandy, or dredge it lightly with flour, so that each piece is coated, before you add it.

[24]

Cake batter for layer cakes should be about the consistency of just-cooked pudding. It should be pourable, but each spoonful added to the pan should leave a mark, and need spreading out. If your cake cracks across the top in baking, or if some of the inside is doughy, the batter was too stiff; if the edges burn before the center is done, it was too runny. (If there are batter problems you cannot correct, some of them can be helped in the baking: a hotter oven for thin batter, a slower one for thick batter.) Fruitcake batters should be stiff, about like thick oatmeal.

BAKING

See the tables on the end papers for normal cake-baking temperatures and times. The oven should always be pre-heated.

Layer cakes should be baked in greased cake pans—those with removable bottoms are easiest to deal with—in which the batter is poured to a depth of 1½–2 inches, and smoothed out.

Loaf and pound cakes should be baked in loaf pans, heavily greased and floured or lined with greased brown paper (paper bags cut up). If you lay them on their sides to cool after baking, they are easier to remove from the pans.

Jelly cakes should be baked in greased and floured baking sheets with rims. The pans may be lined with heavily greased brown paper to make taking the cake out in one piece easier. The batter should be poured no more than ½ inch thick. They should be rolled while warm but not hot.

Sponge and angel cakes are baked in tube pans, greased. If they are baked in loaf pans, do not fill the pan more than half full and raise the temperature slightly. To cool, they should be inverted so that the surface of the cake is off the surface of the counter. It will fall out of the pan when it is ready.

Fruitcakes should be baked in greased loaf pans or in coffee cans, with a shallow pan of water set in the bottom of the oven.

Test cakes for done-ness by inserting a cake tester, a clean broom straw, a knife blade, or a toothpick in the center of the cake: if it comes out clean, the cake is done. All cakes should be cooled on racks, in the pan to keep them from drying out. A towel over them while they cool is not a bad idea. As soon as fruitcakes are cool enough to handle, put the plastic lid on the coffee can or wrap the loaves in plastic and put them away to age. To remove from the coffee cans, use a can opener on the bottom and push them out.

FROSTING

Unless the recipe says otherwise, do not frost cakes until they are cool. Remove them from the pan, place on a plate, covered with brown paper, just the size of the cake. For layer cakes, put the bottom layer top down, and the top layer top up.

"To ice a cake, heap what you suppose sufficient in the center of the cake, then a dip a broad-bladed knife in cold water, and spread the ice evenly over the whole surface. If the sides are to be iced, lay the icing over the sides first." (Mrs. Crowen, *Every Lady's Cook Book*, 1854) The process has not changed.

Cut the brown paper (and the mess from frosting) away around the edge of the cake, and slip it onto the serving plate. An apple in the cake box will help keep cakes fresh longer.

COOKIES

are small cakes, with enough flour added to the batter to roll them out and cut them or to drop them on greased baking sheets. Follow the same general directions.

BASIC PUDDING MAKING

This is an art we have mostly consigned to little boxes of powder. It is possible to make them from scratch, however. Pudding falls into several classes: there are the light, rich creams, the custards, the gelatines, the fruit or suet puddings, and the leftover or bread puddings. None of them, thank goodness, tastes like instant pudding, though some of the cook-it-yourself packages come close in taste to the creams (and are a lot less expensive).

Very little in the way of general directions are necessary, though there are a few general rules:

For creams and custards, cream may be boiled slowly and carefully. Do not boil milk.

If the recipe says to add the yolks to the hot milk or cream, put a little hot mixture into the eggs first, then add them. If the recipe says to add the hot mixture to the yolks, pour it in slowly and steadily, whisking the whole time.

After you add the eggs or egg yolks, do not cook at all except in a double boiler, and then do not let the mixture sit over the hot water after cooking or the eggs will curdle.

Since custards were often used as sauces for fresh fruit, cake, or other desserts, most custard recipes will thicken only enough to pour, or "to coat a silver spoon thinly" while they are hot. If you want a thicker custard, add an egg yolk or so, or use gelatine or rennet according to the directions on the package. Creams will thicken more if you set the molds in a covered pan of water and simmer them for about 20 minutes after adding the egg yolks.

In adding chocolate or other flavoring ingredients to creams, check the contents carefully. Anything with coconut butter in it will separate, depositing a thin, very unattractive layer of waxy fat on the surface of the pudding.

For gelatines, if you use unflavored gelatine instead of isinglass, which most old recipes specify, do not boil after you add the gelatine, or it will not gel.

To boil puddings: Wring the heavy muslin pudding cloth out in very hot water, and flour the inside well, so the pudding will not stick to the cloth. Tie the pudding up well, allowing room for expansion if it contains breadcrumbs or meal or anything that is likely to swell. Coat the tied opening with a little flour to keep the water out. Drop it into boiling water, enough to cover it. If water evaporates too much during the cooking, add *boiling* water to it (if the temperature drops below boiling at any point, the pudding will be heavy). Depending on the size of the pudding, 1½–2 hours' boiling time is usually enough. Plum puddings take much longer.

Steamed puddings should be put into heavily buttered molds and set in water to reach about three-fourths of the way up the mold. The mold should be covered if possible. In fact, the whole thing is easier in a specially made mold for steamed puddings. Again, if water has to be added, use only boiling water. You can test the pudding as you would a cake: when a broom straw inserted in the middle comes out clean, it is done.

Baked puddings bake better if they are set into pans of hot water when they are put into the 350°–375° oven. The usual baking time is 30–40 minutes.

BASIC JELLY AND JAM MAKING
(*with thanks to the Ball Bros. Co., which still makes the jars*)

JELLY

Jelly is fruit juice and sugar, pectin and acid, so treated that it congeals into something you can spread on bread. The pectin and the acid, without which jelly will not gel, are natural ingredients of the fruit. They can be augmented (though I tend to consider it cheating) by store-bought pectin and lemon juice, should your fruit be deficient. Fruit that is just ripe, or very slightly underripe, is highest in pectin. With apples and with grapes, which have a lot of pectin anyway, there should be no problem. For fruits like strawberries, which do not naturally have much, use only just-ripe fruit, or underripe fruit blended with ripe fruit (*not* overripe fruit).

Do not make more than 4 to 6 cups of jelly at a time. It works better in smaller batches, and 1 or 2 quarts of one kind of jelly is about all the jelly the average family can manage to eat during the year.

PREPARING THE FRUIT: Most jelly recipes will give directions. However, wash fruit thoroughly, removing all stems and bruised or soft spots. Chop it up, peels, cores (they contain pectin) and all. Put on the stove with as little cold water as possible for berries, or cold water to cover for hard fruits. Bring to a boil, then simmer about 10 minutes for berries, 20–25 minutes for hard fruits. Mash the fruit against the sides of the pot with a wooden spoon.

While it is hot, pour it into a damp jelly bag. Hang the bag from a stand if you have one, or from the dishtowel rack or the kitchen faucet, so that it can drain freely into a bowl placed below it. Do not squeeze the bag if you want clear jelly.

Commercial jelly bags are available, or you can make one from several thicknesses of cheesecloth or some tightly woven flannel, nap side in, sewn into a cone shape.

MAKING THE JELLY: Taste the juice. It should be tart but not bitter. Add lemon juice if you have to, then to each cup of juice add ¾–1 cup of sugar (honey may be substituted for half the sugar). The process of jellying will go faster if you heat the sugar in the oven first.

Put the juice and sugar over the fire and heat it rapidly to a boil. Boil it until it will sheet from a spoon—a term that is not really all that descriptive. When you take up a metal spoonful and tip the spoon to pour the syrup back into the pot, the mixture will at first run out in single drops. Then it will run out in two drops at a time, and finally the two drops will hesitate, then flow toward each other before falling. That is sheeting. It usually takes about 20 minutes for the jelly to reach this point. You can test it by putting a little on a cold dry saucer. If it quickly starts to gel, the jelly is ready (if you have a candy thermometer, it will gel at 8° above the boiling point of water). Try not to overcook it, as overcooking damages the flavor. If it simply will not gel, the only thing to do is to add more heated sugar and some pectin, and bring it to a boil again, boiling it hard for one minute after the pectin is added.

Pour the jelly immediately into hot sterilized jars, leaving ½ inch at the top of the jar. You can seal it by putting a canning lid on it immediately (invert the jar a minute or so to sterilize the lid, check the seal when the jelly is cool), or you can seal it by spooning a little hot (not smoking) paraffin over it. When the jelly has cooled, add another layer of paraffin if the first looks precarious, and cover with a lid.

Many fruits may be processed for juice, and the juice canned (see p. 32) or frozen for future use if you do not feel like making jelly right away.

JAM

Jam is even easier to make than jelly. Wash the fruit, peel and core it if it is peelable fruit. You will lose pectin with the peels, which can partially be made up by using water in which peels and cores have boiled for your jam, by adding a little more sugar, or, if you do not like your jam too sweet, by adding store-bought pectin according to the directions on the package.

Chop or grate or slice the fruit, add the sugar, and boil it in a pan with a large surface and a flat bottom—like the old preserving kettles. Jam can be flavored or varied with fresh ginger, cinnamon, sliced lemon or orange rind, or a mixture of fruits. Flavoring is added with the sugar.

It is harder to tell when jam is ready, since the large lumps of fruit prevent clear-cut evidence of sheeting. The process usually takes 20–30 minutes. Then try a little on a cold saucer to see if it is ready to gel.

Bottle it like jelly.

BASIC PICKLING

Pickling is preserving in brine and/or vinegar, with or without spices. It is one of the oldest and most interesting ways of dealing with garden over-abundance. Pickles were as common on nineteenth-century tables as salad is in the twentieth century, and they served much the same purpose—a little crunch, a little sharpness, a little chill to set the hot cooked food in artistic relief or to provide a change of pace.

EQUIPMENT AND INGREDIENTS

Pickles should be made in unchipped enamel, glass, stainless steel, aluminum, or stoneware utensils—never in copper, or brass, or iron, since the brine or vinegar will react with them to change the color of the pickles and sometimes to produce dangerous verdigris.

Use pickling salt or kosher salt if at all possible. Salt that has been treated to keep it free-flowing will make cloudy brine.

Look for lime in drugstores or farm supply stores or, in some parts of the country at some times of the year, in grocery stores. Alum can be found in grocery stores. Saltpetre for pickling meat can be found in drugstores or farm supply stores. Alum and lime are used to make pickles crisp and green. Vine leaves or cabbage leaves, boiled with the fruit to be pickled, are nearly as good.

Use whole herbs and spices, as fresh as possible. They once were left in the pickle, where they will eventually cause a slight color change. Nowadays, people tend to tie them in cheesecloth bags, which are removed just before the pickle is packed for storage. Personally, I don't mind the color change and I think leaving the spices in adds something to the flavor.

Cider vinegar is fuller-bodied and fruitier than white vinegar, but either may be used for pickling. It should be about 5% acid—the usual acidity of store-bought vinegar. If you use home-made vinegar, try to make sure it is no weaker than 4% acid, no stronger than 6%, or the pickles will suffer.

Use soft water for making brine. To soften hard water, put 1 teaspoon of baking soda to 1 gallon of water, boil it 15 minutes, then let it stand 24 hours. Ladle it carefully off the sediment in the bottom.

Store the pickles in glass jars or in stoneware crocks.

3: Processes

THE PROCESS

Use only young, underripe, undamaged fruit and vegetables for pickles. Follow the recipe.

Most nineteenth-century pickles were first cured in brine, a process that can be tricky, for which reason it is omitted from most modern books. The problem is controlling the salinity and the temperature of the brine. The brine should be "strong enough to float an egg," and the temperature should be cellar temperature, or about 50°–60°—a hard temperature to maintain in newer, cellarless homes. If the brine is strong enough, checked regularly, and replaced if it looks cloudy, the temperature is less important. Pickles in brine should be covered with a board weighted down to keep them under the brine.

TO MAKE BRINE STRONG ENOUGH TO FLOAT AN EGG

For each two and a half quarts of water take two cups of pickling salt. Boil it up for ten minutes, then let it stand until cold (*unless the recipe says to pour the scalding brine directly on the pickles*). Test it with a medium-sized uncooked egg, when it is cool. The egg should float with a piece the size of a shilling (*or a quarter*) showing above the brine. If the brine is not strong enough, add more salt and boil it up again.

After the brine cure, cook the pickles or pour boiling vinegar over them, as the recipe directs. Pack them in sterilized jars, hot. Canning lids put on immediately will usually form a seal without further ado, if jar and pickles are hot enough. A seal is not absolutely essential to keep pickles.

Like wine, they are better if they age in the bottle, for three or four months or more, before they are used.

Meat can be pickled in brine or—more commonly now—dry-pickled with salt, sugar, and saltpetre. See pp. 381–384 for directions. Pickling is a necessary step before meat is smoked, and it can also preserve meat (especially pork) without further processing.

Once the pattern of pickle making is understood, pickles can become a private art, an area for personal expression and experimentation. The best pickles I ever ate were made from sliced green tomatoes by a Virginia lady, and no amount of coaxing would induce her to part with the secret.

BASIC CANNING AND FREEZING

Canning and freezing are both aspects of the same process: preserving food, stretching the family food budget, eating and living better. Home-canned foods, properly processed, will keep for as long as store-bought cans. Almost indefinitely, in other words, though some foods lose color and texture gradually over a period of years without those artificial preservatives. If you have the right equipment handy, it is ridiculously easy. And the right equipment is still available new—or old, if you want to pay more for the atmosphere. Systematic home freezing is impossible without a large freezer, but if you do have one, it makes sense to buy meat by the quarter or half—half the whole carcass—for two-thirds the usual supermarket price, and get better meat. Freezing also enables you to take full advantage of the seasons.

Everyday canning and freezing couldn't be simpler. Make the turkey bones into soup and process it in cans for 20 minutes instead of letting it spoil in the refrigerator. Make the giblets and necks of chicken into soup while the chicken cooks. Prepare three times too much of whatever vegetables are in season and can the excess while you eat dinner. After dinner, pack away the leftovers in one-meal-sized packages and freeze them (three weeks later they will seem fresh and new), or can the stock you boiled the meat in while you wash the dishes. Make two meat loaves at a time and freeze one. Make more than enough pie crust, or pies, and freeze the extras. There will be whole days when you will hardly have to cook at all—just open cans and TV dinners.

To cut the work involved in annual canning and freezing, and to keep from getting bored, I try to prepare a two-year supply of whatever is plentiful and cheap, so that I can put up something else the following year. (Note, though: canned goods are better after two years than most frozen goods—especially meat. Fresh flavor, for foods to be used reasonably soon, lasts better in the freezer. Pick your preserving method carefully, according to the kind and amount of your food.)

EQUIPMENT

A number of canning jars in quart or pint sizes (pints are more practical for small families). Many peanut-butter jars, mayonnaise jars, etc., have tops that will fit standard canning lids (available in canning season at most supermarkets). If tops are nonstandard, use the jars for jam or jelly. Grocery stores in smaller towns usually carry Mason jars.

Freezer containers. Plastic bags are better than aluminum foil or freezer paper, can be reused, tear less easily—and come free, wrapped around other foods. Do not buy them. Square plastic containers are nice for space-saving, but the lids have a tendency to come off. Wide-mouth glass freezer-canner jars are cheaper and can do double duty.

A canner. Water-bath and steam pressure canners come in 4-, 7-, 8-, and 9-quart sizes. Big ones are useful for annual canning, but the smaller ones are better for everyday. Water-bath canners are less expensive, but pressure canners are necessary if you plan to can much meat, since they can raise the processing temperature to 240° or better.

Tongs to lift the hot glasses.

Wooden spoons for stirring, a ladle for ladling.

The usual measuring cups, paring knives, peelers, etc.

A sieve and a colander.

A large pot and a wire basket that will fit into it, for scalding and blanching.

Tape for labeling.

A wide-bottomed funnel, to put things into jars without slopping over. Best is a large plastic funnel which you can cut yourself to have a bottom opening 2 inches in diameter.

Optional but nice: a food mill, a juicer, a food grinder, a scale, a ricer (that cone-shaped metal colander on legs).

THE PROCESS: CANNING

Prepare the food. Fruits should be washed, then scalded and peeled, or, if you want to leave the skin on, pricked with a needle. Halve them, slice them, or cut them up as you please, and drop them into cold water with a little vinegar or lemon juice in it, to prevent discoloration while you work. As you do this, have the water heating in the canner. When you have enough for a canner-full, pack the fruit in hot jars tightly, but without crushing it. Berries, scalded 15 to 30 seconds in boiling water, can be processed in their own juice, but most other fruits are covered with boiling sugar-syrup, poured over them after they are in the jar. The sweetness of the syrup depends mainly on your own taste. Leave half an inch of head space, make sure the rims of the jars are clean, put the tops on and screw them down tightly but not viciously. (If you have glass-top Mason jars, settle the rubber ring around the neck of the jar, put on the dome and fit the wire bail into its groove, but do not snap down the locking bail.)

Immerse the jars in the boiling water in the canner. Average processing time—counting from the moment the water in the canner comes to a rolling boil—for soft fruits like berries and strawberries is 15 minutes for a pint, 20 minutes for a quart. For harder fruits, allow 20–25 minutes for pints, 25–30 minutes for quarts.

To MAKE SUGAR-SYRUP: Add 2 cups sugar to 1 quart water for light syrup, 3 cups sugar to 1 quart water for medium syrup; 4¾ cups sugar to 1 quart water for heavy syrup (honey may be substituted for half the sugar). Boil until the sugar dissolves.

To can high-acid vegetables like tomatoes whole, wash, scald, and peel them, pack them, adding 1 teaspoonful of salt to each quart. Tomatoes need no added liquid, and, given reasonable care and cleanliness, are foolproof canning successes. They can be cooked into sauce, blended and strained for juice, combined with other vegetables—just about anything you like. Processing time is 30 minutes for pints, 40 minutes for quarts.

Low-acid vegetables—beans, peas, beets, carrots, corn, etc.—should be processed at 10 pounds pressure in a pressure canner. If you haven't got a pressure canner, a touch of ascorbic acid, lemon juice, or vinegar in the liquid you pour over them will help their keeping qualities and color.

Wash raw beans, asparagus, peas, carrots, corn. Trim them, cut them up if they need it, pack them into hot jars. Add 1 teaspoonful of salt per quart, a sprig of whatever herb you like, if you like, and pour boiling water over them, leaving ½ inch at the top. Fit the lids and process, 30–40 minutes for pints, 40–50 minutes for quarts (a little longer for corn). Peppers should be blanched and folded up into jars, beets should be cooked and peeled and potatoes parboiled before you pour the boiling water over; pumpkin should be cooked and mashed, then packed hot into jars. Broccoli, Brussels sprouts, cauliflower, cooked parsnips, and turnips are better frozen. So is corn, for that matter.

Sauces and soups, and all leftover dishes, should be packed hot, into hot jars, and processed longer than you would process the same ingredients fresh.

Anything with meat in it should be processed by pressure at least 1¼ hours for pints, 1½ hours for quarts.

FINISHING

Take the jars out of the canner immediately, check the lids—tightening them if necessary, locking the bails on glass-top jars—and let them stand until cold. Then check the seal by unscrewing the bands of dome lids, then lifting the jar by its lid, or by undoing the wire bails on glass lids and lifting. If a seal has not been made, the lid will come off. If you do not get a seal (probable causes: nicked or dirty rims, old rubber or dome lids, too little processing, cooked food that was cold when you put it into the jar, or food that was too ripe and already beginning to spoil when you canned it), re-process the jar—and if that doesn't work, forget it.

BOTULISM: If it is properly processed, home-canned food will be free of botulism, which is caused by a spore carried by wind, dust, or dirt that sometimes clings to raw foods. It can grow only in the absence of air and does not normally thrive in foods high in acid. Heat kills it, so processing time should never be skimped. If there is any question about the food in a jar when it is opened, *DO NOT TASTE IT* to see whether it is good. Boil the food 15 minutes in an uncovered pan, stirring occasionally. This will kill any possible toxin.

THE PROCESS: FREEZING

FRUIT: Wash, peel, slice, or otherwise fix it as you would like. Pack it raw, or sprinkled with sugar to taste, or pour over it a sugar-syrup (see p. 34) to which ½ teaspoonful of ascorbic acid has been added just before you pour it over the fruit. The last method is best for fruits like peaches, which are apt to discolor. Label and date the packages: you may think you will remember what they are, but you won't. Cool them before freezing, since a hot package will expand more in the freezer, will cause the freezer to work harder (thereby depositing more frost which you will eventually have to clean away), and may affect the already frozen food around. Freeze it.

If you have the space, freeze applesauce and rhubarb instead of canning it: the flavor seems to keep better.

VEGETABLES: Wash them, cut them up as you like, scald 2–5 minutes —no longer than absolutely necessary. Dip them instantly into ice water, drain, pack into meal-sized packages, and freeze. Fruits and vegetables will keep a year or more in a freezer that holds them at 0° temperature.

MEAT: Trim it and pack, without salt, as it comes from the butcher. Beef will keep a year, veal and lamb or mutton will keep 9 months, but pork should be kept frozen no longer than 3 months. Wash and dry chicken and turkey: they will keep a year. Wash and dry fish. It will keep a week without losing flavor, and should not be kept more than 2 months frozen.

Cooked foods may be packed as they are (omit salt, if possible), chilled and frozen. Frozen leftovers should be eaten within 2 or 3 months.

THAWING

Thaw meat thoroughly before you cook it. Some books claim meat can be cooked partly frozen. It is not true. Unless you intend to stew it for hours, you will end up with a tough, nasty piece of meat.

Soups and stocks and most vegetables can be put on to cook while still frozen. Use a low heat. Fruits should be thawed first. If you cook them slowly, turkey, chicken, and fish need not be completely thawed.

Thawing can be speeded up if you immerse the (leakless) freezer bag in lukewarm water. Do *not* try to speed up meat thawing.

BASIC ICE CREAM MAKING

Electric ice cream freezers are available, or reproductions of the old hand-crank ones. The crank machines probably make slightly smoother ice cream, since they allow you to vary the speed of the churning (slower at first), but either of them will make better ice cream than can be made in a refrigerator freezer.

You will need crushed ice, rock salt (or a mixture of 3 parts table salt to 1 part saltpetre), and the ice cream mixture (see pp. 197–200 for recipes) as well as the freezer.

Fill the ice cream pail two-thirds full of mixture to be frozen, and set it temporarily in the refrigerator to chill while you prepare the freezer. Break up the ice as fine as possible. The more it is crushed, the finer the texture of the ice cream will be. Put it in the wooden part of the freezer in layers with the rock salt, strewn in in a proportion of 8 parts of ice to 1 part of rock salt. Pack the ice down solidly. Put the tin ice cream pail on a bottom layer of ice and continue to fill the freezer around it. The ice and salt should fill the freezer to a level a little above the level of the ice cream mixture in the pail.

Fit in the dasher, let it stand a few minutes, then begin to churn. When the ice cream is done, the crank becomes very hard to turn—or the electric churn shuts off automatically.

Drain the water out of the freezer and repack it, using twice as much salt to the ice as before. Remove the churn from the ice cream, pack it down solidly in the pail with a wooden spoon, then put the lid on, and surround it with the

ice-salt mixture. Cover the whole freezer with old carpet or layers of old newspaper to insulate it, and let it stand half an hour to an hour. Then serve, or put
it away in the deep-freeze.

WINE MAKING

Making wine is one of the more delightful ways of preserving fruit. It is
perfectly legal: all you have to do is file a copy of Form 1541 (no fee) with
the regional office of the U.S. Alcohol and Tobacco Tax Division of the Bu-
reau of Internal Revenue, and you can make up to 200 gallons a year for home
use. It doesn't take much space (at least, under about 50 gallons it doesn't),
and the rewards are high in satisfaction, lessened liquor bills, and taste.

My own rule is to make wine only from ingredients I can get free for the
picking or from friends—dandelions, rhubarb, elderberries, apples, pears,
wild grapes. I make exceptions for wines we particularly like (peach and
honey), and buy the ingredients in bulk, in season. The finished product, if
you don't put a price on your time, costs about 25¢ a bottle, once you have the
equipment.

The theory of wine making is simple enough: yeast plus sugar and water
and a little acid equals alcohol. The fruit supplies the flavoring, and some of
the sugar.

The process is not difficult, but is full of pitfalls for the careless. Wine,
once under way, is a living creature, shy, touchy, sometimes deceitful, each
bottle with its own personality and problems but docile when handled with
skill—or even a little luck.

The wine maker needs certain equipment to begin with. A polyethylene
wastebasket with a cover, sterilized, will do to hold the mash, though stone
crocks are more glamorous and probably do a better job of keeping the temperature steady. You'll also need something to hold the wine, a fermentation
lock to keep the air out, a siphon to move the wine from one bottle to another,
bottles, corks, finicky cleanliness, and patience. All except the last two are
available at the wine supply stores that can be found in most major cities, or
by mail order, or they can be improvised with a little determination.

GATHERING THE INGREDIENTS

The general rule is, pick in the middle of the day, in full sunshine; process as soon as possible. The instant a plant is severed from its roots the sugar begins to degenerate, so the quicker the wine-making process is begun, the better the wine will be. Do not wash the fruit, unless the recipe says you should, or unless you suspect that it has been sprayed for insects. All grapes, and most other fruits with peels, have wild yeasts on the skins that are fully capable of carrying on a fermentation once the skin is broken to let them at the sugar in the fruit, should you decide to rely on them. Wild yeasts can be a tricky business, however, and most wine makers add wine yeasts, available at wine supply stores, in order to control the fermentation.

PROCESSING THE INGREDIENTS

Follow the recipe. In general (and in wine making, be wary of general rules), the fruit is crushed or chopped up, and boiling water is poured on this mash, or it is boiled briefly (never more than 20 minutes for fruit wines, or they will not clear properly). Sugar may or may not be added at this point. The mash is then set aside to work for two or three days, either tightly covered or loosely covered with a towel as the recipe directs, and is stirred daily. Here and throughout, fruit or vinegar flies are your greatest enemy. As few as five or six, if they get in, can cause the fermentation to change from alcohol-producing to vinegar-producing. (Should this happen, do not throw the wine out. Just continue, sadly, following the directions for making vinegar; but with care, vinegar can be avoided. I have lost only one batch in five years.)

At the end of the two or three days, the juice is strained off the fruit (and sometimes boiled again). The pulp is discarded. Sugar is added to the juice if it was not put in before. When the mixture is at blood-heat, yeast and acid (see p. 40) are added, and the whole is poured into its sterile fermentation vessel and fitted with a lock to keep the air out (air is almost as deadly an enemy as fruit flies) while the carbon dioxide of fermentation escapes.

Then the wine is set in an out-of-the-way place with an even temperature, preferably about 70°, though I have found that an exact temperature is less important than an unvarying temperature. If the temperaure fluctuates more than about 10° very often, the wine has difficulty in clearing. For this reason, city wine makers would do best to make wine in the late fall, after the heat has been turned on.

3 : PROCESSES

The best vessel for the amateur is a 5-gallon glass water jug, like those used on bottled-water fountains. Five gallons is a minimum size, I think, since the smaller the quantity of wine made, the greater the chances of failure. The jug should be filled to its shoulder first; then, when the first vigorous fermentation is over, in about two weeks, it should be topped up, or filled to its neck, with juice withheld for the purpose.

THE FERMENTATION

The first fermentation, during which about 90% of the sugar turns to alcohol, takes only about two weeks. The froth will subside, the bubbles coming through the air filter will slow down, and a sediment will probably start to settle on the bottom of the jug. The second fermentation, which renders the wine fit to drink, takes much longer. For that, if possible, the wine should be kept at 50° to 60°. It will not be finished until the wine is perfectly clear and there is no sugar left, which can be determined by using a sacchrometer, also available at wine supply stores, or until the yeasts have exhausted themselves. (Fermentation can be stopped at any point after the first furor, if a sweet wine is desired, by adding about 1½ quarts of brandy to each 5 gallons of wine. The jump in alcoholic content will kill the yeasts. Wine made this way, however, requires longer aging.)

The wine should be racked, or siphoned off its dregs into clean, sterile jugs, about every three months—though this timing is subject to judgment tempered by your experience of the state and needs of that particular wine. Racking stirs and aerates the wine just enough to encourage the fermentation to keep going and improving the wine.

When wooden barrels are used, it is essential that they be kept topped up, filled with wine right to the bung-holes. If the wine is in glass jugs, topping up is desirable, but not crucial.

Most fruit wine is clear and ready to bottle in about a year, but only your eye, your experience, and your sacchrometer can tell you *exactly* when. It will not hurt it to age for a while in the fermentation vessel, and if you bottle too soon, fermentation in the bottle can pop the cork, or produce an unexpected and rather cloudy carbonation—rather like a cheap champagne. If you *want* champagne, bottle in champagne bottles (which have heavier glass) when about 2% of sugar is left, tie down the corks and store the bottles standing on their heads, to try to trap the dregs that will naturally form on the cork so you can pop them out when you open the bottle.

When you bottle, use clean, sterile wine bottles saved or cadged from friends. Nothing else is *right* for something you have spent so long producing. Five gallons will fill 25 of them. Wine corks, bought new (used corks will damage the wine; screw tops won't let it age properly and don't seal tightly enough to keep out air), should be soaked 24 hours in a solution of potassium metabisulphite and inserted with a corking machine. Store the bottles on their sides to keep the corks damp, as you would any respectable wine.

Bottling starts the wine's aging process, which produces the difference between a mere alcoholic beverage and something with character. Each wine will take it differently, but in general, light light-colored wines need less time than heavy dark wines. A dry mead, for instance, is perfectly ready to drink after 6 months in the bottle. The elderberry was still improving after 2 years when, through sheer greed, we drank the last bottle.

Potassium metabisulphite, by the way, is an invaluable chemical. By killing unwanted yeasts, it sterilizes clean bottles with a lot less effort than boiling them would take. It is available at wine supply stores.

THE FINE POINTS

The general rule for adding sugar to fruits other than grapes is, 2½ pounds per gallon for a dry wine, to 3½ pounds per gallon for a sweet wine. *This rule should not be taken seriously.* The amount of sugar the fruit contains already will affect what you add. The sacchrometer can tell you exactly; the juice before fermentation should contain somewhere between 24% and 28% sugar.

The amount of acid the fruit contains affects it just as much. Acid is essential to fermentation. If the fruit is low in acid, as honey, pears, and peaches are, you will have to add it, either in the form of lemon and/or orange juice, or as a combination of citric acid and tartaric acid, 1 teaspoonful of each more or less, for 5 gallons. If the fruit is high in acid, as rhubarb and elderberries are, you will have to increase the sugar content to keep the wine from getting sour, or ending its fermentation too soon. Until you know by experience, the best plan is to follow the recipe *exactly*. It is a good idea to sample the wine when you rack it (who wouldn't want to, anyway?). You should be able to taste it if things are not going as they should.

If it has turned vinegary, there is nothing that can be done to save wine —or the barrel either, if it was in wood. But cloying sweetness can sometimes be helped by adding a little acid, and a thin or sour wine can sometimes be improved by adding a little sugar made into a syrup of 2 pounds of sugar boiled with 1 cup of water or juice until it dissolves, then cooled, and added as needed. An exception to the taste test is mead, which tastes awful, almost until it is ready to bottle. But the key to mead success is to boil it with water for a full 40 minutes, skimming it well, before it is fermented.

Home-made wines are more likely to throw down a sediment in the bottle than store-bought ones. Sediment just means that the aging process is proceeding as it should. But to have clear drinking wine, it is best to stand the bottles upright for an hour or so before opening, then to decant them carefully into a decanter for serving.

If the wine, before you bottle it, is not clearing properly, it could be due to a flaw in the original processing of the fruit, to too rapidly changing temperature, or to a disease of the wine. Often the problem will solve itself if you can wait it out. Or you can beat about 4 egg whites (for 5 gallons) to a soft froth and gradually mix wine with them until they are well stirred into the whole batch, and hope that the egg will surround the suspended sediment and carry it to the bottom. There are commercial preparations for clearing wine, but most of them also affect the taste. If the wine won't clear by itself, or with egg whites, and if it tastes all right, you can always drink it cloudy—hiding it carefully from those friends to whom you have bragged of your wine-making prowess.

PART II

Recipes:
Food According
to Its Seasons

[4]

JANUARY

Bread; yeast; more or less quick breads; rolls, muffins,
biscuits; crackers; doughnuts and fried cakes; pancakes
and waffles; pastry, batter, noodles; dried beans, peas;
dried fruits

January is the first month of the year, and bread is the first fact of nineteenth-century life. It is all, always, home made, its quality the first hallmark
of a housewife's skill. For a detailed description of the process of bread making, see pp. 14–18. Here are the recipes. Baking your own bread does have
this disadvantage; it makes it nearly impossible to buy the plastic foam sold
as bread in supermarkets today.

Since we're baking—a hot stove in a cold month is a comforting thing—
here are also recipes for pastry, commonly called paste back then, for shortcakes and rusks, pancakes and doughnuts; for the dried beans that must eke
out the year until spring, and the dried fruits that hang in strings in the attic
(or in cartons in the supermarket), tenacious reminders of summer. And here
are Hopping John and bean porridge, the hearty traditional dishes with which
the family woodcutter can fortify himself to meet the cold and the snow.

NEW YEAR'S CAKES

Seven pounds of flour, two pounds and a half sugar; two pounds of butter and a pint of water, with a teaspoonful of saleratus (*baking soda*) dissolved in it. Work the paste well; roll it thin and cut it in small cakes with a tin cutter; lay them on pie plates (*or cookie tins*) and bake in a quick oven for fifteen minutes.

BREAD

Baking day in the early nineteenth century was a production that is hard even to imagine now. The oven was either set into the masonry of the fireplace behind an iron door, with a small flue leading into the central chimney, or was built separately, outside. In both cases, a fire built of the hardest, hottest wood had to be kindled in the oven and kept burning behind the closed door until the stones or bricks of the oven were almost as hot as the coals. The embers were then swept out and the things to be baked popped in, to cook in the heat gradually dying out of the oven. Bread, which needs the highest heats, went first, then cakes and finally puddings or beans, or things that could simmer all night until the oven was almost cold. Small wonder that the following bread recipes are for such huge batches.

When the kitchen range came in, later, things got easier, but households were generally larger than they are now, including servants (even for very middle-class families; one cookbook authoress, writing in 1885, decries the common assumption that readers had cooks, "since only one housewife in four now has servants") as well as children, and frequently family business employees joined them for the midday main meal. Bread consumption must have been prodigious.

Early nineteenth-century bread is usually made only of flour, water, salt, and yeast. It comes close to being the kind of loaf now available in the better bakeries. Late nineteenth-century breads tend to include shortening and sweetening, and milk is frequently substituted for water for a denser-textured bread. Flour and water recipes can be improved (at least for my tastes) by adding 1 tablespoon of shortening, either butter or lard, and 2 tablespoons of sugar, honey, or molasses per quart of flour. If milk is used instead of water, it is best to scald it first, and let it cool to lukewarm before adding the yeast. The milk yeasts confuse the bread yeasts, and can turn the fermentation to lactic—which makes the bread less good.

The modern oven will hold four to five loaves comfortably. It is silly to bake less. In our bread-starved world, at least one loaf is likely to disappear before it even has a chance to cool—and enjoyable as I find bread making, I wouldn't want to do it every other day. (The extras can always be frozen to keep them fresh.) So most of the recipes here will have to be halved or quartered. A rough guide: 1 pound (4 cups) of flour, more or less, makes 1 large loaf.

In translating the recipes, yeast is the main trouble maker. Sourdough can be substituted, but needs more rising time than the recipes indicate. (For a simple sourdough starter, see p. 56.) If you decide to make your own yeast, there is no translation problem. If you use dried yeast—each package holds 1 tablespoonful—add as much more liquid to the recipe as the yeast would have added. One package of yeast equals about ½ cup of liquid yeast.

FOR A GOOD BAKING

Take two and a half pecks of wheat (*white*) flour (*this would be 20 pounds; five pounds, or one-quarter of the recipe, makes 5 long loaves*); put it into a kneading trough or an earthen pan well glazed; make a hole in the centre of the flour and pour in a pint or more of good brewer's yeast, or still more of home-made, well mixed with a pint of milk-warm water. Stir in, with a spoon, enough flour to make a batter; sprinkle this with dry flour and cover it entirely. Cover the whole lightly with a cloth and set it by the fire. This is *setting the sponge*. When the batter has swelled and risen so as to form cracks in the flour covering it, scatter through it two tablespoonfuls of fine salt, and mix the flour with (*about 4 quarts of*) soft warm water, adding by degrees. Work and mold the dough thoroughly, kneading it till smooth and light, and till not a particle will stick to the hands. Then sprinkle the mass of dough with flour, cover it with a warm cloth and let it stand near the fire for an hour, or less in warm weather. It has now risen to its height. Divide it into seven loaves. (*Make your loaves long and narrow, like French bread; perhaps because of its quick rising time, this bread has a very hard flaky crust when fresh, better for tearing than for cutting. It softens the next day—which may explain why old books instruct you never to eat bread that is less than a day old.*) Mould and form them lightly on the paste-board, put them on floured tin or earthen plates (*let rise 20–30 minutes*) and place them in the oven.

Bake at 400° for about 40 minutes; beware of over-baking, as the crust does not color easily. This recipe makes excellent bread sticks: see p. 63; or Kaffee kuchen, p. 55.

FRENCH BREAD

1 quart of water	About 5 quarts of flour
1 pound of potatoes	6 hop flowers
1 cup of good yeast, or half a compressed cake (or two packages of dry yeast)	1 tablespoon of salt

Put the hops in the water, and boil five minutes. Boil the potatoes in their skins; when done, peel and mash them fine. Put three cups of flour into the bread pan, pour one pint of boiling water over, and heat quickly until smooth; add the mashed potatoes, and then strain into this the hop-water; add the salt and a teaspoonful of the sugar; beat thoroughly; and, when lukewarm, add the yeast; stand in a warm place for nine hours, or over night. In the morning add sufficient flour (*about 3½ quarts*) to make a dough; knead thoroughly and continuously for ten minutes, using as little flour as possible; then wet the hands in lukewarm water, raise the dough about three feet from the board, and throw it back with force, and continue this process for fifteen minutes, or until large air bubbles are formed in the dough (*this is excellent for the chest muscles*). If properly worked the dough will be very elastic and soft, but will not stick to the hands. Now put it back in the bread pan, cover, and stand in a warm place to rise, about two hours. When light, take out gently, enough of this dough to make one loaf (about 1 pound), sprinkle the board lightly with flour, knead so as to make a kind of ball; then roll it gently with the palms of the hands, giving it an elongated shape; now flour a rolling-pin lightly, place it on top of the loaf, right in the centre, and press and roll a little to make a furrow in the middle of the loaf. Now dust a towel or bread cloth well with flour, place the loaf just made upside down on the towel, pulling out the ends a little to give the loaf a long form, and so continue until all the loaves are made; then cover with a towel, let rise as ordinary bread; then turn into floured bread pans (*baking sheets*), the furrowed side up. The loaves must be a little distance apart, if you place two in one pan. Sprinkle plenty of flour on top of each loaf, and bake in a moderately quick oven (*375°*), forty minutes. (*Makes 6–8 long loaves.*)

"Bread baked in flower pots approximates brick-oven bread."
Marion Harland, *Common Sense*, 1883

POTATO BREAD

Rub a dozen peeled and boiled potatoes through a very coarse sieve, and mix with them twice the quantity of flour, mixing very thoroughly. Put in a coffee-cup full of home-brewed or of potato yeast, or half that much of distillery yeast, also a teaspoonful of salt. Add whatever water may be needed to make a dough as stiff as for common flour bread. (*Proceed as for any other bread—see p. 47. Makes 3 loaves.*)

An ounce or two of butter rubbed into the flour and an egg, beat and put into the yeast, and you can have fine rolls or warm cakes for breakfast.

This kind of bread is very moist, and keeps well.

BREAD RAISED WITH PURE POTATO YEAST

Scald a pint and a half of milk. Have ready four and a half pounds of sifted flour in a pan; make a hollow in the centre and pour in half a pint of the milk, stirring in enough of the flour to make a rather thick batter; add a gill of cold water, and let it stand until lukewarm; to a pint of hot milk add half an ounce of butter, two even teaspoonfuls of sugar (*or 1 tablespoonful of honey*) and a tablespoonful of salt; then cover, and set it aside; add three gills of yeast to the batter, mixing in more of flour, and leave it to rise an hour at from 90° to 95°; add a pint of the hot water to the milk (hot enough to make it lukewarm), pour it in on the sponge, and stir in all of the flour; flour the board, place the dough on it, leaving the pan perfectly clean, and knead it into a smooth mass, using as little flour as possible; flour the pan, replace the dough, and leave it to rise two hours; knead it again, and mould into loaves; put them in evenly but slightly greased pans which they will but half fill, and in an hour, or when risen to the top, prick and bake. The bread may remain in the second rising over night, but, of course, in a very much cooler place than when intended to rise quickly; 60° would not be too low. (*Makes 4 loaves; see p. 56 for home-made yeasts.*)

MILK BREAD

One pint milk, scalded and cooled; one tablespoonful butter, melted in the hot milk; one tablespoonful sugar; one teaspoonful salt; one-half cup yeast, six or seven cups flour.

Measure the milk after scalding, and put it in the mixing bowl; add the butter, sugar and salt. When cool, add the yeast, and then stir in the flour, adding it gradually after five cups are in, that it may not be too stiff; use just enough to knead it. Knead till smooth and elastic. Cover; let it rise till light; cut it down; divide it into four parts, shape into loaves or biscuit. Let it rise again in the pans. Bake forty to fifty minutes. (*Makes 2 loaves.*)

BLUE ISLAND BREAD

One yeast cake, one and a quarter pounds of potatoes (*3 or 4, preferably unpeeled*), one pint of the water in which the potatoes are boiled, one gill of flour, two tablespoonfuls of salt, two quarts of warm water, seven pounds of flour.

Soak the yeast-cake in two tablespoonfuls of tepid water, boil the potatoes, mash them through the colander with the boiling water (*or blend them with the water*) onto the flour and salt. When lukewarm, add the yeast and leave it to rise, allowing seven hours in a temperature of from 70° to 75°, so, if the sponge is made at two P.M., the bread may be mixed at nine P.M. When the sponge is light, put the flour in the bread-pan and pour the water in the centre; when enough of the flour is stirred in to make a batter, add the sponge, stir well, and mix in all of the flour; then flour the board, place the dough on it, and knead for twenty or thirty minutes, using barely enough flour to prevent the dough from sticking to the board and hands; lay it in the floured pans, and rub half an ounce of butter on the top, cover the pan, and leave it to rise till morning, when it should be twice its bulk. Then make it into eight or nine loaves, as they must but half fill the pans and when risen to the top, prick and bake. (*Makes 6–7 loaves.*)

FAMILY BREAD

To one quart of sweet milk, take one-third of a compressed yeast cake and three teaspoons of white sugar; stir in flour until you have a dough so stiff that it will not run or drop from a spoon (*but too soft to knead*); set it in a moderately warm room (*moderately warm in 1875 was around 65°*) and let it rise until morning; then put flour on your kneading board, (*knead,*) mould your loaves about two inches thick, and put in pans (handling as little as possible) and let it rise again. When ready for the oven prick the loaves through to the bottom with a fork; bake half an hour. When taken from the oven, roll lightly in a cloth until cool. (*Makes 4 loaves.*)

In the morning, if you wish delicious gems (*rolls*), dip with a spoon some of this same dough and fill your gem-pans two-thirds full and bake for breakfast. If you wish hot biscuit for lunch, you have only to save a small portion of this dough, roll it thin and spread with butter or shortening, fold it a few times, using all the time just flour enough to handle, roll to about half an inch thick, and put in your pans and let rise again, which takes from two to three hours. Your biscuit will bake in from seven to ten minutes. Fold in a napkin, unless you wish the crusts crisp, and send to table.

TO MAKE CROUTONS OUT OF SLIGHTLY STALE BREAD

Slice the bread into ¾-inch slices, then cut off the crusts and slice it into ¾-inch cubes. Heat equal parts of butter and olive oil quite hot in a frying pan (if it isn't hot enough the croutons will be soggy with oil) and add garlic, dill, caraway, thyme, or whatever flavoring you want. Throw in bread cubes and stir quickly to coat; turn down the heat and fry, stirring continually, until they are the proper color, or put the frying pan in a moderate oven and stir the croutons occasionally until they are golden brown.

THIRDED BREAD

1 cup wheat (white) flour	1 teaspoonful salt
1 cup rye flour	3 tablespoonsful sugar
1 cup yellow cornmeal	½ cup yeast

Mix with milk (*scalded and cooled*) till thick enough to be shaped. (*Knead, sprinkle some flour over it.*) Let it rise until it cracks open. Put into a brickloaf pan, and when well risen, bake it one hour. (*Makes 1 loaf. This can be made by using ⅓ each of any 3 flours.*)

SALT-RISING BREAD

It is light, sweet, tender, and very white, and is especially convenient where yeast can neither be made nor obtained. The peculiar odor which it often has does not necessarily belong to it; it is the result of carelessness in allowing the bread to stand too long in rising.

Pour a pint of hot water in a two-quart pail or pitcher, over half a teaspoonful of salt; when the finger can be held in it, add one and one-third pints of flour; mix well, and leave the pitcher in a kettle of water as warm as that used in mixing; keep it at the same temperature until the batter is nearly twice its original bulk, which will be from five to eight hours; it may be stirred once or twice during the rising. Add this to a sponge made of one quart of hot water and two and a half quarts of flour, adding as much more as may be necessary to make a soft dough; mix well, and leave it in a warm place to rise; when light, mould into loaves, keeping them soft as possible; lay them in buttered pans, and when light again, prick and bake. (*Makes 2 loaves.*)

WHEAT AND INDIAN BREAD

Put three pints of water over the fire; when it is boiling hot, add a large tablespoonful of salt, stir into it sweet white corn meal (*about 2 cups*), until it is a thick batter; continue to stir it for ten minutes, that it may not burn, then turn it into a dish, stir into it a quart of cold water; when it is cool enough to bear your hand in it, pour it into a bowl, in which is seven (*or less*) pounds of white flour, heaped round the sides, so as to leave a hollow in the center; add to it a gill of baker's yeast (*2 packages of dry yeast*), and a half a teaspoonful of saleratus (*baking soda*) dissolved in a little hot water, then work the whole into a smooth dough, work it or knead for nearly an hour, then strew a little flour over it, lay a thickly folded cloth over, and set it in a warm place for five or six hours in summer, or mix at night in winter; when light, work it down, set it to rise again for one hour, then heat the oven, work the bread down and divide it into loaves (*let rise 20 minutes*), and bake according to their size in a quick oven; when taken from the oven, turn them over in the pans, and set them to become cold; if the crust is hard, wrap them in a towel as soon as taken from the oven. (*Makes 6–7 loaves.*)

GRAHAM BREAD

4 cups graham (wheat) flour
3½ cups Pillsbury's best wheat (white) flour
2 tablespoonfuls molasses
3 cups lukewarm milk
1 cake yeast

1 heaping teaspoonful salt
2 tablespoonfuls brown sugar
½ teaspoon soda
2 tablespoons butter
½ cup lukewarm water

Sift together the graham flour, wheat flour, brown sugar and salt, then rub in the butter (*or melt the butter with the molasses in the milk and add together*). Add the molasses with the soda dissolved in it. Next add the luke-warm milk and lastly the yeast dissolved in the lukewarm water. Knead the dough well for twenty minutes and set it to rise covered up. After rising form it into two loaves, put them in pans and let them rise again. Graham bread requires longer to rise than white flour bread. Bake in a moderately hot oven for an hour and a quarter (*about 45 minutes—our flour is finer*). If graham bread is baked too quickly it is apt to become doughy in the center. (*Makes 2 loaves.*)

GRAHAM BREAD WITHOUT FINE FLOUR

Three quarts of graham flour; one quart of warm water, two gills of yeast, one gill of syrup (*either sugar and water, maple, corn, or golden syrup*), one tablespoonful of salt. Mix all the ingredients thoroughly, put it in well-buttered pans, and leave it in a warm place to rise, or let it rise overnight at 60°. If left to rise slowly, let it remain in the bowl in which it was mixed, and unless *very* light when put into the pans, let it stand fifteen or twenty minutes before putting it in the oven. (*Makes 2–3 loaves.*)

"*When cutting fresh bread, dip the knife in hot water.*"
The Caloric Book of Recipes, 1907

RYE BREAD

Make the same as wheat and Indian bread, substituting rye for wheat flour. Or thus: —To a quart of warm water, stir in as much wheat flour as will make a smooth batter, stir into it half a gill of baker's yeast, and set it in a warm place to rise; in the morning, put three pounds and a half of rye flour into a bowl, make a hollow in the middle, pour in the sponge, add a dessert-spoonful of salt, and half a small teaspoonful of saleratus, make the whole into a smooth dough, with as much warm water as may be necessary; knead it well, cover it, and let it set to rise in a warm place for three hours, then knead it again, and make it in two or three loaves; bake in a quick oven one hour, if made in two loaves, or less if the loaves be smaller. (*Makes 4 loaves.*)

RYE BREAD CAKE: Take from the risen dough, the size of a small loaf, work into it a small teacup of shortening, make it in a flat cake, rather more than an inch thick, and bake twenty-five minutes in a quick oven.

RAISED BROWN BREAD

One pint yellow corn meal, one-half cup yeast, one-half cup molasses, one-half teaspoonful salt, one saltspoonful soda, one pint rye meal. Put the corn meal in the mixing bowl, and scald it with boiling water, just enough to wet it; let it stand ten minutes, then add cold water enough to make a soft batter. When lukewarm, add the yeast, molasses, salt, soda and rye meal. Beat it well, and let it rise overnight, or until it cracks open. Stir it down, put it in a buttered and floured tin to rise again; sprinkle flour over the top. Bake in a moderate oven two hours. This has been made in the same house regularly every week for thirty years, and proves just as good now as it was in the olden time. (*Makes 1 loaf.*)

BOSTON BROWN BREAD

This is similar to pumpernickel.

Take one pound of white potatoes, peeled, boiled and mashed. Mix it with one pound of white flour, one pint of water with a cake (*or 2 envelopes*) of yeast dissolved in it. Let rise five or six hours. Mix two pounds of rye flour, four pounds of cornmeal, two pounds of graham flour, and one teacup of brown sugar or syrup. Mix all rapidly, thoroughly and lightly with warm water to make a thin dough. Put in a warm place till the surface cracks and shines. Pour into deep pans, not quite full. Bake four to six hours in a moderate oven. You can add one teacup of molasses and one teaspoonful of baking soda instead of the sugar. (*Makes 7–8 loaves.*)

BEAUFORT RICE BREAD

A pint of boiled rice, half a pint of hominy (*cooked*), three pints of rice flour, mixed with water enough to make a thick batter; add a teacup of yeast and a teaspoonful of pearlash (*soda*). Put the mixture into a deep pan, well greased, and let it rest for eight to ten hours. Bake in a rather brisk oven. (*Makes 1 large or 2 small loaves.*)

KAFFEE KUCHEN

The original, of course, for coffee cake; a way of using bread dough amenable to numerous variations.

One pound of risen dough (*about enough to make 1 loaf, taken after its first rising, or in the morning*) ready for the oven, four ounces of sugar, three ounces of butter, one egg. Cream the butter and beat it well with the sugar and the egg; add the dough and mix thoroughly with the hand; leave it in a warm place to rise; when light pour it in a small dripping pan (*a cookie sheet with a rim*) and let it stand ten or fifteen minutes, put it in the oven, and while it is baking prepare an icing. Blanch two dozen almonds and shred them; add to the beaten white of two eggs about half the usual quantity of sugar (*about ½ cup*), stir in the almonds, and when the cake is baked, cover it with the icing and leave it to dry in the mouth of the oven. The almonds may brown a little, if liked. When served, it is cut in oblong pieces.

BROWN, OR DYSPEPSIA BREAD

Take six quarts of wheat (*white*) flour, rather coarsely ground, one teacup of good yeast, and one half teacup of molasses, mix with these a pint of milk, warm water and a teaspoonful of saleratus. Make a hole in the meal and stir this mixture in the middle till it is like batter. Then proceed as for fine flour bread. Make the dough, when sufficiently light, into four loaves, which will weigh two pounds each when baked. It requires a hotter oven than a fine flour bread and must bake one and one half hours. (*The molasses rather than the flour gives this bread its color. It is rather plain—salt is obviously lacking —and undoubtedly very good for the digestion. Makes 5–6 loaves.*)

BROWN BREAD

One pint milk scalded and cooled; two tablespoonfuls of sugar; one teaspoonful salt; one quarter yeast cake dissolved in one half cup cold water; two cups white flour, sifted, three and a half cups graham flour. Mix a little softer than white bread. Let it rise till light; stir down and pour into well-greased pans. Let it rise again, and bake a little longer in a slower oven than white bread. (*Makes 2 small loaves.*)

YEAST

Getting and maintaining a good yeast culture was absolutely essential, particularly for the farm housewife isolated by geography or weather from the local baker or brewer, the usual source of yeast. But once she had the culture, the starter, the nineteenth-century housewife could keep it going indefinitely with home-made yeast. It gives bread a slightly different, interesting flavor, so here are several recipes.

SOURDOUGH

Mix two quarts of soft water with wheat (*white*) flour to the consistency of thick gruel (*oatmeal*); boil it gently for half an hour, and when it is almost cold, stir into it half a pound of sugar and four spoonful of good yeast (*2 packages of dried yeast or 1 compressed cake will do as a starter*). Put it into a large jug or earthen vessel with a narrow top, and place it before the fire (*in a warm place*) so that it may by a moderate heat ferment. The fermentation will throw off a thin liquor, which pour off and throw away; the remainder keep for use in a cool place, in a bottle or jug tied over (*covered well*). The same quantity as of common yeast will suffice to bake or brew with (*but more time is needed for rising*). Four spoonful of this will make a fresh quantity as before.

HOP YEAST

Peel four large potatoes or six small, and put them with a double handful (*about ½ ounce*) of hops tied in a coarse muslin bag into two quarts of water. Cover and boil until the potatoes break and fall apart. Take these out with a perforated skimmer, leaving the water still boiling; mash them fine and work in four tablespoonfuls of flour and two of sugar. Moisten this gradually with the boiling hop tea, stirring it to a smooth paste. When all the tea has been mixed in, set it aside to cool. While still slightly warm, add four tablespoonfuls of lively yeast, and turn all into a large open vessel to "work." Keep this in a warm place until it ceases to bubble up, or until next day. In summer it will work well in a few hours. When quite light, put in earthen jars with small mouths, in which fit corks, or bottle it (*in screw-top soda bottles*), and remove to the ice-house or cellar (*or refrigerator*). It will keep a fortnight, longer in winter (*or in a refrigerator*). When you wish to use it for baking, send a small vessel to the cellar for the desired quantity, and re-cork at once. A half hour in a hot kitchen may spoil it. (*Makes 3 quarts, too much unless you bake daily.*)

This can be made without the hops, but will not keep as long—and is a less interesting flavor.

SELF-WORKING YEAST

Tie two ounces of hops (*available from wine supply or herb stores, should you not have your own hop vine*) in a coarse muslin bag, and boil one hour in four quarts of water. Let it cool to lukewarmness before removing the bag. Wet with the tepid liquor—a little at a time—one pound of flour, making to a smooth paste. Put in half a pound of white sugar and one tablespoonful salt, beat up the batter three minutes before adding the rest of the tea. Set it away for two days in an open bowl covered with a thin cloth, in a closet which is moderately and evenly warm (*warming closets were frequently built alongside the chimney for purposes like this*). On the third day, peel, boil and mash eight potatoes, and when entirely free from lumps and specks, stir in gradually the thickened hop-liquor. Let it stand twelve hours longer in the bowl, stirring often, and keeping it in the warm kitchen. Then bottle or put away in corked jars, which must be kept perfectly sweet and freshly scalded. This will keep a month in a cool cellar (*a refrigerator doubles its life-span; makes 4 quarts*).

YEAST CAKES CALLED TURNPIKE CAKES

Put a quart of hops into two quarts of water, cover it and let them boil, then strain it hot over a quart of fresh corn meal, stir it well together. When cooled, so as to bear your hand in, add a teacup of good yeast, or one turnpike cake (*from the last batch you made*) dissolved in warm water, stir it well, make it in cakes a size of the top of a tumbler, or rather less, half an inch thick, lay them on a board, and set them in a dry, warm, but rather airy place, to rise and harden, do not put them in the sun; when one side is dry, turn the other and so turn them from side to side until they are thoroughly dry and hard; should the weather prove damp, these cakes may be dried near the fire. Keep them in coarse paper bags, in a dry cool place. Half of one of these cakes, dissolved in a cup of warm water, is enough for seven pounds of flour. These will remain good for months.

MORE OR LESS QUICK BREADS

Some of the following contain yeast, and need time for rising, but do not require kneading, and are generally less of an art than risen bread. Some of them are famous. Sally Lunn, Johnny (or journey) cake and corn pone probably had as much to do with the foundation of the country as the deer and the antelope ever did, and they are now nearly as extinct as the buffalo, available only in old country kitchens, a few regional restaurants, or in sleazy supermarket imitations.

SOUR MILK BROWN BREAD

1 cup white corn meal	1 full teaspoon soda
1 cup rye flour	½ cup molasses
1 cup graham (wheat) flour	1 pint sour milk
1 teaspoon salt	

Mix in the order given, sifting the soda, and adding more milk or water if not thin enough to pour. Steam three hours. One cup of raisins, stoned and halved, may be added to this, or any of the receipts for brown bread.

EXCELLENT DIET BREAD

Flour fresh from the mill was damp with the juices of the grain. It wouldn't work properly in recipes until it was dried, and usually aged for a month or so. Diet bread is not bread with fewer calories, but an enriched bread that was supposed to be good for you.

Sift a pound of the finest flour and dry it well before the fire. Beat up eight eggs for a short time, then add a pound of beaten and sifted sugar by degrees. Continue beating them together for an hour and a half (*or, in the electric mixer until very light*). Then, having taken the flour from the fire, strew it in cold, with half an ounce of coriander and caraway seeds mixed together and slightly bruised. The beating, in the meantime, must not cease or be at all discontinued till the whole is put into the paper mould or hoop and set in a quick oven, but not too hot. One hour will be sufficient to make it.

"Try ground caraway seed as flavoring for a simple cake; the ground spice being preferred by man in place of seeds."
                                        The Caloric Book of Recipes, 1907

JOHNNY CAKE

½ cup of sugar	1½ teaspoons of soda
Butter the size of an egg	1 cup of yellow corn meal
1 egg	1 cup of white flour
1½ cups sour cream or butter-milk	Pinch of salt

Grease a flat pan, bake in a 350° oven. (*Split pea soup is traditionally served with it. Makes 1 pie-sized cake. See p. 309 for Apple johnny cake.*)

CAROLINA CORN-CAKE

One quart of thick, sour milk, one and a half pints of corn-meal, half a pint of flour, three tablespoonfuls of melted butter, two even teaspoonfuls of salt, two and a half even teaspoonfuls of soda, three eggs, well-beaten. Sift the soda in the flour; add the meal, salt, two-thirds of the milk, and the eggs; mix thoroughly and add the rest of the milk; bake in patty pans or in large pans, and send it to table cut in square pieces.

SPIDER CORN CAKE

Three-quarters of a cup of corn meal, flour to fill the cup, one tablespoon-ful of sugar, one-half teaspoonful salt, one-half teaspoonful soda (scant), one egg, one cup sweet milk, one cup sour milk, one tablespoonful of butter; mix the meal, flour, sugar, salt, soda, beat the egg, add one-half of the sweet milk and all of the sour milk; stir this into the dry mixture, melt the butter in a hot spider (*cast-iron frying pan*) and pour the mixture into it; pour the other half-cup of sweet milk over the top, but do not stir. Bake 20 minutes in a hot oven.

NONPAREIL CORN BREAD

Receipt for bread made of Northern (*yellow*) Indian meal

2 *heaping cups of Indian meal*	2 *teaspoonfuls white sugar*
1 *cup of flour*	1 *teaspoonful soda*
3 *eggs*	2 *teaspoonfuls cream-tartar*
2½ *cups milk*	1 *teaspoonful salt*
1 *teaspoonful lard*	

Beat the eggs very thoroughly—whites and yolks separately—melt the lard, sift the cream-tartar and soda into the meal and flour while yet dry, and stir this in at the last. Then, to borrow the direction scribbled by a rattle-tongued girl upon the above receipt, when she sent it to me—"beat like mad!" Bake quickly and steadily in a buttered mould (*in a 400° oven*). Half an hour will usually suffice. In cutting corn bread hold the knife perpendicularly and cut toward you.

SALLY LUNN #1

Five teacups flour, one teacup butter and lard mixed, four eggs, three tablespoons sugar, half-teacup yeast, one teacup sweet milk. Stir the yeast into the dry flour, then add the milk and butter slightly warmed together. Then the yolks of eggs well beaten with the sugar. Last the beaten whites. Have the batter stiff enough to drop from the spoon clean. Let rise twice before putting in a well greased (*sponge-cake*) pan. Bake 50 minutes in moderate oven. One yeast cake can rise in ½ day.

SALLY LUNN #2

1 quart of flour	4 tablespoonfuls yeast (1 pack-
4 eggs	age dry)
½ cup melted butter	1 teaspoonful salt
1 cup warm milk	½ teaspoonful soda, dissolved in
1 cup warm water	hot water

Beat the eggs to a stiff froth, add the milk, water, butter, soda and salt; stir in the flour to a smooth batter, and beat the yeast in well. Set to rise in a buttered pudding-dish, in which it must be baked and sent to table. Or, if you wish to turn it out, set to rise in a *well*-buttered (*sponge-cake*) mould. It will not be light under six hours. Bake steadily three-quarters of an hour, or until a straw thrust into it comes up clean. Eat while hot.

This is the genuine old-fashioned Sally Lunn, and will hardly give place even to the newer and faster compounds known under the same name.

GRAHAM BREAD

One pint sour milk, one cup molasses, one heaping teaspoonful soda, one half teaspoonful salt, and graham flour enough to make a thin batter. Bake one hour in a moderate oven. (*Makes 2 small loaves.*)

RICE BREAD

One pint rice flour; one pint milk; one tablespoonful butter; one egg; one level teaspoonful soda; one of cream of tartar; a little salt. Scald the milk and mix as for corn bread. (*Bake 20 minutes in a quick oven, in a square pan.*)

BATTER BREAD, AN OLD VIRGINIA RECIPE

Two cups of sour milk, two cups of sweet milk, one cup of white corn meal, half a teaspoonful of baking powder, one small spoonful of salt, one teaspoonful of baking soda, two eggs (*well beaten*). Bake in a deep dish about half an hour. It should be served very hot, with a spoon and much butter.

ANOTHER: One pint sifted meal; three eggs; one pint of sweet milk; one pint boiling water; one heaping teaspoon of salt; one rounding tablespoon of lard. Add salt and lard to meal and pour over them boiling water, stirring rapidly. Add milk and eggs beaten very light and turn into a well-greased and very hot baking dish. Bake in a hot oven. The water must be boiling when poured over the meal or bread will be ruined. If in a hurry for the bread to cook, heat milk also. (*A broom straw inserted in the middle, if it comes out clean, will tell you the bread is done.*)

INDIAN MEAL BREAKFAST CAKES

Pour boiling water into a quart of yellow cornmeal; stir it until it is wet; then add two well-beaten eggs and milk enough to make a thick batter; measure a small teaspoon of dry saleratus (*baking soda*) and dissolve it in warm water, and put it to the batter with the same quantity of salt; butter (*two*) square tin pans, fill them two thirds full, and bake in a quick oven for one hour; when done, cut it in squares, and serve hot.

HOE CAKES

Scald a quart of Indian meal with just sufficient water to make a thick batter; stir in two spoonfuls of butter and two teaspoonfuls of salt. Turn into a buttered cake pan and bake about half an hour.

ALBANY BREAKFAST CAKES

Ten eggs, three pints of milk, fourth of a pound of butter, two teaspoonfuls of salt, half a teaspoonful of saleratus and white Indian meal to make thick batter; butter scalloped oval tins, two thirds fill them (they should hold about a pint), bake for half an hour in a quick oven. (*Makes 6 pint molds-full.*)

ROLLS, MUFFINS, BISCUITS

CORN-MEAL PONE

Mould with the hands into thin, oblong cakes 1 quart Indian meal, 1 teaspoonful salt, a little lard, melted, and cold water to make a soft dough. Lay in a well-greased pan, and bake very quickly. The common way is to mould into oval mounds, higher in the middle than at the ends, shaping these rapidly and lightly with the hands, by tossing the dough over and over. This is done with great dexterity by the Virginia cooks, and this corn-meal pone forms a part of every dinner. (*Bake in a hot oven.*) It is broken, not cut, and eaten very hot. (*Cast-iron pone pans, with cups shaped like miniature ears of corn, are still available.*)

FRIED PONE: Instead of moulding the dough with the hands, cut into slices with a knife. Try out (*fry*) some fat pork in a frying pan and fry the slices in the gravy (*grease*) thus obtained to a light brown (*or chop up some slices of bacon, brown them, then fry the pone, letting the scraps of bacon adhere to the outside*).

ITALIAN BREAD STICKS

One pound of bread dough (*about the amount it would take to make one loaf taken after its first rising*), a quarter of a pound of softened butter. Work the butter well into the dough (*adding a little flour if necessary*), and roll out about half an inch thick; cut into strips nearly an inch wide, and about seven or eight inches long; sift over them fine corn meal, place them apart on a buttered pan, and when light, bake in a quick oven. (*Brush with beaten egg white and coat with sesame or caraway seeds and salt, if you like. Makes 24–30.*)

VIENNA BREAD (*A HARD ROLL*)

The Vienna bread that became so famous on the Centennial Exhibition grounds in 1876 was made on the following recipe:

Sift in a tin pan four pounds of flour; bank up against the sides; pour in one quart of milk and water and mix into it enough flour to make a thin batter, and then quickly and lightly add one pint of milk in which is dissolved one ounce of salt and one and three-quarters ounces (*2 packages*) of yeast; leave the remainder of the flour against the sides of the pan; cover the pan with a cloth and set it in a place free from draught for three-quarters of an hour; then mix in the rest of the flour until the dough will leave the bottom and sides of the pan, and let it stand two and a half hours; finally, divide the mass into one-pound pieces, to be cut in turn into twelve parts each; this gives square pieces about three and a half inches thick, each corner of which is taken up and folded over to the center, and the cases are turned over on a dough-board to rise for half an hour, when they are put in a hot oven that will bake them in ten minutes. (*Makes 5 dozen.*)

PARKER HOUSE ROLLS

Scald one pint of milk with a little sugar, salt and butter the size of an egg; when cool, break into it half a yeast-cake, and add flour to knead smooth. Let it rise, and when light, cut down with a knife. If for tea (*at 4 o'clock*), mix in the morning, cutting down at noon. Roll out an hour and a half before tea, cut round, double over with a piece of butter in the middle of each. Bake fifteen minutes. (*Makes about 2 dozen.*)

FRENCH ROLLS

Pour a quart of lukewarm milk to a quart of flour; melt two ounces of butter, and add to it, with two eggs and a teaspoon of salt; when cool, stir in six spoonfuls of yeast (*1 package dry yeast*) and flour till sufficiently stiff to mould up. Set it in a warm place. When light, mould it into small rolls; lay them on flat, buttered tins, and let remain twenty minutes before baking. (*Makes about 4 dozen.*)

FRENCH ROLLS

Names traveled. "French rolls" could include a number of different ingredients. I doubt they had anything to do with France, since there was a tendency to call any good recipe "French."

One pound of flour, nine ounces of potato (*one good-sized potato*), one teaspoonful of sugar, one teaspoonful of salt, one gill of warm milk, one egg, one and a half ounces of lard, two gills of cold water, half a yeast cake soaked in a tablespoonful of tepid water.

Pare and slice the potato, cover it with the cold water; and boil until tender, then rub it through a sieve with the water (*or blend*), add the lard, sugar, and salt, and a tablespoonful of the flour; leave this to rise in a warm place. When light, beat in the egg, add the milk, and knead in the flour; leave it to rise again, and when light make into oblong rolls, and lay them in buttered pans. When light again, prick (*a curious practice which involves jamming a kitchen fork through to the bottom of the roll*), and bake (*in a hot oven; makes about 2 dozen*).

RICE CAKES

Pick and wash half a pint of rice, and boil it very soft. Then drain it, and let it get cold. Sift a pint and a half of flour over the pan of rice and mix in a quarter of a pound of butter that has been warmed by the fire, and a saltspoon of salt. Beat five eggs very light, and stir them gradually into a quart of milk. Beat the whole very hard, and bake it in muffin rings or in a waffle-iron. Send them to table hot, and eat them with butter, honey or molasses. (*Makes 1–1½ dozen.*)

ST. JOHN'S RICE ROUND BREAD

One-half pint of rice boiled soft, three eggs, one teaspoonful of butter, one teacupful of milk, and as much wheat (*white*) flour as will make the consistency of pound cakes. Drop on a hot pan; bake, do not turn over. (*Makes about 1 dozen.*)

TO MAKE CRUMPETS

Mix a gill of brewer's yeast, free from bitter (*not made with hops*), with two quarts of water, just lukewarm, to which add sufficient flour to make thinnish batter, and just let it stand six hours in a warm place, then stir it well with a wooden spoon, and let it remain four hours longer, have the muffin stove hot, upon which lay a number of tin hoops, the size of crumpets. Pour a small ladleful of the batter into each hoop, and when the top is covered with small bladders (*like the small bubbles that appear when a pancake is ready to be turned*), turn them quickly over (*hoops and all*), with a large palate knife (*spatula*), and in about five minutes afterwards, they will be sufficiently baked. (*Makes 2–3 dozen.*)

LAPLANDERS

A kind of popover.

One pint (*8 ounces*) of graham flour, one pint of warm water, half a teaspoonful of salt, one egg, well-beaten.

Have the gem-pans (*muffin tins*) heating in the oven, which must be very hot, much hotter than for biscuit (*about 450°*). Beat the egg with one or two spoonfuls of the water; add the salt, half of the water, and the flour; beat thoroughly, then stir in the rest of the water. Put the pans on the range, butter them, using a swab on a stick, pour in the batter, and put them immediately in the oven. The batter may be mixed in a pitcher and poured. Made with milk instead of water, the above are sometimes called German puffs. (*Makes 1 dozen.*)

CARAWAY BUNS

Half an ounce of caraway seeds; half a pound of currants; a little nutmeg, a little lemon peel; two eggs; one quart of new milk; one ounce of butter; two pounds of flour; a quarter of a pound of sifted sugar; one or two spoonfuls of yeast (*1 package of dry yeast*). Make a hole in the middle of the flour, and pour the milk in, with one or two spoonfuls of the yeast. Stir the dough, cover it over, and let it stand before the fire to rise for an hour. Then mix the caraway seeds, lemon peel, and nutmeg with one half, and the currants with the other, and cover all up together till the oven is ready. Make up the buns of a proper size, and put them on a baking sheet buttered. Beat up an egg, and brush over them with it. Cover them again, and put them before the fire for another half an hour. Then bake them twenty minutes. Do not make them too big. (*Makes about 2 dozen.*)

POTATO ROLLS

Boil six pounds of potatoes and work them well with four ounces of butter and as much milk as will make them pass through a cullender, add yeast and warm water enough to mix up ten pounds of flour with some salt, knead it well and let it stand until raised; bake it in a hot oven. (*Makes 75–80.*)

CREAM TEA CAKES

To a pound of flour, put a pint of sour cream, and a cup of butter; dissolve half a teaspoonful of saleratus in a little hot water, and put to it; mix it lightly, flour your hands well; make it out in small cakes, each about the size of an egg; lay them close in a buttered basin, and bake in a quick oven. (*Makes 12–15. They are best served hot.*)

VELVET CAKES

To one quart of flour put a pint of warm milk and a gill of yeast; stir it well; then set it in a warm place to rise for two hours: then work into it two large tablespoonfuls of melted butter or beef dripping; flour your hands well, and make it in small cakes; rub a bit of butter over a pan, and lay them in; dip your hand in milk, and pass it over the tops of them; and bake in a quick oven. (*Makes 1 dozen.*)

MUFFINS

Two eggs lightly beaten, one quart of flour, one teaspoon of salt, three teaspoons of Durkee's baking powder, one tablespoon of melted butter, one pint of milk, and two teaspoons of vanilla extract if liked. Beat up quickly to the consistency of cake batter; bake in buttered gem-pans (*muffin tins*) in a hot oven. (*Makes 24–30.*)

RAISED MUFFINS

One cup of home-made yeast or half of a compressed yeast cake, one pint of sweet milk, two eggs, two tablespoons of melted butter, two tablespoons of sugar. Beat the sugar, butter and eggs well together; then stir in the milk, slightly warmed, and thicken with flour to the consistency of griddle cakes. (*Fill muffin rings half full and set, covered, in a warm place to rise. Bake in a quick oven when they are light, in about 6 hours.*) If wanted for tea, the batter should be mixed immediately after breakfast. Muffins should never be cut with a knife, but be pulled open with the fingers. (*Makes 2 dozen.*)

[67]

INDIAN MUFFINS

Pour boiling water into a quart of yellow corn-meal, stir it well, let it be a thick batter; when it is cooled a little, add to it a tablespoonful of yeast, two eggs well beaten, and a teaspoonful of salt; set it in a warm place to rise, for two hours; then butter (*two*) square tin pans, two-thirds fill them, and bake in a quick oven; when done, serve hot, cut in squares; or bake as wheat muffins.

Berries may be added at will to muffins. If they are floured first, they won't sink.

CREAM SHORTCAKES

Add 1 teaspoon of salt to 1 quart of flour. Dissolve 1 scant teaspoon of soda in 2 tablespoonfuls of boiling water (*no longer necessary*), add it to ½ pint of thick cream; then add the cream to the flour, mix quickly, and form into cakes the size of a breakfast-plate, and a half-inch thick. Place on a hot griddle. Brown on one side, then turn and brown on the other. (*Makes 8–12.*)

If flour is very heavy, it may require a little more cream to make a soft dough.

POTATO BISCUIT

To four good-sized mealy potatoes, boiled soft, peeled, and mashed, add a piece of butter as big as a hen's egg, and a teaspoonful of salt. When the butter is melted, put in half a pint of cold milk. If the milk sufficiently cools the potatoes, put in a gill of yeast, and flour enough to make them of the right consistency to mould up. Place them where warm; when risen, mould them up with the hand; let them remain ten or fifteen minutes, and bake. (*Makes 12–15.*)

BUTTER BISCUIT

Mix a teacup of melted butter with two thirds of a pint of milk (*warm*), add a teaspoonful of salt, six spoonfuls of milk yeast, or other yeast, and stir in flour till sufficiently stiff to mould up. The addition of two eggs will improve the biscuit. Place the dough where warm; when risen, mould it with the hands into small cakes, and place them on flat buttered tins. Bake them, after standing half an hour. (*Makes 1½ dozen.*)

BUTTERMILK BISCUIT

Dissolve two teaspoonfuls of saleratus in a teacup of sour milk; mix it with a pint of buttermilk, and two teaspoonfuls of salt; stir in flour till sufficiently stiff for moulding up. Make them into small cakes and bake them immediately. (*Makes 2–2½ dozen.*)

SALERATUS (*SODA*) BISCUIT

Put two teaspoonfuls of saleratus to a pint of sour milk. If you have no sour milk, put a spoonful of vinegar to a pint of sweet milk, and set it in a warm place. As soon as it curdles, mix it with the saleratus, put in two spoonfuls of melted butter, and flour enough to roll out. Mould into small biscuits and bake immediately. (*Makes 1½ dozen.*)

GRAHAM OR BRAN BISCUITS

Three cups of graham or bran flour, one cup of white flour, three cups of milk, two tablespoonfuls of lard, one tablespoonful of white sugar, one saltspoonful of salt, one teaspoonful of carbonate of soda, two teaspoonfuls of cream of tartar.

Mix the dry ingredients together, then rub in the lard and make a dough with the milk. Roll out, cut into round cakes, and bake in a hot oven until beginning to brown. (*Makes 2 dozen.*)

MARYLAND, OR BEATEN BISCUIT

Rub ¼ cup lard and ½ teaspoon salt into 1 quart flour, and mix with 1 cup cold water to a very stiff dough (*like pie dough; some recipes call for a little soda*). Knead ten minutes, or until well mixed; then beat hard with a biscuit beater or heavy rolling pin (*or, traditionally, with the flat of an ax on a smooth tree stump*), turning the mass over and over until it begins to blister,

[69]

and looks light and puffy, or "till pulling off a piece quickly, it will give a sharp, snapping sound." When in this condition, pull off a small piece suddenly, form it into a round biscuit (about silver dollar size), then pinch off a bit from the top. Turn over and press with the thumb, leaving a hollow in the centre. Put the biscuits some distance apart in the pan. Prick with a fork. Bake twenty minutes in a quick oven. They should be of a fine, even grain, and crack at the edges like our crackers. In Maryland, no young lady's education was formerly considered finished until she learned the art of making beaten biscuit. (*Makes 50.*)

These are hard and flaky in the fingers, soft in the mouth, and are to be eaten cold, with chicken salad or lobster salad.

MISS YANDES' RUSK

1 pint of milk, scalded	*1 cup potato yeast*
½ cup butter and lard, mixed	*3 eggs*
¾ cup sugar	*Flour as required*

Mix early in the morning, in order given, adding flour enough to make a thin batter. Let it rise till full of bubbles, then add flour enough to knead it. When well risen, shape into rounds, or roll out and cut them. Let them rise in the pans until very light; then bake in a hot oven about half an hour. (*Makes 2 dozen.*)

Dried rusks, when risen, are rolled thin, cut into rounds, and put two together in the pan. When baked, they are pulled apart and left in a very moderate oven to dry. Or they are cut in slices when cold and dried until crisp and brown. They are delicious soaked in milk and eaten with butter.

RUSK

One pint of milk, one teacup of yeast, mix it thin (*with a little flour and set it to rise*); when light, add twelve ounces of sugar, ten ounces of butter, four eggs, flour sufficiently to make it as stiff as bread; when risen again, mould and sponge it (*let it rise briefly*) upon tin. (*Makes 2–2½ dozen.*)

CRACKERS

CRACKERS

One pound of flour, and two ounces of butter, mixed to a stiff paste with milk; beat it smooth with the rolling pin, then roll it thin, and cut it in round or square cakes; prick each with a fork, and bake on tin. (*Makes 3–4 dozen.*)

LEMON CRACKERS

2½ cups sugar
3 eggs
1 cup lard
1¼ cup sweet milk
5 cents worth baking ammonia
  (1 teaspoon of baking powder)

5 cents worth of lemon oil (1 teaspoon of lemon extract)
flour enough to make a stiff dough

Pulverize the ammonia and soak overnight in the milk (*not necessary with baking powder*). Mix a stiff dough and roll thin, cut into squares and pierce with a fork. (*Makes 8–10 dozen.*)

DOUGHNUTS AND FRIED CAKES

DOUGHNUTS

One pint milk; three eggs; two cups sugar; one cup butter or lard; one gill fresh yeast; grated orange peel or nutmeg; flour enough to make a stiff paste. (*Knead it well; let it rise.*) Roll into balls, and cook like crullers. (*Deep fry; makes 2 dozen.*)

"Try putting a pinch of ginger in your doughnuts and they will not absorb the fat or grease."

The Caloric Book of Recipes, 1907

[71]

DOUGHNUTS

Two cups of sugar, half a cup of butter, one cup of sour milk, three eggs, one teaspoonful of carbonate of soda, one saltspoonful of salt, flour sufficient to roll it out.

Rub the sugar and butter to a cream, add the yolks of the eggs and the milk. (*Add the soda.*) Then stir in enough sifted flour, in which is the salt, to make a dough stiff enough to be rolled. Flavor with a little ground cinnamon or nutmeg. Roll out to the thickness of half an inch and cut into round cakes, making a hole in the middle with a doughnut cutter if you have one. Have ready a large shallow saucepan nearly full of boiling lard; about two pounds will be necessary the first time, but, of course, it may be used many times over for frying doughnuts and other things, if it is strained through muslin after using. When the lard is boiling hot—this you can tell by dropping in a small piece of dough, which will rise immediately if the fat is hot enough—drop your doughnuts carefully in, putting as many in as will float in the pan barely touching one another. Fry till a delicious brown color on one side: when turn and fry till the other side is colored brown; by this time the doughnuts will be done. (*Keep checking the temperature of the fat. If too hot, the doughnuts will brown before the inside is cooked. If too cold, they will be greasy and soggy.*) When cold, sprinkle with icing (*confectioner's*) sugar. (*Makes 1– 1½ dozen.*)

Doughnuts may also be made with bread dough, into which 2 ounces of lard or butter per pint of dough has been worked or cut (with a little flour to prevent sticking). Let it rise, roll, cut, and fry.

CRULLERS

1 *tablespoon melted butter*	½ *saltspoon cinnamon or mace*
2 *heaping tablespoons sugar*	½ *saltspoon salt*
1 *egg, white and yolk beaten*	*Flour enough to roll out*
separately	(1 cup milk)

Roll dough one-quarter of an inch thick. Cut in rectangular pieces, two and a half by three and a half inches; then make five length-wise incisions, cutting to within one-third of an inch of the end. Take up every other strip, fold each together slightly in the middle, and drop them in hot fat. (*Makes 1 dozen.*)

ANOTHER: Beat nine heaping tablespoons of brown sugar, rolled, yolks of five eggs and one cup of butter together. Spice (*with nutmeg, ginger, or lemon rind*) to taste. Stir in the whites of the eggs (*stiffly beaten*). Stir in half a cup of wine, then one tablespoon of saleratus in one cup of milk. Add flour to thicken it for rolling. Roll out, cut and fry in hot lard. (*Makes 1 dozen.*)

CREAM FRITTERS

Take a quart of sweet milk and a teacup full of cream, four eggs beat to a froth, one half a nutmeg or a grated lemon peel, and one teaspoonful salt. Stir them with sufficient flour to make a thick batter. Dissolve half a teaspoonful of saleratus and stir in. Have your lard hot and drop them in by the spoonful and fry to a light brown. Serve them with liquid pudding sauce (*p. 94*) or sprinkle over them sugar and nutmeg. (*Makes 2 to 2½ dozen.*)

BATTER FOR FRITTERS

Yolks of two eggs beaten well; add half a cup of milk or water, and one tablespoonful of olive oil, one saltspoonful of salt, and one cup of flour, or enough to make it almost a drop batter. When ready to use, add the whites of the eggs, beaten very stiff. If intended for fruit, add a teaspoonful of sugar to the batter. If for clams, tripe or meat, add one tablespoonful of lemon juice or vinegar. This batter will keep several days. (*Makes 2 cups.*)

PANCAKES AND WAFFLES

LEMON TURNOVERS

A dessert crêpe.

Four dessertspoonfuls of flour, one of powdered sugar, the (*grated*) rind of one lemon, two ounces of melted butter, two eggs and a little milk. Mix flour, sugar and lemon with milk to the consistency of batter; add the butter and eggs well-beaten. Fry (*like pancakes*) and turn over. (*Spread lightly with jam or sprinkle with powdered sugar and roll up; serves 4.*)

A square piece of salt pork, speared on a fork and rubbed over the *griddle or frying pan, will grease for pancakes better, leaving no fat in the pan to soak into the cakes and no burned-on fat to clean later.*

THE JUSTLY FAMED WAFFLES OF FLATBUSH, RECEIPT HANDED DOWN THROUGH FOUR GENERATIONS FOR THE WAFFLES ALWAYS TO BE HAD IN FLATBUSH AT ANY HIGH TEA AMONG THE OLD FAMILIES

One pound of Sugar, One Pound of Butter, One Pound of Flour, Ten eggs (*Cream the butter and sugar. Separate the eggs and beat the yolks into the creamed mixture until light. Add the flour, then fold in the egg whites, beaten to stiff peaks.*) Bake in a window-pain waffle-iron (*a grid, like modern ones*) and when slightly cool, sprinkle with powdered sugar. (*Serves 6–8.*)

RAISED WAFFLES

Mix at night, one pint of milk, one-third of a cup of yeast, and one pint of flour. In the morning, add half a teaspoonful of salt, two eggs, yolks and whites beaten separately, and one tablespoonful of melted butter. Cook. (*Serves 4.*)

Use only one egg, make the batter a little thinner, and fry on the griddle, and you have flannel cakes.

The nineteenth-century cook got up long before she ate breakfast, and did a lot of housework while the fire reached a good heat for cooking. Because of the time needed for rising, these are better for brunch than breakfast.

WHITE MOUNTAIN FLANNEL CAKES

Mix two eggs with one cupful molasses and two cupfuls sweet milk, add one pound flour sifted with one heaping teaspoonful baking powder in it and a good pinch salt. Mix together and add enough milk to make a thin running dough. Fry on a hot griddle. (*Serves 6–8.*)

"Snow *will serve instead of eggs for pancakes. It should be taken when* just *fallen, and quite clean. Two tablespoonfuls of snow will suppy the place of one egg.*"

Ella E. Myers, *The Home Cook Book,* 1880

LEMON SYRUP FOR WAFFLES AND CAKES

Boil 1 cup sugar with ¼ cup water until it thickens slightly, add 1 teaspoonful butter and 1 tablespoonful lemon juice. Serve as soon as the butter is melted. (*Makes 1 cup.*)

BUCKWHEAT CAKES

One quart of buckwheat flour, one gill of wheat (*white*) flour, one quart less one gill of warm water, one gill of yeast, two teaspoonfuls of salt.

Mix the batter at night in order to have the cakes for breakfast; if very light, an hour before they are required stir the batter down and let it rise again. Bake the cakes on a smooth, nicely-greased griddle, and send them to the table the moment they are baked, piled regularly in the middle of the plate. If some of the batter is left from the baking, it will serve as yeast for the next baking; put it away in a cold place, but where it will not freeze; bring it out at night, add buckwheat, etc., and leave it to rise. With a little care, no fresh yeast will be necessary the whole winter. A gill of oatmeal may be used in addition to the wheat flour. (*Serves 8.*)

GRIDDLE CAKES

1 pint of flour	1 teaspoon soda
1 scant pint sour milk or cream	(2 tablespoonfuls melted butter)
2 well-beaten eggs	
½ teaspoonful salt	

Mix the dry ingredients thoroughly. Add the milk and beat well; then add the beaten yolks, and lastly the whites, beaten stiff. Bake on a hot, well-greased griddle; turn when full of bubbles, and bake on the other side until they stop puffing. (*Serves 4.*)

Use ½ or ⅓ corn meal, or graham flour, to make a variety.

Substitute sweet for sour milk, 2 teaspoonfuls baking powder for soda, and add ½ cup cottage cheese for very light pancakes.

FINE HOMINY CAKES

Hominy, fresh-boiled or cold, can be used. If the latter, break into grains with a fork and heat it in a steaming pail, stir in a little butter. For a pint, two eggs, whites and yolks beaten separately. A saltspoonful of salt, if the hominy was well salted at first. Drop in spoonfuls on well-buttered tin plates, and bake to a nice brown. Nice and light as sponge drops. (*Serves 4.*)

PASTRY, NOODLES

Puff paste, light, crisp and flaky, crackling with butter, was used in most of the places where we now use plain old pie crust, as a top for pies, as a crust for meat pies, to make fancy shells for tarts or seafood, to enclose custards and puddings. It was one of the tests of the housewife: a light, delicate puff paste marked the expert. It takes more time to make than pie crust, but it is no more difficult, and it is far more impressive.

PUFF PASTE #1

One pound of butter; one pound of flour. Divide the butter into quarters; put one quarter into the flour and with a knife (*or a pastry cutter, not with the hand, since the warmth of the hand makes the butter oily*) cut it through very fine. Then with cold (*iced*) water, make it a stiff dough. Flour the board, turn out the paste, dredge with flour, and roll quite thin. Then cut another quarter of the butter into thin slices, and lay over the paste. Dredge (*lightly*) with flour, and fold over the sides, forming a square. Then roll until of a moderate thickness, and add another quarter (*the paste improves if it rests in the refrigerator under a damp towel, between rollings*); and so continue until all the butter is rolled in, observing to roll quickly, and handle as little as possible, as the warmth of the hand softens the butter. When the last quarter is in, roll until about half an inch thick, then cut the paste into quarters, place it on a dish and set it in a very cold place. (*This makes enough for 2 pies.*)

"For the best puff paste, make each pound of butter into a flat cake about an inch thick; put it on a dish, and set it in a cold place until needed. When the weather is cold, half lard (if fresh and pure)

may be used (vegetable shortening will NOT do); and if speedily and carefully made will be of equal lightness and flavor, as that made with all butter. In winter, as soon as the paste is made, put it on a dish, cover with a cloth and set it in a cold place until perfectly hard. By letting it remain (in this way) two or three hours, it will puff much more than if baked soon after mixing. Never take a larger piece of paste (at a time) than sufficient to line the plate, which roll of a moderate thickness. Then dredge with a little flour, fold it over, and roll again until the size of the plate, in which it is to bake. Always roll it much thinner in the center than at the edge. Slightly butter the plate, put in the paste, pat in close at the sides (being careful not to touch the edge). Then trim round with a knife, put in the filling, and cover with paste rolled moderately thin. Then, trim round again and notch tastefully."

Mrs. Widdifield's New Cookbook, 1856

"Puff paste should not be used for the under crust of pies; when not having space enough to rise, it becomes greasy and heavy. Puff paste requires a quicker oven heat; a hot oven would curl the paste and scorch it. Tart or short paste requires a degree less of heat."

Mrs. Crowen, The American System of Cookery, 1870

PUFF PASTE #2

Mix 1 pint flour, a tablespoonful of butter, 1 beaten egg yolk and 1 gill icewater into a paste with a wooden spoon. Flour your pastry board, and roll out the crust very thin. Put the rest of ½ pound butter, when you have washed it, in the centre of this sheet, in a flat cake. Turn the four corners of the paste over it, and roll out carefully, not to break the paste. Should it give way, flour the spot that it may not stick to the roller. When very thin, sprinkle lightly with flour, fold up, and roll out four times more. Set in a cool place for an hour, roll out again, and cut into tartlet-shells or top crust for (*two*) pies. (*It will keep three days in the refrigerator, rolled in a damp cloth.*)

PLAIN PIE CRUST

Two cups of flour, ¾ cup of lard or vegetable shortening (which is flakier than butter in plain crust), ½ teaspoonful of salt, perhaps a little grated lemon rind. Chop the shortening into the flour and salt, until fine and crumbly. *Add ice water gingerly—between ½ and ¼ cup of it—stirring it in quickly with a fork, until the paste just holds together. Then roll it out about ¼ of an inch thick on a floured board with a floured rolling pin. Fold it in half to slip into the pie plate, then unfold and trim to fit with pastry scissors. To put on a top crust, moisten the rim of the bottom crust, lay the top on, trim to fit and pinch together or press all around the edge with the tines of a fork. Unless the recipe says otherwise, slash the top to let the steam escape or your pie will spring leaks around the edges.*

POTATO PIE CRUST

is good (*for meat pies*). Peel and mash fine eight boiled potatoes; mix with them half a pint of milk, a teaspoonful of salt, a hen's egg-size piece of butter, and flour enough for rolling out. (*Makes enough for 1½ pies.*)

TART PASTE

Rub into eight ounces of flour, six ounces of butter and a spoonful of powdered sugar. Form it into a thick paste with hot water.

NOODLES FOR SOUP

Take a quarter of a pound of flour, a little salt, and as many egg yolks as will make it a stiff dough. (*Pour the beaten egg yolks into a hollow in the flour and work them well together.*) Roll it out very thin, flour it well, and let it remain on the pastry board to dry; then roll it up as you would a sheet of paper, and cut with a sharp knife into slips as thin as straws; after all are cut, mix them lightly together, and to prevent them from adhering, keep them well floured.

DRIED BEANS, PEAS

DRY BEANS

Wash, pick them over, and soak overnight. Cut a new piece of salt fat pork, not too large, cut the rind in thin strips and change the water on the beans, and boil them together until the beans become soft. Take them out (*reserve the liquid*) into a bean dish or deep dish of some kind, lay the pork in the center, having the rind just above the beans, pepper them, and have gravy (*the reserved liquid*) enough to almost cover. It should be even with the beans, then set in the oven and bake one hour (*at 350°*) or until the pork is crisped. Some add a little molasses, and they are more healthy cooked with a little saleratus. Soft water should be used, if possible, to boil in, or saleratus is necessary. (*I like pinto beans best for baked beans, and a chopped onion, a couple of teaspoonfuls of dried mustard, and a little salt added with the molasses. This is the basic Boston baked bean recipe. A pound of dry beans will serve 8–10.*)

"*Much of the excellence of baked beans depends upon the bean-pot. It should be earthen, with a narrow mouth, and bulging sides. This shape is seldom found outside of New England, and is said to have been modelled after the Assyrian pots. In spite of the slurs against 'Boston baked beans,' it is often observed that strangers enjoy them as much as natives.*"

Mrs. Lincoln's Boston Cook Book, 1896

WHITE HARICOT BEANS

Nothing is so cheap or so solid a food as haricot beans; get a pint of fine white beans, put them into half a gallon of cold soft water, with one ounce of butter; they take about three hours to cook, and should simmer very slowly, drain them and put into a stewpan with a little salt, pepper, chopped parsley, two ounces of butter, and the juice of a lemon, place on the fire for a few minutes, stir well and serve. The longer sort (*of beans*) requires to be soaked a few hours before boiling. (*Serves 8.*)

ANOTHER: Take a pint of beans, pour one quart of boiling water over them and let them remain in soak until the next day; cut a (*small head of*) lettuce in four pieces and put it with the beans in some fresh hot water, throw in a small fagot of parsley and a slice of ham, boil them until the whole is tender. Chop up some onions with a clove of garlic, fry them, and put them into a stewpan, put the beans to them with a well-beaten egg and some spice, heat them and send them to table. (*Serves 8.*)

RED BEANS WITH BURGUNDY

Take a quart of sound red beans; pick out all the small stones that are likely to be mixed with them; wash them thoroughly, lay them in plenty of cold water, and let them soak for six hours. Drain, and put them in a saucepan, covering them with fresh water, adding an ounce of butter, a bouquet (*parsley, a bay leaf and a sprig of thyme or marjoram tied around a celery stalk*), and a medium-sized onion with two cloves stuck in it. Boil for twenty minutes, stirring in a good glassful of red wine; season with a pinch of salt and half a pinch of pepper, and let it cook again for forty-five minutes. Remove, take out the bouquet and onion, and place the beans in a hot deep dish. Decorate with six small glazed onions around the dish and serve. (*Serves 15–18.*)

TO COOK DRIED LIMA BEANS (*OR OTHER DRIED BEANS*)

At night wash one pint of beans, put them in a small tin pail, pour over them one quart of boiling water, cover closely and let them stand until two and a half hours before dinner; then add more water, and let them boil until tender, keeping them well covered with water (*a light stock, or the water from boiled vegetables, improves limas and white beans and adds vitamins*). When nearly done, throw in two even teaspoonfuls of salt; be careful to keep them from breaking. When perfectly soft, drain in the colander, return them to the kettle, and add three ounces of butter, half a teaspoonful of white pepper, and one gill of cream. Shake them about gently, and when very hot, serve. (*Serves 8.*)

Salt pork may be boiled with beans, or small bits of bacon, fried crisp, added with the cream.

WINTER SUCCOTASH

Parboil a pint of beans (*dried limas*) and throw off the water; add one quart of boiling water, and when they have boiled twenty minutes, throw in a gill of cold water, and twenty minutes afterwards, throw in another. In this way the beans will be cooked in an hour and a quarter. Have ready a pound of salt pork that has been boiled two hours (*this was pork salted, not the salted fatback we call salt pork now; fresh pork or pork butt make approximate substitutes, or a half-pound slab of lean bacon*) and a (*quart*) can of sweet corn boiling hot; add them to the beans, with two tablespoons of white sugar, three ounces of butter rolled in flour, and salt and pepper to the taste; add a little water if necessary. Let all simmer together for half an hour, then serve very hot. (*Serves 8.*)

HOMINY

Two quarts of (*dried*) white corn, three half-pints of white beans; two pounds of pickled pork. Wash the corn and put it on to boil in water sufficient to cover it; and as the corn swells, more water must be added so as to keep them covered all the time it is cooking. After boiling four hours, then add the beans and pork, which when done, the hominy must be sent to the table. Should the pork not make it sufficiently salt, more may be added. This is very nice warmed over the next day. (*A Yankee version of a Southern dish. Serves 20.*)

HOMINY BROWNED FOR BREAKFAST

In a small but rather deep frying-pan put a bit of butter, a little more than enough to prevent sticking. When hot, fill the frying-pan with cold boiled hominy, press it evenly, cover until thoroughly heated, then remove the cover and let it remain on the range until a brown crust has formed below and on the sides; loosen it with a knife, lay a dinner plate upon the frying pan, turn them together, then raise the pan and you will find a beautiful brown mound of hominy.

BEAN PORRIDGE

Five pounds of corned beef, not too salt, or four pounds of beef and one of salt pork; one pint of dry white beans, four tablespoonfuls of corn meal, pepper and salt to taste, one pint of hulled (*dried*) corn. Soak the beans overnight. In the morning parboil in fresh water with a pinch of soda until soft. Put the corned beef and pork in cold water, skim carefully and simmer for four or five hours, or until tender. Take out and cut into two-inch pieces, and remove the bone and gristle; also the fat from the liquor. Put the meat and beans into the meat liquor and simmer very slowly three or four hours, or till most of the beans are broken. Half an hour before serving stir in the meal, first wetting it to a smooth paste with cold water. The meal should thicken the porridge to about the consistency of thick soup. The meat should be cooked till it falls apart. Season to taste with salt and pepper. Add the hulled corn (*cooked; home-frozen corn may be substituted*), and serve with brown bread. Sometimes the vegetables usually served with a boiled dinner (*p. 347*) are cooked with the meat, then removed and the beans cooked as above. (*Serves 12.*)

This was a staple for winter woods-workers around 1800. It was poured into small bowls, a length of string was laid into it, the loop dangling over the edge, and then it was put outside to freeze. When the dish was held in hot water, the porridge could be slipped out, then hung by the string in the freezing-cold buttery. It was considered "best when nine days old," and would be hung from the sledge when wood had to be cut in the forest, to be heated in a pot over a fire for lunch.

BLACK BEAN SOUP

Soak one pint of black beans all night. Then boil in two and a half quarts of water. To four quarts of stock add the beans (strained through a sieve), one teaspoon of cloves, a half teaspoon of cinnamon, one teaspoon of pepper, one lemon sliced, four hardboiled eggs. Just before serving, add forcemeat balls, one glass of port wine and half a glass of brandy to every three quarts of soup. (*Serves 20.*)

FORCEMEAT BALLS: Cook veal or sweetbreads till tender, chop very fine, with one third suet, and bread crumbs, a very little onion, pepper and salt. Roll in yolk of eggs and fry in lard.

ANOTHER: Soak over night one pint black beans. In the morning pour off the water, put on to boil in two quarts of cold water, add an onion fried in butter, and a bit of celery, if you have it. Simmer four or five hours till the beans are soft, adding more cold water as it boils away, leaving about two quarts when done. Rub the beans through a steamer (*or blend*), put the soup on to boil, adding three tablespoonfuls of salt, one saltspoonful of black pepper, one saltspoonful of mustard, one tablespoonful of whole cloves, and a dash of cayenne pepper. When boiling, thicken with one tablespoonful of flour mixed with two tablespoonfuls of butter. Slice into the tureen one lemon and two hard-boiled eggs; pour the soup over them and serve. Add half a can of tomatoes before straining, if you like. (*Serves 8.*)

SCOTCH BARLEY BROTH

Throw three quarters of a pound of barley into some clean water; when thoroughly cleansed place it with a knuckle of veal in a stewpan, cover it with cold water, let it slowly reach a boil, keep it skimmed, add seven onions and simmer two hours; skim again and add two heads of celery and two turnips cut in slices or any shape it pleases the cook, add as much of salt as required to make it palatable, let it stew for one and a half hours; it must be well skimmed before the broth is dished; the meat must be previously removed and the broth alone sent to table. If it is intended to send the veal to the table with it, dress it as follows: take two pints of the broth and put it into a stewpan over a clear fire, add two tablespoonfuls of flour to the broth, and keep the broth stirring as you shake it in until it boils; add a little cayenne pepper, two tablespoonfuls of port, boil it for two minutes, strain it over the veal and send to table. (*Serves 10.*)

MADEMOISELLE JENNY LIND'S SOUP

Mlle. Lind was in the habit of taking this soup before she sang, as she found the sago and eggs soothing to the chest and beneficial to the voice.

Wash one quarter pound of the best pearl sago (*barley can be substituted*) until the water poured from it is clear; then stew it tender and very thick in water or thick broth (it will require nearly or quite a quart of liquid, which should be poured on it cold and heated slowly). Then, mix gradually with it a pint of good boiling cream, and the yolks of four fresh eggs, and mingle the whole carefully with two quarts of strong veal or beef stock, which should be kept ready boiling. (*Season with salt and pepper.*) Send the soup immediately to table. (*Serves 10.*)

LENTIL SOUP

Cut three onions, a turnip and the half of a carrot into very thin slices, which put into a stewpan, with a quarter of a pound of butter, a few sprigs of parsley, a sprig of thyme and two bay-leaves, add also two pounds of leg of beef, cut into small dice; set the stewpan upon the fire, stirring with a wooden spoon, until the contents are fried rather brownish, when add one quart of

[83]

lentils and three of water, let the whole simmer until the lentils are very tender, when season with nearly an ounce of salt and half that quantity of sugar; it is then ready to serve. (*Serves 16.*)

To make a purée of lentils: When the soup is made, strain off the broth, add a good spoonful of flour to the lentils, which mash with the spoon against the sides of the stewpan, then again put in the broth, boil all up together, keeping it stirred with the spoon; rub it through a tammy or hair sieve (*not necessary if you blend it*), again boil and skim, and it is ready.

HOPPING JOHN

One pound of (*unsliced lean*) bacon, one pint of red (*-eyed*) peas, one pint of rice. First put on the peas, and when half boiled, throw in the rice, which must be first washed. When the rice has been boiling for half an hour, take the pot off the fire and put it on the coals to steam, as in boiling rice alone. Put a quart of water on the peas first, and if it boils away too much, add a little more hot water. Season with salt and pepper, and if liked, a sprig of green mint. In serving up, put the rice and peas first on the dish, and the bacon on top. (*Serves 6.*)

DRIED FRUITS

PRUNE JELLY, WITH ALMONDS

One pound of prunes, one-half box of gelatine. Soak the prunes overnight, and stew until tender in the water in which they have soaked. Remove the stones and sweeten to taste.

Dissolve the gelatine in a little hot water, and add to the prunes while hot. Lastly, add the juice of a lemon and two tablespoonsful of blanched almonds. Pour the jelly into molds and set it on the ice to harden. Eat with cream.

DRY PLUM BEVERAGE

Put a quart of water in a saucepan upon the fire, and when boiling, throw in twelve fresh dry French plums (*prunes*), and let them boil twenty minutes, then pour them in a basin with the liquor to cool; when cold, take out the plums, which put into a basin; add two tablespoonfuls of brown sugar and a very small quantity of port wine. They are excellent to eat and the liquor to drink. (*Makes 1 quart.*)

DRIED APPLE CAKE

Half a pound of butter; one and a half pints of sour, dried apples; one and a half pints of molasses; half a pint of raisins; fourteen ounces of flour (*3½ cups*); one tablespoonful of soda, one tablespoonful of mace, cinnamon, cloves; one egg. Cover the apples with cold water and soak them overnight: pour off any water that may remain, chop, and stew them twenty minutes with the spices in the molasses. When cold, add the creamed butter and egg, the soda, the flour and raisins. Bake (*in 2 loaf pans*) in a moderate oven.

SNOW CREAM

Add a quarter of a pound of sugar to half a pint of cream, and flavor highly with vanilla or lemon; if fresh lemon is used, more sugar will be required. Stir in newly-fallen snow until thick as ice cream. The syrup of any kind of sweetmeats (*jams or preserved fruits*) may be used instead of cream. In either case, the snow must not be added until just before serving. (*Serves 4.*)

Snow can be used instead of crushed ice to freeze ice cream: this makes winter ice cream making very simple.

[5]

FEBRUARY

Invalids' dishes; infants' dishes; puddings and creams; maple sugar

INVALIDS' DISHES

The care and feeding of invalids was one of the favorite pastimes of the nineteenth century, and probably with reason. A winter cold, without penicillin, vitamin B-12, or even aspirin, was no laughing matter.

The invalid was confined rigidly to bed, cosseted and coddled, and expected to be irritable and unreasonable. Tempting his appetite was a subject of much concern. The only foods that were considered proper for invalids were concentrates or bland concoctions that would not tax the delicate constitution in the least, so it is little wonder that the appetite needed coaxing. Since February is still a favorite month for colds, and since some invalids' dishes still are warm and cozy with nostalgia, here are a few of the old recipes.

BEEF-TEA

Take one pound of lean fresh beef cut thin; put it in a jar or wide-mouthed bottle, add a little salt, place it in a kettle of boiling water (*on a rack*) to remain one hour, then strain it, and there will be a gill of pure nourishing liquid. This has been retained on the stomach when nothing else could be, and has raised the patient when other means have failed.

PANADA

One of the most simple and least hurtful dishes for the sick, is cracker panada. Take half a bowl of boiling water, two or three large lumps of loaf sugar, roll a Boston (*soda*) cracker into fine crumbs, and when put in the bowl, grate over a little nutmeg. If wine is given, a little improves it.

CHICKEN JELLY

Cut a chicken into small pieces, bruise the bones, and put the whole in a stone jar, and cover it close. Set the jar in a kettle of boiling water and keep it boiling three hours. Then strain off the liquid and season it with a little salt, pepper, mace, etc., or with loaf sugar and lemon. Return the chicken to the jar and boil again; it will produce nearly as much as before of jelly. It can be made just as well of an old fowl.

LAIT DE POULE, FRENCH REMEDY FOR COLDS

Break a fresh egg, separate the white from the yolk, put the yolk in a basin, with a quarter of a gill of good cream or milk, which mix well with a spoon. Have half a pint of broth boiling, which pour gradually over the egg and cream, mixing it (*as you pour the broth*) with a wooden spoon; it is then ready and ought to be taken when going to bed, if only for a cold.

SWEET LAIT DE POULE: This is also reckoned very good for a cold. Put two yolks of egg into a cup, with two teaspoonfuls of pounded sugar, a few drops of orange-flower water, or the eight part of the rind of a fresh lemon grated, beat them well together for ten minutes, then pour boiling water gradually over, keep it stirred, until the cup is nearly full. Drink this very hot when in bed; I can strongly recommend it from experience.

"Let those who love to be invalids drink strong green tea, eat pickles, preserves, and rich pastry."
            Sears' New Family Receipt Book, 1852

[87]

Part II: *Recipes*

WINE WHEY FOR INVALIDS

Sweeten one pint of milk to taste, and when boiling, throw in two wine glasses of sherry (*remove from the fire*): When the curd forms, strain the whey through a muslin bag into tumblers.

BARLEY WATER

Pick and wash two ounces of pearl barley, put it in a saucepan with one quart of water. Let it boil slowly until the barley is soft, then strain and sweeten to taste. A little lemon juice may be added if preferred.

COOLING DRINK FOR A FEVERISH THIRST

One tablespoonful of cream of tartar; juice of two large lemons; a pint of boiling water; sugar to taste; one wineglass of gin. Mix all together.

OYSTER TOAST FOR INVALIDS

Make a nice slice of toast and butter it, lay it on a hot dish; put six oysters, a teacup of their own liquor, into a tin cup and boil one minute. Use half milk if preferred. Season with a little butter, pepper and salt, and pour over the toast.

MOLASSES POSSET

Put into a saucepan a pint of the best West Indian molasses; a teaspoon of powdered white ginger; and a quarter of a pound of fresh butter. Set it on hot coals and simmer slowly for half an hour; stirring it frequently. Do not let it come to a boil. Then stir in the juice of two lemons or two tablespoonfuls of vinegar; cover the pan and let it stand by the fire five minutes longer. This is good for a cold.

It is the preparation absurdly called by the common people a stewed quaker.

A healthy splash of rum brings it even closer to its vulgar description.

[88]

INFANTS' DISHES

Babies had a rough time of it. Their systems were considered too delicate for anything save nature's perfect provision, milk: "Confine a child under three years of age to a very limited bill of fare. His stomach is too delicate an organ to be tampered with. Let milk—scalded or boiled, as a rule—be the staple, mixed with farina, barley, or something of the sort. Let him munch graham bread and light crackers freely. Remove far from him hot bread and griddle-cakes. When he has cut his carnivorous teeth (*molars*), Nature says—'this creature wants meat.' . . . The inner part of a well-roasted apple, and, in their season, ripe peaches and apples, will not harm him, taken in moderation, if he be well and strong. . . . Raisins—skins and all—are unfit for anybody to eat. Pulp and pits, they are poisonous for baby. Ditto, pickles, pastry and preserves. Ditto, most kinds of cake and all sorts of fruit puddings. . . . Give him light suppers and put him to bed early in a dark room. . . . Always see for yourself that his last waking thoughts are pleasant; that he shuts his eyes at peace with the world and in love with you." (Marion Harland, *Common Sense*, 1880)

Few of the items of an infant's diet are more interesting than pabulum. However:

CAUDLE FOR A CHRISTENING

This was for the adults, not the baby. A curious drink, but mentioned often enough that it seems to have been customary.

Two papers of Robinson's groats (*enough oatmeal to make a very thin gruel*); six quarts of water boiling. Rub the (*dry*) groats smoothly and add four tablespoonfuls of ground cinnamon, half of a teaspoonful of ground mace, two grated nutmegs (*2 teaspoonfuls*), sugar to taste. Add as much cold water as would make a thick gruel and mix well. Throw into a kettle of the boiling water and boil for one and a half hours, stirring well. Add two and a half quarts of sherry, the juice of four lemons, sugar to the taste. Boil for ten minutes. Strain through a hair sieve and add stoned raisins. Serve hot to drink.

Part II: *Recipes*

PORRIDGE

The best method of making porridge is to strew oatmeal with one hand into a vessel of boiling water, so gradually that it does not become lumpy, stirring the mixture all the time with the other hand (*which holds a spoon*). After about four ounces of coarse oatmeal have been stirred into a quart of boiling water, the whole should be allowed to stand by the side of the fire, so as to simmer gently and thicken for twenty or thirty minutes. Porridge is usually eaten with milk. It is excellent for children.

FARINA

Stir 1 large tablespoonful Hecker's Farina, wet up with cold water, into 1 cup boiling water (*slightly salted*) in the farina kettle (*double boiler*). Boil fifteen minutes, stirring constantly until it is well-thickened. Then add 1 cup fresh milk, stirring it in gradually, and boil fifteen minutes longer. Sweeten, and give to the child as soon as it is cool enough. You may make enough in the morning to last all day; warming it up with a little hot milk as you want it. Keep in a cold place. Some of the finest children I have ever seen were reared upon this diet.

GRAHAM HASTY PUDDING

Stir 1 cup Graham flour, wet up with cold water, into 1 large cup boiling water, slightly salted. Boil fifteen minutes, stirring almost constantly. Add a cup of milk and cook, after it has again come to a boil, ten minutes longer. Give with sugar and milk for breakfast.

Eaten with cream, nutmeg and powdered sugar, this is a good plain dessert for grown people as well as children.

RICE FLOUR HASTY PUDDING: is made as above, substituting two heaping tablespoonfuls of rice flour for the graham.

EGG GRUEL, FOR OLDER INFANTS

Beat the yolk of one egg with one tablespoonful of sugar; pour one teacup of boiling water on it; add the white of the egg beaten to a froth, with any seasonings or spice desired. To be taken warm.

This does not offer much in the way of alternatives to commercial baby foods —which are at best questionable in quality (read the list of ingredients carefully), and at their most commercial, cost more than twice what the same foods cost in adult packages. But the solution is simple: any food a baby is allowed may be put in the blender with enough water, milk or broth to make it the proper consistency, and puréed. Before the seasonings are added (it is still agreed that babies' diets should be bland), almost any dinner for adults can be puréed for babies and frozen in ice-cube trays to give you a quick supply in a handy amount. The work involved is perhaps less than that of opening and warming a glass jar from the supermarket.

PUDDINGS AND CREAMS

Next to bread making, pudding making was *the* skill that a girl had to acquire before she was considered fit for marriage. Pudding appeared for dinner and for supper and possibly for breakfast too.

Jell-O has taken over most of this section of modern cookbooks—it once ran as long as the section on bread—but here are some relics. Details of pudding making can be found on p. 26.

Creams, basically custards made with cream, are the aristocrats of old puddings. For a mousse-like Bavarian cream, try whipping half the cream and folding it in last.

CHOCOLATE CREAM

Time, 20 minutes. Break a bar of chocolate into small pieces (*use a 6-ounce bar of milk chocolate or a 6-ounce package of semisweet chocolate bits with a little sugar*), and pour over them a pint and a half of cream (*heated*), let it remain until it is dissolved (*or blend it*), and then boil it (*very*) slowly for ten minutes. Well beat the yolks of five eggs with a spoonful and a half of good sugar, mix it with the cream, and pour it into cups. Stand them in a stewpan of boiling water, which must only cover half-way to the edge of the cup, and let them remain simmering twenty minutes with the lid of the stewpan kept on. When done, place them in a very cold place. Milk may be used instead of cream if a less expensive cream is desired.

This is richer and more expensive than chocolate pudding—and worth it. Serves 6–7.

COFFEE CREAM

One large cupful of made coffee; four ounces of sugar, three quarters of a pint of milk; yolks of eight eggs; two ounces (*2 envelopes*) of gelatin.

Put three quarters of a pint of boiled milk into a stewpan with a large cupful of coffee, and add the yolks of eight well-beaten eggs, and four ounces (*½ cup*) pounded loaf sugar. Stir the whole briskly over a clear fire until it begins to thicken, take it off the fire, and stir it for a minute or two longer, and strain it through a sieve on the two ounces of gelatin. Mix together thoroughly, and when the gelatin is dissolved, pour the cream into a mould previously prepared. (*Serves 6–8.*)

WINE CREAM

Boil the rind of half a lemon in a quarter of a pint of cream with two ounces of sugar, for twenty minutes; then take out the lemon-peel, and stir in a pint of cold cream and a quarter of a pint of sherry or Madeira; beat up well into a froth, and fill the glasses. (*Serves 6–8.*)

BAVARIAN CREAM

Whip a pint of cream to a stiff froth. Boil a pint of rich milk with a teacup of sugar, and add a teaspoonful of vanilla. Soak half a box of gelatine for an hour in half a cup of warm water and add to the milk. Add the yolks of four eggs beaten smooth, and take from the fire instantly.

When cold, and just beginning to thicken, stir in the whipped cream. Put in molds and set in a cold place. For chocolate, add two tablespoonfuls of grated chocolate dissolved in half a cup of boiling water; for coffee add one teacup of clear, strong coffee. (*Serves 8–10.*)

BRANDY CREAM

Boil in a quarter of a pint of milk two ounces of blanched almonds and two or three bitter almonds (*or ½ teaspoon almond extract*), with three ounces of sugar; when soft, pound all together till smooth (*the blender leaves them*

[92]

grainy, so it has to be pounded), and leave to cool; then beat up the yolks of five eggs, two glasses of brandy and a quart of cream; set it over the fire for a quarter of an hour, stirring it to thicken, but not allowing it to boil; pour it into cups or glasses, and when cold (*sprinkle with slices of almond*), sift sugar over and brown with a salamander. (*Chestnuts, peeled, skinned and pounded, may be used instead of almonds. Whipping half the cream and folding it into the almost-cool custard improves this. Serves 8.*)

CARAMEL CREAM

One ounce of brown sugar, one pint of cream, a half a gill of caramel, (*see below*) one egg and the yolks of three.

Scald the cream, add the caramel, beat the eggs, stir in the hot cream, and add the sugar; pour in a buttered mold, place it in a saucepan with hot water about two-thirds of the depth of the mold; cover both the mold and the saucepan, keep the water as near boiling as possible; when stiffened, let it cool, then place it on the ice. It may be served with vanilla custard poured round it, or eaten with cream. (*Serves 4–6.*)

CARAMEL, FOR CREAM OR SAUCE

One and a half pounds of moist brown sugar, half a pint of hot water. Put half a pound of the sugar in a small iron frying-pan or a small kettle (one with a round (*bowl-shaped*) bottom is more convenient), let it heat gradually, then stir it with a knife until it is melted and like a smooth batter; the color should not change much. Add the water by slow degrees, mixing thoroughly; let it simmer a few minutes, while you scrape down the sugar that adheres to the sides of the kettle; then stir in the pound of sugar, and when dissolved let it boil and become clear; when chilled, it is ready. (*Makes about 2 cups.*)

VELVET CREAM, AN EXCELLENT FAMILY RECEIPT

Cover the bottom of a glass dish with apricot jam, and pour over it a large tablespoonful of lemon-juice and a glass of sherry; dissolve half an ounce of isinglass (*or 1 envelope gelatine*) in a quarter of a pint of water; add to it a pint of cream and three ounces of sugar; simmer it over the fire ten minutes, stirring it all the while; then strain it into a jug; when half cold, hold the jug high above the dish, and pour the cream over the sweetmeat (*jam*); let it stand to cool and stiffen. (*Serves 4–6.*)

CARAMEL PUDDING

Melt in a saucepan one-half cupful granulated sugar, then add one-quarter cupful cold water (*carefully: the melted sugar is very hot*). Stir until thick and smooth. Take a pudding mold holding one quart, and pour caramel over bottom and sides, or line individual dishes with caramel. Let get cold. Make a custard of two cupfuls of milk, one-half cupful sugar, four eggs, and flavor with lemon extract. Put in mold over caramel. Put mold into hot water and bake in oven until firm. Remove, and serve with its own sauce. (*Serves 6–8.*)

Sugar melted slowly, stirred constantly, without water, will make a candy-like coating on molds that colors the outside of the custard and dissolves slowly into a syrup as the custard chills. Be careful: melted sugar is much *hotter than boiling water.*

CUSTARD

One quart of milk, five ounces of sugar, eight eggs, leaving out the whites of six, two teaspoonfuls of vanilla, or half a vanilla bean, a pinch of salt.

Put in (*the top of a double boiler*) the milk, sugar and salt; beat the eggs thoroughly, and when the milk is boiling hot (this will be indicated by a froth or film on the top) pour half of it on the eggs, mix well, and pour it back into the rest of the milk, and stir constantly to prevent curdling. When thick as desired, pour it at once through a strainer into a pitcher; it curdles if allowed to remain in a hot basin; add the vanilla, and when thoroughly cold, serve it.

This makes about twice as much as you are likely to want. It is used as a sauce for cakes or more sharply flavored puddings.

Chocolate custard: This may be made with the addition of four ounces of sweetened chocolate. Put it over the boiling water, hardly covered with milk; mash and stir it perfectly smooth, then add the rest of the milk and proceed as above.

FIG CUSTARD PUDDING

One pound best white figs, one quart milk, yolks of five eggs, whites of two, one half box gelatin (*2 envelopes*) soaked in a little cold water, one cup wine or other jelly, one tablespoonful sugar, flavor to taste. Soak the figs in warm water till soft; split them; dip each piece in the jelly and line a buttered mould with them. Make a custard of the milk, yolks and sugar. Boil till it begins to thicken, take from the fire, and cool. Melt the soaked gelatin in a very little hot water; stir till clear, when cool, stir gradually into the two beaten egg whites; when white and thick, add the custard. Whip together and fill the fig-lined mould. (*Serves 8–10.*)

RENNET CUSTARDS

Take half a pint of cream and a quart of new milk mixed, four ounces of powdered white sugar, a large glass of white wine in which an inch of washed rennet has been soaked (*see p. 128 for home-made rennets, or use rennet tablets, available in most supermarkets*), and a nutmeg; mix together, in a pitcher, the milk, cream and sugar; stir in the wine; and pour the mixture into your custard cups. Set them in a warm place near the fire, till they become a firm curd. Then set them on ice, or in a cold place. (*Serves 8.*)

Grate nutmeg over them (*or sprinkle them with red cinnamon candy hearts*) for a Valentine's dish.

RICE PUDDING

Beat half a pound of rice to a powder (*or take ½ pound of rice flour*), set it with three pints of milk upon the fire, let it boil well, and when cold, put to it eight eggs well-beaten, half a pound of butter, half a pound of sugar, cinnamon, nutmeg and mace; add raisins, candied lemon, citron or other sweetmeats, and lay a puff paste all over the sides and rim of the dish; half an hour will bake it. (*Serves 10–12.*)

CHINESE RICE PUDDING

Whip one pint of sweet cream to a froth; add one third cup sugar; flavor with vanilla and sherry; add one ounce of rice that has been boiled in one cup of milk until soft and tender; then cool. Just before serving, add one half cup preserved ginger or figs chopped into fine pieces. (*Serves 6–8.*)

TURKISH PUDDING

Half pound bread crumbs, half pound figs chopped fine, six ounces sugar, six ounces suet, two eggs, one cup milk, one teaspoonful brandy, half a nutmeg grated, boil four hours (*in a floured pudding cloth*) and serve with wine sauce. (*Serves 8–10.*)

WINE SAUCE FOR SUET PUDDINGS: Work equal quantities of butter and (*powdered*) sugar together with a glass of wine, add more or less as you prefer it liquid or otherwise; a little nutmeg is an improvement. A fine sauce may be made of sugar and butter flavored with lemon essence.

SOFT SAUCE: One pint hot water; one tablespoonful butter; three full tablespoonfuls sugar. While boiling, stir in one tablespoonful cornstarch dissolved in cold water. Flavor with vanilla, or lemon and nutmeg.

CABINET PUDDING

Boil three quarters of a pint of cream and mix one quarter of a pint, cold, with the well-beaten yolks of six eggs and a glass of brandy. Pour the boiling cream over this, and stir as you pour it till it becomes a custard. Butter a plain mould, and line it with dried cherries and slices of dried apricots in a tasteful pattern. Put into the mould lightly four ounces of sponge biscuit (*ladyfingers*) and two ounces of macaroons, mixed: strew an ounce of powdered sugar amongst them; then fill up the mould with the custard perfectly cold. Tie up and steam for an hour. Let it stand a few minutes, then turn out carefully and serve with wine sauce (*p. 99*). (*Serves 4–6.*)

ALMOND PUDDING

Beat six ounces of almonds in a mortar, with three ounces of butter, four ounces of sugar, and a teaspoonful of grated lemon peel; then mix the paste into two tablespoonfuls of cream; beat up with the yolks of six eggs. Butter small cups, pour in the mixture; bake half an hour; turn out and serve with custard (*p. 94*) or whip cream. (*Serves 4.*)

AMBROSIA

One pound of sponge cake, two ounces of almonds, one pint of boiled custard, hot, half a pint of preserved fruits.

Prepare the nuts, of which there may be two or three kinds, blanch the almonds, drain the fruit from the syrup; it must be richly preserved fruit (*candied fruitcake mix, or canned fruit cocktail or berries stewed with sugar, or fresh grapes, peaches and pears with sugar, or almost any of the home-preserved fruits made from recipes in this book*), including a little ginger. Slice the cake, lay it in a shallow dish, and pour the custard over it. When cold, wet two smooth bowls, holding about one pint each; put in a layer of (*custard-soaked*) cake, a sprinkling of almonds and bits of fruit, then another layer of cake, almonds and fruit, and cover with cake. Let stand on ice for an hour, then serve. (*Top with whipped cream laced with brandy, or put a little whipped cream between each layer. Serves 8.*)

CHARLOTTE RUSSE

One quart of cream, whites of eight eggs; place the cream on ice for two or three hours; beat it well; beat the eggs to a stiff froth, mix together, sweeten to taste, and flavor with vanilla (*or sherry or Madeira*). Take half a box of (*unflavored*) gelatine, pour on a little cold water and let it stand an hour; then pour on boiling water enough to dissolve and stir it into the cream. When about half set, pour into the mould, which must be lined with sponge cake. (*Serves 8–10.*)

Part II: Recipes

ROYAL DIPLOMATIC PUDDING

Line the bottom of a jelly mould with fruit arranged in fanciful patterns, then pour in wine jelly (*below*) to a depth of half an inch. Put in a cold place until firmly chilled. When it is chilled, fill another, smaller mould with ice and set it into the first mould. Pour wine jelly between the two and chill until it is well set. You may also line the space between the two moulds with fruit if you like. When it is chilled, remove the smaller mould by taking out whatever remains of the ice and filling the mould briefly with hot water, to allow it to slip out. Now fill the space where the mould was with Bavarian cream (*p. 92*) and chill. When ready to serve, invert over a plate and remove the mould. (*Serves 8.*)

WINE JELLY

"Jelly" means gelatine as well as spread for bread. Jell-O dates from about 1895.

One box (*unflavored*) gelatin, one and a half pounds of sugar, two quarts of water, one pint of wine, two lemons. Pour one pint of cold water on the gelatin and the rind of the lemons; let it stand an hour; then add three pints of boiling water, the sugar, wine and lemon-juice; strain it and put in moulds, which must be placed on ice to stiffen. (*Makes 2½ quarts.*)

MACEDOINE OF FRUITS

Wine jelly and fruit in alternate layers, frozen together; the fruits may be of any or all sorts, and may be candied or preserved, or the slices of pear, apple, etc., may be boiled in syrup and then drained. The mould must be filled after the jelly has begun to form, but before it is stiff, and the first layer should be of jelly.

PAIN PERDU

Half a pound of bread, half a pint of boiling milk, three tablespoonfuls of sugar, the rind of half a lemon, one egg, grated bread.

Put the milk, the lemon-peel and sugar over boiling water (*in a double boiler*). Cut the bread in slices two-thirds of an inch thick and cut off the crust evenly and divide the slice in two or three regular pieces (*do not attempt this recipe with flimsy store-bought bread*); lay them in a pan with a surface so large that they need not lie one upon the other, and pour the milk over them; in a few minutes, turn the pieces, then let them stand half an hour or more; beat the egg in a saucer, dip a piece of the bread in it, and then in the bread crumbs, lay it in the frying basket, and sink it in hot lard. Serve in a platter on a napkin, standing in two rows, two or three inches apart and meeting at the top like a miniature roof. To be eaten with a liquid wine sauce (*below; serves 8*).

CITRON PUDDING

Beat three eggs with two spoonfuls of flour; add half a pint of boiled milk and a quarter of citron (*about 4 ounces*) cut small. Put it in buttered cups, bake in a quick oven. When done, turn them out in a large dish. (*Serves 4.*)

QUAKING PUDDING

Grate a small loaf of stale bread; add to it six well-beaten eggs and half a spoonful of rice flour. Stir into it a quart of milk; add the essence of lemon and some nutmeg and boil (in a mold or in a cloth) two hours; or bake in a buttered basin. Wine (*below*) or brandy (*p. 433*) sauce. (*Serves 8.*)

TAPIOCA PUDDING

Tapioca is made from the root of a tree of South America. It makes a delicate pudding. Stir three tablespoonfuls of tapioca into boiling milk; continue to stir for twenty minutes, add two ounces of loaf sugar. Put it into a basin, and while cooling, stir in an ounce of butter, and when cold, add three well-beaten eggs. Pour it into a buttered dish, and bake for an hour. Serve with wine sauce.

WINE SAUCE: In a quarter of a pint of water boil for fifteen minutes the thin rind of a small lemon and an ounce of sugar; strain the liquor into half a pint of melted butter, and stir into it, over the fire, a glass or a glass and a half of brandy, and serve immediately. (*The sauce is runny and will separate as it stands, but it makes the pudding. It should be served with a ladle or poured from a pitcher.*)

[99]

MAPLE SUGAR

SUGARING OFF FOR MAPLE SYRUP

The traditional day to tap the trees is Washington's birthday.

Use a cauldron deeper than it is wide and never fill it more than half full to allow room for boiling up. Prepare a thick bed of faggots for fast, hot kindling. Since few people have the new sugaring-off houses, pile some brush to break the wind. He who figures to get more than one gallon of syrup from less than 35 gallons of sap is not good at figuring nor at making maple syrup.

Sugaring off is a time for parties in New England. The syrup is boiled until it reaches 240°, the soft-ball stage, when it is spread lightly over pans of clean snow to cool. The guests then eat it, like taffy. It is not for those with loose fillings.

FROZEN MAPLE-SUGAR PUDDING

Beat the yolks of three eggs with a cup of grated maple sugar and a level teaspoonful of cinnamon until light; add slowly a cup of boiling-hot milk, beating as you pour it over the egg mixture. Then place in a double boiler and stir constantly until the custard coats the spoon. When cold, add a cup of rich cream, flavored with vanilla to taste, and freeze as you would ice cream. (*Or whip the cream first and freeze in an ice-cube tray in the freezer.*) When half frozen, a cup of candied fruits may be stirred in, and the cream returned to the freezer to attain the proper consistency. Transfer to a (*quart*) melon mold and let it stand packed in ice until it is served with sweet whipped cream flavored with vanilla.

MAPLE-SUGAR SAUCE FOR ICE CREAM

Butter the inside of a granite saucepan and pour in a cup of maple syrup and a third of a cup of cream. Boil (*2 or 3 minutes*) until the syrup forms to a (*very*) soft ball when tested by dropping a bit into cold water. Pour (*hot*) over each serving of ice cream.

For PUDDINGS: Break half a pound of maple sugar into small bits, put it into a thick saucepan with half a gill of cold water, set the saucepan over the fire, and melt the sugar until it forms a clear syrup; then remove it from the fire and stir in two heaping tablespoonfuls of butter cut into small bits. Serve the sauce very hot with any fruit (*or bland pudding; you can get the same effect, of course, with heated maple syrup and butter*).

[6]

MARCH

Milk and cream; butter; cheese and cheese dishes; shad

March is a month to drive you mad. At least in the Northeast, it is the month you always think will bring spring—and it never does. The stores sprout seed packages while the ground remains rock-hard. But on farms, baby animals are being born.

The fact that cows calve and freshen in the spring, thereby guaranteeing a new supply of milk, has no noticeable effect on milk, butter, and cheese prices in stores. But it's nice to think about in March, when practically nothing else is going on. So here are dairy products.

MILK AND CREAM

MILK SOUP

A late night supper dish.
Boil two quarts of milk with a quarter of a pound of sweet almonds, blanched and broken to pieces; add a large stick of cinnamon broken up. Stir in sugar enough to make it very sweet. When it has boiled, strain it. Cut some

thin slices of bread, and (having pared off the crust) toast them. Lay them in the bottom of the tureen, pour a little of the hot milk over them and cover them close that they may soak. Beat the yolks of five eggs very light. Set the milk on hot coals, and add the eggs to it by degrees, stirring it all the time till it thickens. Then take it off instantly, let it curdle, and pour it into the tureen, boiling hot, over the bread. (*Serves 8.*)

This will be better still if you cover the bottom with slices of baked apple (*instead of bread*).

BLANC MANGE

This is the simplest of simple puddings, still familiar in England and France, but ever since reading Little Women, *I've wondered what it was.*

Boil a quart of milk with a pint of cream; clarify an ounce and a half of isinglass (*break it up, pour on it a cup of boiling water and set it on the stove to dissolve; when it is entirely dissolved, take off any scum that may rise—or simply use 3 envelopes of unflavored gelatine, added at the end*), stir it into the milk, add fine white sugar to taste, one teaspoonful of fine salt, and flavor with essence of lemon or orange flower water. Let it boil up, stirring it well (*add the gelatine*), then have ready your moulds dipped in cold water, and strain the blanc mange through a coarse white muslin into them; turn it out when perfectly cold. (*Serves at least 12.*)

Three ounces of almonds pounded to a paste and stirred into the milk with the isinglass is considered an improvement by some, and by boiling cinnamon-sticks in the milk, it may have that flavor.

ORNAMENTAL FROTH FOR BLANC MANGE OR CREAMS: Beat to a froth the whites of four eggs, and then stir in half a pound of preserved raspberries, cranberries or strawberries; beat the whole well together and turn it over the top of your blanc mange or creams.

BURNT CREAM

Boil (*very slowly*) a pint of cream with two ounces of sugar, the thin rind of half a lemon, and a stick of cinnamon for twenty minutes; take it off, and remove the lemon and cinnamon; pour the (*hot*) cream by degrees over the well-beaten yolks of four eggs; beat all well together and pour into a dish or into glasses. (*Set in a pan of hot water, halfway up the sides of the molds, and cook, covered, another 20 minutes.*) When cold, sift sugar thickly over,

[103]

and brown with a salamander (*under the broiler*). Use any flavoring you like.

THE RECEIPT USED BY THE JEFFERSON FAMILY AT MONTICELLO: Boil two quarts of milk with a large piece of orange peel. To half a pound of sugar add the yolks of seven eggs and the whites of two. Stir them well together and add two to three handfuls (*about 1 cup*) of flour and pour in (*by degrees, whisking*) the boiling milk. Stir all well together and strain it through a sieve and put it on the fire and stir it until it thickens. Add one ounce of fresh butter and pour it into a deep dish. Sift powdered sugar over it and glaze it with a hot shovel (*under the broiler*). Use any flavoring you like. (*Serves 16.*)

FRIED CREAM

One pint of milk; half a cup of sugar; yolks of three eggs; two tablespoons of cornstarch and one of flour mixed; half a teaspoonful of vanilla, and two inches of stick-cinnamon; a teaspoonful of butter.

Boil the cinnamon in the milk. Stir the cornstarch and flour smooth in a little cold milk or water, and add to the milk. Beat the yolks light with the sugar, and add. Take from the fire; take out the cinnamon, and stir in the butter and vanilla, and pour out on a buttered tin or dish, letting it be about half an inch thick. When cold and stiff, cut into pieces about three inches long and two wide. Dip carefully in sifted cracker crumbs; then in a beaten egg, and in crumbs again, and (*deep*) fry like croquettes. Dry in the oven for four or five minutes and serve at once. Very delicious. (*Serves 4–6.*)

A TRIFLE

Place a half pound of macaroons or Naples biscuits (*ladyfingers*) at the bottom of a large glass bowl. Pour on them as much white wine (*or brandy*) as will cover and dissolve them. Make a rich custard, flavored with bitter almonds or peach leaves (*boiled in the milk and strained out; almond flavoring may be substituted*), and pour it when cold on the macaroons. Then add a layer of marmalade or jam (*or chopped fresh fruit*). Take a quart of cream, mix with it a quarter of a pound of sugar, and half a pint of white wine (*or brandy*) and whip it to a stiff froth. Pile the frothed cream upon the marmalade in a high pyramid. To ornament it, take preserved water-melon rind that has been cut into leaves or flowers; split them nicely to make them thinner, place a wreath of them round the heap of cream, intersperse with spots of stiff red currant jelly. Stick on the top some real flowers. (*Serves about 20.*)

It isn't properly proper, but try small bits of peaches, strawberries, pre-served ginger, green grapes, pineapple, etc.,—whatever harmonizes or con-trasts with the jam—scattered thinly through the whipped cream.

DISH OF SNOW

To a quart of cream, add the whites of three eggs well beaten; four spoonfuls of sweet wine (*sherry, Madeira, or port*); sugar to taste and a tea-spoonful of essence of lemon; whip it to a froth, and serve in a deep glass dish. (*Serves 12.*)

DEVONSHIRE CREAM

Put a panful of (*pasteurized, not homogenized—or better yet, if you have a cow, raw*) milk in a cold place for twenty-four hours, or in summer for twelve hours. Then place it on the fire and let it come very slowly to the scald-ing-point, but do not let it boil. Put it again in a cool place for six to twelve hours and then take off the cream, which will be firm and of a peculiarly sweet flavor.

Devonshire cream is thick and clotted and is used on fruits, mush, etc. It will keep for some time, and is particularly delicious.

TO PRESERVE CREAM FOR STEAMBOAT VOYAGES,

(*or to keep it a couple of weeks in the refrigerator*) mix fresh cream with half its weight of loaf sugar; cork it tight in bottles. When used, no sweeten-ing need be added.

BUTTER

Some of the butter and cheese recipes will be useless for those without access to fresh raw milk—those without cows, in other words. The recipes are included because they are interesting.

[105]

BUTTER TO CHURN, KEEP AND STORE

In cold weather, heat the milk to blood heat before straining it. Never allow the milk to stand over forty-eight hours; in summer not more than thirty-six, and twelve hours will often be found to be quite enough (*to bring the cream to the top for skimming*); churn twice a week even if there be but a small quantity of cream. Keep the crock of cream, during the summer, in the coolest place you have, and every time cream is added, stir it well. In cold weather, place the crock of cream before the fire the night before churning, turning it occasionally and stirring the cream until it is milk-warm; then re-move it to a cold room; in the morning put it in the churn, when a few minutes churning will bring the butter. In hot weather put ice in the churn, broken into small bits, one and a half pounds to four gallons of cream; let it stand about ten minutes before churning to equalize the temperature of the cream. When the butter has "come" or "gathered" take it up in the hand, squeeze out the butter-milk quickly; put it in the wooden butter-bowl, and work into it one ounce of fine salt to every pound of butter; lay in it, for the above quantity, a piece of ice weighing one and a half pounds and leave it in as cool a place as possible. The next day, work out all the water and milk, but be careful not to go beyond this, as the grain of the butter is often broken by too much working. Make it into rolls, or pack it in stone crocks or firkins (*wooden buckets*). If not to be used at once, pour brine over it.

BRINE FOR PRESERVING BUTTER DURING THE SUMMER: Half a pail of water, one quart of fine salt, one ounce of salt-petre, two ounces of white sugar. Boil all together, skim, and when cold pour it over the top of the butter.

FOR COLORING BUTTER: (*The lack of fresh pasturage in winter made the butter pale, which was thought to be undesirable.*) For four gallons of cream grate two, three or four carrots, according to their size and color; add enough new milk to extract the juice; make it about milk warm, and strain it into the churn.

TO CLARIFY BUTTER

Put your boat into a saucepan of cold water, and set it over a slow fire until it melts; then take it off the fire; take off the scum and again warm it gently. After being used, it will still serve for basting, or for meat-pie paste.

"If there are bits of butter (left) *on the plates, free from specks, let them be put away carefully for greasing tins. As butter is used with*

the knife only, and the knife never touches the lips, this piece of economy will shock no one."

Elisabeth S. Miller, *In the Kitchen*, 1875

TO DRAW OR MELT BUTTER

Nothing is more simple in the doing; yet nothing is done so badly so often. Take four ounces of good butter; rub into it two teaspoonfuls of flour; put it in the saucepan, with one spoonful of water and a little salt; cover it, and set the saucepan in a larger one of boiling water; shake it continually until entirely melted and beginning to boil. If the pan containing the butter be placed on the coals, the heat will reduce the butter to oil, and so spoil the butter.

A great variety of savory sauces may be made by adding different herbs to drawn butter, all of which are fine to eat with boiled butcher's meat, fish, or fowl. Chervil, burnet, tarragon, young fennel, and cress or peppergrass, all may be used; and they must be prepared in the same mode as parsley: wash a large bunch very clean, pick the leaves from the stems carefully; boil them ten minutes in salt and water; drain them perfectly dry; mince them exceedingly fine; and stir them in the butter when it begins to *draw*. When herbs are added to the butter, you must take two spoonfuls of water instead of one for the preparation.

ANOTHER: Wet 1 heaping teaspoonful of flour to a smooth paste with a little cold milk, and add to a half-pint hot water in the inner vessel (*of a double boiler*), stirring until thick. Have ready a beaten egg in a cup. Take a teaspoonful of the mixture from the fire and beat with this until light; then another and still another. Set aside the cup when this is done and stir three ounces of butter into the contents of the inner saucepan gradually, until thoroughly mixed, then add the beaten egg in the same way. There is no danger of clotting the egg, if it be treated as I have described.

MELTED BUTTER

Put into a saucepan two ounces of butter, not too hard, also a good tablespoonful of flour, mix both well with a wooden spoon, without putting it on the fire; when forming a smooth paste, add to it a little better than half a pint of water; season with a teaspoonful of salt, not too full, the sixth part of (*a teaspoonful of*) pepper; set it on the fire, stir round continually until on the point of boiling; take it off, add a teaspoonful of brown (*cider*) vinegar, then add one ounce more of fresh butter, which stir in your sauce until melted, then use where required; a little nutmeg may be introduced.

BUTTER À LA MAÎTRE D'HÔTEL, A MOST REFINED, EXQUISITE SAUCE FOR BOILED FISH

Half a pound of fresh butter, one and a half tablespoonfuls of parsley chopped fine, half a teaspoon of salt, one pinch of white pepper, the juice of two lemons.

Cream the butter perfectly, beat in the salt, pepper, and lemon juice, add the parsley, and serve. If preferred, a tablespoonful of vinegar and a teaspoonful of mixed mustard may be added.

CHEESECAKE

I have yet to see a nineteenth-century cheesecake that contains any form of cheese. Rennet (p. 128) is used in a process like that for making cheese (p. 109), so perhaps that explains the name. Cheesecake was frequently made into individual tarts.

Take four quarts of milk and turn it with some fresh rennet (*after you have let it sit in a warm place 12–24 hours, carefully lift the curd and put it in a cheesecloth bag to drain*); when dry crumble it and sift it through a coarse sieve into a bowl, beat it well up with a quarter of a pound of butter until it is quite smooth (it may require more butter, depending on the quality of the milk); mix in another bowl the yolks of four eggs and a quarter of a pound of very fine biscuit powder (*cracker crumbs or sifted vanilla-wafer crumbs*) the rind of four lemons, the juice of two, a quarter of a pound of powdered sugar (some add a little grated nutmeg or cinnamon), beat these all well together, until forming a stiff cream, then put it by degrees into the bowl with curd, and mix them well together; line some tartlet pans, previously buttered, with some paste, and place some of the above mixture in, and bake quick. (*Makes 12 tartlets.*) In some places milk is used instead of egg. Should you not have rennet, procure some good milk and turn it with the juice of a lemon, or a teaspoonful of soda: drain the curd and proceed as before.

MISS BRATTY'S CHEESECAKES

The yolks of eight eggs, eight ounces of finely powdered sugar, sifted, eight ounces of sweet almonds powdered; beat all together until very light and white. Line the pans (*one pie pan*) with a thin paste; immediately before you put them into the oven, mix butter the size of a walnut, melted, with them. If the oven be too hot, they will fall when taken out.

Or: Ten eggs, leave out half the whites, one pound finely powdered sugar, sifted, one-half pound of flour, three ounces of butter, three ounces of sweet almonds with a glass of brandy put into them while they are (*i.e., you are*) pounding. Beat them all well together and butter the (*two small*) pans very well.

CHEESE AND CHEESE DISHES

You must have raw milk to make real cheese, but pasteurized milk will make a farmer's cheese and sour milk of any kind will make a quick cottage cheese.

TO MAKE CHEESE

To each gallon of milk warm from the cow, add a piece of rennet six inches long and three wide, or two tablespoonfuls rennet water—i.e., water in which rennet has been boiled (*or a rennet tablet*). Cover, and set in a warm place until it becomes a firm curd; this should be, at the most, not more than three-quarters of an hour. When the whey has separated entirely, and looks clear and greenish, wash your hands very clean, and with them gently press all the curd to one side of the pan or tub, while an assistant dips out the whey. Have ready a stout linen bag, pour the curd into it, and hang it up to dry until not another drop of whey can be pressed out; then put the curd into a wooden dish, and chop it fine. Empty into a finer bag, and put into a small cheese-box or other circular wooden box with a perforated bottom, and a lid that slides down easily but closely on the inside. Your bag should be as nearly as possible the same shape and size as this box. Lay heavy weights upon the top, in lack of a cheese-press, and let it stand an hour. The cloth should be wet inside as well as out when you put the curds in. At the end of the hour, take out the cheese and chop again, adding salt this time. Have ready a fresh wet cloth; pack in the curd hard. There should be a circular cover for this bag, which must be basted all around and very smooth on top. Scald the box and cover, then rinse with cold water, and put the cheese again under press for twelve hours. Next day, take it out, rub all over with salt, and fit on a clean wet cloth. Look at it sixteen hours later, pare off the rough edges, and scrape the sides of inequalities before returning to the press for the last time. Let it remain under the weights for twenty-four hours. Strip off the cloth, rub the cheese well with butter, and lay upon a clean cloth spread on a shelf in a cool, dry place. A wire-safe is best. Wipe clean; then rub every day with butter for a week, and turn also every twenty-four hours. (*It can be coated with cracked pepper instead of butter.*) At the end of the week, omit the greasing, and rub hard with a coarse cloth. Do this every day for a month. Your cheese will then be eatable, but it will be much finer six months later.

Stilton cheeses—renowned over the world—are buried in dry heather when they are firm enough to remove from the shelves, and kept there a month. This is called "ripening."

Sage cheese: Bruise the tops of young red sage in a mortar, with some leaves of spinach, and squeeze the juice; mix it with the rennet in the milk, the more or less according as you like for color and taste.

TO POT CHEESE

Cheese that has begun to mould, may be kept from becoming more so, if treated thus: cut off the mouldy part, then grate it (*the cheese*) if the cheese be dry. If not, pound it fine in a mortar, crust and all. To each pound, when fine, put a spoonful of brandy. Mix it well with the cheese, press it tight in a clean stone pot, and lay a paper wet in brandy on the top. Cover the pot tight and keep it in a cool dry place. Dry pieces of cheese may be potted in the same manner. Potted cheese is best a year old. It will keep several years without breeding insects.

Tag ends of cheese may be grated after they have dried out completely, or they may be frozen. Frozen cheese will crumble very easily, which is handy for use in recipes calling for grated cheese. Slice it thin without thawing it, and it will be ready instantly. This does not apply to processed cheese, but most processed cheese is hardly worth saving anyway.

[110]

COTTAGE CHEESE

Take one or more quarts of sour milk (*or sour skim milk*), put it in a warm place (*about 80°*), and let it remain until the whey separates from the curd (*about 12 hours; 1 tablespoonful of sour cream or ¼ of a rennet tablet per gallon dissolved first in a little cold water speeds the process; when the curd is risen and solid, cut it into inch-sized squares with a long knife and heat the whole thing carefully to about 100°, or a temperature comfortably warm to the finger; hold it there 10 to 30 minutes—the longer it is heated, the drier the cheese will be—stirring the mass occasionally*); then pour it into a three-cornered bag (*or a square of cheesecloth*), hang it up, and let it drain until every particle of whey has dripped from it (*about 6 hours*); then turn it out, and mash with a spoon until very fine, after which add a little milk or cream, with salt to taste; before sending to table (if liked), dredge a little black pepper over the top. (*1 gallon of skim milk makes about 1 pound of cheese.*)

Moist cottage cheese, mixed with onions and dill, makes a very good dip. Let it rest a day before serving.

The whey from cheese making is full of vitamins and may be substituted for milk in making bread and rolls.

CURDS AND WHEY

Have ready in a deep dish or pan, a quart of unskimmed milk (*or 3 cups of milk and 1 cup of cream*) that has been warmed but not boiled. Put rennet (*or junket*) into it, cover the pan, and set it by the fireside or some other warm place. When the milk becomes a firm mass of curd, and the whey looks clear and greenish, set the pan in ice, or in a very cold place. Send to table with a bowl of sweetened cream, with nutmeg grated over it.

FONDUE, FROM BRILLAT-SAVARIN

Weigh as many eggs as you have guests. Take one-third their weight of Gruyère cheese, and one-sixth their weight of butter. Beat the eggs well in a saucepan; add the cheese, grated and the butter. Put the saucepan on the fire and stir until the mixture is soft and creamy; then add salt, more or less, according to the age of the cheese, and a generous amount of pepper, which is one of the positive characters of the dish. Serve on a hot plate. Bring in the best wine, drink roundly of it, and you will see wonders.

FONDUE OF STILTON CHEESE

Neither of these recipes makes a normal fondue—but most modern cookbooks contain instructions for the Gruyère-and-white-wine variety. This recipe resembles little cheese pies, a good first course.

Put six ounces of butter and half a pound of flour in a stewpan (*off the fire*), rub well together with a wooden spoon, then add a quart of warm milk, stir over the fire a quarter of an hour, then add the yolks of eight eggs, three quarters of a pound of grated Parmesan, and half a pound of Stilton cheese in small dice, season rather high with pepper, salt and cayenne, add the whites of the eggs whipped very stiff, which stir in lightly; have a dozen and a half small paper cases (*muffin cups*), fill each one three parts full, place them in a moderate oven, bake about twenty minutes; when done dress them upon a napkin on your dish, and serve very hot. (*Serves 10–12.*)

RAMAKINS, OR RANAQUIN À LA UDE
(FROM THE COOK TO LOUIS XVI)

Four ounces of grated cheese, two ounces of butter, two ounces of bread (without crust), half a gill of milk, one-third of a teaspoonful of mustard, one-third of a teaspoonful of salt, small pinch of cayenne, two eggs.

Crumb the bread and let it boil soft in the milk; add the butter, mustard, salt, pepper and cheese, and the yolks of the eggs, beat thoroughly, then stir in the whites of the eggs, whisked to a stiff froth. Pour in a soup-plate, or in small squares of stiff white paper pinched at the corners, and bake fifteen minutes. A delightful dish for tea. (*Serves 4.*)

WELSH RAREBIT

¼ lb rich cream-cheese (Cheddar is commonly used now)
½ cup of cream or milk
1 teaspoonful mustard
½ teaspoonful salt

A few grains cayenne
1 egg
1 teaspoonful of butter
4 slices toast

Break the cheese in small pieces, or if hard, grate it. Put it with the milk in a double boiler. Toast the bread, and keep it hot. Mix the mustard, salt and pepper; add the egg, and beat well. When the cheese is melted, stir in the egg and butter and cook two minutes, or until it thickens a little, but do not let it curdle (*should it curdle, a little flour or cornstarch dissolved in a little water and stirred in may smooth it out again*). Pour it over the toast. Many use ale instead of cream. (*Serves 3–4.*)

EGGS WITH CHEESE

Put into a stew-pan about two ounces of grated Parmesan, or Gruyère, or old Cheshire, with one ounce of butter, two sprigs of parsley, two spring onions (*scallions*) chopped up, a little grated nutmeg, and half a glass of sherry; put it on the fire, and keep stirring until the cheese is well melted; break six eggs in a basin, put them (*unbeaten*) in the stew-pan, stir and cook them on a slow fire; when done, serve with fried sippets (*triangles*) of bread around. (*Serves 4–6.*)

MACARONI

Six ounces of macaroni, three ounces of grated cheese, one and a half ounces of butter, half a pint of milk, three-quarters of a tablespoonful of dry mustard, one teaspoonful of salt, a pinch of cayenne. More than cover the macaroni with cold water, and let it boil gently until half done. It must not be stirred; if it sticks to the kettle, use a fork to loosen it; drain it and put it in layers in a baking dish with a little of the butter and some cheese between them, reserving a part of both for the top; mix the mustard, salt and pepper smooth in a little of the milk, add the rest, and pour it over the macaroni; cover with cheese dotted with butter, and bake half an hour. (*Serves 3–4.*)

SAVORY MACARONI: Half a pound of macaroni, three ounces of uncooked ham, half a pint of tomato juice, half an onion chopped fine, one teaspoonful of white pepper, two ounces of grated cheese. Boil the macaroni in water, until tender; chop and brown the ham and onion in a frying pan, and add the tomato, macaroni, pepper and salt (*bake it 15 minutes*); just before serving sprinkle the cheese over the whole (*and brown it under the broiler; serves 4*).

[113]

SHAD

Shad comes into season on March 15 and goes out of season toward the end of May. One of the few really seasonal fish, it isn't available at any other time. Shad cooked with its roe (in season only until the middle of April) was, and still is, considered a special delicacy. See May (*pp. 163–179*) and Index for other fish recipes.

BAKED SHAD

In the first place make a stuffing of the head and cold boiled ham, seasoned with salt and pepper, cloves and sweet marjoram; moisten it with the beaten yolk of an egg. Stuff the fish, rub the outside with the yolk of an egg, and some of the stuffing. Lay the fish in a deep pan, putting its tail in its mouth. Pour in the pan a little water, a piece of butter rolled in flour. Bake two hours, pour the gravy round it, garnish with lemon sliced, and send to table. Any fish may be baked in this way. (*Serves 3–6, depending on size of fish.*)

SHAD WITH SORREL

Select a small, fine shad, pare and scale it, then let it steep as long as possible in a marinade composed of one tablespoonful of oil, half a sliced lemon, a quarter of a bunch of parsley roots (*generally unavailable now unless you grow them: try the stems of parsley*), and half a sliced onion. When ready, place it in a buttered stewpan, with half a glassful of white wine, three tablespoonfuls of mushroom catsup (*p. 250*), also a good bouquet. Take two handfuls of picked and washed sorrel, mince it very fine, then put it in the stewpan with the fish, adding a good pinch of salt and half a pinch of pepper; cover it, and let it cook as long as possible on a slow fire, at least two hours; then arrange the shad on a dish. Add one tablespoonful of white roux (*1 ounce of butter melted with 1 tablespoonful of flour*) to the juice, thicken well, and pour the sauce over the fish when serving, with some more of its own gravy in a sauce-bowl. (*Serves 2–4.*)

PLANKED SHAD

A thick oak board is prepared for this purpose with wooden pegs; the fish is opened, spread, and laid on the board, and secured with the pegs (*or it can be nailed*); the plank is then placed before a clear fire, the end resting in a shallow iron pan, with a little salt and water, with which the toasting fish is basted; when almost cooked, baste with butter also. In serving, add a little walnut ketchup (*p. 251*) to the gravy; pour it over the fish, and garnish with pickled walnuts (*p. 194; serves 2–4*).

Fried shad roe makes a good garnish along with the pickled walnuts.

FISH ROES, FRIED

Wash the roes and cook them ten minutes in boling salted water with one tablespoonful of vinegar. Then plunge them into cold water. Drain and roll in beaten egg, then in seasoned crumbs, and fry them till brown in smoking hot fat.

SCALLOPED: Boil as above. Drain, and break up lightly with a fork. Sprinkle a layer of the roe in a shallow dish; then rub the yolk of a hard-boiled egg through a fine strainer. Add a sprinkling of parsley and a little lemon juice. Moisten with a thin white sauce. Then another layer of roe, egg, and seasoning and sauce. Cover with buttered crumbs and bake until brown. If a larger dish be required, use with the roes any cold flaked fish, or a small quantity of cooked rice.

SPICED SHAD

Scale the fish, cut off the heads and tails, and divide them into four pieces. Chop four or five small onions, and sprinkle a layer on the bottom of a stone jar; on this place a layer of fish, packing closely. Spice with black and cayenne pepper, cloves, allspice, whole pepper, and a little more onion. Then add another layer of fish, and so on till the jar is full. Arrange the roe on top, spice highly, and fill the jar with the strongest vinegar that can be procured. Place five or six thick folds of paper on the jar under the cover and bake for twelve hours (*overnight in a cooling brick oven; 12 hours is a bit excessive—5 or 6 in a 200°–250° oven will do*). The vinegar will dissolve the bones, and the fish can be sliced for a tea table relish.

[115]

[7]

APRIL

Veal; innards; veal soups; lamb; kid; salmon

VEAL

Like other meats, veal no longer has a real season. Calves are born, raised, fatted, and slaughtered at any time of year. Once, however, calves were born almost exclusively in late winter. "Milk veal" was ready by April or May, while "grass veal" could be had throughout the summer. Veal was not eaten at all during the winter.

ROAST VEAL

Fry a piece of butter with a spoonful of flour and a slice of ham or bacon cut in thin slips. When this has taken a fine golden color, put in the veal to be roasted, and let it get brown on both sides. Then salt it and throw on a glassful of milk and let it boil without covering the pan. (*Put it in a 325° oven allowing 20–25 minutes to the pound.*) When this is consumed, throw on another glassful, and continue adding milk until the meat is done, which generally requires about five glassfuls of milk to be consumed. This roast will

[116]

be found very savory, specially as it is to be served with the dense and brown juice or crust, which remains at the bottom of the pan. With roast veal serve pickled mushrooms (*p. 235*).

ROAST MEAT

For veal and other white meats, use a basting of yolk of eggs, grated biscuits and juice of an orange.

To froth, only three minutes before done (*this is a process by which meat roasted in the open fireplace was sealed at the last minute, to keep all the juices in while the spit was withdrawn and the meat was served; the roast was first dusted with flour, then basted with butter*): Do not use too much flour; the meat should have a light varnish, not a covering of paste. The process plumps the skin and improves its appearance.

"Veal stands lowest among the heat-producing meats, and should be eaten with potatoes or rice, which stand highest, or with bacon and jelly."

Mrs. Lincoln's Boston Cook Book, 1896

NECK OF VEAL

Lard it (*make holes through the meat with your thinnest knife blade, or with a larding needle, and insert slivers of salt pork; this is one way of tenderizing lean meat and is less necessary, now that animals are bred to produce meat, than it once was; the flavor of bacon larded into veal is still quite delicate and nice*), and plain roast it, or braise it in plain gravy (*place it in a tightly covered pan with a very little liquid and cook slowly either on the stove top or, preferably, in the oven*). Serve it with piquant sauce (*see p. 436*), brown cucumber sauce, tomato sauce (*p. 281*) or white mushroom sauce. Serve the loin with drawn butter (*p. 107*).

BROWN CUCUMBER SAUCE: Peel a small fresh cucumber; chop it, stew with a little sugar and half an ounce of butter over a slow fire, stirring it occasionally. Add twelve tablespoons of brown sauce (*p. 436*), four tablespoons of broth. Simmer till tender, skim and remove the cucumber. Reduce a little, taste and serve.

WHITE MUSHROOM SAUCE: Use small white ones, cut the dark part out and remove the tail, wash in several waters, put in a stewpan with a little butter, salt, pepper, juice of lemon, sauté it a few minutes, add a gill of white sauce (*p. 438*), four tablespoonfuls of broth, milk or water; boil and serve under any white meat.

FRICANDEAU OF VEAL

The fricandeau is the most choice cut of veal. It is taken from the upper round of the leg, and is one side of the filet. As it destroys this cut, it commands the highest price. It should be cut four inches thick, and is usually larded and braised. Place it in a baking-pan on a layer of sliced salt pork, and chopped carrot, onion and turnip. Add a bouquet of herbs (*parsley, bay, thyme, and perhaps marjoram, tied around a celery stalk*), a cupful of stock, and enough water to fill the pan one and a half inches deep. Cover closely, and let cook in a moderate oven, allowing twenty minutes to the pound; baste frequently. Remove the cover for the last half hour, so the meat may brown. Strain the gravy from the pan to serve it. (*Parboiled potatoes may be put in the pan with it, to brown for the last half hour.*)

HORSERADISH

This most refreshing and appetizing relish is used chiefly in the spring, and is especially valuable in country towns, where the reign of *veal* is so long and wearisome. It must be washed clean, grated, and moistened with vinegar; add a little salt.

Horseradish is ready to pull in late October or November after a frost, but can be left in the ground all winter. It is most plentiful in cities, fresh, around Passover time.

TO ROLL A BREAST OF VEAL

Bone it, take off the thick skin and gristle, and beat the meat with a rolling pin. Season it with herbs chopped very fine, mixed with salt, pepper and mace. Lay some thick slices of fine ham in it—or roll it about two or three calves' tongues, of a fine red, boiled first an hour or two, and skinned. Bind it up tight in a cloth and tape it. Set it over the fire to simmer, in a small quantity of water, till it is quite tender—this will take some hours. Lay it on the dresser, with a board and weight on it till quite cold. The different colors laid in layers look well when cut—and you may put in yolks of eggs boiled, beet-root, grated ham, and chopped parsley in different parts. (*Serves 4–6.*)

VEAL CUTLETS

Take two or more cutlets, pound them with a rolling pin, then wash, and dry them on a clean towel, and season with salt and pepper. Have ready half a pint of bread crumbs, or fine cracker, which season with salt and pepper. Whisk two eggs with one gill of milk, and pour over the cutlets; then take one at a time and place in the crumbs, pat well with the back of a spoon, in order to make the crumbs adhere. Put them in hot lard, and fry slowly until well done, and handsomely browned on both sides; then serve hot (*with tomato sauce, piquant sauce, or butter and lemon juice; serves 2 or more*).

VEAL CUTLETS AND TOMATOES

Wash two (*or more*) cutlets, and season them with pepper and salt. Have ready some hot lard and butter in a pan; put the meat into it, and fry it on both sides of a nice brown; when done, take it up on a dish.

(*Scald, peel, and*) stew about a quarter of a peck (*5 or 6*) of tomatoes, drain, mash and season them with red pepper and salt. Pour the tomatoes into the pan with the gravy, after the cutlets have been dished, and stir them well together. Pour them over the cutlets and send to table hot. This dish is very much admired by many. (*Serves 2–4.*)

ESCALOPS OF VEAL À LA CHICORÉE

Pare and cut two pounds of veal (from the hip is preferrable) into six even steak-forms. Season with a pinch of salt and half a pinch of pepper. Then brown them in a sauté-pan in one ounce of butter, on a very hot range, for four minutes on each side. Then dress half a pint of chicory on a plate, place the escalops over it, and send to the table. (*Serves 6.*)

CHICORY AND GRAVY: Take six large fine fresh heads of chicory, pare any outer leaves that may be damaged, leaving the root intact; wash well in two waters, remove and pat them to blanch for ten minutes in boiling salted water. Take them out, put them back into cold water, and let them cool off thoroughly; drain neatly, and cut them in halves. Put a piece of lard skin (*bacon rind or salt pork*) at the bottom of a frying-pan. Add one carrot, one onion, both cut up, and a bouquet. Place the chicory on top, season with half a pinch of salt, half a pinch of pepper, and a third of a pinch of nutmeg, and cover with a buttered paper. Place the frying pan on the stove, and when the chicory is a golden color (not letting it take longer than ten minutes), moisten with half a pint of white broth. Put it in the oven for thirty minutes; arrange the chicory on a hot dish, strain the sauce over, and serve.

ESCALOPS WITH STUFFED PEPPER

Proceed as above, adding the juice of half a medium-sized, sound lemon and a gill of hot Madeira sauce (*p. 439*). Cook for three minutes longer, and decorate the dish with six stuffed peppers (*p. 241*) three minutes before serving.

TO MAKE A SAVORY DISH OF VEAL

Cut some large scallops from a leg of veal, dip them in rich egg batter (*p. 73*), season them with cloves, mace, nutmeg, beaten fine; make force-meat of some of the veal, some beef suet, oysters chopped, a few bread crumbs, sweet herbs shred fine; strew these all over the collops (*scallops*), roll and tie them up; put them on skewers and roast them (*roasting meant over an open fire; to broil, skewers are not necessary*). To the rest of the force-meat, add two raw eggs, roll them in balls and fry them. Put them into a dish with the meat when roasted and make the sauce with a strong broth, an anchovy or a shallot, a little white wine and some spice. Let it stew, and thicken it with a piece of butter rolled in flour. Pour the sauce into the dish, lay the meat in with the force-meat balls, and garnish with lemon.

VEAL OLIVES

1½ pounds of veal cutlet cut out very thin	1 tablespoon of sweet marjoram
	½ pound of bacon
1 tablespoon of chopped parsley	1 tablespoon of flour
1 tablespoon of melted butter	1 bay leaf
1 pint of stock or boiling water	1 tablespoonful of mushroom
1 cup of stale bread crumbs	catsup (p. 250)
1 teaspoon of salt	Pepper to taste

Cut the veal into strips about three inches long and two inches wide. Make a filling from the bread crumbs, salt, pepper to taste, parsley, sweet marjoram, and melted butter. Mix thoroughly and spread on the strips of veal, roll them up and tie them tightly with twine; now roll them in flour. Put the bacon in a frying-pan and try out all the fat. Put the olives in this, and brown them on all sides. Now put them in a saucepan, add the flour to the fat remaining in the pan, and stir until a nice brown; then add the stock or boiling water, and stir until it boils; add salt and pepper to taste; pour it over the olives; add the bay leaf and mushroom catsup, cover the saucepan and let *simmer* two hours. Then take up, cut the strings with a sharp knife, and remove them. Put the olives in a row on a dish, strain the sauce over them, and serve. (*Serves 4.*)

ANOTHER: Cut thin slices off a filet, and flatten them; season them highly with pepper, salt, mace and grated lemon peel; roll up in each a bit of fat and tie it with a thread. Fry them of a light brown, and stew them in white stock (*p. 438*) with two dozen of fried oysters, a glass of white wine, a spoonful of lemon pickle (*p. 404*) and some small mushrooms. Stew them nearly an hour. Take off the threads before serving.

Thin slices of beef can also be made into "olives."

BLANQUETTE OF VEAL

Cut into two-inch square pieces, two and a half pounds of breast of veal. Soak it in fresh water for one hour (*some older books show a conviction that young meat like veal or lamb, and innards, are pernicious unless soaked*); drain it well, then lay it in a saucepan; cover with fresh water; boil, and be careful to skim off all the scum. Add a well-garnished bouquet (*parsley, bay, thyme, rosemary, and/or marjoram tied around a stalk of celery*), six small, well-peeled, sound white onions, two good pinches of salt, and a pinch of white pepper. Cook for forty minutes. Melt about an ounce and a half of butter in another saucepan, add to it three tablespoonfuls of flour, stir well for three minutes; moisten with a pint of broth from the veal; boil for five minutes. Set it on the side of the stove. Beat up in a bowl three egg yolks with the juice of a medium-sized sound lemon and a very little grated nutmeg. Take the preparation into the saucepan gradually. Add to it the egg yolks, etc., briskly mix with a wooden spoon meanwhile until all is added. Throw this over the veal, lightly toss the whole, and be careful not to allow to boil again, and serve. (*Serves 6.*)

All blanquettes are prepared the same way, adding different garnishings (*as, for instance, mushrooms or quenelles or peas or asparagus or crumbled bacon—but rarely more than a single garnishing*).

VEAL PIE

Take two pounds of veal out from the loin, filet or the best end of the neck. Remove the bone, fat and skin, and put them (*the trimmings*) into a saucepan with half a pint of water to stew for their gravy. Make a good paste, allowing a pound of butter to two pounds of flour. Divide it into two pieces, roll it out rather thick, and cover with one piece the bottom and sides of a deep dish. Put in a layer of veal, seasoned with black pepper, then a layer of cold ham sliced thin, then more veal, more ham, and so on until the dish is full; interspersing the meat with the yolks of eggs boiled hard. If you can procure some button mushrooms, they will be found an improvement. Pour in, at the last, the gravy you have drawn from the trimmings, and put on the lid of the pie, notching the edge handsomely and ornamenting the centre with a flower made of paste. Bake the pie at least two hours and a half (*at 325°; serves 6–8*).

MOCK LOBSTER

Take some cold veal (either boiled or roasted), cut it in small pieces, season with salt, pepper, (*dry*) mustard, vinegar and sweet (*olive*) oil. If preferred hot, leave out the mustard and oil, and put in a piece of butter instead. Put all together in a saucepan, place it on the fire, and let it get hot; then serve immediately. This makes a fine relish for breakfast, or for tea.

PÂTÉ DE VEAU

Of veal three and one-half pounds of fat and lean, a slice of salt pork about half a pound, six small crackers powdered very fine, two eggs, a bit of butter the size of an egg, one tablespoonful of salt, one of cayenne pepper, one of black or white pepper (*this is a lot of pepper, and it is conceivable that, given the distances it had to travel and the time involved, it was weaker than our pepper is now; in any case, season to taste*), one grated nutmeg (*about 1 teaspoonful*). Chop the meal all very fine and mix the ingredients thoroughly, put it in a dripping pan with a little water, make it into a loaf pyramidical in shape, or round, from a bowl. Bake about two hours, basting it constantly. Leave it to get cold, and slice as headcheese. A very palatable and convenient lunch or tea relish.

MOCK PÂTÉ DE FOIE GRAS

This is an imported delicacy too expensive for the average housekeeper. This recipe is simple and the results hard to detect as an imitation.

Boil one calf's liver; when cold, put through the finest blade of the chopper; add two cupfuls of melted butter, the juice of one lemon, half a pound of mushrooms stewed until tender (*and chopped roughly*), paprika, and celery salt to taste. Mix well, putting in some cut-up truffles (*which once were less expensive than they are now*). Place in a buttered mould (*cover with waxed paper and place a weight on top of it*) and serve cold.

MARBLED VEAL

Take some cold roasted veal, season with spice, pound in a mortar; skin a cold boiled tongue, cut up and pound it to a paste, adding to it nearly its weight of butter; put some of the veal into a pot, then strew in lumps of the pounded tongue; put in another layer of veal and again more tongue; press it down and pour clarified butter (*p. 106*) on top. This cuts very prettily like veined marble. White meat of fowls may be used instead of veal.

ONIONS STUFFED WITH VEAL

Peel twelve large onions, cut a piece off at the top and bottom to give them a flat appearance, and which adds a better flavor if left, blanch them in four quarts of boiling water twenty minutes, then lay them on a cloth to dry; take the middle out of each onion, and fill them with a veal forcemeat (*with a little chopped shallot, parsley, and mushroom mixed into minced veal*), put them in a sauté pan well buttered. Cover them with white broth (*p. 131, or with chicken bouillon*), let them simmer over a slow fire until well covered with a glaze, and tender; turn them over and serve where required.

VEAL FORCEMEAT

Take a pound and a half of lean veal, cut it in long, thin slices, scrape with a knife until nothing but the skin remains; put it (*the meat*) in a mortar, pound it ten minutes, or until a purée, pass it through a sieve (*or chop in a blender*), then take one pound of good fresh beef suet, which shred and chop very fine (*or chop in a blender*), put it in your mortar, and pound it, then add six ounces of panada with the suet, pound them well together, and add the veal, season with a teaspoonful of salt, a quarter of one of pepper, half that of nutmeg; continually pounding the contents of the mortar; when well mixed, take a small piece in a spoon, and poach it in some boiling water, and if it is delicate, firm and of a good flavor, it is ready for use. You can vary the flavor by the addition of a spoonful of chopped parsley, eschalot, mushroom, etc., and the flesh of rabbit, or pheasant, grouse, etc.

PANADA: Put two-thirds or half a pint of water into a stewpan holding a quart, with nearly an ounce of butter; when boiling, stir in a quarter of a pound of flour; keep it moving over the fire until it forms a smooth and toughish paste; take it out of the stewpan, and when cold use it as directed.

FORCEMEAT BALLS (*AN EASIER RECIPE*)

To a pound of lean of the leg of veal, allow a pound of beef suet. Mince them together very fine, then season it to your taste with pepper, salt, mace, nutmeg, and chopped sage or sweet marjoram. Then chop a half-pint of oysters, and beat six eggs very well. Mix the whole together, and pound it to a paste in a marble mortar. If you do not want it immediately, put it away in a stone pot, strew a little flour on the top, and cover it closely.

When you wish to use the forcemeat, divide into equal parts as much of it as you want; and having floured your hands, roll it into round balls, all of equal size. Either fry them in butter, or boil them.

This forcemeat will be found a very good stuffing for meat or poultry. (*Make it when you have the ingredients around and freeze it, if you must keep it longer than a week.*)

OYSTER SAUSAGE

Take one pound of veal and a score of oysters bearded (*beards removed*), then pound the veal very finely in a mortar with a little suet, season with a little pepper, soak a piece of bread in the oyster liquor, pound it, and add it with the oysters cut in pieces to the veal; beat up an egg to bind them together, and roll them into little lengths, like sausages; fry them in butter a delicate brown. (*Serves 4–6.*)

INNARDS

People ate more innards in the nineteenth century than we do now. Rich in iron, minerals, and vitamins, they are delicious when well prepared. We have been missing something.

CALF'S-LIVER SAUTÉ

Cut it into slices, put a little butter in the sauté or frying pan, when melted, lay the liver in, season with salt and pepper, a teaspoonful of chopped eschalot, parsley and grated nutmeg; sauté on a sharp fire; when rather brown on both sides, dredge a tablespoonful of French vinegar (*wine vinegar*) or a glass of wine, and stir it well and boil for a few minutes; dish the liver; if the sauce is too pale add a little mushroom catsup or coloring (*p. 250*), and it had better be too thin than too thick; taste if well seasoned, and serve: the above is for about two pounds of liver. (*Serves 4–6.*)

CALF'S-LIVER ROASTED

Wash and wipe it; then cut a long hole in it and stuff it with crumbs of bread, chopped anchovy, herbs, a good deal of fat bacon, onion, salt, pepper, a bit of butter, and an egg (*beaten and mixed with the other ingredients to bind them*); set the liver up, then lard it, or wrap in a veal cawl (*or a thin sheet of salt pork*), and roast it—serve with a good brown gravy and currant-jelly. (*Serves about 8.*)

[125]

Steer liver, soaked overnight in milk, will be almost as tender as calf's liver, and far less costly.

LARDED CALF'S-LIVER

Take a calf's liver and wash it well. Cut into long slips the fat of some bacon or old ham, and insert it all through the surface of the liver by means of a larding pin. Put the liver into a pot with a tablespoonful of lard, a few sliced tomatas, or some tomata catchup; adding one large or two small onions minced fine, and some sweet marjoram leaves rubbed very fine. The sweet marjoram will crumble more easily if you dry it before the fire on a plate.

Having put in all these ingredients, set the pot on hot coals in a corner of the fire-place (*or in a 350° oven*), and keep it stewing, regularly and slowly, for four hours (*15 minutes to the pound in the oven*). Send the liver to table with the gravy around it. (*Serves about 8.*)

TO PREPARE SWEETBREADS

Put them in cold water; remove the pipes and membranes. Cook them in boiling salted water, with one tablespoonful of lemon juice, twenty minutes, and plunge into cold water to harden. They may then be cooked in any way you please.

To serve, either larded, broiled, or (*breaded and*) fried, arrange around a centre of tomato sauce, mushrooms or peas. Or put sweetbreads in the centre of a nest of boiled macaroni. Sprinkle the macaroni with cheese and pour white sauce or tomato sauce over it; or garnish the sweetbreads with stuffed tomatoes.

DELICATE PIE OF SWEETBREADS AND OYSTERS

The sweetbread of veal is the most delicious part. Boil it tender (*see above*); stew some oysters; season with salt and pepper, and thicken with cream, butter, the yolk of eggs, and flour; line a deep dish with a puff paste (*p. 76*); take up the oysters with an egg (*slotted*) spoon; lay them on the bottom; cover them with the sweetbreads; fill the dish with gravy (*from the oysters*); put over it a paste top, and bake it (*in a 350° oven, until the crust is delicately brown*).

CALF'S BRAINS

Soak the brains for an hour in cold water; then simmer in water containing a tablespoonful of vinegar for twenty minutes; an onion, thyme, bay-leaf, salt and peppercorns in the water also will improve the flavor of the brains; place again in cold water to blanch; remove the skin and fibres, and cook by any of the recipes given for sweetbreads. (*One set serves 4.*)

The boiled brains may also be served with any of the following sauces poured over them: a plain white sauce (*p. 438*), a hollandaise sauce (*p. 165*), a tomato sauce (*p. 281*), a sauce made of browned butter and a dash of vinegar.

MARINADE OF BRAINS: Boil the brains, remove the skin and veins; cut them into pieces the size of half an egg; let them stand an hour in a marinade of oil, vinegar, onion (*chopped*), pepper and salt; then wipe and dip them into fritter batter (*p. 73*) and fry in hot fat. Arrange them on a napkin and serve with tomato sauce.

CALF'S BRAINS WITH BLACK BUTTER

Place three fine, fresh calf's brains in cold water, and then peel off the skins. Wash again in cold water; neatly drain; put them in a sautoire (*frying pan*), and cover with fresh water. Add two pinches of salt, half a cupful of vinegar, one medium-sized sliced carrot, one sprig of thyme, one bay-leaf and twelve whole peppers. Boil for five minutes, drain well, and cut each brain in two. Dress them on a dish, and serve with a gill of very hot black butter. (*Serves 8–10.*)

BLACK BUTTER: Warm good butter in a frying-pan until it becomes brown; add parsley leaves, heat again for one minute, then throw in vinegar, five drops to an ounce of butter. Pour it into a sauce-bowl and serve.

BEEF HEART WITH VEAL STUFFING

Soak and clean (*cut open to remove the ventricles, soak in water half an hour, then parboil it about 10 minutes*). Make a filling as follows: one pound of uncooked veal, chopped fine, a quarter-pound of salt pork, chopped fine, or a quarter-pound of sausage-meat, two heaping teaspoonfuls of dried bread crumbs, a tablespoonful of onion juice, one teaspoonful of salt, a quarter-teaspoonful of black pepper, if you like, a dozen mushrooms, chopped fine, and one egg slightly beaten. Mix all these ingredients well together, and stuff the heart. Wrap tightly in a cloth and sew it. Stand it in a small saucepan, with the point down, cover with boiling water, and *simmer* slowly three hours; then take it out and remove the cloth. Bake in a quick oven one hour, basting every ten minutes with a little melted butter. Serve with a brown sauce, the same as baked heart. (*Serves 4–6.*)

This is also a nice cold dish, cut in thin slices, using no sauce.

CALVES' FEET JELLY

A kind of jellied consommé, a predecessor of gelatine, this is a base for a number of puddings, as well as the recommended dish to take to neighborhood invalids.

Boil four calves-feet or cow heels in two gallons of water until it is reduced to two quarts; strain it, and when cold skim off the fat; then put the jelly to boil, with a pint of sherry, a glass of good brandy, the peel and juice of three lemons, enough loaf sugar to sweeten it, and the whites and *shells* of six eggs, well-beaten. Stir all together till it comes to a boil; let it boil quickly for a few minutes, then strain it through a flannel bag until it is quite clear. A little saffron boiled with it gives a rich color. (*Makes 3 quarts.*)

TO PREPARE RENNET TO TURN MILK

This has been largely outdated by handy little rennet tablets. However, should you have an extra calf's stomach lying around . . .

Take out the stomach of a calf as soon as it is killed, and scour it inside and out with salt. After it is cleared of the curds always found in it, let it drain a few hours; then sew it up with two handfuls of salt in it, or stretch it on a stick well salted; or keep it in the salt wet (*in a strong brine*); and soak a piece of it for use, which will do over again by washing it in fresh water. (*Rennet may also be preserved in wine or brandy, and the wine used to curdle milk.*)

VEAL SOUPS

CRÈME DE RIZ

Three pounds of veal (leg is best), pulled with forks (*shredded*), five pints of water, one-quarter pound of rice. Simmer very gently until reduced to half the quantity; strain through a sieve (*or purée in a blender*), and season to your taste (*try salt, white pepper, chopped fresh parsley, a sprinkling of paprika on top*). It is very nourishing and well made is of the thickness of good cream. (*Serves 4–6.*)

RICH VEAL SOUP

Take three pounds of the scrag of a neck of veal, cut it in pieces and put it with the bones (which must be broken up) into a pot with two quarts of water. Stew it till the meat is done to rags, and skim it well. Then strain it and return (*the broth*) to the pot.

Blanch and pound in a mortar to a smooth paste a quarter of a pound of sweet almonds, and mix them with the yolks of six hard-boiled eggs grated, and a pint of cream, which must first have been boiled, or it will curdle in the soup. Season it with nutmeg and mace. Stir the mixture into the soup (*first adding a little hot soup to the cream mixture*) and let it boil afterward about three minutes, stirring all the time. Lay in the bottom of the tureen some slices of bread without the crust. Pour the soup upon it and send it to table. (*For an even richer soup, purée a little of the best meat and add it. Serves 6.*)

"*Malaga-Tawny signified Pepper Water. The progress of inexperienced peripatetic Palaticians has lately been arrested by this outlandish word being pasted on the windows of our Coffee Houses; it has, we believe, answered the Restauranteur's purpose, and often excited John Bull to walk in and taste; as the more familiar name of Curry Soup would, perhaps, not have had sufficient of the charms of novelty.*"

Dr. Kitchener, *The Cook's Oracle*, 1822

Part II: Recipes

MULLAGATAWNY SOUP MADE IN INDIA

Take a quarter of an ounce of China turmeric (*sharp spices tended to lose pungency when they had to travel long slow distances; two teaspoonfuls should be enough for most tastes*), one-third of an ounce of cassia (*no longer generally available; a scant teaspoon each of ground cardamom and cumin may be substituted*), three drachms (*⅓ ounce*) of black pepper, two drachms (*¼ ounce*) of cayenne pepper and an ounce of coriander seeds (*or 2 tablespoons, ground*). These must all be pounded fine in a mortar and well mixed and sifted. (*Commercial curry powder may be substituted, but it does not have nearly the subtlety or delicacy of this mixture. For another recipe for curry powder, see p. 443.*) They will make a sufficient quantity of curry powder for the following quantity of soup:

Take two large fowls, or three pounds of the lean of veal. Cut the flesh entirely from the bones in small pieces, and put it into a stew pot with two quarts of water. Let it boil for a hour, slowly, skimming it well. Prepare four large onions, minced and fried in two ounces of butter. Add to them the curry powder and moisten the whole with broth from the stewpot, mixed with a little rice flour (*or cornstarch*). When thoroughly mixed, stir the seasoning into the soup and simmer it until it is as smooth and thick as cream (*10–15 minutes*), and until the chicken or veal is perfectly tender. Then stir into it the juice of a lemon; and five minutes after take up the soup with the meat in it, and serve it in the tureen. (*Serves 6–8.*)

The rice is to be put into the soup by those who eat it.

SOYER'S STOCK FOR ALL KINDS OF SOUP

Alexis Soyer was a chef and cookbook author, as well-known in the nineteenth century as Julia Child is now.

Procure a knuckle of veal about six pounds in weight, which cut into pieces about the size of an egg, as also a half pound of lean ham or bacon; then rub a quarter-pound of butter upon the bottom of a stewpan (holding about two gallons) into which put the meat and bacon with half a pint of water, two ounces of salt, three medium onions, with two cloves stuck in each, one turnip, a carrot, half a leek, and half a head (*bunch*) of celery; put the cover on the stewpan, which place over a sharp fire, stirring occasionally with a wooden spoon until the bottom of the stewpan is covered with a thick whitish glaze, which will adhere to the spoon; fill up the stewpan with cold water, and when upon the point of boiling, draw it to the corner of the fire where it must simmer gently for three hours, carefully skimming off every particle of grease and scum; pass your stock through a hair (*fine*) sieve and it will be ready for use. (*Makes 1 gallon, more or less.*)

WHITE STOCK

Take scrag or knuckle of veal, ox-heel or calf's head together with an old fowl and the trimmings of any white poultry or game which can be had, and lean ham in proportion to one pound for every fourteen pounds of meat. Cut it all into pieces (add three or four large unroasted (*and unpeeled*) onions and heads of celery with a few blades of mace (*whole if you can get it, otherwise 1 teaspoonful of ground mace*), but neither carrots, pepper, nor spice of any kind but mace); put it into a stockpot with just water enough to cover it: and let it boil for five hours and then it is fit for use.

See p. 438 for another recipe.

HOT CROSS BUNS

These are traditional Easter-morning rolls.

Three cupfuls sweet milk; one cupful of yeast (*or 1 package, dissolved in a cup of lukewarm water*); flour enough to make a thick batter. Set this as a sponge overnight. In the morning, add one cupful of sugar, one-half cupful butter, melted; half a nutmeg (*grated*); one saltspoonful of salt, and flour enough to roll out like biscuit. Knead well, and set to rise five hours. Roll half an inch thick, cut into round cakes, and lay in rows on a buttered bakepan. When they have stood half an hour, make a cross upon each with a knife, and put instantly into the oven. Bake to a light brown, and brush over with a feather or soft bit of rag (*or pastry brush*), dipped in the white of an egg beaten up stiff with white (*powdered*) sugar. (*Makes 2½–3 dozen.*)

LAMB

Lamb, like veal, is a springtime meat although it is now available year-round, and traditionally, it is eaten on Easter Sunday. Lambs do not turn into mutton until they are a year old, but the younger they are, the whiter and more tender the meat is, and the more amenable it is to outside flavorings. Unlike mutton, which is good rare, lamb should be served fairly well done, just pink in the middle. See November (*pp. 360–368*) for mutton recipes, most of which can be adapted for lamb.

SADDLE OF LAMB, RUSSIAN FASHION

Roast a small saddle of lamb (*the entire back, excluding the haunches, up to and including the first couple of ribs; it is roasted with the flaps of the flank curled under it, sometimes over a mound of stuffing*), keeping it pale; having had it covered with paper. Take ten good-sized boiled potatoes, mash them with about two ounces of butter, a teaspoonful of salt, a quarter ditto of pepper, a tablespoonful of chopped parsley and a little grated nutmeg; mix all well together with a fork, adding half a gill of milk and one egg (*beaten in the milk*); when cold, roll them in long shapes the size of a plover's egg (*about half hen's-egg size*), egg and bread-crumb twice (*roll in crumbs, then in beaten egg, then in crumbs again*), and (*deep*) fry light-colored; dress the saddle, surround it with the potatoes, make a sauce of melted butter (*p. 107*) and pour it round, and serve. All joints of lamb can be dressed thus.

Roast lamb is good basted occasionally while roasting with a cup of coffee to which cream and sugar have been added. A sauce of olive oil, soy or Worcestershire sauce, lemon juice, salt and pepper, minced garlic and herbs, rubbed into the lamb about an hour before roasting, gives it a crunchy crust and a good flavor.

"*Roast lamb should be eaten with mint sauce (if you fancy it), currant jelly, and asparagus or green peas. Lettuce-salad is likewise a desirable accompaniment.*"

Marion Harland, *Common Sense*, 1883

MINT SAUCE

One cup fresh chopped mint, one-half cup vinegar, one-fourth cup sugar. Use only the leaves and tender tips of the mint. Let it stand an hour before serving. Use more sugar if the vinegar be very strong.

LEG OF LAMB À LA BRETONNE

Choose one about six pounds weight, peel four cloves of garlic, make an incision with the point of a knife in four places around the knuckle, and place the garlic in it, and hang it up for a day or two (*to age; not generally necessary now*), then roast (*at 325°, 15–18 minutes to the pound*) it for one hour and a half. At the same time you have procured a quart of small dry French haricot (*white beans*), which after well washing put into a saucepan with half a gallon of water, add about half an ounce of salt, the same of butter, set them on the side of the fire to simmer for about three hours or till tender, when pour off the liquor into a basin, and keep the haricots hot; peel and cut two large onions into thin slices, put some of the fat from the dripping (*roasting*) pan into the frying pan, put in the onions and fry a light brown, add them to the haricots with the fat and gravy the lamb has produced in roasting, season with salt and pepper, toss them a little, and serve very hot on a large dish, put the leg on it, with a frill of paper on the knuckle. This if well carved is an excellent dish for eight or nine persons. Shoulder and loin may be dressed the same way.

Roast lamb, like roast beef, should be removed from the oven and allowed to set for about 15 minutes before carving.

INDIAN PILAU

Slice a large onion very fine, and divide it into shreds. Then fry it slowly in a quarter of a pound of butter until it is equally, but not too deeply browned. Take it out and fry in the butter half a pound of rice. As the grain easily burns, it should be done over a very slow fire (*stirring constantly*) until it becomes a light yellow tint. Then add sufficiency of boiling broth to boil the rice soft in the usual way, each grain remaining separate. Also add a quarter of an ounce each of (*whole*) cloves, peppercorns, and allspice, tied in a piece of muslin, three onions, if you like their flavor, and salt to the taste. Before serving, take out the spices and the onions, and serve with the meat the broth was made from. It ought to be a loin of lamb, cut in joints, which after being taken out of the broth should be peppered, salted, and fried. Place the meat on a large flat (*warm*) plate, and pour over it the stewed rice, which ought to be a rich brown color. Garnish with hard-boiled eggs cut in quarters. This dish must be eaten hot. Malaga raisins are often boiled with the rice, and chicken substituted for lamb. (*Serves 6.*)

SAUSAGE PILAU: This is made as the rice pilau, using sausage that has been stuffed but not smoked.

MIGNONS OF LAMB, SAUCE BÉARNAISE

Procure a fine, tender leg of lamb, bone it with a sharp knife so as to detach the meat from the knuckle, beginning from the hip-side downwards. Cut out from this six even pieces or steaks (*or have your butcher do it*), one inch thick by two and a half in diameter, pare them nicely, and with a small, keen knife remove any sinews that are liable to adhere to the meat. Lay them on a cold dish, and season with a good pinch of salt, and a light pinch of pepper, and roll them well, so that the seasoning be equally distributed. Put half an ounce of good butter in a frying-pan, set it carefully on a brisk fire, and add the pieces, or mignons, immediately, being careful that they do not lay one on top of the other, and cook them very briskly for two and a half minutes on each side. Prepare half a pint of Béarnaise sauce, pour it on a hot serving dish, dress the six mignons nicely over, one overlapping the other, and send it to table immediately. (*Serves 6.*)

Any lamb that may be left over after cutting the mignons can be utilized for minced lamb, soup (*kababs, stew*), or any other purpose desired.

BÉARNAISE SAUCE: Chop very fine two-medium-sized, sound, well-peeled shallots; place them in a small saucepan on the hot range, with two tablespoonfuls of either tarragon or chervil vinegar, and five whole crushed peppercorns. Reduce until nearly dry, then put away to cool. Mingle with it six fresh raw egg yolks, sharply stirring meanwhile, then gradually add one and a half ounces of good fresh (*melted*) butter, seasoning with half a tablespoon of salt, half a teaspoon of grated nutmeg, and twelve finely chopped tarragon leaves. Have a much wider pan on the fire with boiling water (*a double boiler*), place the small one containing the ingredients into the other, and see that the boiling water reaches up to half its height; thoroughly heat up, beating briskly with the whisk; when the sauce is firm, add one teaspoonful of melted meat glaze (*p. 438; this seems to be an addition to the classic sauce and may be omitted*), beat lightly for two seconds longer, then strain through an ordinary clean kitchen towel, neatly arrange the sauce on a hot dish to be sent to the table; and dress over it any article required to be served.

STEAKS OF LAMB OR MUTTON AND CUCUMBERS

Quarter cucumbers, and lay them into a deep dish, sprinkle them with salt, and pour vinegar over them. Fry the chops of a fine brown, and put them into a stewpan; drain the cucumbers, and put over the steaks; add some sliced onions, pepper and salt; pour (*a very little*) hot water or weak broth on them; stew (*about 15 minutes*) and skim well.

LAMB CHOP À LA MAINTENON

Each chop is cut thick and has the larger end split open for the stuffing. To put in this incision, take: four tablespoons of chopped mushrooms, one tablespoon chopped onion, one tablespoon butter, one tablespoon flour, three tablespoons of stock, one teaspoon salt and one-fifth teaspoon of pepper. Prepare this by melting the butter and browning the flour in it, then add the stock, and other ingredients. After this has cooked, add one-quarter teaspoon Worcestershire Sauce and one tablespoon chopped parsley, and set away to cool. Then put one teaspoonful into each chop and broil.

BROCHETTE OF LAMB À LA (*ALEXANDRE*) DUMAS

Take a raw leg of lamb weighing about three pounds; remove the bone and pare off the skin. Then cut into six square pieces of equal size. Put them into a vessel with two very finely chopped shallots, one teaspoonful of chopped chives, one teaspoonful of parsley and a crushed clove of garlic. Add the juice of half a lemon, a tablespoonful of salt, a teaspoonful of pepper, and half a teaspoonful of nutmeg. Let them steep for about two hours, stirring at times; then take the pieces out, run a skewer through the centre of the six pieces, interlarding them with pieces of salt pork; dip them in bread-crumb and broil for four minutes on each (*of the four*) sides. Serve with half a pint of Colbert sauce poured on the serving dish, and place the brochette over, arranging them nicely. (*Serves 2–3.*)

COLBERT SAUCE: Put in a saucepan half a pint of very thick Madeira sauce (*p. 439*); add to it very gradually one ounce of good, fresh butter, also two tablespoonfuls of meat glaze (*p. 438*). Mix well together without boiling; then squeeze in the juice of half a sound lemon, and add one teaspoonful of chopped parsley before serving.

CURRY OF LAMB WITH ASPARAGUS TOPS

Have three pounds of shoulder of lamb cut into pieces about two inches square. Wash well in fresh water, drain, put into a saucepan, and cover with fresh water. Let it come to a boil, then strain through a colander, and wash again in water (*I think this first boiling rather unnecessary*). Place the pieces in a saucepan, cover them with boiling water; season with two tablespoonfuls of salt, one teaspoonful of pepper, six small onions, and a bouquet (*parsley, bay, thyme, or marjoram, tied around a celery stalk*). Put the lid on, and cook for forty minutes. Then strain off the liquor into another saucepan containing half a pint of white roux (*flour stirred into an equal amount of melted butter; ½ cup should be enough*), stirring well until it boils, and then let it stand on a corner of the stove. Break into a separate bowl four egg yolks with the juice of half a lemon, beaten well together. Add this to the sauce, dropping it in little by little, and stirring continually. Pour all over the lamb and add one pint of cooked asparagus tops, but be careful not to boil again. (*Serves 4–6.*)

LAMB STEW

Cut up from three to four pounds of lamb—the inferior portions will do as well as any other—crack the bones and remove all the fat. Put on the meat—the pieces not more than an inch and a half in length—in a pot (*and brown them in hot butter; when brown, dredge over them 3 tablespoons of flour, stirring to coat them; then add*) enough cold water to cover well, and set it where it will heat gradually. Add nothing else until it has stewed an hour, closely covered; then throw in half a pound of salt pork cut into strips, a little chopped onion (*and some minced garlic*), and some (*whole*) pepper; cover and stew an hour longer, or until the meat is very tender. Make out a little paste, as for the crust of a meat pie (*p. 344 or p. 387*); cut in squares and drop in the stew. Boil ten minutes, and season further by the addition of a little parsley and thyme. Thicken with two spoonfuls of flour stirred into a cup of cold milk. Boil up once and serve in a tureen or deep covered dish. (*Serves 8–10.*)

If green corn (*or sweet corn*) is in season, this stew is greatly improved by the addition, an hour before it is taken from the fire (*corn is tenderer now: 10 minutes will do*), the grains of half a dozen ears, cut from the cob. Try it for a cheap family dinner, and you will repeat the experiment often.

Turnips, carrots, peas, or onions, any one, may be used.

HOT LAMB PIE

To make this an oval, a tin or copper pie mould (*available at kitchen specialty shops*) would be required. Butter the inside of the mould, which stand upon a baking sheet, then make the following paste: put a quarter of a pound of butter and the same of chopped suet into a stewpan, with half a pint of water, and let the whole boil together one minute, when strain it through a sieve into a basin containing two pounds of flour, mixing it first with a spoon, then with the hand when cool enough, until forming a smooth paste; when partly cold, roll it out into a sheet half an inch in thickness, with which line the mould, pressing the paste evenly at all points; have ready cut sufficient small lamb chops from the loin, neatly cut away the bone, and lay them round the interior of the pie, alternating with slices of raw potato (a quarter of an inch in thickess), season rather highly as you proceed, with pepper, salt, chopped onion, and parsley; make a neat cover of the trimmings of the paste, and bake it rather the better than two hours in a moderate oven; when done, lift the cover, pour out as much of the fat as possible, add a little gravy, (*unfasten the mold to leave it free-standing*) and serve (*to 8–10*).

ANOTHER: Take two or three pounds of nice lamb chops; wash and put them into a stew kettle with water just sufficient to cover them; then season with salt, black and cayenne pepper mixed, and dredge in flour (*rubbed with butter to make a roux*) sufficient to make the stew of the proper consistency; then stew them over a slow fire until tender, taking care the gravy does not scorch. When done, remove the kettle from the fire, and put in twenty-five or more oysters, according to the size of pie required, first taking them from their liquor and seeing that every particle of shell has been removed. Stir all together, and if not sufficiently seasoned, add more to taste. Roll out a puff paste (*p. 76*) moderately thin, and line the sides of your dish, which first grease with a little butter; then place in the meat and oysters, and pour over the gravy, though not a sufficient quantity to boil out whilst the pie is baking. Then roll out a lid of moderate thickness, which place over the top. Cut an opening in the top and turn over the edges, and bake in a quick oven. When done, and handsomely browned, send to table hot. (*Serves 6–8.*)

KID

TO ROAST A KID

A kid should be cooked the day it is killed, or the day after at the far-thest. They are best from three to four months old, and are only eaten while they live on milk.

Wash the (*skinned, drawn, whole*) kid well, wipe it dry, and truss it. Stuff the body with a force-meat of grated bread, butter or suet, sweet-herbs, pepper, salt, nutmeg, grated lemon-peel, and beaten egg; and sew it up to keep the stuffing in its place. Put it on the spit and rub it over with lard or sweet oil. Put a little salt and water into the dripping-pan (*a pan placed under the spit to collect the drippings from the meat*), and baste the kid first with it, and afterwards with its own gravy. Or you may make it very nice by basting it with cream. It should roast about three hours. At the last, transfer the gravy to a small sauce-pan; thicken it with a little butter rolled in flour, give it a boil up, and send it to table in a boat. Garnish the kid with lumps of currant jelly laid round the edge of the dish. (*Serves 6–8.*)

A hare or a couple of rabbits may be roasted in the same manner.

You may send to table, to eat with the kid, a dish of chestnuts boiled or roasted, and divested of their hulls.

SALMON

Commercial fishermen fish for salmon off the mouths of the rivers where they go to spawn. They are fattest just before they spawn. The best, I understand, are royal king salmon caught by ocean trolling, in season at April's end. Once, they were so common that bondservants' contracts some-times specified that salmon would be served to them no more than three times a week. Now they are neither as plentiful nor as good.

TO BAKE A SALMON WHOLE

Clean the fish and season well outside and inside with pepper and salt; mix some butter together and lay it in bits over the inside, and stick it over the fish outside. Form it into a circle by running a string through the head and tail and tying them together (*the whole nineteenth century held strait-laced ideas as to the form in which a fish should appear on the table; salmon must be in circles, as must herring, but most fish had to be slashed across the back to keep them from snapping straight, and trussed into S-shapes, to simulate swimming, I suppose*), put three or four muffin rings (*or a rack*) in a deep dish or pan, lay the fish on (*to keep it from resting on a surface*), and baste, while baking, with melted butter.

TO BOIL FRESH SALMON

Scale and clean, cutting open no more than is necessary. Place it in a kettle of cold water with a handful of salt. Let it boil slowly, but it should be well cooked, about a quarter of an hour to a pound of fish. Skim it well, and as soon as done, lift it carefully into a napkin to absorb the moisture, and wrap it close. Send to table on a hot dish. Garnish with horseradish and curled parsley, or boiled eggs cut in rings, laid round the dish. Oyster sauce (*p. 277*) is best with fresh boiled fish.

TO BROIL SALMON

Cut slices an inch thick and season with pepper and salt; lay each slice in half a sheet of white paper, well buttered (*fold over to enclose fish*), twist the ends of the paper, and broil the slices over a slow fire (*this can be done outdoors over embers or in a broiler*), six to eight minutes. Serve in the paper with anchovy sauce (*p. 340*).

SALMON COLLARED

Split such a part of the fish as may be sufficient to make a handsome roll (*a large fillet*), wash and wipe it, and, having mixed salt, white pepper, pounded mace, and Jamaica pepper (*allspice*), in quantity to season it very highly, rub it inside and out, well. Then roll it tight, and bandage it; put as much water and one-third vinegar, as will cover it, with bay leaves, salt and both sorts of pepper. Cover close and simmer till done enough (*15 minutes to the pound*). Drain and boil quick the liquor, and put it on (*the fish*) when cold. (*Remove the bandage when the fish is cold, just before serving.*) Serve with fennel. It is an elegant dish and very good.

SALMON À LA ST. MARCEL

Separate cold boiled salmon into flakes and free them from the skin; break the bones and boil them in a pint of water half an hour. Strain off the liquor into a clean pan and stir into it by degrees as it begins to boil two ounces of butter melted with one large (*heaping*) teaspoonful of flour, and when the whole has boiled, add one teaspoonful of essence of anchovies (*or, if you cannot find essence, one finely minced anchovy*), one of good mushroom catsup (*p. 250*), half as much lemon juice or chili vinegar, one-half saltspoonful mace, cayenne and a very little salt; shell from one-half to a pint of shrimp, add them to the salmon and heat the fish in the sauce very slowly by the side of the fire. Do not allow it to boil. When very hot, dish and send it quickly to table.

SPICED (*PICKLED*) SALMON

Boil a salmon, and after wiping it dry, set it to cool; take of the water in which it was boiled, and good vinegar, equal parts, enough to cover it; add to it one dozen cloves, as many small blades of mace (*1 tablespoonful, ground, if you cannot find it whole*), or sliced nutmeg, one teaspoonful whole pepper, and the same of alspice; make it boiling hot, skim it clear, add a small bit of butter (the size of a small egg) and pour it over the fish; set it aside in a cool place. When cold it is fit for use, and will keep a long time, covered close, in a cool place. Serve instead of pickled oysters for supper.

DRIED SALMON

This recipe was written down in 1805 by Captain William Clark, as he and Meriwether Lewis descended the headwaters of the Columbia River through the Nez Percé Indian tribes.

About their lodges I observe great numbers of stacks of pounded Salmon neetly preserved in the following manner, i.e. after (*being*) suffiently (*sic*) Dried it is pounded between two Stones fine, and put into a speces of basket neetly made of grass and rushes better than two feet long and one foot in Diamiter, which basket is lined with the Skin of the Salmon Stretched and dried for the purpose. in this it is pressed down as hard as is possible, when full they Secure the open part with the fish Skins across which they fasten th(*r*)o. the loops of the basket that part very securely, and then on a Dry Situation they Set these baskets the corded part up, their common custome is to Set 7 as close as they can Stand and 5 on the top of them, and secure them with mats which is raped around them and made fast with cords and covered also with mats, those 12 baskets of from 90 to 100 lbs. each form a Stack, thus preserved those fish may be kept Sound and sweet Several years, as those people inform me.

DRIED SALMON

Cut the fish down the back, take out the inside, and roe. Scale it, and rub the whole with common salt, and hang it to drain for twenty-four hours. Pound four ounces of saltpetre (*still available in drugstores, and in supermarkets at pickling time, in more rural areas*), two ounces of coarse salt, and two ounces of brown sugar; mix these well, and rub into the salmon, and lay it on a large dish for two days; then rub it well with common salt, and in twenty-four hours more it will be fit to dry; wipe it well after draining. Stretch it open with two sticks, and hang it in a wood chimney or in a dry place (*or smoke it over a wood fire, not too close*).

Dried salmon is eaten broiled in paper, and only just warmed through (*after soaking overnight in lukewarm water*). Egg sauce (*p. 167*) and mashed potatoes are usually served with it; or it may be boiled; or rub the gridiron over with a bit of suet, lay on the salmon, shake a little pepper over, and serve.

[8]

MAY

Rhubarb; asparagus; watercress; dandelions; poke; primroses; tropical fruits; shellfish; salt-water fish; fresh-water fish; fish soups

RHUBARB

Rhubarb is the first sure sign of spring. The knobby red fiddleheads, poking up while everything else is still locked in the ground, fill the gardener with delight. Like dandelions, it is perhaps as thoroughly seasonal an edible plant as there is. After the end of May the stalks turn tough, and are best left to get on with preparing for next year's crop.

If you have never eaten rhubarb straight from the garden, you have never eaten rhubarb. Like that of sweet corn, its sweetness begins turning to starch the minute it is pulled. The stuff sold in supermarkets isn't worth buying.

RHUBARB

Choose tender, medium-sized stalks. Trim off the leaves and peel the dry skin from the bottom of the stalk. Peel the larger, tougher stalks if you have to, but the color is better if they are left unpeeled. Cut them into 1-inch lengths and sprinkle them with a cup of sugar per quart of rhubarb. Let it stand 2 or 3 hours, then pour off the syrup which will have formed. Bring it to a hard boil (a little lemon or orange juice added to the syrup is a nice flavor variation). Add the rhubarb and cook it until just tender, about 5 minutes.

Serve as a dessert, with custard, over plain cake, or with pork instead of apple sauce.

RHUBARB PIE

Cut the large stalks off where the leaf commences, strip off the outside skin, then cut the stalks into pieces half an inch long, line a pie dish with paste rolled rather thicker than a dollar piece, put in a layer of the rhubarb nearly an inch deep (*or more*); to a quart bowl of cut rhubarb put a large teacup of sugar, strew it over with a saltspoonful of salt and half a nutmeg grated; cover with a rich pie crust, and bake in a quick oven (*about 45 minutes*) until the pie loosens from the dish. Rhubarb pies made in this way are altogether superior to those made of the fruit stewed. (*Also good made with half apples, half rhubarb. Use a little less sugar.*)

SWEET VOL-AU-VENT WITH RHUBARB

In the spring of the year this makes a very inviting and wholesome dish, and its qualities purify the blood, which the winter's food has rendered gross; cut about twelve sticks of rhubarb into lengths of one inch, put it in a stew-pan holding about two quarts, put over it a quarter of a pound of sugar, and a tablespoonful of water, set it on a sharp fire, stirring it, do not let it get brown, or it would spoil and lose its sharp flavor; it will take but a few minutes to do; when tender, put it in a basin to cool; a few minutes before serving, fill the vol-au-vent with it (*top with whipped cream*), and serve cold.

VOL-AU-VENT: *Make a rich puff paste (p. 76); divide it in half and roll out each piece about half an inch thick; cut 2 circles about 8 inches* in diameter. *Cut the inside out of one, leaving a pastry ring about an inch and a half wide. Brush the whole circle with water and put the ring on top of it, matching the edges. Bake in a quick oven until golden. If a deeper vol-au-vent is wanted, put another ring on top of the first, brushing the surface of the first with water to make it adhere.*

RHUBARB FILLING FOR CAKES

One pint of chopped rhubarb, half a pound of chopped raisins, one and a half pounds of sugar, juice and grated rind of one lemon. Boil all together. (*Cut each layer of a layer cake in half horizontally and spread this between the layers before icing.*)

TO PRESERVE RHUBARB AND ORANGE

Six (*small*) oranges; one quart of rhubarb; one pound and a half of loaf sugar. Peel the oranges carefully, take away the white rind and the pips, slice the pulps into a stewpan, with the peel cut very small, add one quart of rhubarb cut very fine, and from a pound to a pound and a half of loaf sugar. Boil the whole in the way usual with all preserves (*p. 29*). (*Makes 4–5 pints.*)

RHUBARB GINGER

Six pounds of rhubarb, six pounds of lump sugar, two ounces of whole ginger. With a damp towel rub well the stalks (*this lessens the chance of the jam fermenting*); cut them into lengths. Place the ginger between the folds of a kitchen towel, and bruise it with a hammer. Place the ginger in a large basin, and place over it alternate layers of the rhubarb and sugar. Allow this to stand twenty-four hours. At the end of this time pour the syrup from the rhubarb. Pour the syrup into a preserving pan; stir it over the fire until it boils. Pour the boiling syrup over the rhubarb, and allow this to stand twenty-four hours longer. Pour all now into a large preserving pan, place the pan over a brisk fire, and stir the contents until boiling. Skim well, draw the pan to one side, and let all simmer slowly half an hour, when the preserve is ready to pour into the pots. (*Makes 10 pints.*)

RHUBARB WINE

In the month of May, when rhubarb is green, the stalks of the leaves should be used in the following proportion: five pounds of stalks are bruised in a suitable vessel, to the whole is added one gallon of spring water; and after lying in mash three or four days, the liquor juice is poured off, when to every gallon of this juice three pounds of sugar is added, and allowed to ferment for four or five days in a suitable vat (*covered against flies with a towel*); as soon as the fermentation has ceased, the liquor must be drawn off into a cask and allowed to remain until the month of March, when all fermentation will have finished; it must then be racked off, and more loaf sugar added (*if necessary; then leave it another six months to a year before bottling; see p. 37 for details of wine making*).

ASPARAGUS

Asparagus appears not long after rhubarb, and is usually good until some time in June. The fresher you can get it, the better it is.

ASPARAGUS

Cut when two or three inches long, wash and place the heads all one way and tie in bundles with thread or twine. Have your water boiling, with a little salt, and lay it in; keep it boiling half to three quarters of an hour, according to its age (*the nineteenth century had a tendency to cook vegetables to mush; for cooking a pound at a time, 10–20 minutes is plenty*). Toast two slices of bread, moisten it with the water in which the asparagus is boiling, season it with salt, and lay on a small platter or dish. Then drain the asparagus a moment, and, laying the heads inward, spread it on the toast, pouring over it melted butter and pepper.

ASPARAGUS AS YOUNG PEAS, AN ENTREMET

Entremets are the optional dishes, usually vegetables, which follow or accompany the roast at a formal dinner.

Take the green heads of very young asparagus, and cut them into small pieces no larger than peas; put them into boiling water with a little salt; and boil for ten to twelve minutes; drain them a minute or two on a clean napkin, then put them into a stewpan with an ounce of butter, a sprig of mint, a table-spoonful of cream, a teaspoonful of salt and as much powdered sugar. Stew for ten minutes, shaking round the pan; then stir in the beaten yolks of two eggs, and in three minutes more turn the asparagus out on a dish and serve in the sauce, with sippets (*fried triangles*) of bread.

ASPARAGUS IN AMBUSH

Wash 1 quart of asparagus tops, boil fifteen minutes, and drain them in a colander. Cut the tops off 9 stale breakfast rolls, and take out the crumbs, then set them open in the oven to dry, laying each top by the roll from which it was taken. Put 1 pint milk on to boil in a farina (*double*) boiler. Beat 4 eggs until light, then stir them in the boiling milk, and stir until it begins to thicken; add 1 large tablespoonful of butter, salt, and pepper, and take from the fire. Chop the asparagus tops, then add them to the milk. Take the rolls from the oven, fill them with this mixture, put on the tops, and serve hot. Good. (*Serves 9—or less if they are hungry.*)

SOUP DE L'ASPERGE

Cut into thin slices half a pound of bacon, lay them in the bottom of the stewpan, cut into lumps six pounds of lean beef and roll it well in flour, cover the pan close, shake occasionally until the gravy is all drawn, then add half a pint of old ale and two quarts of water; throw in some whole peppers and a spoonful of salt, stew gently for an hour, skim the fat and when an hour has elapsed strain off the soup, then put in it some spinach, two cabbage (*head*) lettuces, the leaves of the white beet (*chard may be substituted, or any leafy top*), a little mint, powdered sweet aroma (*herbs*), and sorrel; boil them (*and when they are tender, if you like, purée in a blender*), then put in the tops of the asparagus, cut small; when they are tender the soup is done. Serve up hot with a French roll (*or croutons*) in the middle.

Serve the beef up separately, as boiled beef.

WATERCRESS

Cress is difficult to grow, so you have an excellent excuse to poke along swift-running clear streams in the springtime, looking for the wild cress. It has more bite than supermarket cress, but supermarket cress is better than no cress at all.

SPRING SALAD

In a salad bowl put first a layer of fresh, crisp watercress, then a layer of thinly sliced cucumbers, which have been soaked in cold water fifteen minutes, then a teaspoonful of minced chives, then another layer of cucumbers and around the edge a light border of the cresses. When ready to serve, pour a French dressing (*oil and vinegar*, *salt and pepper*) over it and toss it until well mingled. This is appropriate to serve with a course of broiled fish.

WATER-CRESS AND APPLES

Prepare the water-cress by letting it become crisp in cold water, then drying it thoroughly. Mix it with a French dressing (*oil and vinegar*). A few thin slices of sour apple with water-cress makes a good salad to serve with ducks.

STEWED WATER-CRESS

Lay the cress in strong salt and water, to clear it from insects. Pick and wash nicely and stew in water for about ten minutes; drain and chop, season with salt and pepper, add a little butter and return it to a stewpan until well heated. Add a little vinegar first before serving: put around it sippets of toast or fried bread.

DANDELIONS

Dandelion greens are good only while they are very young. Once the dandelions come into bloom, the leaves acquire a strong taste.

DANDELION SALADS

Procure a quart of very white (*light green*), fresh dandelions (*young plants, not flowers*); pare the root and stale leaves, if any; then wash thoroughly in two different waters, drain nicely on a cloth, and place in a salad bowl. Dilute a pinch of salt and half a pinch of pepper in a salad-spoonful (*3 tablespoons*) of vinegar, adding one and a half (*4½ tablespoons*) of sweet olive oil; mix thoroughly together and serve (*to 3–4*).

Or: Add to the dandelion two medium-sized cooked and pickled beets cut into thin slices.

Or: Crumble crisp bacon over it, and douse with a quarter of a cup of very hot vinegar to which one tablespoon of sugar has been added.

DANDELIONS,

when gathered young, are good for greens. They require half an hour (*to cook, like spinach*). Drain and press them, to accompany boiled meats.

Young horse-radish leaves, dock leaves, plantain, patience, etc., also make nice greens in the spring.

WILTED DANDELION

Cut the roots from a quarter-peck (*2 quarts, or, 8 cups*) of dandelions, wash the leaves through several cold waters, drain and shake until dry. Take a handful of the leaves and cut them with a sharp knife into small pieces, and so continue until you have them all cut. Beat one egg until light, add to it a half-cup of cream, and stir over the fire until it thickens; then add a piece of butter the size of a walnut, two tablespoons of vinegar, salt and pepper to taste. Now put the dandelions into this, and stir over the fire until they are all wilted and tender (*a matter of a couple of minutes: lettuce or endive may be cooked the same way*). Serve hot (*to 6*).

DANDELION BEER

Sparkling, and very lightly alcoholic.

Use one-half pound of (*peeled*) dandelion root to one gallon of water. Boil well. Cool to lukewarm and add one pound of maple sugar (*light brown sugar may be substituted*), one ounce ginger, one teaspoonful good vinegar yeast (*dry yeast*). Let ferment, covered, about ten days. Bottle and tie down well (*or use soda bottles and cap them with a capper; see p. 37 for wine-making directions*).

Wild mushrooms are good in May and early June, and will be even better in late August and September—they do not like the hottest weather. See August for recipes.

POKE

POKE

The young stalks and leaves of the poke-berry plant when quite small and first beginning to sprout up from the ground in the spring, are by most persons considered very nice, and are frequently brought to market. They are in a proper state when the part of the stalk nearest the ground is not thicker than small asparagus.

Scrape the stalks, letting the leaves remain on them, and throw them into cold water. Then tie up the poke in bundles, put it into a pot that has plenty of boiling water, and let it boil fast an hour at least. Serve it up with or without toast, and send melted butter with it in a boat.

PRIMROSES

PRIMROSE WINE

Use seven pecks of primroses gathered while thirty pounds of honey boils in fifteen gallons of water until one gallon of liquid boils away. Skim and remove from the fire. Add sixteen lemons, halved, to one gallon. Put the flowers to the remainder and steep overnight. Add lemonade, eight spoonfuls of new yeast. Stir well and let stand three to four days. Strain, put in cask. Bottle at six months. (*This will be a very light, dry wine. For more body, use more honey. See p. 37 for details of wine making.*)

TROPICAL FRUITS

Tropical fruits begin to come into season in Florida, California, and Hawaii early in May.

The following recipes were published by the Ladies' Society of the Central Union Church in Honolulu, in 1888. I make no claim for them since I have no experience with tropical fruit—but they look good.

MANGO CUSTARD PIE

Stew and strain through a sieve the fruit, taking it when underripe. Then take one quart milk, one cup mango, six eggs and one cup sugar. Use more sugar if desired. Line pie plates with paste and fill with the mixture. The above is enough for two pies.

MANGO MERINGUE

Two to three cups of stewed green mangoes (not too sweet) flavored with lemon, or a little nutmeg, and poured into a shallow baking dish. Cover with a meringue made of the whites of three eggs and two tablespoonfuls of powdered sugar. Brown slightly and eat cold for luncheon or with nice cake for dessert.

POTATO AND MANGO

Pare and quarter the potatoes and boil till done. Pare green mangoes (not too green), slice and boil till tender, drain and add them to the potatoes, mixing them moderately, and season with butter and salt. This is a German dish and in the original receipt pears are used with potatoes. The pears should be quartered and core taken out, then boiled without paring.

MANGO CHUTNEY

Four pounds green mangoes, one pound almonds, one-quarter pound green ginger, one-half pound white salt, two pounds raisins, one-quarter pound garlic, three pounds brown sugar, two ounces yellow chilies, one bottle (*1 quart*) vinegar. The mangoes must be skinned and ground on a curry stone (*grated or chopped in a blender would probably do*), as also the other ingredients, putting in nearly a bottle of vinegar, or enough to make it of proper consistency. Put it into wide-mouth bottles, tie muslin over, and let them stand in the sun for a fortnight, when it will be fit to use, though it will be better to be kept in the sun for six weeks.

DELICIOUS GREEN MANGO SAUCE

Take the fruit when fully grown but quite hard and green, pare, and, with a large grater, grate the pulp from the seed. Then to a bowl of the fruit add half a bowl of sugar—more if you prefer. Put in a close container and stand in boiling water till the fruit is thoroughly cooked. (*See canning details, p. 32. This sauce might be served with custard, or plain cake.*)

BREADFRUIT

If you like it very sweet, wait till it is quite soft, and then bake it for an hour. If you want it not so sweet, bake before it is so soft.

STEWED BREADFRUIT

Take the full-grown fruit before it is so ripe as to be sweet and soft; peel and cut into small pieces; boil in just sufficient salted water to keep from burning. When the breadfruit is about cooked and the water nearly all evaporated, pour in milk made from the cocoanut (*by soaking grated coconut in a little water, then squeezing the juice through a cloth*). When thoroughly heated, it is ready for the table. Of course the quantity of breadfruit and milk should be regulated by the number of persons for whom it is prepared. Breadfruit may be used in every way in which potatoes are used in potato-growing countries.

AUNT MARY'S PAPAIA PUDDING

Cook the half of a ripe papaia for one pudding. After cooking the fruit till quite soft, strain off the water, season with sugar, a little nutmeg, and the juice of one Chinese orange. Then beat up three eggs with milk to make a custard, sweeten to taste and mix with the fruit. Bake well and brown.

SLICED PAPAIA PIE

Slice the fruit, a little under-ripe, as you would ripe apples. Pile the pie-plates and squeeze over the fruit the juice of a lime; add sugar, half a cup to a pie. Cover with an upper crust and bake. Papaia can also be used like squash for pies.

MERINGUE OF PAPAIA

Take the fruit a little under-ripe, steam until quite soft. Put through a sieve (*or purée*); then take two cups of the sifted papaia, one coffee-cup sugar, one large tablespoon butter, yolks of three eggs, juice of two limes and rinds grated. Make a rich butter paste (*p. 76*) and line two pie plates, put in the mixture and let it bake till the paste is done. While baking, beat the whites of the eggs light and add one teacup sifted sugar. Remove the pies from the oven and spread this frosting on them and return to the oven till the frosting is nicely browned.

[152]

GUAVA JELLY

Take one hundred guavas rather large, cut off skins and slice, add as much water as will cover them and boil to a pulp, over a slow fire. Take care not to burn. Strain without squeezing (*see p. 28 for jelly-making details*); three pounds of sugar to be boiled to a thick syrup, and the guava juice added and kept boiling until reaching the proper consistency. Then add a wineglass or one and a half of lime juice.

GUAVA MARMALADE

Wash and cut the ends off the guavas, and boil till quite soft. When cool, strain through a sieve (*blend*) and add an equal quantity of sugar to the pulp. Cook for one or two hours, stirring constantly to prevent it from burning. If cooked thoroughly, it can be kept a year.

GUAVA WHIP

Take ripe guavas, sweet and sour mixed. Wipe these with a cloth; if not perfectly clean, cut off the ends with a silver knife, mash them well, strain them through any cloth that will allow the juice and pulp to pass through but not the seeds. Beat into the pulp powdered sugar, about one cupful to a pint of the guava. It is difficult to give the exact amount of sugar to be used. It is best to sweeten to taste.

TAMARIND CHUTNEY

One-half pound tamarinds, one-half pound dates, one-half pound green ginger, one-half pound raisins, one-half pound onions (it is said Burmese are nicest), one-quarter pound chilies, four tablespoons brown sugar, two tablespoons salt. Pound all with vinegar, and rub through a sieve. Bottle and cork.

TARO BAKED

Scrape all the outside off the taro, wash clean, and bake the same as potatoes. If the taro is large, cut it in two lengthwise. Bake for an hour and a quarter to an hour and a half. When serving, do not cut it with a knife, but gently press the taro with your hands and break it open. It will be mealy like a potato. Eat with salt and pepper.

FRIED TARO: Boil your taro with the skin on. When done, peel it as you would a boiled potato. Cut it in slices, sprinkle with salt, and fry in hot lard.

LUAU

Put the young, tender taro leaves (luau) into hot water, and when they have boiled ten or fifteen minutes, pour this water off through a colander and put in water and milk, and let it boil till the leaves lose their form and are very tender. Season with salt and butter. The milk overcomes the sting which some luau has.

HA-HA

Take the inner stalks from a taro head, peel off the thin skin and put on to boil in hot water salted a little, and boil till tender. Then drain and lay the stalks on toast and pour over them drawn butter, sprinkling chopped hard-boiled eggs on top.

SHELLFISH

Lobsters show more seasonal variation in price and availability than any other shellfish except oysters (for which, see September, p. 273). Although they can be bought all year long, they begin to come in, in quantity, about the middle of April, and are at their cheapest around May 15.

With most other fish and shellfish, season is merely a matter of finding them—and fishermen can find them more easily when they do not have to contend with winter storms and icy water, so both tend to be more plentiful in late spring and summer.

TO BOIL A LOBSTER

Choose a lively one—not too large, lest he be tough. Put a handful of salt into a pot of boiling water, and having tied the claws together, if your fish merchant has not already skewered them, plunge him into the prepared bath. He will be restive under this vigorous hydropathic treatment; but allay your tortured sympathies by the reflection that he is a cold-blooded animal, destitute of imagination, and that pain, according to some philosophers, exists only in the imagination. However this may be, his suffering will be short-lived. Boil from half an hour to an hour, as his size demands. When done, draw out the scarlet innocent, and lay him, face downward, in a sieve to dry. (*Send him hot to the table with parsley and drawn butter.*)

When cold, split open the body and tail, and crack the claws to extract the meat, throwing away the "lady fingers" and the head. Lobsters are seldom served without dressing, upon private tables, as few persons care to take the trouble of preparing their own salad after taking their seats at the board.

SOUR SAUCE FOR BOILED LOBSTER OR FISH

Make half a pint of good vinegar hot, stir it into a quarter of a pound of fresh butter, add a teaspoonful of made mustard, and a little pepper.

LOBSTER CUTLET

One pint lobster meat chopped fine, season with a saltspoonful of salt and one of dry mustard, and a little cayenne pepper. Moisten with one cupful cream sauce before the wine is added. Roll in bread crumbs, egg, and bread crumbs again, and fry by spoonfuls in boiling grease, flatten each one to look like a cutlet, using a claw of the lobster to decorate each piece when served. (*Serves 4.*)

CREAM SAUCE: Melt two tablespoons fresh butter in fryer on stove, add four tablespoons flour, or two tablespoons corn starch (*for a clearer sauce*), and stir until mixed, season with salt and pepper, add one pint sweet cream, stir till it thickens, take out one cupful for chops, and to the other add one wineglass of sherry or Madeira wine and remove from fire. Serve over lobster cutlets.

EXCELSIOR LOBSTER SALAD WITH CREAM DRESSING

1 fine lobster, boiled and when cold picked to pieces, or two small ones	1 teaspoonful (dry) mustard wet up with vinegar
1 cup best salad oil	1 tablespoonful powdered sugar
½ cup sweet cream, whipped light to a cupful of froth	1 teaspoonful salt
	A pinch of cayenne pepper
1 lemon—the juice strained	4 tablespoonfuls vinegar
	Beaten yolks of 2 eggs

Beat eggs, sugar, salt, mustard, and pepper until light; then, add very gradually, the oil (*or make it like mayonnaise in the blender, adding oil drop by drop through the lid*). When the mixture is quite thick, whip in the lemon. Beat five minutes before putting in the vinegar. Just before the salad goes to table, add half the whipped cream to this dressing and stir well into the lobster. Line up the salad bowl with lettuce-leaves; put in the seasoned meat and cover with the rest of the whipped cream. This salad deserves its name. (*Serves 4.*)

LOBSTER SOUP

Extract the meat from the shells of two hen lobsters which have been boiled; put the spawn aside, beat the fins and small claws in a mortar; then place both in a saucepan with two quarts of water until the whole goodness of the fish has been drawn; then strain the liquor. Beat in a mortar the spawn with a lump of butter and flour, rub it through a sieve into which the soup has previously been strained; simmer without boiling, that the color may be preserved, ten minutes; squeeze in a piece of a lemon with a little of the essence of anchovies (*1 anchovy pounded fine in a mortar will do*). When this dish is sent to table as a feature, forcemeat balls are served with it; they are made of minced lobster spawn, crumb of French roll, egg, and mace pounded; roll it in flour and serve in the soup. (*The meat of the lobster is added to the soup just before serving.*)

Langoustine, from Chile, can be substituted for lobster in recipes. It has less flavor, but is cheaper and, like king crab, can be frozen without hurting its taste too much.

LOBSTER SAUCE FOR FISH

Put twelve tablespoonfuls of melted butter in a stewpan, cut up a small-sized lobster into dice, make a quarter of a pound of lobster butter with the spawn, as directed: when the melted butter is upon the point of boiling, add the lobster butter, season with a little essence of anchovy (*or 1 anchovy pounded to a paste*), the juice of half a lemon, and a quarter of a saltspoonful of cayenne pepper; pass it through a tammy into another stewpan, and add the flesh of the lobster; when hot, it is ready to serve. This sauce should be quite red; if no red spawn is in the lobster, use live spawn.

LOBSTER BUTTER: Procure half a lobster, quite full of spawn, which take out and pound well in a mortar; then add six ounces of fresh butter, mix well together, then rub it through a sieve and put it in a cold place until wanted. The flesh can be used for any other dish.

LOBSTER SAUCE À LA CRÈME (*FOR FISH*)

Cut a small lobster into slices the size of half-crown (*50¢*) pieces, which put into a stewpan; pound the soft and white parts with an ounce of butter, and rub them through a sieve; pour ten spoonfuls of melted butter (*p. 107*) and two of cream over the pieces in the stewpan, add half a blade (*¼ teaspoon*) of mace, a saltspoonful of salt, a quarter ditto of pepper, and a little cayenne; warm gently, and when upon the point of boiling, add the butter and two tablespoonfuls of thick cream, shake over the fire until quite hot, when it is ready to serve.

TO POT SHELL-FISH

Boil lobsters and shrimp in salt water; pick the meat out of the tail and claws (*and chop it*); put them into a stewpan with a little butter, some chopped mushrooms or truffles, and simmer a short time over a gentle fire. When nearly done, beat the yolks of two or three eggs, with a teacup of cream and a little chopped parsley; let all stew together for a few minutes, until rendered as consistent as a paste. When the meat is perfectly cold, pack well down into a jar and cover well with clarified butter and tie it over with oiled paper (*or plastic*) to exclude the air.

OR: When boiled, take them out of their shells and season them with salt, white pepper, a very little mace and nutmeg. Press them into a pot; lay a little butter over them; and bake in a slow oven for ten minutes. When cold, cover with clarified butter. They will keep a week.

SHRIMPS may also be potted whole, by putting them for a few minutes in clarified butter, seasoned as above, and gently heated; then put into pots and cover with more butter, to totally prevent the admission of air.

"Prawns, shrimp and crabfish: the first two, if stale, will be limber and cast a kind of slimy smell, their colour fading and they slimy; the latter will be limber in their claws and joints, their red colour blackish and dusky, and will have an ill smell under their throats; otherwise all of them are good."
                              Hannah Glasse, *The Art of Cookery*, 1812

TO BOIL SHRIMP

Leave them in their shells; put into boiling water or court bouillon (p. 164) and boil about 4 minutes, or just until they assume a pinkish color. Over-cooked shrimp are tough and tasteless. Then shell them and take out the dark vein that runs just under the skin down their backs.

TO SAUTÉ SHRIMP

Shell and vein the raw shrimp; put them into a generous amount of melted butter, flavored with garlic or whatever herb you want, and sauté quickly 5 to 7 minutes, or until they are pinkish. Take them out and use the butter to flavor rice or a sauce to go with them.

SHRIMP SALAD

Shrimp salad may be made by following any lobster salad recipe.
Wash the shrimps and lay in vinegar two hours, then pour over an oil mayonnaise (*p. 440*) to which has been added mustard, salt, cayenne and sugar.

8: MAY

"Wild Roses, Buttercups, Daisies, or Nasturtium blossoms are pretty for garnishing salad dishes."

Mrs. Ludlum, *The New and Old in Cookery*, 1891

SHRIMP PIE

Boil one quart of rice dry (*1 quart of cooked rice*) with this mix well two teacups of tomato juice, one pound of butter, three eggs, pepper to taste, one-half teaspoon of curry. Sprinkle black pepper over the shrimps. Put layers of mixture and layers of shrimp until the pan is filled. Pour a gill of milk over the top before baking (*about 30 minutes*). This is for six plates of shrimp.

SHRIMP SAUCE

This is a delicious sauce for salmon, trout, and many kinds of fish; but is rather tedious to prepare. For a large party you will require a quart of shrimps, perfectly fresh, as they will be easily shelled; put the heads and shells into a saucepan with two tablespoonfuls of water, and boil for a quarter of an hour to extract the flavor. In the meantime, make three-quarters of a pint of melted butter (*p. 107*), strain into it the liquor in which the shells have been boiled; then stir in the shrimps, and shake over the fire two or three minutes before you serve. No seasoning is required for shrimp sauce.

TO BOIL CRABS

Throw a handful of salt into a pot of boiling water, when it boils very hard, put in the crabs. Let them boil a quarter of an hour, and when you take them out, lay them on a sieve and wipe with a dry cloth. Eat with a dressing made of a saltspoonful of salt and about the same quantity of cayenne, mixed with two tablespoonfuls of sweet (*olive*) oil and a teaspoonful of made mustard, adding at least one tablespoonful of vinegar and two more of oil. Many persons add a teaspoonful of powdered white sugar, thinking that it gives a mellowness to the whole. You may put in some yolk of hard-boiled egg, mashed in the oil.

Part II: Recipes

CRAB FRICASSEE

Have the crabs boiled. When they are cold, take the meat out of the claws and the fat out of the tops of the shells, and the rest of the meat from one-third the number of crabs. Cut the rest of the bodies into quarters, removing the deadmen's fingers. To one and a half pints of crab put two gills of cream, four ounces of butter, cayenne pepper, salt and a wee pinch of black pepper. Simmer for half an hour. If this is too thick, add a little hot milk or cream.

HOT CRABS

Having boiled the crabs, extract all the meat from the shells, cut it fine, and season to your taste with nutmeg, salt, and cayenne pepper. Add a bit of butter, some grated bread crumbs and sufficient vinegar to moisten it. Fill the back shells of the crab with the mixture; set it before the fire and brown it (*under the broiler or*) by holding a red-hot shovel or a salamander a little above it.

Cover a large dish with small pieces of dry toast with the crust cut off. Lay on each slice a shell filled with the crab. The shell of one crab will contain the meat of two.

CRABS ST. LAURENT

1 cupful of boiled crab meat (6 crabs)	*1 tablespoonful flour*
	½ cupful stock
2 tablespoonfuls grated Parmesan cheese	*½ cupful cream or milk*
	½ teaspoonful salt
2 tablespoonfuls white wine	*¼ teaspoon pepper*
1 tablespoonful of butter	*dash of cayenne*

Put into a saucepan one tablespoonful of butter; when melted, add the flour; cook, but not brown; add slowly the stock and stir until perfectly smooth; then add the cream, and when thickened, add the salt and pepper, then the crab-meat and the cheese; simmer for a few minutes, then add the wine; spread this mixture over pieces of buttered toast cut in squares or circles; sprinkle with grated Parmesan cheese, and place on each piece a small bit of butter; set in the oven for three minutes; serve very hot on a napkin garnished with parsley. (*Serves 4–6.*)

This dish may be prepared in a chaffing dish, in which case the mixture must be placed on the toast and served directly from the chaffing dish.

Boiled halibut may be substituted for the crab meat.

CRAB SOUP, A PURELY AMERICAN SOUP, A GREAT FAVORITE AT THE SOUTH, AND ESTEEMED A GREAT LUXURY BY THOSE WHO HAVE EATEN OF IT

Open and cleanse twelve young fat crabs (raw) and cut them into two parts; parboil and extract the meat from the claws, and the fat from the top shell. Scald eighteen ripe tomatoes; skin them and squeeze the pulp from the seed and chop it fine, pour boiling water over the seed and juice and, having strained it from the seed, use it to make the soup. Stew a short time, in the soup-pot, three large onions, one clove of garlic, in one spoonful of butter, two spoonfuls of lard, and then put in the tomatoes, and after stewing a few minutes, add the meat from the crab claws, then the crabs, and last, the fat from the back shell of the crab; sift over it grated bread-crumbs or crackers. Season with salt, cayenne and black pepper, parsley, sweet marjoram, thyme, half-teaspoonful lemon juice, and the (*grated*) peel of a lemon; pour in the water with which the seed were scalded, and boil it moderately one hour. Any firm fish may be substituted for crab. (*Serves 12.*)

STUFFED CLAMS

Fry an onion, chopped very fine, in one ounce of good butter until it is of a golden brown color, adding one tablespoonful of flour to make a roux. Moisten with half a pint of white stock (*p. 438*), stirring well and constantly until the sauce hardens. Season with half a tablespoonful of salt, a teaspoonful of white pepper, the same of cayenne, one tablespoonful of English (*Worcestershire*) sauce, half a teaspoonful of (*dry*) mustard, a crushed grain (*clove*) of garlic, and one teaspoonful of chopped parsley. Stir well, adding the meat of twenty-four clams, blanched well and chopped exceeding fine. Refill the shells (*of about 8 large ones*) with the forcemeat, besprinkle them with fresh bread-crumb, smooth the surface with the blade of a knife, moistening the top with a little clarified butter. Place them on a baking pan, and bake a little brown for six minutes. Serve hot with parsley greens. (*Serves 4.*)

DEVILED CLAMS

Chop fifty clams very fine; take two tomatoes, one onion chopped equally fine, a little parsley, thyme, and sweet marjoram, a little salt, pepper and breadcrumbs, adding the (*clams and the*) juice of the clam until the mixture is of the consistency of sausage; put it in the shells (*20 of them*) with a lump of butter on each; cover with bread-crumb and bake half an hour. (*Serves 6–8.*)

Clams can be scalloped, like oysters. See p. 275.

CLAM CHOWDER

The classic New England version.

½ *peck* (1 gallon) *clams in their shells*	1 *teaspoonful of salt*
1 *quart of potatoes, sliced thin*	½ *teaspoonful of white pepper*
A 2 inch cube of fat salt pork	1 *large tablespoonful of butter*
1 *or 2 onions*	1 *quart milk*
	6 *butter crackers*

Clams in their shells are better, as you then have more clam liquor. Wash with a small brush, and put them in a deep kettle with half a cup of water, or just enough to keep the under ones from burning; set them over the fire. When the clams at the top have opened, take them out with a skimmer, and when cool enough to handle, take the clams from their shells; remove the thin skin; then with scissors cut off all the black end, cut the "leather straps" into small pieces, leaving the soft parts whole. Let the clam liquor settle, and pour it off carefully. Use half water and half clam liquor. Cut the pork into dice, dry it, then brown the onions, sliced thin, in the pork fat. Pour the fat through a strainer into the kettle, leaving the scraps of pork and onions in the strainer; add the potatoes, which have been soaked and scalded, and pour through the strainer enough boiling water to cover. When the potatoes are soft, add the clam liquor, the seasonings and the clams; when warmed through, add the hot milk, and turn into the tureen. Do not put the clams into the chowder until the potatoes are nearly done, as prolonged boiling hardens them. (*Serves 10–15.*)

CLAM CHOWDER

This later became known as Manhattan chowder.

One-half gallon chopped clams; boil half an hour, liquor and all, adding water if necessary. To this add one and one-half cans (*6 cups: home-canned cans hold 1 quart*) tomatoes, a small handful chopped celery, a pinch of thyme. Cut four slices of salt pork into narrow strips and fry, adding grease and all to the clams. Boil very slowly half an hour; then add one quart of milk and six hard-tack, or crackers broken up small; take from the fire and stand fifteen minutes before serving.

TO PICKLE OYSTERS AND CLAMS

Take the oysters from the liquor, rinsing off the pieces of shell, if any; strain, boil and skim it; then put the oysters into the boiling liquor with whole peppercorns, spice and mace, with a little salt, and boil all one minute. Take the oysters out immediately, and let them cool; add as much vinegar as the oyster liquor, and boil fifteen minutes, and then turn it hot on the oysters. Keep them cool and air tight, and they will retain their natural flavor. Pickle clams in the same way, only boil them longer.

TO STEW SCALLOPS

Boil them very well in salt and water, take them out and stew them in a little of the liquor, a little white wine, a little vinegar, two or three blades of mace (*1 teaspoonful*), two or three cloves, a piece of butter rolled in flour, and the juice of a Seville orange. Stew them well, and dish it up.

Scallops may also be breaded and fried.

SALT-WATER FISH

Salt-water fish, with only a few exceptions, are not seasonal. What comes into the market depends upon what the fishermen find and catch. The more they get of a certain kind, the lower its price will be. Fish are brought in all year, but in winter, with storms, the catch is less, so the cost is usually higher.

It is not a new situation: "The wind cannot be fair for all; the consequence then is, frequently, a great abundance of some sorts, and none, or little of many others. Persons send their servants to market, to get, perhaps, a Turbot, or Cod's head and shoulder; it very likely happens that the articles are scarce and extravagant: the servants have no other order, or perhaps will not take the trouble to get other orders, but order a Turbot at thirty Shillings or forty Shillings . . . If masters or mistresses were to go to market themselves, if one sort was dear, they could have another." (Wm. Tucker, Fishmonger, London, 1819)

Fish "ought to be made an article of diet more often than it is, as the particles it contains tend to purify the blood from the grossness it receives in partaking of animal food." (Alexis Soyer, *The Modern Housewife*, 1850)

TO BOIL A FISH

The nicer the fish, the more simply it should be prepared. A long, narrow fish kettle with a rack is the best to boil fish in, but even a deep frying pan and a cheesecloth sling, which lets you remove the fish from the water without breaking it, will do. Start the fish in cold water, with salt and vinegar in it, or in cold court bouillon. Bring it slowly to a boil and simmer gently until just done, 8 to 10 minutes to the pound. Serve hot, with lemon wedges or a sauce.

COURT BOUILLON

Court bouillon is used for boiling fresh-water fish or others which are without much flavor. It may be prepared before-hand and used several times, or the vegetables may be added at the time the fish is boiled.

Fry in one tablespoonful of butter one chopped carrot, one chopped onion, one stalk of celery. Then add two quarts of hot water, one cup of vinegar or wine, three peppercorns, three cloves, one bay-leaf, and one teaspoonful of salt.

A good liquid for boiling fish can be made from any assortment of green leafy vegetables; celery tops, beet tops, lettuce, spinach, dandelion greens, kale, etc., and with a few slices of unpeeled cucumber added. After the fish is boiled, the stock makes a vitamin-rich base for seafood soups.

"And with all boiled fish, you should put a great deal of salt and horse-radish in the water, except mackerel, with which put salt and

mint, parsley and fennel, which you must chop to put into your butter; and some love scalded gooseberries with it."
Hannah Glasse, The Art of Cookery, 1812

SOME SAUCES FOR BOILED FISH

BURNT BUTTER: Put two ounces of butter into a frying pan; set on the fire; when of a dark brown color, put in six spoonfuls of vinegar, a little pepper and salt. (*Also good with eggs.*)

SAUCE FOR COLD FISH: Boil two eggs three minutes; mix with them a mustardspoonful (*½ teaspoonful*) of prepared mustard, a little pepper, salt, six spoonfuls of drawn butter (*p. 107*) or salad oil, six of vinegar, and one of catsup. (*Use also for cold meat.*)

SAUCE TARTARE: 1 teaspoonful (*dry*) mustard, ½ saltspoonful pepper; 1 teaspoonful powdered sugar; 1 saltspoonful salt; few drops onion juice; yolks of raw eggs; ½ cup oil; 2 tablespoonfuls vinegar; 1 tablespoonful chopped olives; 1 tablespoonful chopped capers; 1 tablespoonful chopped cucumber pickles; 1 tablespoonful chopped parsley. Mix in the order given; add the yolks and stir well; add the oil slowly (*as for mayonnaise*), then the vinegar and chopped ingredients. This will keep several weeks (*and is also good for tongue or broiled chicken. A few shallots may be added if you like.*)

HOLLANDAISE SAUCE: One-half cup of butter, one and one-half tablespoons of lemon juice, one-half teaspoon of salt, one-tenth teaspoon of cayenne, and the yolks of four eggs. Heat a bowl slightly; put in butter; cream it and add eggs, one at a time, then the other ingredients; finally, add one-half cup (*or a little less*) of boiling water (*whisking constantly; cook until creamy over hot water*). Serve with boiled fish, asparagus or cauliflower.

Serve Spring salad, p. 147, with boiled fish.

FISH MOULTEE, AN INDIAN RECEIPT

Take any nice fish, (*roll it in*) egg, bread-crumb, and fry it with a little turmeric and butter, after cutting it to a nice fillet. Scrape half a fresh cocoanut, take the milk from it (*or soak dried coconut a couple of hours in a little warm water, then use the water*), cut some green ginger, and green chilies in slices, boil them with the cocoanut milk and a little water. Add the fish and let stew until the sauce is slightly thickened. Send to table with rice.

[165]

TO MAKE A CHOWDER

Lay four or five slices of salt pork in the bottom of the pot, let it cook slow that it may not burn; when done brown, take it out, and lay in fish cut in lengthwise strips, then a layer of crackers, sliced onions and very thin sliced potatoes, with some of the pork that was fried, then a layer of fish again, and so on. Strew a little salt and pepper over each layer; over the whole pour a bowl of flour and water (*or half water and half milk, 1 tablespoon of flour to 1 cup of water*), well stirred up, enough to come up even with what you have in the pot. A sliced lemon (*and some parsley*) adds to the flavor; a few clams improves it. Let it be so covered that the steam cannot escape. (*Bake it in a 325° oven for 2 hours or more.*) It must not be opened until cooked. Serve with pickles.

TO FRY FISH

Fillets of fish may be rolled in corn meal, dredged in flour, dipped first in beaten egg and then in fine bread crumbs, or fried plain. Small fish or small pieces of fish may be dipped in batter and deep-fried. For deep-frying, the fat should be moderately hot; for sautéing, the pan should be hot but not smoking. Lay the fish in and fry it according to size and thickness, about 10 minutes per pound. Turn it only once. Serve it with slices of lemon.

"Fry them in hot lard or beef dripping, or you may use equal parts of lard and butter; butter alone takes out the sweetness and gives a bad color. Fried parsley, grated horse-radish, or lemon, are used as garnish."

Mrs. Crowen, *Every Lady's Cook Book*, 1854

Like beef, fish should be room temperature before you cook it. Freezing it for a week won't hurt the flavor much, but after that, it suffers.

STUFFING FOR BAKED FISH WEIGHING FROM FOUR TO SIX POUNDS

1 cup cracker crumbs	1 teaspoonful chopped parsley
1 saltspoonful of salt	1 teaspoonful capers
1 saltspoonful of pepper	1 teaspoonful (minced) pickles
1 teaspoonful chopped onion	¼ cup melted butter

If a *moist* stuffing be desired, moisten it with one beaten egg and use stale, not dry, bread crumbs. (*Serves 8.*)

Slash it lightly, diagonally, in two or three places so the skin, shrinking, will not pull it out of shape; rub butter, plain or seasoned, in the slashes; bake in a 375° oven, and baste with butter melted in a little water while baking.

Cod, haddock, blue-fish, small salmon, bass and shad may be stuffed and baked whole.

Fish is perfectly nice baked without stuffing, too—just allow a little less time, about 12 minutes to a pound instead of 20, in a moderate oven, uncovered.

OYSTER STUFFING FOR BAKED FISH

One pint of oysters, one cup seasoned and buttered cracker crumbs. Drain and roll each oyster in the crumbs. Fill the fish with the oysters and sprinkle the remainder of the crumbs over.

SMALL FISH BAKED IN A CRUST

Clean the fish and wipe dry. Cut gashes one inch apart on each side; sprinkle with salt and pepper. Make a rich biscuit crust with baking powder, or make a pastry crust; roll it out half an inch thick; wrap the fish in the crust, pinch the edges together, and bake about half an hour. Serve with egg sauce.

EGG SAUCE: Make a drawn butter (*p. 107*), chop two hard-boiled eggs quite fine, the whites and the yolks separately, and stir them into the sauce before serving. This is also used for boiled fish or vegetables.

Part II: Recipes

Almost any small whole fish, or any fish steak may also be broiled. Baste it with butter, or with butter-flavored lemon juice, tarragon, dill, chervil, or any other single appropriate herb.

BASS À LA BORDELAISE

Cut a deep incision down the back of a three-pound sea bass, put it in a baking-dish with half a glassful of red wine, half a pinch of salt, and a third of a pinch of pepper. Besprinkle with a finely chopped shallot, cover with a buttered paper, and cook in a moderate oven for fifteen minutes. Lay the bass on a dish, put the juice in a saucepan with a gill of good Espagnole (*p. 439*), four finely shred mushrooms, and a thin slice of finely chopped garlic; finish cooking for five minutes more, then pour it over the fish. Decorate with six cooked cray-fish or shrimp, and serve very hot. (*Serves 4–6.*)

BASS WITH WHITE WINE

Lay a three-pound, well-cleaned bass on a well-buttered baking-dish; season with half a pinch of salt and a third of a pinch of pepper; moisten with half a glassful of white wine and three tablespoonfuls of mushroom catsup (*p. 250*). Cover with a heavy piece of buttered paper and cook in a moderate oven for fifteen minutes, then lay the fish on a dish; put the juice in a saucepan with half a pint of good Allemande; thicken well with a tablespoonful of butter till well dissolved, and throw it over the bass, serving with six heart-shaped croutons. (*Serves 4–6.*)

ALLEMANDE SAUCE: Cook together two ounces of butter and three tablespoons of flour; add one pint of white broth (*or chicken bouillon*) and stir until smooth; thicken with three beaten egg yolks; finish by adding half an ounce of butter and the juice of half a lemon.

COD FISH SAUCED OVER WITH OYSTER SAUCE

Haddock and halibut are more delicate fish, but cod is more generally available. It needs a good cook, since it is relatively flavorless.

Boil three slices of the fish in salt water, one pound of salt to every six quarts, slowly, from twenty minutes to half an hour, drain and dress them upon a dish without a napkin, blanch three dozen oysters, by putting them into

[168]

a stewpan with their juice, upon the fire, move them around occasionally, do not let them boil; as soon as they become a little firm, place a sieve over a basin, pour in the oysters, beard them, and throw them again into their liquor, put them into a stewpan; when boiling, add two cloves, half a blade of mace, six peppercorns, and two ounces of butter to which you have added a table-spoonful of flour, breaking it into small pieces; stir well together, when boiling; season with a little salt, cayenne pepper, and essence of anchovies; finish with a gill of cream or milk and sauce over. (*A half cup of white wine or sherry may be added with the oysters instead of the cream. Serves 3.*)

"Cod and codling: chuse him by his thickness toward his head, and the whiteness of his flesh when it is cut; and so of codling."
Hannah Glasse, *The Art of Cookery*, 1812

CODFISH CAKES

First boil soaked (*fresh or salt*) cod, then chop it fine, put to it an equal quantity of potatoes boiled, then mashed; moisten it with beaten eggs and milk, and a bit of butter and a little pepper; form it in small, round cakes, rather more than half an inch thick; flour the outside, and fry in hot lard or beef dripping until they are a delicate brown: like fish, these must be fried gently, the lard being boiling hot when they are put in; when one side is done, turn the other. Serve for breakfast.

CELIA'S SUCCESS

A quarter of a pound of butter, one quart of cream or milk, two pints of fresh cod, boiled, and picked from the bones, one pint of boiled potatoes, three even teaspoonfuls of salt, one even teaspoonful of white pepper. Put the fish and potatoes in a wooden bowl, with the salt and pepper, and pound and mix them with a pestle until thoroughly incorporated; stir in the cream, put the whole in a baking-dish, smooth the surface, cover with the beaten yolk of an egg, and bake one hour. (*Serve with a sharp fish sauce to 4.*)

BAKED HADDOCK

"This is also the fish that it is said St. Peter took the tribute money from and thus gave the impression of his finger and thumb, where it remains in confirmation of the miracles."
Alexis Soyer, The Modern Housewife, 1850

Fill the interior of the fish with veal stuffing (*p. 124*), sew it up with pack thread, and truss it with the tail in its mouth, rub a piece of butter over its back, or egg and bread-crumb it over, set it on a baking-dish, which put in a warmish oven (*275°*) to bake. A common haddock would require but half an hour. Dress it upon a dish without a napkin, and serve a Beyrout sauce, or any other, round. (*Serves 4–8.*)

BEYROUT SAUCE: Put a tablespoonful of chopped onions into a stew-pan, with one of chili vinegar, and one of common ditto (*vinegar*), a pint of melted butter (*p. 107*), four spoonfuls of brown gravy, two of mushroom cat-sup (*p. 250*), and two of Harvey sauce; place it over the fire, keeping it stirred until thickish, then add two tablespoonfuls of essence of anchovies (*or 1 anchovy pounded to a paste*) and half a teaspoonful of sugar; it is then ready to serve.

The above, although a fish sauce, may be used for meat or poultry by omitting the anchovy and adding more Harvey sauce. If no brown gravy, add water and a little coloring.

See p. 167 for another way to stuff haddock.

BAKED HALIBUT

This method of cooking halibut is very superior to either boiling or frying, as the flesh of the fish is firmer and the flavoring better.

Take a piece of halibut weighing five or six pounds and lay it in salt and water for two hours, wipe dry and score the outer skin. Put it in a baking-dish in a moderately hot oven, and bake for an hour, basting often with butter and water heated together in a saucepan or tin cup. When a fork will penetrate it easily, it is done. It should be of a fine brown. Take the gravy in the dripping pan, add a little boiling water, should there not be enough, stir in a tablespoonful of walnut catsup (*p. 251*), a teaspoonful of Worcestershire sauce, the juice of a lemon, and thicken with browned flour (*p. 438*) previously wet with cold water. Boil up once, and pour into the sauce-boat. (*Serves 8–10.*)

Halibut may be substituted in Crabs St. Laurent, p. 160.

A FRICASSEE OF SOLES

"How to chuse soals: these are chosen by their thickness and stiff-ness. When their bellies are of a cream color they spend the firmer."
Hannah Glasse, *The Art of Cookery*, 1812

Fry them a nice brown, drain them, and make a few balls with a small sole boned and chopped, a little grated bread and lemon peel, parsley chopped, pepper, salt, nutmeg, yolk of egg, a piece of butter; fry these; thicken some good gravy (and some port wine, not too much) with a little flour, boil it up; add cayenne, ketchup, lemon juice; lay in the fish and balls, simmer a few minutes. Garnish with lemon.

SOLES AUX FINES HERBES

Put a spoonful of chopped eschalots into a sauté-pan with a glass of sherry and an ounce of butter, place the sole over, pour nearly half a pint of melted butter over it, or four spoonfuls of brown gravy or water, upon which sprinkle some chopped parsley, place it in a moderate oven for half an hour, take the sole out of the pan, dress upon a dish without a napkin, reduce the sauce that is in the pan over a sharp fire, add a little Harvey sauce and essence of anchovy, pour over the sole and serve.

SLIPS, OR SMALL SOLES

When cleaned, season them with a little pepper and salt, dip lightly into flour, and broil them slowly over a moderate fire about ten minutes, or accord-ing to their size; when done, place them upon a hot dish, pour two tablespoon-fuls of cream over, and serve immediately. Nothing but small white fish could be tolerated for breakfast.

FILLETS BAKED WITH CUSTARD OR TOMATO

Remove the fillets from any white fish, dredge them with salt and pepper, and lay them in a baking-pan, one on top of the other. Beat 2 eggs, and add to them: 2 cupfuls of milk, 1 saltspoonful of salt, 1 saltspoonful of pepper, 1 saltspoonful of nutmeg, and 3 soda crackers rolled to a powder. Put two table-spoonfuls of butter into the pan with the fish, and set it in the oven. When the butter is melted, add half the milk mixture, and baste the fish with it fre-quently. When the custard becomes set, add a little more of the milk, and continue the operation until the fish is cooked. Lift the fish carefully from the pan with a pancake turner and broad knife. Place it on a hot dish, and pile on top the flakes of custard. Instead of the milk mixture, tomatoes may be used if preferred.

To half a can of tomatoes (*2 cups*), add 1 teaspoonful of salt, ½ tea-spoonful of thyme, ¼ teaspoonful of pepper, 1 slice of onion, 1 bayleaf, 3 cloves. The whole of the tomato mixture must be put in the pan as soon as the butter is melted.

TURBOT

To cook it, cut an incision in the back, rub it well with salt, and then with the juice of a lemon; set it in a turbot kettle, well covered with cold water, in which you put a good handful of salt; place it over the fire, and as soon as it boils, put it at the side, where it must not be allowed to more than simmer slowly, or the fish would have a very unsightly appearance. A turbot of ten pounds weight will take about an hour to cook after it has boiled; take it out of the water, let it remain a minute upon the drainer, and serve upon a napkin, with a few sprigs of fresh parsley around, and lobster (*p. 157*) or shrimp (*p. 159*) sauce in a boat.

TURBOT, THE NEW FRENCH FASHION

Boil your turbot as in the last, but dress it upon a dish without a napkin, sauce over with a thick caper sauce (having made a border of small new pota-toes), sprinkle a few capers over the fish, and serve.

CAPER SAUCE: Put twelve tablespoons of melted butter (*p. 107*) into a stewpan, place it on the fire, and when on the point of boiling, add two ounces of fresh butter and one tablespoonful of capers; shake the stewpan round over the fire until the butter is melted, add a little pepper and salt, and serve where directed.

STURGEON

This fish is best fried, but good baked or broiled. Cut it in slices about an inch thick, fry some slices of pork; when brown, take them up, and put in the sturgeon. When well browned, take up, and stir in a little flour, and water, mixed smoothly together. Season the gravy with pepper, salt, and catsup, stir in a little butter, and wine if liked, then put back the sturgeon, and let it stew a few minutes in the gravy. While the fish is cooking, make forcemeat balls of part of the sturgeon and salt pork (*minced fine*); fry them and use them for garnish.

MACKEREL

Are generally served plain boiled: put them in a kettle containing boiling water, well salted; let simmer nearly half an hour, take them up, drain, and dish them upon a napkin; serve melted butter in a boat, with which you have mixed one tablespoonful of chopped fennel; boil it a few minutes.

Gooseberry sauce, p. 207, was traditionally served with mackerel in France.

TO BAKE MACKEREL

Clean the fish, cut off the heads, take out and wash the roes, and then put them again in the fish; powder the fish lightly within and without with a mixture of salt, pepper, and finely-chopped parsley; arrange them neatly on a baking dish. Pour over them a quarter of a pint of vinegar and half a pint of clarified butter. Then put into the oven and bake for half an hour; remove them in a hot dish, pour the gravy (*juice*) over them, and serve with parsley butter.

MACKEREL WITH BLACK BUTTER

Take the mackerel and soak it for a couple of hours in oil, season it with salt and pepper, and then broil it, basting with oil. For sauce, melt a tablespoonful of butter in a frying-pan till quite hot, fry some parsley in it, and a tablespoonful of vinegar and two of stock; boil up and pour over the mackerel, and serve very hot.

[173]

Part II: Recipes

"A smoke of corncobs while it is broiling, improves it much."
Mrs. Webster, *The Improved Housewife*, 1854

BROILED HERRINGS

"The delicacy of these fish prevents them being dressed in any other way than boiled or broiled; they can certainly be bread-crumbed and fried, but scarcely any person would like them."
Alexis Soyer, *The Modern Housewife*, 1850

Clean and dry the fish, cut off their heads, flour them and broil them. Break up the heads and boil them for a quarter of an hour in a little table beer or ale, with a little whole pepper and a slice of onion; strain off the liquor, thicken it with butter and flour, beat mustard up with it, and serve it in a tureen to eat with the herrings.

HERRING SALAD

Take three medium-sized smoked herrings, lay them on the corner of the stove for half a minute on each side, then tear off the skin, cut off the heads, and split them in half; remove the bones, and cut them up into small square pieces. Place them in a salad-bowl with half a hashed onion, two hard-boiled eggs cut in pieces, a cold boiled potato cut the same, and a teaspoon of chopped parsley. Season with half a pinch of salt, one pinch of pepper, three tablespoons of vinegar and two of oil. Mix well together, and decorate with a small cooked beet-root cut in slices, also twelve capers; then serve. (*Serves 4–6.*)

ANOTHER: Soak three nice fat (*smoked*) herring in cold water for three hours. Then remove the head and tail and bones. With a scissors cut in pieces as small as dice, add a handful of English walnuts cut fine, a tablespoonful boiled beets cut fine, two tablespoonfuls capers, one large apple cut in small pieces, and one dill pickle cut up. Then take the soft egg (*roe*) and mix with two cups white vinegar until soft, add one teaspoon sugar, three cloves and allspice, and pour the sauce over the ingredients. The sauce should not be too thick. Mix all well together, and serve a spoonful on a lettuce-leaf for each person. (*Serves 4–6.*)

TO SMOKE HERRINGS

Clean and lay some fresh herrings in salt and a little saltpetre for one night; then run a stick through their eyes and hang them in a row. Put some sawdust into an old cask, or in the midst of a *heater red hot;* hang the stick on which you have threaded the fish over the smoke, and let them remain for twenty-four hours.

WHITINGS

Of all the modes of preparing and dressing whitings for breakfast, I cannot but admire and prize the system pursued by the Scotch, which renders them the most light, wholesome, and delicious food that can possibly be served for breakfast: Their method is, to obtain the fish as fresh as possible, clean and skin them, take out the eyes, cover the fish over with salt, immediately after which take them out, and shake off the superfluous salt, pass a string through the eyeholes, and hang them to dry in a passage or some place where there is a current of air; the next morning, take them off, just roll them lightly in a little flour, broil them gently over a slow fire, and serve very hot, with a small piece of fresh butter rubbed over each, or serve quite dry if preferable.

SMELTS

This fish, when fresh, has a beautiful smell of violets or cucumbers, but the Germans call it stinck-fish, I know not why.

Dry them in a cloth, and dip them in flour; then have half an ounce of butter or clear fat melted in a basin, into which break the yolk of two eggs, with which rub the smelts over with a brush, dip them in bread-crumb, fry in very hot lard, dress them on a napkin, garnish with parsley, and serve with shrimp sauce (*p. 159*) in a boat.

TO BROIL EELS

The eel is greatly esteemed in all countries but this. Nothing is more difficult to kill than eels; and it is only by knocking their heads upon a block or hard substance, and stunning them, that they suffer least. Take the head in your hand with a cloth, and just cut through the skin round the neck, which turn down about an inch; then pull the head with one hand and the skin with the other, it will come off with facility; open the belly, take out the intestine without breaking the gall, and cut off the bristles which run up the back.

Joint them in suitable lengths, or coil them on your fish plate; rub them with the yolk of an egg, strew over bread-crumbs, minced parsley, pepper, salt, and sage; butter them well, and lay them in a dripping pan to broil. Use drawn butter and parsley for a sauce.

FRIED EELS

After cleaning the eels well (eels to be good, must be as fresh-caught as possible), cut them in pieces two inches long; wash them and wipe them dry; roll them in flour or rolled cracker; and fry as directed for other fish, in hot lard or beef dripping, salted; they should be browned all over and thoroughly done.

FRESH-WATER FISH

Fresh-water fish, except for some brook trout and some pike, are rarely available in fish markets any more. For commercial purposes, they have either been fished out or lost to pollution—and since the mercury scares, people have not been buying them. Here are recipes, however, for the home fisherman.

TO FRY BROOK TROUT OR ANY OTHER SMALL FISH

"The most approved way to dress trout is to fry them simply; the flavor of the delicate fish is best preserved by this mode of cooking."
The Cuisine, by An Eminent French Caterer, 1872

Clean the fish, and let them lie a few minutes wrapped singly, in a clean, dry towel; season with pepper and salt, roll in corn-meal, and fry in one-third butter and two-thirds lard; drain on a sieve, or on coarse brown paper, and serve hot.

TO BOIL TROUT, ISAAK WALTON'S RECIPE

Wash and dry your trout with a clean napkin, empty, and wipe very clean within; but wash him not, and give him three scotches (*slashes*) to the bone, on one side only. Take a clean kettle, and put in as much hard, stale beer vinegar (*p. 445*), and a little white wine and water, as will cover your fish; and throw in a good quantity of salt, the rind of a lemon, a handful of sliced horseradish, and a handsome light fagot of rosemary, thyme and winter-savory (*tied up together*). Set the kettle on a quick fire, and let it boil up to the height before you put in your fish; and if there be many, put in one at a time, that they may not so cool the liquor as to make it fall; and while your fish is boiling, beat up the butter for your sauce with a ladleful or two of the liquor from the fish; and being laid on a dish, pour the sauce over them, and strew horse-radish and a little chopped ginger. Garnish with sliced lemon.

TO BAKE TROUT

If the anglers bring in a full pannier of trout, it is sometimes convenient to bake a dish, which is delicious to eat cold (*and can be kept 2 or 3 days*). Place the fish properly cleaned, in a baking dish; make a seasoning of the usual proportions of salt, pepper and mace, with a tablespoonful of chopped parsley, and sprinkle each layer (*of fish*), add a thin slice of butter on each fish. Bake for half an hour. If served hot, the gravy must be mixed with plain melted butter to send up as a sauce.

THE REMAINS OF TROUT, SALMON, OR MACKEREL ARE EXCELLENT PICKLED:

Put three onions in slices in a stewpan, with two ounces of butter, one turnip, a bouquet of parsley, thyme and bay-leaf; pass them five minutes over the fire, add a pint of water and a pint of vinegar, two teaspoonfuls of salt and one of pepper, boil until the onions are tender, then strain it through a sieve

[177]

over the fish; it will keep some time if required, and then will do to pickle more fish by boiling again.

PIKE

Stuff the interior as directed for haddocks (*see p. 167*), only adding some fillets of anchovy and chopped lemon-peel with it; curl round and put in a baking dish, spread a little butter over all, put in a moderate oven; when half done, egg over with a paste-brush (*brush with 1 egg beaten with 1 tablespoon of water*), and sprinkle bread-crumbs upon it; a middling-size pike will take about an hour, but that according to the size and heat of the oven; when done, dress upon a dish without a napkin and sauce round. (*Serves 4–6.*)

TO DRESS A PIKE

Gut it, clean it, and make it very clean, then turn it round with the tail in the mouth, lay it in a little dish, cut toast three-corner ways, fill the middle with them, flour it, and stick pieces of butter all over; then throw a little more flour, and send it to the oven to bake. When it is done, lay it in your dish, and have ready melted butter, with an anchovy dissolved in it, and a few oysters or shrimps; and if there is any liquor in the dish it was baked in, add it to the sauce, and put in just what you fancy. Pour your sauce into the dish. Garnish it with toast about the fish and lemon about the dish.

You should have a pudding (*stuffing*) in the belly, made thus: Take grated bread (*crumbs*), two hard-boiled eggs chopped fine, half a nutmeg grated, a little lemon-peel cut fine, and either the roe or the liver, or both, if any, chopped fine; and if you have none, get either a piece of the liver of a cod, or the roe of any fish; mix these together with the raw egg and a good piece of butter; roll it up, and put it into the fish's belly before you bake it. A haddock done this way eats very well. (*Serves 6.*)

TO DRESS A BRACE OF CARP

Take a piece of butter, and put into a stewpan to melt it, and put in a large spoonful of flour. Keep it stirring till it is smooth; then put in a pint of gravy, and a pint of red port or claret, a little horse-radish scraped, eight cloves, four blades of mace, and a dozen corns of allspice, tie them in a little linen rag, a bundle of sweet herbs, half a lemon, three anchovies, a little onion chopped very fine; season with pepper, salt and cayenne pepper, to your liking; stew it for half an hour, then strain it through a sieve into the pan you intend to put your fish in. Let your carp be well cleaned and scaled, then put the fish in with the sauce, and stew them very gently for half an hour; then turn them, and stew them fifteen minutes longer; put in along with your fish some truffles and morels (*or mushrooms*), some pickled mushrooms (*p. 235*), an artichoke bottom, and about a dozen oysters. Squeeze the juice of half a lemon in, stew it five minutes; then put your carp in your dish, and pour all the sauce over. Garnish with fried sippets and the roe of the fish, done thus:

Beat the roe up well with the yolks of two eggs, a little flour, a little lemon-peel chopped fine, some pepper, salt, and a little anchovy liquor; have ready a pan of beef-drippings boiling, drop the roe in to be about as big as a crown piece (*about the size of a quarter*), fry it of a light brown, and put it round the dish with some oysters fried in butter and some scraped horse-radish. (*Depending on their size, a brace of carp can serve as many as 12.*)

N.B.: Stick your fried sippets in your fish. You may fry the carp first, if you please, but the above is the most modern way.

TO BAKE CARP

Scale, wash, and clean a brace of carp very well; take an earthen pan deep enough for them to lie in, butter it a little, and lay in your carp; season with mace, cloves, nutmegs, and black and white pepper, a bundle of sweet herbs, an onion and anchovy. Pour in a bottle of white-wine, cover it close, and let them bake an hour in a hot oven, if large; if small, less time will do them. When they are enough, carefully take them up, and lay them on a dish; set it over hot water to keep it hot, and cover it close; then put all the liquor they were baked in into a sauce-pan, let it boil a minute or two, then strain it, and add half a pound of butter rolled in flour. Let it boil, keep stirring it, squeeze in the juice of half a lemon, and put in what salt you want; pour the sauce over the fish, lay the roes round, and garnish with lemon. Observe to skim all the fat off the liquor.

FISH SOUPS

CATFISH SOUP

Cat-fish caught near the middle of the river are much nicer than those that are taken near the shore where they have access to impure food. The small white ones are the best.

Having cut off their head, skin the fish and clean them, and cut them in three. To twelve small cat-fish allow a pound and a half of ham. Cut the ham into small pieces, or mouthfuls, and scald it two or three times in boiling water, lest it be too salt. Chop together a bunch of parsley and some sweet marjoram stripped from the stalks. Put these ingredients into a soup kettle and season them with pepper; the ham will make them salt enough. Add a head (*small bunch*) of celery cut small, a large tablespoonful of celery seed tied up in a bit of clean muslin to prevent it dispersing. Put in two quarts of water, cover the kettle, and let it boil slowly till every thing is sufficiently done, and the fish and ham quite tender. Skim it frequently. Boil in another vessel a quart of rich milk, in which you have melted a quarter of a pound of butter, divided into small bits and rolled in flour. Pour it hot to the soup, and stir in at the last the beaten yolks of four eggs. Give it another boil, and then put it into a tureen, taking out the bag of celery seed, and adding some toasted bread cut in squares. Before you send it to table, remove the backbones of the cat-fish. (*Serves 12.*)

BOUILLABAISSE

Nearly all kinds of fish, except the fat or oily kinds, like Mackerel, etc., are supposed to be good for the bouillabaise, and the more varieties used together, the better is the dish produced.

Separate the small fish, unfit to eat, from the larger ones. Take the former and boil them alone with salt and abundance of water. When thoroughly cooked, strain the fish through a sieve or a towel wrung by two persons, so as to extract all the juice which is mixed with the water in which the fish have been boiling. Then prepare in a saucepan the condiments, tomatoes pealed (*sic*) and cleaned of seeds, onions, chopped parsley, garlic, sage, nutmeg, lemon peel, pepper, salt, etc., with a good quantity of the best olive oil

[180]

(if olive oil is not to be found, I suppose butter might be used instead, but the character of the dish would certainly be changed). After ten minutes of good frying, add the broth and juice of the fish and some peeled potatoes, and boil on a good fire until the oil has ceased to float on the liquid and been thoroughly incorporated in this last. Now take the large fish you have kept in reserve, and which must be as fresh as possible, clean it, and if too large, cut in halves. Put it to boil briskly with a little saffron in the liquid just described; fifteen or twenty minutes will suffice. Take it out with a skimmer, pass the liquid through a sieve, throw it on slices of bread, or on soda crackers, and serve the fish and tomatoes (*and potatoes*) with these slices. The fish livers, which only require a few minutes of cooking, are best boiled separately in a little fish broth, after which they are poured in together with a few yolks of eggs or a little tomato sauce, to be then served as a sauce on the fish. (*This makes as much as you have fish.*)

FISH STOCK

Take a dozen flounders, or any small flat fish, and the same number of perch; gut them carefully; put them into a stewpan with two quarts of strong veal broth; add a few slices of lean ham, two or three carrots, celery, and onions cut in slices, some sweet herbs and salt, with a little cayenne; stew until the fish will pass through a coarse sieve; then return it to the stewpan, with a good lump of butter and some flour to thicken it (*slightly*); add a couple of large glasses of white wine and a large spoonful of garlic vinegar. The gravy from potted herrings, or anchovies, will also improve the flavor.

Any species of fish (*or even the heads, tails, and bones trimmed off at the fish market and usually thrown away*) may be made into soup in the same manner. If meant to be brown, the onions should be fried and a good spoonful of mushroom ketchup (*p. 250*) or India soy should be added; and red wine will be better than either sherry or Madeira. But if kept *white*, cream should be substituted for ketchup or soy; a glassful of ginger wine will answer the purpose of red wine.

[9]

JUNE

Wedding cakes; June vegetables; strawberries;
walnuts; roses; candied flowers; ice cream; sherbets

WEDDING CAKES

Wedding cakes in those days were light fruitcakes, not the foam rubber and air confections foisted upon friends at wedding receptions now. Following are two wedding cake recipes. The first, with a whipped cream icing, is spectacular. I baked it for my own wedding. Two or three weeks of keeping, in an airtight container, improves the flavor.

WEDDING CAKE, 1813

4 *pounds of flour*	4 *pounds of currants*
4 *pounds of butter*	1 *pound of almonds, blanched*
2 *pounds of loaf* (granulated)	*and slivered*
sugar	1 *pound of citron*
¼ *ounce mace*	1 *pound candied orange peel*

¼ ounce nutmeg	1 pound candied lemon peel
32 eggs, separated	½ pint brandy

First work the butter to a cream with your hands, then beat in your sugar a quarter of an hour (*or until light, with an electric mixer*), and work up the whites of your eggs to a very strong froth (*stiff peaks; it is best if these are folded in last*). Mix them with your butter and sugar, beat your yolks half an hour at least (*or until light and lemon-yellow*) and mix them with your other ingredients. Then put in your flour, mace and nutmeg, and keep beating well till the oven is ready (*the batter will be very stiff*). Put in your brandy, and beat lightly in your currants and almonds. Tie eight sheets of paper around the bottom of your hoop (*a device like a spring-form pan; use well-buttered pans in graduated sizes, and sift flour over the butter*) to keep it from running out, and rub it well with butter. Then put in your cake and place your sweet-meats (*the citron and candied peel*) in three layers with some cake (*batter*) between every layer. As soon as it is risen and colored, cover it with paper and send it to a moderate oven. (*Bake it at 250°. If the edges brown before the cake is done, cover it with a tent of aluminum foil. The recipe is huge and should be baked in sections. This amount will make two layers, one 18 inches in diameter, the other 12 inches.*) Three hours will bake it (*depending on the shape of the pan and the depth of the batter; use a cake tester or a straw to check it occasionally; put a shallow pan of water in the bottom of the oven while it is baking*).

BRIDE'S CAKE

1 lb. powdered (granulated) sugar	1 lb. raisins seeded and chopped
1 lb. butter	½ lb. citron, cut in slips
1 lb. flour	2 teaspoonfuls nutmeg
12 eggs	1 tablespoonful cinnamon
2 lbs. currants well washed and dredged (with flour)	1 teaspoonful cloves
	1 wineglass brandy

Cream the butter and sugar, add the beaten yolks of the eggs, and stir *well* together before putting in half of the flour. The spice should come next, then the whipped whites stirred in alternately with the rest of the flour, and lastly the brandy.

The above quantity is for two large cakes (*but is much smaller than the recipe for Wedding cake*). Bake at least two hours in deep tins lined with well-buttered paper.

The icing should be laid on stiff and thickly. This cake, if kept in a cool, dry place, will not spoil in two months. I have eaten wedding-cake a year old. Test the cakes well, and be sure they are quite done before taking them from the oven.

Almond icing for bride-cake: The whites of three eggs; one pound of sweet almonds; one pound of loaf sugar; a little rosewater. Beat the whites of the eggs to a *strong* froth, beat a pound of almonds very fine, with a little rose-water (*or lemon or orange flavoring*), mix the almonds with the eggs lightly together, and one pound of common white sugar, beaten very fine and put in by degrees. When the cake is sufficiently done, take it out, lay the icing on, and then put it back to brown (*this is an undercoating, and for between the layers*).

Sugar icing for the top of the bride-cake: Two pounds of double-refined (*powdered*) sugar; whites of five eggs; a little extract of lemon (*or orange*). Whisk the whites of five eggs stiff enough to bear the weight of an egg. Then with a spatula or wooden spoon (*or an electric mixer*), mix gradually with them two pounds of sugar; work them together for a few minutes, and add a teaspoonful of strained lemon juice. Spread it evenly all over the cake, covering the almond icing thickly and evenly. Dry it very slowly in a cool oven (*or in a sunny window*), or if it is put on as soon as the cake is taken from the oven, the icing will be hard by the time the cake is cold.

JUNE VEGETABLES

GREEN PEAS

These are reason enough for the existence of June. They will be good till the end of the month but they cannot stand hot weather. In some parts of the country, they can be planted again in the fall.

They are best when first gathered and shelled. But if kept, do not shell them until they are needed. Put them in while the water boils, and have only just enough (*water*) to cook them done. Season with salt and pepper and a good supply of butter (*and a little mint, if you like; cook until just tender, about 15 minutes. Overcooked peas lose their sweetness*). If they have been kept, they are greatly improved by the addition of a spoonful of sugar, or if a little old and yellow, a piece of saleratus (*baking soda*).

Another method is said to be an improvement. Place in your saucepan several leaves of head lettuce, put in your peas, with an ounce of butter to two quarts of peas, cover it close, and place over the fire; in thirty minutes (*or less, of very slow simmering*), they are ready for the table. Season with pepper, etc. It is said they are better than when cooked in water.

GREEN PEAS WITH BACON

Put a pint of (*fresh*) peas into a stewpan, with five spoonfuls of brown sauce (*p. 436*), two of brown gravy, a teaspoonful of butter, two button onions, and a bunch of parsley; let it boil ten minutes; have ready braised about a quarter of a pound of lean bacon, cut in dice about a quarter of an inch square; add it to the peas. Take out the onions and parsley, season with an ounce of butter and half a teaspoonful of sugar; mix well together, stew twenty minutes and serve. (*Serves 4.*)

FRESH PEAS PUDDING

Boil two quarts of shelled peas for fifteen minutes until tender; press through a colander; add two teaspoonfuls of salt, half a cup of cream and a dash of pepper. Fill custard-cups and stand in a pan of hot water and bake in a moderate oven for twenty minutes. This may be made in the morning and cooked just at serving time. (*Serves 12–15.*)

GREEN PEA SOUP

Put two quarts of green peas into a stewpan with a quarter of a pound of butter, a quarter of a pound of lean ham cut into small dice, two onions in slices, and a few sprigs of parsley; add a quart of cold water, and with the hands rub all well together; then pour off the water, cover the stewpan close, and stand it over a sharp fire, stirring the contents round occasionally; when very tender, add two tablespoonfuls of flour, which mix well in, mashing the peas with your spoon against the sides of the pan, add two quarts of stock, a tablespoonful of sugar, and a little pepper and salt if required; boil all well together five minutes, when rub through a hair sieve (*or purée in a blender*);

then put it into another stewpan with a pint of boiling milk; boil five minutes, skim well, pour it into your tureen. Serve with croutons of bread. (*Serves 20.*)

CREAM OF GREEN PEA, ASPARAGUS, STRING BEAN, SPINACH, CORN OR CELERY SOUP

These soups are very delicate and are much esteemed. They are all made in the same way. The vegetable is boiled until soft, and is then pressed through a sieve (*or puréed in a blender*). A pint of vegetable pulp is diluted with a quart of stock (veal, beef or chicken). It is thickened with a roux made of one tablespoonful of butter and two tablespoonfuls of flour, seasoned with pepper and salt, and is then strained again, so it will be perfectly smooth. It is replaced on the fire, a cupful or half a cupful of cream added, and the whole beaten with an egg-whisk to make it light, and is served at once very hot.

The French thicken cream soups with egg-yolks. In this case, two yolks would be used for the above quantity. The beaten yolks are diluted with cream and cooked only just long enough to set the egg. It would curdle if allowed to boil. Butter is needed for seasoning, and where eggs are used it should be added in small bits before the cream and eggs. Where roux is used for thickening, there is enough butter in the roux.

GREEN PEA TIMBALE FOR SOUP

Mix one-half cupful of mashed green peas with one tablespoonful of soup stock and three whites of eggs; season with salt, pepper and a little nutmeg. Beat well together and place in a small mould of flat tin. Set the mould into hot water and place in a slow oven until the mixture is set. When it is firm, unmould, cut into small cubes, and put them in the soup just before serving.

TO PRESERVE PEAS FOR WINTER USE

Shell, scald and dry them; put them on tin or earthen dishes, in a cool oven, once or twice, to harden. Keep them in paper bags hung up in the kitchen. When they are to be used, let them lie an hour in water; then set them on with cold water and a bit of butter to boil till ready. Put a sprig of dried mint to boil with them.

ANOTHER WAY TO DRY PEAS: Put them into a pot with two or three tablespoonfuls of sugar, put over a fire, and as soon as they begin to sweat, pour out, drain, spread on paper in an airy place, not in the sun, and turn frequently to dry them rapidly.

HOTCH POTCH

To three quarts of water put vegetables according to the season. In summer, peas, french beans, cauliflower, lettuce and spinach; in winter, beet-root, and endive; carrots, turnips, celery, and onions in both, all cut small; and stew with two pounds of neck of mutton, or a fowl, or one pound of pickled pork (*or lean salt pork*) until quite tender. On first boiling, skim. One-half hour before serving, add a lobster or crab cleared from the bones. Season with salt and cayenne. A small quantity of rice should be put in with the meat. Some people choose very small suet dumplings (*p. 363*) boiled with it. Should any fat arise, skim nicely; and put one-half cup water with a little flour (*to thicken it*). (*Serves 10–12.*)

It may be made of various things using a due proportion of fish, flesh, fowl, and vegetable. In the West Indies it is the universal dish, but seasoned so highly with capsicums (*a variety of pepper*) and peppers that it is there called "pepper-pot."

SPINACH WITH CREAM

The usual way of cooking spinach now is to wash it well, pick off the tougher stalks, put it into a pot with only the water that clings to its leaves, and cook it, covered, until it is wilted; then drain and serve with salt and butter, and perhaps a little vinegar. But once spinach was boiled ruthlessly.

This vegetable is very light and good for invalids. It must be washed in several waters, after having been well picked. Then put a quarter of a sieve of spinach to a gallon of water, and three ounces of salt, boil for ten minutes till tender, drain on a sieve, press a little with your hands to extract part of the water, chop it up fine, put in a stewpan with a quarter of a pound of butter, a teaspoonful of salt, half ditto of pepper, a tablespoonful of flour, half a pint of milk or cream, and a tablespoonful of sugar. Cut three slices of bread, lay on a dish, sift sugar over, put in the oven, salamander over (*toast*), cut in various shapes, and serve under or over spinach.

[187]

CHARTREUSE OF SPINACH OR CABBAGE

Boil a large carrot and turnip; cut them into slices lengthwise three-eighths of an inch thick, then into strips of the same width. Butter well a tin basin, with slightly flaring sides, or a plain mold. Ornament the bottom with hard-boiled egg. Around the sides of the mold place close together alternating strips of (*cooked*) carrot and turnip. If the mold is well-buttered, they will hold easily in place. Fill the center with (*cooked, creamed*) spinach or with well-seasoned chopped cabbage, and press it down so that it is quite firm. Smooth the top and cut the strips so they are even. Heat the chartreuse by placing the mold in a pan of hot water and putting both in the oven for ten or fifteen minutes. Turn the chartreuse on a flat dish to serve. A white or vinaigrette sauce goes well with this dish.

Birds, veal cutlets, chicken or sweetbreads may be placed on top of the chartreuse, if desired.

BEIGNETS OF SPINACH

Take some washed and picked spinach; mix the yolks of four eggs, some butter, and four ounces of sugar, with some bread-crumbs; add this to the chopped spinach; form it into round cakes, and fry them in butter.

BAYBURY SALAD

Cook about a peck of spinach until very tender, then drain and chop very fine, with two cucumbers and two hard-boiled eggs. Mix with this a dressing made of four tablespoons of (*melted*) butter (*or oil*), four tablespoons of vinegar, one-half saltspoon each of salt, pepper and mustard. Fill crisp, curly lettuce leaves with the spinach, and serve with a mayonnaise dressing.

CHIFFONADE

Wash well, drain, and chop up very fine one quart of sorrel with the green leaves of a lettuce-head. Brown in a saucepan, with two ounces of butter and a sliced onion, seasoning with half a tablespoon of salt and a teaspoon of pepper. Moisten with three pints of white broth (*p. 131*), add a handful of peas, the same of string beans and asparagus tops; boil for three-quarters of an hour with an ounce of butter; serve with six slices of toasted bread. (*Serves 6.*)

Make with asparagus only, and thicken with the yolk of one egg in half a cup of cream. Serve with sippets of toast.

SORREL AU MAIGRE

Pick off the stems of half a peck of sorrel; wash it in several waters, drain and chop up with a head of well-cleansed lettuce. Add half a bunch of chervil, and chop all together very fine. Place all in a saucepan, stir well together on the hot stove for three minutes, and then place it in the oven until the vegetables are well dissolved; then add an ounce and a half of butter, and stir again for about ten minutes, or until the sorrel is reduced to a pulp. Season with a pinch of salt, and half a pinch of pepper, and pour into it a thickening of two egg yolks (*beaten with*) half a cupful of cream; stir well without boiling, and serve. (*Serves 6–8.*)

SORREL SAUCE (*FOR ROASTS*)

Wash well four handfuls of sorrel, put it nearly dry into a middle-sized stewpan, with a little butter; let it melt, add a tablespoonful of flour, a teaspoonful of salt, half one of pepper, moisten to a thick purée with milk, or broth, or cream; pass it through a sieve (*or blend*), put it back in a stewpan, warm again, add two whole eggs, two ounces of butter, and stir well, and serve where directed.

AUTUMN SOUP

From its ingredients, this should rightfully be called Summer soup.

Cut up four cabbage-lettuces, one cos ditto (*lettuce*), a handful of sorrel, a little tarragon and chervil, when well washed and drained, put them into a stewpan, with two cucumbers finely sliced, and two ounces of butter. Place them over a brisk fire, stirring occasionally, until very little remains, then add two tablespoons of flour, stirring it in well, then pour over three quarts of stock, adding a quart of young and fresh green peas; half an hour's boiling will suffice for this delicious soup, and the flavor of the vegetables will be fully preserved; season with a teaspoon of salt and two of sugar. (*Serves 12–15.*)

DUTCHED LETTUCE

Wash carefully two heads of lettuce, separate the leaves and tear each leaf in two or three pieces. Cut a quarter-pound (*four or five slices*) of ham or bacon into dice, and fry until brown (*but do not drain off the grease*); while hot, add two tablespoonfuls of vinegar. Beat one egg until light, add to it two tablespoonfuls of sour cream, then add it to the ham, stir over the fire one minute until it thickens, and pour, boiling hot, over the lettuce; mix carefully with a fork and serve. Endive may also be cooked in this way. (*Serves 6–8.*)

SALAD OF ALLIGATOR PEAR

Mash the pear and put it, in a pretty shape, in the center of a dish with crisp lettuce leaves around the edge, and pour over it a nice mayonnaise dressing; or the pear may be sliced instead of mashed; or mash the pear and beat it with the mayonnaise dressing and pour over the lettuce.

SALAD DRESSING STOCK

One tablespoonful of vinegar, one egg yolk, one spoonful of butter, or a piece the size of an egg yolk. Allow the vinegar to come just to a boil; thoroughly beat the egg and pour into the vinegar off the fire; stir over the fire till it thickens; add the butter while still hot. It can be kept for an indefinite time. In this state it is called Salad Dressing Stock. (*Enough for 3–4.*)

CREAM MAYONNAISE: Thin Salad Dressing Stock with cream.

BOILED DRESSING FOR SALAD

Mix yolks of 3 eggs, beaten, 1 teaspoon (*dry*) mustard, 2 teaspoons salt, ¼ teaspoon cayenne, 2 tablespoons sugar, 2 tablespoons (*melted*) butter or oil, 1 cup cream or milk, ½ cup hot vinegar and whites of 3 eggs, beaten stiff. Cook in the double boiler until it thickens like soft custard. Stir well. This will keep in a cool place two weeks, and is excellent for lettuce, celery, asparagus, string beans and cauliflower.

9: JUNE

"Sallets in general consist of certain Esculent Plants and Herbs, improv'd by Culture, Industry, and the art of the Gard'ner; or, as others say, they are a composition of Edule Plants and Roots of several kinds, to be eaten Raw or Green, Blanch'd or Candied; simple, and per se, or intermingl'd with others according to the Season."

John Evelyn, *Aceteria*, 1706

MINT JELLY FOR ROAST

Wash one cup of mint leaves, pour over them a cup of boiling water and let stand for an hour or more; strain through a cheese cloth bag, pressing out all the juice. Prepare apple juice for jelly (*p. 311*). To each cup of strained juice add a large tablespoonful of mint juice; then add sugar and make the jelly. (*See p. 28 for details.*) If a stronger flavor is desired, add more mint juice.

The juice can be canned for later use.

"Gather wild mint, put it where you wish to keep mice out, and they will not trouble you."

Mrs. Abell, *Ladies' Guide: or, The Skillful Housewife*, 1852

WAYS OF COOKING RADISHES

A favorite way is to slice them thin and fry them with steak, or fry with potatoes.

Some readers slice them thin, cook eight minutes, drain and serve with butter, salt and pepper.

Others fix raw radish and mayonnaise sandwiches.

Some readers parboil sliced radishes for five minutes, turn them into a buttered baking dish, cover with cream and buttered crumbs, and bake until tender.

Others cook them and mash them, adding a little butter.

Many readers assure us that they have cooked strong, rather old radishes with splendid results.

Young carrots will be ready toward the end of June, but are cheapest in the early fall. Carrot recipes are in September (pp. 284–285).

STRAWBERRIES

STRAWBERRIES IN ORANGE JUICE

Wash and stem two quarts juicy, ripe strawberries. Make a syrup of half a cup of sugar and a quarter of a cup of water. Boil five minutes, cool, and add one and a half cups of orange juice to which has been added a dash of grated orange rind. Pour over berries in a glass dish and serve cold. Strawberries are also delicious when served in canned peach, apricot, currant or plum juice. (*Serves 6–8.*)

SALAD OF STRAWBERRIES (*A DESSERT*)

Pick the stalks from a pottle (*quart basket*) of very fine strawberries, which put into a basin with half a teaspoonful of powdered cinnamon, two glasses of brandy and an ounce of powdered sugar, toss them lightly over, and dress them in pyramid upon your dish, pouring the syrup over; these should only be dressed a few minutes before serving. If handy, a glass of maraschino (*liqueur*), substituted for the brandy, makes them delicious. (*Serves 4.*)

STRAWBERRY AND CURRANT SALAD

A pretty dessert dish may be made of mixed early fruits, strawberries, white or red currants, gooseberries, and cherries, all carefully picked, placed in alternate layers stewed with sugar, and piled up with taste. Either simple cream, or wine or brandy cream, should be poured over the salad.

Strawberries served in white wine, in champagne, in orange liqueur, or in kirsch are also delicious.

STRAWBERRY SHORTCAKE

Two cups of flour; one cup of sour milk; a piece of butter the size of a walnut; one-third of a teaspoonful of soda, one salt-spoonful of salt; one quart of strawberries. Mix the dry ingredients with the flour, rub together through a

[192]

sieve; then work in the butter and add gradually the milk. Butter two round shallow tins and spread the mixture in them. Bake for fifteen minutes. When done, split the cakes open, butter them and sprinkle with sugar. Crush one quart of strawberries, sugar them to taste, and spread between the layers. Serve at once (*topped*) with whipped cream.

See p. 68, for another shortcake recipe.

STRAWBERRY PIE

Have a pie-plate lined with paste (*brush the unbaked pastry with white of egg, beaten with a tablespoonful of water, so that it will not be soggy*), lay in one-half of a pound of apple sauce, then place it in the oven for thirty minutes. Take it out and let it get thoroughly cold. Fill the interior with a pint and a half of well-picked and cleaned strawberries, mixed with two ounces of powdered sugar. Spread two ounces of apple jelly (*gelatine*) evenly over the strawberries, and serve.

TO PRESERVE STRAWBERRIES IN WINE

Stem the finest and largest strawberries; put them into wide-mouthed pint bottles. Put into each bottle four large tablespoonfuls of pulverized loaf sugar; fill up the bottles with Madeira or Sherry wine. Cork them closely, and keep them in a cool place.

STRAWBERRY JAM

Put an equal weight of good ripe scarlet strawberries and broken loaf (*granulated*) sugar into a preserving pan; let them boil very slowly until the sugar is all dissolved. The fruit should be kept as much unbroken as possible, therefore stir very carefully; remove the scum as it rises; the addition of half a pint of white currant juice to every four pounds of fruit is a great improvement, strawberry jam being rather a luscious preserve. Boil from forty minutes to an hour, until the fruit looks clear.

Gooseberry jam may be made the same way.

STRAWBERRY SAUCE

Make a hard sauce (*p. 398*); add the whipped white of one egg and a cupful of strawberries mashed to a pulp. Any fruit pulp may be added in the same way, and makes a good sauce for fruit pudding.

Elderberries bloom in June. Mark the locations for berry-picking in late August or early September. The white blossoms, which look like Queen Anne's lace, are easier to spot than the purple berries. The blossoms also make a nice light wine.

GREEN CURRANT PIE

Currants usually ripen in early July. See pp. 207–209 for other recipes.
Currants will make good and wholesome pies at nearly all stages of their growth. They only require to be stewed, and sweetened according to their degree of acidity, and baked between two crusts in the ordinary manner. The addition of a little dried or green apple gives a fine flavor.

Gooseberry pie is made in the same way, but requires a larger proportion of sugar.

WALNUTS

PICKLED WALNUTS

100 walnuts
1 ounce of cloves
1 ounce of (whole) black pepper
½ ounce of mace

1 ounce of stick cinnamon
½ ounce of race (green) ginger
1 ounce of mustard seed
Cider or white vinegar sufficient to cover them

The nuts should be collected about the middle of June. Make a pickle of salt and water strong enough to bear an egg, which boil and let stand until cold. Put the walnuts into jars, cover them with the pickle, and let them remain in a cold place three weeks. At the expiration of this time, take them out of the brine, put them in a colander and let them drain. Wash and wipe the jars; then replace the walnuts, and cover them with the best cider vinegar, in which let them remain one month. Then take them out, remove the vinegar, rinse and wipe the jars, put in the nuts, and sprinkle with the mustard seed. Boil the spice ten minutes in a sufficient quantity of the best cider vinegar to cover them. When cold, pour the whole over the nuts, and cover very close, to exclude every particle of air. These are fit to eat when soft, but are better if kept for one or two years.

ROSES

ROSE BRANDY

Rosewater, a frequent ingredient in old cake and pudding recipes, is nearly impossible to get these days. Druggists who mix their prescriptions still carry it, but it is perishable once opened, so it is unwise to buy large amounts. It is even more difficult to make your own, since it requires a still. Rose extract can be substituted—or this rose brandy makes a pleasant stand-in.

Nearly fill a glass jar with freshly-gathered rose leaves, and pour in sufficient French white brandy to fill it quite up; and then cover it closely. Next day put the whole into a strainer, and having squeezed and pressed the rose leaves and drained off the liquor, throw away the leaves, put fresh ones into the jar and return the brandy to it. Repeat this every day while roses are in season, and you will find the liquid much better than rose water for flavoring cakes and puddings.

ROSE BUTTER

Take a glass jar, put on the bottom a layer of butter, and each day put in rose leaves, adding layers of butter, and when full, cover tight and use the butter for articles to be flavored with rose water.

CANDIED FLOWERS

TO CANDY FLOWERS

Gather your flowers when dry, cut off the leaves as far as the color is good. Boil sugar and water (*1 pound of sugar to ½ cup of water*) to a thick syrup, put in your flowers—primroses, violets, cowslips—or whatever they may be, take them out as quickly as you can with as little of the syrup as possible, spread them on a warm dish (*or a screen or sieve*) over a gentle fire to allow the syrup to drain from them. When they have drained sufficiently remove to another warm dish and sprinkle with granulated sugar. Then rub the flowers gently with your hands to open the leaves, sprinkling them every now and then with more sugar, until they are thoroughly open and dry. Then place them in a collander and sift the sugar from them. Keep in a box lined with paraffined (*waxed*) paper in a dry place.

Rosemary flowers must be put whole into the syrup; young mint leaves you must open with your fingers; but rub all blossoms with the hands as directed.

TO MAKE CANDY CAKES OF FLOWERS

Boil the syrup until it candies, then strew in your flowers, let them come up to a boil, then scatter in a little granulated sugar, then as quickly as possible pour into little shaped pans or boxes of cardboard, the bottom of which has been pricked with holes. Set aside to cool. Keep them in boxes very dry.

ICE CREAM

With a good freezer, ice cream is easy to make, impressive, and fun. You probably do not save any money by doing it yourself, but at least you know what ingredients went into it.

Brand-new electric imitations of old ice cream freezers are available almost anywhere now. So are new hand-crank ones. Ice cream may be made in the freezing compartment of a refrigerator—put the mixture in ice-cube trays;

take it out and beat it up when it is half frozen; beat it up again when it is completely frozen; and once more, for good measure—but the result is not as creamy as if it were done in an ice cream freezer, or even following the old method of freezing cream without a freezer.

Ice cream doesn't keep well, even in very cold freezers, for more than three months. See p. 36 for ice-cream-making details.

Ice cream tastes better in June—but if you make it in January, snow mixed with rock salt freezes it even better than crushed ice.

PHILADELPHIA ICE CREAM

This is the simplest, and to many the most delicious form of ice cream. Scald 2 quarts cream; if thick, add one pint milk; melt 2 cups sugar in it, and flavor when cool. Freeze. The cream should be very sweet and highly flavored, as both sweetness and flavor are lessened by freezing. To make it lighter and more delicate, whip the cream until you have a quart of froth, and add the froth after the cream is partly frozen. (*The custom when whipping cream was to skim off the froth as it formed.*) Many prefer to add the white of eggs, beaten till foamy but not stiff. Use two, three or four eggs to each quart of cream. The proportion of sugar should vary according to the flavoring used. (*Makes 3 quarts to 1 gallon.*)

NEAPOLITAN ICE CREAM

Make a boiled custard with 1 quart milk, 1 cup sugar and yolks of 6 to 8 eggs (*p. 94*). Cook it slightly till smooth, but not curdled. Strain, and when cool add 1 pint to 1 quart of cream, sugar to make it quite sweet, and any flavoring desired. The custard, when made with cream instead of milk, makes the richest kind of ice cream. If cream cannot be obtained, beat the white of the eggs till foamy, and add them just before freezing. No matter how many eggs are used, a little cream, if not more than half a cupful, is a decided improvement to all ice-creams. It is better to make a sherbet, or fruit or water ices, than an inferior quality of ice cream with milk. (*Makes 3 quarts.*)

To make the following ice creams, use either of the preceeding bases:
VANILLA: Use one tablespoon of extract (*or simmer a vanilla bean with a little of the milk until the flavor is extracted*).
CHOCOLATE: Melt two bars of sweetened vanilla (*milk*) chocolate with one to two tablespoons of water; add a little cream or custard, and when

smooth, stir into the remainder of the custard. Add half a tablespoon of vanilla. Confectioners sometimes mix half a teaspoon of Ceylon cinnamon with the chocolate. It gives a rich, spicy flavor.

COFFEE: Make half a cup of very strong black coffee for two quarts of ice cream.

PINEAPPLE: Add half a can (*2 cups, drained*) of grated pineapple, or a pint of the ripe fruit, grated.

STRAWBERRY: Sprinkle sugar over the berries; mash and rub through a fine sieve (*or blend*). Measure, and use one pint (*of berries*) to two quarts of cream or custard.

BANANA: Add six bananas, sifted (*strained or puréed*) or cut in thin slices. Add a little lemon juice if the bananas lack flavor.

BAKED APPLE: Bake and sift six sweet apples. Add one quart of rich cream and sugar to taste. When the sugar is dissolved, freeze. (*Try this with red cinnamon candy scattered through it.*)

PISTACHIO: One cup of pistachio nuts and a quarter of a cup of almonds, blanched, chopped, and pounded to a paste.

MACAROON, ALMOND, WALNUT, COCOANUT, OR BROWN BREAD ICE-CREAM: May be made by adding one pint of any of the ingredients to any receipt for ice-cream. Crumble and brown slightly, or chop fine.

FRUIT: Canned fruit or ripe fruit, sweetened to taste and cut into small pieces, may be added to the partly frozen cream, giving many delicious varieties.

TUTTI FRUTTI: Flavor with two tablespoons of Sicily Madeira wine or Maraschino. When partly frozen, add one pound of French candied fruit, chopped fine. Or, use home-made preserves, drained carefully and cut into dice.

ICE-CREAM WITH CONDENSED MILK: Mix one can of condensed milk with three pints scalded milk, and use in making a rich custard. Flavor highly.

SHERBETS

RASPBERRY OR STRAWBERRY CREAM ICES

Mix with a pound of strawberry or raspberry jam, the juice of two lemons, and a quart of cream, or a pint of milk and a pint of cream mixed; rub the whole through a tamis (*or purée it in a blender*) into the tin freezing pot, place it in the ice pail, and stir it until it is frozen. The pulp of fresh fruit, when in season, has a richer flavor, but will then require to be well-mixed with eight ounces of powdered sugar. (*Makes 2 quarts.*)

APRICOT CREAM ICES

Take very fresh and ripe apricots and press out half a pint of the juice; mix with it the kernels of six stones pounded to a paste, with the juice of a lemon, four ounces of powdered sugar and a pint of cream. Freeze, and serve it in a form or glasses. This is a most delicious ice, next to none but pineapple ice, which can only be obtained by a mixture of the juice of fresh pineapples. (*Makes 1 quart.*)

PINEAPPLE WATER ICE

Take half a pound of fresh pineapple, bruised fine in a mortar, add the juice of one lemon, half a pint of water, one pint of clarified (*syrup*) sugar; pass through a sieve (*or blend*); freeze. One quart. Pineapple (*whole*) may be added.

"Water ices, which are more refreshing and wholesome than ice cream, are now used almost as extensively in England as on the Continent. They are generally made of the juice of fresh fruits, pressed out through a linen bag. Then to each pint of juice, add half a pound of sugar, a quarter of a pint of water, and a dessert-spoonful of lemon juice. When well mixed, freeze it like ice cream."
The Cuisine, by An Eminent French Caterer, 1872

RUM ICE

Put into a pan one pound and a half of loaf sugar, on which is rubbed the outer rind of two lemons; add the juice of one lemon and a quart of cold water. Stir it over the fire, and by degrees, stir into it the whites of six eggs beat to a solid froth. Before it begins to simmer, pour it out to cool, add half a pint of rum, and freeze it to serve in glasses. (*Makes 2½–3 quarts.*)

ROMAN PUNCH ICE

Roman punch glacé is made by adding to a quart of lemon ice (*p. 403*) made with syrup, three whites of eggs beaten stiff and one glassful each of brandy, champagne and maraschino, and freeze it. (*Makes 1½–2 quarts.*)

THE FIVE THREES SHERBET

The juice of three oranges, juice of three lemons, three bananas chopped fine, three scant cups of sugar and three cups of water. Freeze till stiff, then add the white of one egg beaten stiff with a little sugar. It is best to cut one orange up fine and use the juice from the other two. (*Makes 2 quarts.*)

TO FREEZE CREAM WITHOUT A FREEZER

If one wishes to freeze a pint or a quart of cream when there is no freezer at hand, it may be done in a tin pail in from twenty to thirty minutes. Put the cream in a two-quart tin pail and cover it; mix coarse salt with finely pounded ice or snow, in the proportion of one-third salt; put a quart of it in an ordinary wooden pail, place the tin pail in the centre, and pack it firmly with the freezing mixture to within an inch of the top; then remove the cover and stir with a wooden spoon, constantly detaching the frozen cream from the bottom and sides of the pail, until the whole is stiff; smooth it over the top, replace the cover, pour off the water, repack, cover the whole closely with a piece of carpet, and leave it for an hour or two in as cool a place as can be found. In winter, the pail may stand on a chair in the kitchen while the cream is being stirred, in summer in any shady place in the open air.

This mode gives one the pleasure of seeing the freezing process, which is concealed in patent freezers.

[10]

JULY

Berries; bananas; July pickles; July vegetables; turtles; salt fish

BERRIES

July is berry month.

June strawberries start the season, which proceeds lusciously through raspberries, cherries, blackberries, gooseberries, currants, and blueberries. By late July, almost all the berries will be gone. Almost any kind of fresh raw fruit, was a little *déclassé* in the nineteenth century. The accepted mode of "dressing" them was to stew them in a sugar-syrup. But berries are at their best just picked, with a little sugar and a little cream—Devonshire cream if you can get it or make it (*p. 105*)—or with this sauce:

SOUR CREAM SAUCE FOR BERRIES

Mix together 1 cup thick sour cream, ½ cup sugar and the yolk of 1 egg. Flavor it with 1–2 tablespoons of any orange-flavored liqueur, or with grated orange rind, and refrigerate for 1 hour before serving.

BERRY PUDDING

Two cups molasses; one cup milk; three cups flour (*or less*); one-half cup butter; two cups berries; two eggs; one teaspoon saleratus. Bake.

BLACK BUTTER

Allow to any kind of berries, stoned cherries, currants, etc., half their weight of sugar, and boil till reduced one-fourth. (*Put, hot, into sterilized jars; seal with paraffin.*) This is a healthful and nice substitute for butter, for children.

AN EXCELLENT FAMILY WINE

may be made of equal parts of red, white and black currants, ripe cherries and raspberries, well bruised and mixed with soft water, in proportion of four pounds of fruit to one gallon of water. When strained and pressed, three pounds of moist sugar are to be added to each gallon of liquid. After standing open three days (*covered with a towel*), during which it is to be stirred frequently and skimmed as it may require, it is put into a barrel and left for a fortnight to work, when a ninth part of brandy is to be added (*1 part for each 8 parts of juice*), and the whole bunged down; and in two or three years it will be rich and valuable. (*See pp. 37–41 for wine-making details.*)

CHERRY PUDDING

Two eggs, one cupful sweet milk, flour enough to make a stiff batter, two teaspoons baking powder and as many cherries as can be stirred in. (*Steam.*) Serve with cherry sauce. (*Serves 6.*)

CHERRY SAUCE: Fresh red cherries, stewed, sweetened, and passed through a sieve, and slightly thickened with corn starch.

CHERRY PUDDING #2

One coffee-cup of tapioca, soaked overnight. Cook until clear in a quart of water; flavor with nutmeg; add two scant cups sugar, one tablespoon of butter, and two cups of pitted cherries, drained from the juice. Bake one hour, and ice the top. Serve very cold. (*Serves 4–6.*)

Baked in a pie crust, this is a cherry pie.

CHERRY CAKE

Bake a layer cake. Cook together one cup sugar and two of pitted cherries; one teaspoon of butter and one of cornstarch. Place between and on top of the layers, and finish with a meringue of eggs (*whites beaten stiff and sweetened*) and whipped cream.

CHERRY ICE

1 quart cherries, with half the stones pounded in a mortar	1 pint of water, in which dissolve 1 pint of sugar
2 lemons—the juice only	1 glass of fine brandy

Squeeze out the bruised cherries and stones, in a bag over the sugar; add the water, then the brandy, and freeze. It will require a longer time to freeze than other ices, on account of the brandy. (*Makes 2 quarts.*)

WILD CHERRY AND CURRANT JELLY

Two-thirds wild cherries (stones and all) and one of red currants. A pound of sugar to a pint of the juice, and make as you do plain currant jelly. This, besides being very palatable and an excellent table jelly, is highly medicinal, good for coughs and any weakness of the digestive organs.

PRESERVED CHERRIES (*JAM*)

Two quarts best New Orleans molasses, one gallon of pitted cherries, and one teaspoon of cinnamon. Boil all together until thick.

CHERRY BOUNCE

Four pounds of sour and the same quantity of sweet cherries, two and a half pounds white sugar, one gallon best whiskey. Crush the cherries to pieces by pounding in a deep vessel with a smooth billet of wood. Beat hard enough

[203]

to crack the stones. Put into a deep stone jar, mix in the sugar well and cover with the whiskey. Shake around briskly and turn into a demijohn. Cork tightly and let it stand a month, shaking it every day, and another month without touching it. Then strain off and bottle. It is better a year old than six months.

No beverage which contains alcohol in any shape should be used daily, much less semi- or tri-daily, by a well person.

Fruits can be added to this as they come into season (but never bananas or fruits that will rot), and the mixture can be kept going for years. The fruits, with a little of the liquor, make a delicious sauce for ice cream.

CHERRIES IN BRANDY

Dissolve a pound and a half of white sugar-candy in a pint of brandy, and drop in as many fine ripe cherries with the stalks half cut away as the brandy will cover, adding half a pint of fresh clear raspberry juice, which will improve the color; cover up closely, and when the fruit has absorbed the brandy, add a little more till the cherries be fully saturated; keep them still covered with the brandy; cork closely, the corks covered with bladders (*paraffin or plastic*).

CHERRY SHRUB

Pick ripe Morello cherries from the stem; put them in an earthen pot; place that in an iron pot of water; boil till the juice is extracted; strain it through a cloth thick enough to retain the pulp, and sweeten it to your taste. When perfectly clear, bottle it, sealing the cork. By first putting a gill of brandy into each bottle, it will keep through the summer. It is delicious mixed with water.

FRENCH RASPBERRY TART

Choose a pint of very fine ripe raspberries, either red or white; stem them and throw them into a boiling syrup, made with a quarter of a pound of loaf sugar and a tablespoonful of water; withdraw them immediately from the fire; line a tart-dish with a puff paste (*p. 76*) rolled as thin as possible; lay in the fruit and syrup, observing to keep the raspberries as whole as possible; put it into a quick oven for twenty minutes; strew more sugar over it, and glaze it; or, if to be served cold, pour raw cream over it.

RASPBERRY PUDDING

Put into a tart-dish a pint and a half of fresh raspberries, or raspberries and red currants mixed, and strain in ten ounces of sugar. Beat the yolks of six eggs and the whites of four very well, and mix with half a pint of good milk or cream, and two ounces of sifted sugar. Whisk up to a froth, and pour over the fruit the moment before you put it into the oven. Bake half an hour, and serve only when cold, with sifted sugar over it. (*Serves 6.*)

RASPBERRY SAUCE FOR PUDDINGS

Put into a jar a pint of fresh raspberries with half a pint of water, and set it into a pan of boiling water, or a moderate oven, for half an hour; then strain off the liquor, and put it into a saucepan with two ounces of sugar, two glasses of sherry, and a tablespoonful of arrowroot, first blended in a spoonful of the wine.

Sauces thickened with cornstarch or arrowroot will be clearer than those thickened with flour.

RASPBERRY SHRUB

Put one quart of vinegar to three quarts of fresh ripe raspberries; after standing a day, strain it, adding to each pint a pound of sugar, and skim it clear while boiling about half an hour. Put a wineglass of brandy to each pint of the shrub, when cool. Two spoonfuls of this mixed with a tumbler of water is an excellent drink in fevers. (*And mixed with soda water, it is an excellent soft drink any time.*)

RASPBERRY JAM

Select raspberries that are perfectly ripe; weigh them and allow a pound of sugar to a pound of fruit. Mash the fruit and sugar together. Put the whole into a preserving kettle over a clear fire. Stir it frequently and skim it as it boils. It will take from three-quarters to an hour to cook. When done, put it in small pots or glasses, and when cold, cover with brandy paper (*or paraffin*).

BLACKBERRY JAM

merely requires nice picking, half the weight of any kind of sugar, and three-quarters of an hour boiling.

BLACKBERRY WINE

Place your fruit in a large vat, mash and strain them through a hair sieve or wine press, so as to extract the juice. To every quart of pure juice add two quarts of water and three pounds of sugar. Fill your barrel or keg entirely full. Reserve some of the mixture, in order to refill the vessel as it is fermenting. Continue refilling until fermentation has ceased. Close the bung hole. If the barrel or vessel is undisturbed, it does not require to be racked off. To rack it will not injure the wine, it will rather improve it. (*See pp. 37–41 for details of wine making.*)

VOL-AU-VENT WITH GREEN GOOSEBERRIES

A quart of green gooseberries, a quarter of a pound of powdered sugar, the juice of half a lemon and a tablespoonful of water; put on the fire and move it about for ten minutes, or till tender, and forming a thick green marmalade; put it in a basin till cold, serve in pyramid with vol-au-vent (*p. 143*); a little thick syrup, if handy, poured over, improves the appearance.

See p. 194 for Green gooseberry pie.

GOOSEBERRY FOOL

Top and tail (*1 quart of*) gooseberries. Pour some boiling water on them, cover them up and let them set about half an hour, or till the skin is quite tender, but not till it bursts, as that will make the juice run out into the water. Then pour off the water, and mix with the gooseberries an equal quantity of sugar. Put them into a porcelain stewpan and set it on hot coals. In a few minutes you may begin to mash them against the side of the pan with a wooden spoon. Let them stew about half an hour, stirring them frequently. Stir them as soon as they are cold into a quart of rich boiling milk. Grate in a nutmeg, and covering the pan, let the gooseberries simmer in the milk for five minutes, then stir in the beaten yolks of two or three eggs, and immediately remove it from the fire. Keep on the cover a few minutes longer; then turn out the mixture into a deep dish or glass bowl, and set it away to get cold, before it goes to table. Eat it with sponge-cake. It will probably require additional sugar stirred in at the last. (*Serves 15–20.*)

GOOSEBERRY SAUCE

Top and tail them close with a pair of Scissars, and scald half a pint of green Gooseberries, drain them on a hair sieve, and put them into half a pint of melted butter. Some add grated Ginger and Lemon Peel, and the French add minced Fennel, as others send up Gooseberries whole, or mashed, without any butter, etc. (*Serve with mackerel, or with game.*)

PRESERVED GREEN GOOSEBERRIES

Take green walnut gooseberries when they are full grown, and take out the seeds, put them in cold water, cover them close with vine leaves, and set them over a slow fire; when they are hot, take them off, and let them stand and when they are cold, set them on again until they are a pretty green, then put them on a sieve to drain, and have ready a syrup made of a pound of double-refined sugar, and half a pint of spring water; the syrup is to be cold when the gooseberries are put in, and boil them until they are clear, then set them by for a day or two, then give them two or three scalds (*pour off the syrup, bring it to a boil, then pour it back on the berries*), and put them into pots or glasses for use.

CURRANT WATER ICE

Press the juice from ripe currants; strain it clear; to one pint of juice put nearly a pound of loaf sugar. When wanted for use, put to it ice-water enough to make a pleasant drink. Grate nutmeg over, and serve. Or, it may be frozen like ice-cream; for this it should be rich and sweet.

PINK OR RED CURRANT CREAM

Squeeze three gills of juice from red currants, quite ripe, add to it nine ounces of powdered loaf sugar, and the juice of one lemon; stir it into a pint and a half of (*heavy*) cream, and whisk it till quite thick. Serve it in a glass dish. (*Serves 8.*)

Raspberry and strawberry cream may be made in the same way.

CURRANT BREAD

Take three pounds of flour; one pound of raisins; two pounds of currants; one pint and a half of new milk and one gill of yeast. Warm the milk and mix it with the flour and yeast; cover with a cloth and set by the fire. When risen sufficiently, add the fruits and mold it; then put it into a baking tin or deep dish rubbed with sweet (*olive*) oil; after it has risen for half an hour longer, bake it in a moderately hot oven. (*Makes 2–3 loaves.*)

RED CURRANT JELLY

Gather your currants when they are dry and full ripe, strip them off the stalks, put them in a large stewpot, tie paper over them (*or cover very closely*) and let them stand an hour in a cool (*200°*) oven (*or in a larger pan of simmering water*); strain them through a cloth, and to every quart of juice add a pound and a half of loaf sugar; stir it gently over a clear fire till your sugar is melted, skim this well, let it boil pretty quick twenty minutes, pour it hot into your pots (if you let it stand it will not set so well); put papers (*or paraffin*) over them and keep them in a dry place for use. Cranberry and grape jelly are made the same way.

To clarify it if the juice is not completely clear: add the beaten white of 1 egg to each quart of juice, let it boil and skim well; then add the sugar and proceed.

This is served with mutton or venison as traditionally as mint jelly is served with lamb.

CURRANT SAUCE

Six pounds of currants picked from the stems, three pounds of sugar, one cup and a half of vinegar, three-quarters of an ounce of cinnamon, and spices to taste; boil slowly an hour. (*Makes 6–7 pints.*)

To be eaten with mutton or game. Currants may also be cooked with a simple sugar-syrup and frozen.

SPICED CURRANTS

Four quarts currants (ripe), three and a half pounds brown sugar, one pint of vinegar, one tablespoonful of allspice (*whole*), one tablespoonful of cloves and a little nutmeg; boil an hour, stirring occasionally. Gooseberries and cherries may be spiced in the same manner.

RED CURRANT WINE

Take thirty-six pints of fruit and one pint of raspberries. Mix with them twenty pints of water. When these have fermented, add twenty pounds of good sugar; and after the wine is casked, two pints of brandy or whiskey without any special flavor. (*See pp. 37–41 for details of wine making.*)

BLUEBERRY CAKE

Two eggs, one-half cup butter, one-half cup sugar, one cup sweet milk, one teaspoonful of soda, two teaspoonfuls cream of tartar, four cups flour, scant pint blueberries. Bake as any cake (*p. 23*).

BLUEBERRY PUDDING

One cup molasses, one teaspoonful soda, two cups blueberries, two cups flour; mix, and steam three hours; serve with white (*hard*) sauce (*p. 398; serves 6–8*).

BLUEBERRY PIE

Take about 1 cup of blueberries and boil them to a thin jam with ½ cup of sugar and ¾ of a cup of water, flavored with 1 stick of cinnamon and thickened a little with arrowroot or tapioca. Have ready a baked pie shell. Fill it with fresh uncooked blueberries and pour the hot, cooked blueberries over it. Chill, and serve with sweetened whipped cream.

BLUEBERRY SAUCE FOR ICE CREAM

Boil 1 cup of fresh or frozen blueberries to a marmalade with 1 cup of sugar and only as much water as necessary to keep them from burning. Just before you take it from the stove, add a dash of brandy or orange-flavored liqueur.

BANANAS

BANANA PUDDING

Bananas are available all year long, but they seem to go down in price during July and August.

Stew bananas and strain into the baking-pan (*adding a dash of lemon juice to prevent discoloring*), and sweeten. Melt one tablespoonful of butter in a saucepan, add two tablespoons of flour, one cup of milk (*and stir over the heat until thickened and smooth*). Stir until cool, then stir in the yolks of four eggs, beat the whites to a froth and add them (*last*). Stir in thoroughly spice and sugar (*to taste*). Pour on top of the bananas and bake (*at 375°*) about thirty minutes. (*Serve hot, as a soufflé.*)

BANANA FRITTERS

Select and neatly peel six fine sound, not too ripe, yellow bananas, cut each one in halves, crosswise, place them on a dish. Have a well-prepared batter (*p. 73*); gently and carefully roll them in the batter one by one, so as to keep them in their original form. Place them in very hot (*deep*) fat, and fry for ten minutes. Lift them up with a skimmer, thoroughly drain. Dress them on a hot dish, with a folded napkin, and serve (*with a brandy sauce, p. 99; serves 6*).

BANANAS FRIED

Select six very firm sound red bananas; carefully peel them, cut each one into halves lengthwise, place them on a dish, one beside the other, sprinkle two tablespoonfuls of flour over, gently and carefully roll them in the flour without disturbing their shapes.

Have two gills of sweet (*olive*) oil in a frying pan on the hot range, and when very hot, transfer the half-bananas in and fry them for five minutes on one side, then turn them over and fry for five minutes on the other side. Gently lift them up with a skimmer, dress them on a hot dish with a folded napkin, and send to the table. (*Serves 6.*)

CHARLESTON MODE TO DRESS AND COOK PLANTAINS

Peel them; put them into a tin pan, with sufficient water to prevent burning; add a little butter and brown sugar; sift on a little cinnamon; cook them in a stove or dutch oven till tender, and then brown them.

JULY PICKLES

Pickling season starts properly on the fifth of July, when the watermelon rinds produced by picnics on the Fourth are pickled. Below are mostly cucumber pickles. Other pickles will be found in August, September, and October, as the ingredients ripen. See p. 30 for details of pickling.

Almost anything in the way of young vegetables may be pickled, and almost any whole spice used in the pickle. These recipes can serve as guidelines. If you raise your own cucumbers—and pickle making is a little expensive otherwise—you can pick them every day as they are ready, and drop them into a strong brine (1 pound salt per gallon of water), with a weight to keep them under, until you have enough to pickle. Then soak them 36 hours or more in fresh water, changing the water 3 times.

PICKLED WATER-MELON RIND, EXTREMELY NICE

Equal weight of rind and white sugar
½ ounce white ginger to a gallon pickle
1 pint vinegar to every pound sugar

1 tablespoonful turmeric to a gallon of pickle
(Whole) mace, cloves, and cinnamon to taste

Take the thickest rind you can get, pare off the hard green rind, also the soft inner pulp. Lay the pieces—narrow strips or fanciful cuttings—in brine strong enough to float an egg (*p. 31*), and let them remain in it ten days. Then soak in fair water, changing it every day for ten days. Cover them with clear water in a preserving-kettle, heat slowly and boil five minutes. Take them out and plunge them instantly into ice-water. Leave them in this until next day. Give them another gentle boil of five minutes in strong alum-water (*water to which alum is added: this makes them green and crisp*). Simmer carefully, as a hard boil will injure them. Change *directly* from the alum to the ice-water again, and do not disturb them for four hours. After a third boil of five minutes, let them remain all night in the last water to make them tender. Next day add to enough water to cover the rinds, sufficient sugar to make it quite sweet, but not a syrup. Simmer the rinds in this ten minutes, throw the water away, and spread them upon dishes to cool. Meanwhile, prepare a second syrup, allowing sugar equal in weight to the rind, and half an ounce of sliced white ginger to a gallon of the pickle, with a cup of water for every two pounds of sugar. When the sugar is melted and the syrup quite hot, but not boiling, put in the rinds and simmer until they look quite clear. Take it out, spread it upon the dishes again, while you add to the syrup a pint of vinegar for every pound of sugar you have put in the ginger, turmeric, mace, cloves and cinnamon. Boil this up, return the rind to it, and simmer fifteen minutes. Put up in glass jars. It will be fit for use in two weeks.

These are yellow, not green, watermelon pickles. See also Sweet pickle, p. 236.

MOCK GINGER

Cut into strips the thick rind of a water-melon, trim off the green and cut out the inside until the rind is firm; cover with water into which throw enough soda to make the water taste of it; let stand from 12 to 24 hours; take out, boil in clear water until a straw will go easily through; drain, put into syrup made of good brown sugar (*6 pounds per quart of water, boiled and skimmed*) very strongly flavored with pounded ginger. (*Put the whole into Mason jars and process 30 minutes in a water bath. If left uncanned, the sugar-syrup will ferment and spoil the pickles.*) This is almost as good as ginger preserves. Soda makes the rind more brittle than alum or lime.

Use in any way you would use preserved ginger.

UNIQUE PRESERVE

Gather young cucumbers, a little longer than your middle finger, and lay in strong brine one week. Wash them and soak a day and a night in fair water, changing this four times. Line a bell-metal (*or enamel*) kettle with vine-leaves, lay in the cucumbers, with a little alum scattered among them; fill up with clear water; cover with vine-leaves, then with a close lid, and green as for pickles. Do not let them boil. When well greened, drop in ice-water. When perfectly cold, wipe, and with a small knife slit down one side; dig out the seeds; stuff with a mixture of chopped raisins and citron; sew up the incision with fine thread. Weigh them, and make a syrup, allowing a pound of sugar for every one of cucumbers with a pint of water. Heat to a lively boil, skim, and drop in the fruit. Simmer half an hour, take out and spread upon a dish in the sun while you boil down the syrup, with a few slices of ginger root added. When thick, put in the cucumbers again; simmer five minutes and put up in (*sterilized*) glass jars; tying them up when cold.

"Fresh green corn husks, boiled with sweetmeats, will keep them green."

Ladies' Aid Society, *"Still Another"* Cook Book, 1888

PICKLES

Let your cucumbers be small, fresh-gathered and sound. Make a brine strong enough to bear an egg, boil it and skim it, and pour upon the cucumbers and let it stand 24 hours. Take good vinegar, cloves, cinnamon (*allspice*), and pepper, and boil together. Have your cucumbers in a large stone jar, and pour the hot spiced vinegar over them. If you wish them green, add a little alum with the spices, to boil in the vinegar. Cover them well.

ANOTHER: After scalding them in brine, put them into a mixture of one part whiskey and three parts water; secure them closely. By Christmas they will be hard, of a fine flavor, and retain their original color. The liquor will be an excellent vinegar for the table. (*See p. 30 for pickle-making details.*)

CHOW CHOW

Take six cucumbers just before they ripen, peel, cut in strips and remove the seeds; four white onions, six good-sized heads of cabbage; chop all fine, let them stand in salt and water over night; then pour off the water, and add (*scalding*) vinegar and spices to suit the taste.

SEVEN YEAR PICKLE IN THREE HOURS

Cut two dozen cucumbers in rounds about two inches thick. If they are just off the vine, soak in salt water twenty-four hours, drain from water and boil in weak vinegar one hour. Take from this vinegar and put into strong vinegar (about two quarts), with two pounds of brown sugar, one tablespoonful each of (*whole*) cinnamon, celery seed, black pepper, cloves, mustard and ginger cut into small pieces. Simmer all over the fire one hour. When cold, add one teaspoonful of cayenne pepper and one tablespoonful of grated horse-radish.

KALAMAZOO PICKLES

Half a bushel of small cucumbers; one quart of brown sugar; half a pint of white mustard seed, one ounce of broken cinnamon, one ounce of celery seed, two ounces of alum, seven quarts of vinegar.

The cucumbers should not be more than two or three inches long; nip the remains of the flowers from the end; cover with a brine made of two gallons of water and a pound of salt; let them stand twenty-four hours; drain them, boil the vinegar, alum, and spices; put the cucumbers in jars (FILL the jars with them, as the spaces between leave room for a sufficient quantity of vinegar); pour the boiling vinegar over them, and close immediately. Glass fruit-cans are excellent for pickles, but stone jars will do.

CUCUMBER VINEGAR

Pare and slice fifteen large cucumbers, and put them in a stone jar, with three pints of vinegar, four large onions sliced, two or three shalots, a little garlic, two large spoonfuls of salt, three teaspoonfuls of pepper, and one-half teaspoonful cayenne. After standing four days, give the whole a boil; when cold, strain and filter the liquor through paper.

CUCUMBER CATSUP

One dozen full-grown cucumbers, pared; one dozen onions. Grate the cucumbers and leave them on a sieve while the onions are being grated; put both together in a large bowl and mix thoroughly; add salt, spices, mustard, and turmeric to the taste; also, if liked, a little sugar and horse-radish, and vinegar to liquify the mass sufficiently for bottling.

Save catsup bottles, sterilize them and fill with this, and mark them.

PINE-APPLE PICKLE

Pineapples are plentiful in late July.

To fourteen pounds of fruit cut in slices of small pieces, add seven pounds of brown sugar and seven pints of vinegar, as many cloves as you can hold in the palm of your hand, and as many peppercorns, stick cinnamon broken into small bits. Let the sugar, vinegar and spices boil ten minutes before adding the fruit. Let all boil together until the fruit is tender and well-seasoned, then remove the fruit, and let the syrup boil five or ten minutes longer. (*Pack the fruit in hot, sterile jars; pour the syrup over it; seal.*)

Pineapples can also be added to peach preserves (p. 255) to the advantage of both.

JULY VEGETABLES

FRIED CUCUMBERS

When pared, cut them in slices as thick as a dollar. Dry them with a cloth, and season with salt and pepper, and sprinkle them well with flour. Have butter hot and lay them in. Fry of a light brown and send to table hot. They make a breakfast dish.

Cucumbers are easier to find in the garden if you train the vines to grow up a chicken-wire fence.

"Scoop out the inside of a turnip, scallop the edges downward on the earth. Insects will pass into it as a place of refuge and the cucumbers, squashes, melons, etc., will soon be clear of them."
Mrs. Abell, *Ladies' Guide*, 1852

CUCUMBERS FRIED IN BATTER

Pare three cucumbers, cut them into slices one-sixteenth of an inch thick, dredge them with salt and pepper, and let them lie fifteen minutes. Beat one egg (the white and yolk together) until light; add to it a half-pint of milk, a half-teaspoon of salt, two dashes of black pepper, and a cup and a half of sifted flour; beat until smooth. Dip the pieces of cucumber into this batter and fry in boiling fat or oil. The fat must be deep enough to float them. When done, take them out with a skimmer (piercing them with a fork will make them fall), drain them on brown paper and serve very hot.

BIMBO HASH

Take two large cucumbers and wash them. Peel and dice them; slice two onions. Skin and seed and chop tomatoes to equal the bulk of the cucumbers and onions (*about four tomatoes*). Add breadcrumbs to equal the bulk of the whole, and a little water if necessary. Stew until cooked. Serve with butter.

STUFFED CUCUMBERS

Peel six small cucumbers, pare them carefully and shapely; cut off the lower ends, and with a vegetable-spoon empty them, after extracting the seeds. Place them in a slightly acidulated water (*water with a little lemon juice or vinegar in it*); rinse them well, and parboil them in boiling water for three minutes. Remove them, and put in cold water to cool. Drain them, and fill the insides with a cooked forcemeat made of the breasts of chickens. Line a small frying-pan with slices of pork skin (*bacon rind*); add the cucumbers, season with a pinch of salt and half a pinch of pepper, a bouquet (*parsley, bay, thyme, marjoram, celery tied up together*), a glassful of white wine, two cloves, and a spoonful of dripping from any kind of roast. Cover with a piece of buttered paper, and place it in a slow oven to cook gently for twenty minutes. When done, transfer them carefully to a hot dish; free them entirely from any fat, pour half a pint of Madeira sauce (*p. 439*) over them, and serve.

FORCEMEAT: Cut in large pieces two raw chicken breasts, pound them in a mortar, adding the same quantity of bread soaked in milk, a teaspoonful of fresh butter and four egg yolks, seasoning with half a tablespoonful of salt, a scant teaspoonful of pepper, and a teaspoonful of nutmeg. Mix all together; strain and put it in a bowl with three tablespoons of velouté sauce (*p. 439*).

WHITE CUCUMBER SAUCE

Peel two cucumbers, divide each lengthwise in four, remove the pips, and cut into pieces one inch long; add, in stewpan, one ounce of butter, a teaspoonful of sugar, one-half one of salt; let it stew on the fire for fifteen minutes, then add a gill of white sauce (*p. 438*), six spoonfuls of milk, broth, or water; simmer gently and skim, add a tablespoonful of roux (*equal parts of flour and butter, rubbed together*), and serve where directed, but observe that all these garnitures ought to be served under meat, and over poultry.

Serve with chicken or veal or fish. See p. 117 for brown cucumber sauce.

"*Try cucumber peelings for cockroaches; they will act like a poison to them.*"

The Caloric Book of Recipes, 1907

CUCUMBERS WITH DILL

Rake each cucumber with the tines of a fork, in parallel lines, to give each slice a design. Slice thin, then put in a bowl and sprinkle salt over them liberally. Let stand 2 hours. Pour off the liquid and rinse the cucumbers in clear water; drain. Mix 2 tablespoons of sugar into 1 cup of warm cider vinegar; add a little pepper and a generous amount of dill (2 tablespoonfuls fresh, snipped; 1 tablespoonful dried). Pour it on the cucumbers and refrigerate for 2 hours before serving. This will keep at least a week. It goes well as a salad with rich food.

CUCUMBER SOUP

Pare, split and empty (*of seeds*) from eight to twenty well-grown cucumbers; throw a little salt over them and leave them for one hour to drain; then put them with a couple of small onions in a deep stewpan and cover them with nearly one-half inch of pale but good veal stock (*p. 131*), and stew them gently until tender (three-quarters of an hour to an hour and a quarter); work the whole through a hair sieve (*or purée in a blender*); and add as much stock as may be needed to make the quantity desired for tables; stir to it when it boils as much arrowroot or rice flour as will thicken it pleasantly; add from one-half to one pint of boiling cream and serve immediately. Salt and cayenne sufficient to season it should be thrown over the cucumbers while they are stewing. The yolks of six or eight eggs, mixed with a dessertspoonful of chili vinegar, may be used instead of cream; and three dessertspoonfuls of minced parsley may then be strewed into it a couple of minutes before they are added; it must not, of course, be allowed to boil after.

Canned milk, undiluted, can always be substituted for cream in soup.

SAVORY CUCUMBER SOUP

To each 4 washed, unpeeled cucumbers, allow 1 small, unpeeled potato, 1 leek or 3 scallions, and 5 or 6 stalks of parsley. Chop all into large dice. Cover with 1 quart of beef broth and cook until the vegetables are tender. Purée the soup in a blender, then season it with salt, white pepper and summer savory. Just before serving, add 1 cup of cream and reheat, but do not boil.

This freezes well; add the cream after thawing it.

BEETS

Beets will be ready in early July, or ready again in September. They do not like hot weather.

Wash them clean with a cloth, rubbing them well. Be careful not to cut them unless they are very large, and then you may cut them in two, not splitting them. (*Leave about 1 inch of the leaf-stalks on; if the skin is broken, beets will lose color in boiling. After cooking, the peels slip right off.*) When tender all through (*in 1 hour or more*), scrape off the outside, split or cut them in thin round slices, and pour over melted butter and sprinkle with pepper. Boiled beets sliced and put into spiced vinegar until pickled are good. The tops of beets are good in summer boiled as greens. Beets should be kept in the cellar, covered with earth to keep them fresh. It is said that they are nicer roasted as potatoes for the table.

BEET-ROOT

Take two nice young boiled beet-roots, which will take about from two to three hours to simmer in plenty of boiling water, peel when cold, cut in slanting directions, so as to make oval pieces; peel and cut in small dice two middling-sized onions, put in a pan with two ounces of butter, fry white, stirring constantly with a spoon; add a spoonful of flour and enough milk to make a thickish sauce, add to it three saltspoonfuls of salt, four of sugar, one of pepper, a spoonful of good vinegar, and boil a few minutes; put in the slices to simmer for about twenty minutes; have ready some mashed potatoes, with which make a neat border in your dish one inch high, then put the beet-root and sauce, highly seasoned, in the centre, and serve. (*Serves 4–6.*)

FRENCH WAY OF DRESSING COLD BEET-ROOT: Take your cold beet-root, chop it very small and put it in a saucepan to heat, with a little cream; immediately before serving, put in a spoonful of vinegar and a little brown sugar.

BEET SALAD

Boil a deep-red beet until quite tender; pare, and cut in dice. Have a root or two of endive, well-blanched, washed and dried; six button onions, and two stalks of celery cut. Rub the yolk of a hard-boiled egg with a little salt, a little powdered sugar, mustard, and enough thick and slightly sour cream to dress the salad, and vinegar to the taste. Pour it over the beet, etc., garnish and serve.

PICKLED BEETS

Boil a quart of vinegar with an ounce of whole black pepper and an equal weight of dry ginger (*or whole cloves*), and let it stand until quite cold. Pour over cold sliced beets (*and let it stand 24 hours or longer*).

SWEET CORN

Sweet corn will barely be in by the end of July, but it is always eagerly awaited. The tender hybrids we eat now are less than fifty years old. Much of the corn referred to in old recipes is either Indian or field corn, tough, durable stuff that probably needed every minute of the 30 to 60 minutes' boiling it got. No matter what the old recipes say, no modern sweet corn should be boiled for more than five minutes.

The sugar in sweet corn begins to turn to starch the moment it is picked, so the fresher you can get it, the better it will taste.

Season with sweet butter or cream, salt, pepper, a little nutmeg, and a tablespoonful of loaf sugar. It makes a most delightful dish to accompany a nice bit of boiled pork.

Serve melted butter with corn on the cob, to be put on with a small paint or pastry brush.

FRIED SWEET CORN

Cut tender (*raw*) corn off the cob. Put it in a pan, and add sufficient water to moisten it, a little salt and butter, and fry it to your liking.

CREAMED CORN

Boil the corn on the cob or use left-over boiled sweet corn. Cut it carefully from the cob (but do not scrape) and season highly with salt and pepper. There should be a good pint of corn when cut. Melt one rounding tablespoonful of butter, stir in one tablespoonful of flour, then pour over it one cupful of milk, stir until boiling, then add one-half teaspoonful of salt and a dash of pepper, and mix it while hot with the corn. Turn into a shallow buttered baking dish, cover the top thickly with fine buttered bread crumbs, and bake until brown.

CORN PUDDING

One pint of scraped corn pulp, two eggs beaten separately, the (*stiffly beaten*) white added last, one and one-half tablespoons flour, one cup of milk, one-half teaspoon of salt, a heaping teaspoon of sugar, one good pinch of pepper and a tablespoonful of butter melted. Bake (*at 375°*) in a buttered baking dish about thirty minutes (*keeping the dish covered for the first 20 minutes*), or until set in the centre. (*Serves 6.*)

GREEN CORN, BAKED

Green corn is field corn, sown in May, harvested for feed in August —but picked in July for eating, before the outer husk turns yellow and the inner grains turn hard: "When the grains become yellow it is too old. Strip it of the outside leaves and the silk, but let the inner leaves remain, as they will keep in the sweetness." (Miss Eliza Leslie, *Directions for Cookery,* 1870) *Old sweet corn makes a good substitute.*

Cut with a sharp knife through the centre of every row of grains of eighteen ears of corn, and cut off the outer edge; then with the back of the knife, push out the yellow eye, with the rich, creamy centre of the grain, leaving the hull on the cob. Beat six eggs very light, and add a quarter of a pound of butter, creamed and stirred in with a pint of *very* warm milk; mix well, and beat until very light; add two tablespoonfuls of light brown sugar and a little salt; put in a deep dish, and bake in a quick oven for three-quarters of an hour. Serve hot, in the same dish. (*Serves 12.*)

[221]

Or, one dozen ears, cut or grated, one pint of sweet milk, two eggs, and two ounces of butter, mixed well and baked three-quarters of an hour. (*Serves 8.*)

CORN OYSTERS

Six nice large ears of corn, score them by cutting through the centre of the grains, then scrape, not cut, from the cob. Add to this three well-beaten eggs (whites and yolks beaten separately), a half-teaspoonful salt. Drop a tablespoonful of the batter in a frying pan with hot butter and fry them a nice brown. Some add a teacupful of flour and half a cup of butter to this. (*Serves 6.*)

GREEN CORN SOUP

6 *ears sweet corn, or enough to make 1 pint raw pulp*	½ *saltspoon white pepper*
Water to cover the ears	1 *teaspoonful sugar*
1 *pint milk or cream*	1 *teaspoon flour*
1 *teaspoon salt*	1 *tablespoon butter*

With a very sharp knife, scrape the thinnest possible shaving from each row of kernels, and then, with the back of the knife, scrape out the pulp, leaving the hull on the cob. Break the cobs if long, and put them on to boil in enough water to cover them. Boil thirty minutes and strain. There should be about one pint of water after straining. Put the corn water on to boil again, and when boiling, add the corn pulp. Cook fifteen minutes. Add salt, pepper, sugar and the boiling milk. Thicken with one teaspoonful of flour and one tablespoonful of butter cooked together. Boil five minutes and serve. (*Serves 4–6.*)

Corn is better for soup when it is a little old for the table, and the pulp is thick rather than milky.

CORN CHOWDER

1 *quart raw sweet corn*	A *two-inch cube of salt pork*
1 *pint sliced potatoes*	1 *onion*

1 saltspoonful white pepper	1 pint sliced tomatoes
1 large tablespoonful butter	1 pint milk
1 teaspoonful salt	6 crisped crackers

Scrape the raw corn from the cob. Boil the cobs twenty minutes in water enough to cover them; then skim them out. Pare, soak and scald the potatoes. Fry the onion in the salt pork fat, and strain the fat into the kettle with the corn water. Add the potatoes, corn, tomatoes, salt, and pepper. Simmer fifteen minutes, or till the potatoes and corn are tender. Add the butter and milk, and serve very hot with crisped crackers. (*Serves 8–10.*)

CREOLE CORN

Peel and cut in quarters four good-sized tomatoes; put these in a saucepan with a dozen okra washed and cut in thin slices; cover and stew slowly for twenty minutes; add the pulp of a dozen ears of corn, a level teaspoonful of salt, one of sweet pepper chopped fine, a dash of white pepper; cook over hot water for fifteen minutes; add either four tablespoons of cream or two tablespoons of butter and send at once to the table. (*Serves 8.*)

Served with chicken, this forms a most desirable sauce. (*It may be canned.*)

TO DRY GREEN CORN

It must be gathered when just good to boil, strip off the husks and throw them (*the corn*) in boiling water, and let them remain until the water boils over them, then take them out, and shell off the corn by running the prong of a fork along the base of the grain. This method saves the kernel whole and is much more expeditious. Spread it thin until thoroughly dry. When cooked, put it in cold water and boil three hours. Let the water nearly boil off, add a little milk and sweet cream, or butter, pepper and salt, and it is very nice. It is a nice rare dish in winter and spring.

This can be used in making winter succotash or bean porridge. Hulled corn, another means of drying Indian corn, involves soaking the kernels in a lye solution, made by leaching water through wood ashes, until the hulls loosen from each kernel. The corn is then rinsed well in clear water, the hulls are rubbed off, and spread to dry in the shade outdoors, or in a cool oven.

MILKWEED TOPS

are very nice when cut young. They are improved by cultivation. They require nearly an hour to boil. (*Cut them when very tender; drain, press out the water after cooking, serve with butter, salt, and pepper like other greens.*)

Dry herbs just before they begin to flower. They have the most pungency then. Dry on screens in the open air, in shade, not sunlight. Or use the oven to dry them, on a low heat with the door open, if they will not dry outdoors in one or two days. Keep in tightly closed containers and they will last two years or more.

> *"Such as like a variety of herb spicery in soup, will find it convenient to have the following mixture:—When in their prime, take sweet marjoram, sweet basil, thyme, and summer savory; dry them thoroughly; pound them and sift them; steep them for two weeks in brandy. The spirit is then fit for use."*
>
> Mrs. Ellet, *The Improved Housekeeper*, 1854

TURTLES

Turtles and terrapins are almost never available in fish markets any more. So if you need a turtle recipe, it is probably because the snapping turtles are becoming troublesome in the old swimming hole—and that is most noticeable in July. Dressing one is a complicated maneuver.

TO DRESS TURTLE

Cut off the head in the morning, in summer; at evening in winter; hang it up by the hind fins, and let it bleed well; with care, separate the bottom shell from the top, lest you break the gall bladder, which, with care, take out and throw away; throw the liver into a bowl of water; empty the chitterlings (guts), and throw them into water; the eggs also, if any—have a separate bowl for each article; slice all the meat from the under shell; wash clean and put in a pot, completely covering it with water, and add to it one pound of middling (or a flitch of bacon), with four chopped onions, and set it on the fire to boil. Open the chitterlings; clean them thoroughly, take off the inside skin, and put them in the pot with the shell; let them boil three hours steadily; if the water boils away too much, add more.

The top:—wash the top shell neatly, after cutting out all the meat; cover and set it by.

Parboil the fins, clean them perfectly, taking off all the black skin, and throw them into water. Now cut the flesh taken from both shells in small pieces; cut the fins in two, and lay them in a dish with the flesh, sprinkle over some salt, and cover up the dish.

When the shell, chitterlings, etc., are done, or have boiled three hours, take out the bacon, scrape the shell clean, and strain the liquor—about one quart of which must be put back into the pot; reserve the rest of the soup. Pick out the chitterlings, and cut them into small pieces; select the nice bits that have been strained out, and put them with the chitterlings in the gravy; add the fins, cut in pieces, to them, and enough of the flesh to fill the upper shell; add to it, if a large turtle, one bottle of white wine, cayenne pepper, and salt to your taste; one gill of mushroom catsup, one gill of lemon pickle (*p. 404*), mace, cloves and nutmeg pounded to highly season it; mix two spoonfuls of flour with one pound and a quarter of butter; add, with them, marjoram, thyme, parsley and savory tied in a bunch; stew all these together till the flesh and fins are tender; wash out the top shell; place a thin paste round the brim; sprinkle over the shell salt and pepper, then take the herbs out of the stew; if the gravy is not sufficiently thick, add a little more flour, and fill the shell. If no eggs in the turtle, boil six new-laid ones for ten minutes; put them in cold water for a few minutes (*to make them easier to peel*), peel them, cut them in two, and place them on the turtle. Make a rich forcemeat; fry the balls nicely, and place them also in the shell. Place the shell in a dripping pan, with something underneath the sides to steady it, heat the oven as for bread, and bake till a fine brown. Fry the liver, and send it up hot.

TURTLE SOUP

This is for a turtle of from forty to fifty pounds. It should invariably be made the day before it is wanted.

Cut the callipash (upper shell) and the callipee (under shell) into pieces six inches square, which put into a stockpot with some light veal stock. Let it boil until the meat is tender, and then take it out into cold water; free the meat from the bones, and cut it into pieces one inch square. Return the bones to the stock and let it boil gently for two hours, strain it off, and it is then fit for use. Cut the fins across into pieces about one inch wide, boil them in stock with an onion, two or three cloves, a faggot of parsley and thyme, a sprig of sweet basil and marjoram. When tender, take them out and add this stock to the other. Take the lean meat, put into a stewpan with a pint of Madeira, four tablespoons of chopped green shallots (*or scallions*), two lemons sliced, a bunch of thyme, marjoram and savory (about two tablespoons, chopped), one and a half tablespoons sweet basil (chopped) and four tablespoons of parsley. Pound together a nutmeg, two dozen allspice, one blade of mace, five or six cloves, one tablespoon of pepper and salt. Mix the whole together with as much curry powder as will lie on a shilling (*a heaping teaspoon*). Put about two-thirds of this to the lean meat, with half a pound of fresh butter and one quart stock. Let the whole be gently sweated until the meat is done. Take a large knuckle of ham, cut it into very small dice, put into a stewpan with four large onions sliced, six bay leaves, three blades mace (*about 1 teaspoon*), one dozen allspice, three-quarters of a pound of butter; let it sweat until the onions are melted. Shred a small bunch of basil; a larger one of thyme, savory and marjoram; throw these with the onions and keep them as green as possible; when sweated sufficiently, add flour according to your judgment sufficient to thicken the soup. Add by degrees the stock in which the callipash and callipee were boiled, and the seasoning stock from the lean meat. Boil one hour; run through a tammy (*sieve*), and add salt, cayenne and lemon juice to palate. Then put in the meat; let it all boil gently about half an hour; and if more wine be required, it must be boiled before being added to the soup.

SALT FISH

There was once a curious belief that fresh meat was too exciting a food for summer use: "corned beef . . . is used to give variety to your diet in summer when fresh meats prove too stimulating. It is eaten by the working-man to give bulk to his food." Of course, the lack of refrigeration and the hot days may have had something to do with this prejudice—but it seems a good enough excuse to include salt-fish recipes in July. Salt cod, salt herrings, mackerel, and sardines are still available, although somewhat expensive, in some supermarkets.

STEWED SALT COD

Soak salt fish overnight in plenty of clear water, skin side up. Warm water, changed occasionally, speeds the process somewhat, sour milk speeds it even more. But do not be hasty; there is little as inedible as undersoaked salt fish.

Pick some soaked cod in flakes, and put it in a stewpan, with a tablespoonful of butter worked into the same of flour, and as much milk as will moisten it; let it stew gently for ten minutes; add pepper to taste, and serve hot; put it in a deep dish, slice hard-boiled eggs over, and sprigs of parsley around the edge. This is a nice relish for breakfast, with coffee or tea, and rolls or toast.

SALT FISH SOUFFLÉ

One pint of finely shredded boiled salt codfish; eight potatoes; three-quarters of a cup of milk; four eggs; two tablespoons of butter; salt and pepper. Peel the potatoes and boil thirty minutes. Drain the water from them and mash very fine. Then mix thoroughly with the fish. Add the butter, seasoning, and hot milk. Have two of the eggs well beaten, stir them into the mixture, and put in the dish in which it is to be served. Place in the oven for ten minutes. Beat the whites of the two remaining eggs to a stiff froth, and add a quarter of a teaspoonful of salt; then add the yolks, spread this over the dish of fish. Return to the oven until brown, and serve at once.

MOCK OYSTER STEW

Prepare one cup of salt fish by washing, shredding and simmering until soft; when ready to serve, put it in a shallow dish with one pint of oyster crackers or three butter crackers split and browned, and pour over it one pint of hot milk. Add a tablespoonful of butter and half a saltspoonful of pepper, and serve.

[11]

AUGUST

Eggs; pickles; August vegetables; melons; mushrooms; August fruits; elderberries; nasturtiums; frogs

EGGS

Chickens hatch at any time of year, but more of them are hatched in the late winter to take advantage of the summer growing season. They begin to lay at about 26 weeks of age, so pullet eggs are often available in the late spring. But egg prices seem to drop, at least in the country, as the egg supply increases in August.

Most food prices have gone up—but in 1890 eggs cost 40¢ to 50¢ a dozen, perhaps equivalent to $1.50 a dozen now. They were still a bargain, old books insist, since they are pure protein.

BAKED EGGS EN COQUILLE

Take half a cup of soft bread crumbs, an equal quantity of fine-chopped ham or tongue, and a little pepper, salt, parsley, mustard and butter, melted. Make it into a smooth paste with hot milk or cream. Spread this mixture on some scallop shells. Break eggs carefully, and put one in the centre of each shell; sprinkle with a little salt and pepper, and fine cracker crumbs moistened with melted butter. Set in the oven and bake till the egg is firm.

OR: Put the meat and bread mixture in a baking dish, shaping it a little to hold six or seven raw eggs; cover lightly with bread crumbs and bake till the whites of the eggs are firm. (*Serves 6 or so.*)

Grated Parmesan and a little chopped onion can be substituted for the meat.

BAKED EGGS WITH ASPARAGUS

Cut twenty heads of sprue (*asparagus*) into small pieces, keeping only the tender part; boil them for fifteen minutes, put them in a stew-pot with half an ounce of butter, set them on the fire for three minutes, season with a little pepper, salt, and sugar; when done, put them in the dish you intend to serve it in, break six eggs over, which season with one pinch of pepper, half a spoonful of salt, and half an ounce of butter in small pieces; put them into the oven until it sets, and serve. (*Serves 4–6.*)

Eggs can be baked in tomato shells: Slice off the top, scoop out the insides, season with salt, pepper, and butter, and break the egg into it. Sprinkle with bread crumbs and grated cheese. Bake about 20 minutes in a hot oven.

SOUR EGGS, GERMAN STYLE

Melt two tablespoons of butter in a pan, stir in one tablespoon flour and brown well. Then thin with one-half scant cup vinegar and one-half cup water. Season with salt, pepper and a pinch of sugar. Let mixture boil up, then break eggs into it one at a time until the pan is full. Baste the eggs with this gravy until they are cooked to taste.

OMELETS

can be made with just about anything. Beat the egg yolks with a little milk or cream, salt and pepper, then fold in the whisked whites. Pour into a hot, buttered omelet pan, let it set over the fire for a few minutes, then sprinkle the filling carefully over it and finish cooking, so that both omelet and filling are equally hot and done. Fold it over carefully, slide out of the pan, and serve.

Grate the cheese for cheese omelets, or shave it thin. Or use crumbled cheese that has been frozen.

Fry chopped chicken livers first, adding parsley, chervil, mushrooms, and perhaps a little Madeira or Madeira sauce (*p. 439*).

Curry powder, stirred into chopped chicken with a little cream sauce, makes a nice omelet filling.

Add cold cooked rice to the eggs, to make a rice omelet.

Some people, unaccountably, like jelly omelets. The jelly should be added just before the omelet is folded over.

Ham, either in thin slices or minced with onions and mushrooms; raw sliced tomatoes with oregano; cooked clams chopped fine with a little grated lemon rind; raw oysters cut in half; shrimp alone or with chopped green peppers—all make good omelets.

For a thin dessert omelet, grated orange rind with some juice and a little powdered sugar may be beaten into the eggs with cream instead of milk.

"A little boiling water added to an omelet will keep it from being tough."

The Caloric Book of Recipes, 1907

EGG TOAST

Put the yolks of four eggs and the whites of two with four ounces of clarified butter; beat them well together, then stir it over the fire in the same direction till mixed. Make a round of thin delicate toast, spread anchovy paste over it, then put on the mixture with a fork. Cut the toast into pieces and serve very hot. (*Serves 4.*)

"When eggs are poached, put a little lemon juice or vinegar in the water to make the white firm."

Mrs. Ludlum, *The New and the Old in Cookery,* 1891

MRS. G'S STUFFED EGGS

Boil six eggs twenty minutes, remove the shells, divide the eggs in halves, taking a slice from each end so they will stand like cups, take out the yolks and mash fine and put with them one-quarter teaspoon of white pepper, one-half teaspoon salt, one tablespoon melted butter, four tablespoons of milk, three drops onion juice. Mix these thoroughly together, fill the egg cups with it and set in the oven six minutes.

SAUCE FOR SAME: One tablespoon melted butter, one tablespoon flour, one cup of hot milk, one-half saltspoonful of salt, one-quarter saltspoonful of white pepper; put the melted butter in the flour, stirring all the time; then gradually pour on the hot milk; when thoroughly mixed, add the salt and pepper. Take the eggs from the oven, and pour the sauce around them; garnish with parsley.

STUFFED EGGS

Hard-boil eggs, plunge them into cold water and remove the shells; cut them in half, remove the yolks; mash the yolks together, moistening them with a little cream, sour cream, or mayonnaise, season them with salt and pepper; stir in red caviar and chopped parsley.

OR: *Moisten them with pickle brine, season with salt, pepper, dry mustard; stir in capers and pickle relish.*

OR: *Moisten with vinegar or lemon juice; season with salt and white pepper; stir in chopped olives and anchovies.*

Refill the egg whites with the yolk mixture and garnish the whole with paprika, watercress or parsley, or small pickles.

"Egg shells crushed up, will clean your water bottle and vinegar cruet beautifully."

The Caloric Book of Recipes, 1907

Egg shells, dropped into a gallon jug of water and allowed to steep four or five days, make good liquid fertilizer for plants.

TO MAKE EGG BALLS FOR SOUP

Take the yolks of six hard-boiled eggs, pound them in a mortar, with a little flour, a sprinkle of salt, and the yolks of two raw eggs; mix all well together, roll it into little balls, drop each into boiling water.

"A way to test good eggs is to put them in a pail of water, and if they are good, they will lie on their sides always; if bad, they will

stand on their small ends, the large end always uppermost, unless they have been shaken considerably, when they will stand either end up. Any egg that lies flat is good to eat, and can be depended upon. When eggs are stale, the whites will be thin and watery, and the yolk will not be a uniform color, when broken; if there is no mustiness or disagreeable smell, eggs in this state are not unfit. A new-laid egg will generally recommend itself by the delicate transparency of its shell."

Miss E. Myers, *The Home Cook Book*, 1880

Very fresh eggs should not be hard-boiled, since it is almost impossible to remove their shells neatly.

TO PRESERVE EGGS

Chicken farmers coat eggs with a solution that stops up the airholes in the shells, and refrigerate them practically at the moment of laying. This adds to the eggs' shelf-life—in fact, from the way store-bought eggs sometimes act in soufflés, it would surprise me if they even reach city supermarket shelves until they are two or three months old. Fresh eggs are superior, but if it is impossible to get them regularly, they might be bought en masse *when egg prices are lowest and stored according to the following recipe:*

Put into a tub or other vessel, half a peck of unslaked lime, four ounces of salt, and one ounce of cream of tartar, and mix the same together with as much water as will reduce the composition or mixture to that consistence which will cause an egg put into it to swim with its top just under the liquid. Then put and keep the eggs therein, which preserve them perfectly sound for the space of a year at least.

THE FRENCH METHOD OF PRESERVING EGGS

is to dissolve beeswax and olive oil and anoint the eggs all over. If left undisturbed in a cool place, they will remain good for two years.

PICKLES

Almost anything that is grown in August can be pickled. It is a good way to preserve an overabundance, and home-made pickles were as common on nineteenth-century tables, and as necessary, as salt and pepper. (See p. 30 for the details of pickle making.)

TO PICKLE PEACHES

Take some sound cling-stone peaches, remove the down with a brush; make one gallon of vinegar hot, add to it four pounds of brown sugar, boil it and skim well, stick five or six cloves into each peach, then pour the vinegar boiling hot over them, cover them over and set them in a cold place for eight to ten days; then drain off the vinegar, make it hot, skim it, and again pour it over the peaches, let them become cold, then put them into glass jars and secure them as for preserves. (*Makes enough for 10 quarts of peaches.*)

TO PICKLE PLUMS LIKE OLIVES

Take the plums before they are quite ripe, and put them into a saucepan with some white wine vinegar, salt water, fennel seed, and dill, as much of each as will impart a flavor to the pickle; when it boils, put in the plums, let it boil again, then take it off, let it stand till cold, then put in jars.

PEPPERS, PICKLED WITH CABBAGE

Take such as are fresh and green; cut a small slit in them; take the seeds out carefully and neatly with a small knife; and wash them. Pour weak boiling brine over them, and let them stand four days, renewing the brine daily boiling hot. Chop cabbage fine; season it highly with (*whole*) cinnamon, cloves, and mace; then stuff the peppers, adding nasturtiums if liked. Sew them up nicely; and turn the same *sharp* vinegar boiling hot over them (*drain it from them, heat it, then return it*), three successive weeks, adding a little alum at the last.

Tomatoes, if green and small, are good pickled with the peppers.

PICKLED PEPPERS

The bell pepper should be gathered when half grown. Slit the side and carefully take out the seed and core so as not to injure the shell. Pour over them a strong hot brine and keep them warm; some simmer them a whole day. You may take them out next morning, when cool, and lay them in a jar, with (*whole*) mustard sprinkled over them, and fill up the jar with vinegar. They require no spice and should be pickled alone. The vinegar may be put on cold, with a piece of alum to give them a fine green.

GREEN BEANS PICKLED

Gather them half grown, and pickle them in cold vinegar and spices.

TO PICKLE FRENCH BEANS AND RADISH PODS

Gather them while quite small and tender. Keep them in salt and water, till you get through collecting them, changing the water as often as once in four or five days. Then scald them with hot salt and water, let them lie in it till cool, then turn on hot vinegar, spiced with pepper-corns (*whole*), allspice and mace. The radish top, if pickled in small bunches, is a pretty garnish for other pickles.

PICKLED (*GREEN*) BEANS

Select your beans; string and wash them. Make a brine of salt and water strong enough to bear an egg. Put your beans into it, and let them remain until they change color. Then take them out, and wash them in clear water. Line the bottom of your kettle with green cabbage leaves, and put in your beans, and as much vinegar and water, or clear water, as will cover them. Lay cabbage leaves over the top; put them over a slow fire, and let them get scalding hot. When they are green, take them out, and let them drain. Put them in jars with some (*whole*) allspice, cloves, a little mustard seed, and some scraped horse-radish, and enough vinegar to cover them. Tie (*cover*) them close and keep them in a cool dry place.

Brine from pickles can be used for vinegar in salad dressings, for making stuffed eggs, and for flavoring fish sauces.

PICKLED EGGS

Boil twelve eggs quite hard, and lay them in cold water to peel off the shell, then put them in a stone (*or glass*) jar with one quarter-ounce of mace, the same of (*whole*) cloves, a sliced nutmeg, a tablespoonful of whole pepper, a little ginger root and a peach leaf. Fill the jar with boiling vinegar and cover it that it may cool slowly. After three days, boil the vinegar again and return it to the eggs and spices. They will be fit for use in a fortnight.

ANOTHER: Boil the eggs very hard; when cold, shell them and cut them in halves lengthwise. Lay them carefully in a large-mouthed jar, and pour over them some scalding vinegar well-seasoned with whole pepper, allspice, a few pieces of ginger and a few cloves of garlic. When cold, tie up closely, and let them stand a month. They are then fit for use.

MUSHROOMS PICKLED

Choose small white mushrooms; they should be of one night's growth. Cut off the roots, and rub the mushrooms clean with a bit of flannel and salt. Put them in a jar, allowing to every quart of mushrooms 1 ounce each of salt and ginger, ½ ounce of whole pepper, 8 blades of mace (*½ teaspoonful*), a bay leaf, a strip of lemon-rind, and a wineglassful of sherry. Cover the jar close and let it stand on the stove so as to be thoroughly heated and on the point of boiling; so let it remain a day or two till the liquor is absorbed by the mushrooms and spices; then cover them with hot vinegar, close them again and stand till it just comes to a boil, then remove from the fire.

When they are quite cold, divide the mushrooms and spice into wide-mouth bottles, fill them up with boiling vinegar. Be sure the vinegar covers the mushrooms. Seal air tight.

ANOTHER: Gather the buttons, peel them in water, wash and drain. Put them in a saucepan, then add a good quantity of salt, some whole pepper, cloves, mace and nutmegs; let them boil in their own liquor for one-quarter hour over a brisk fire. Remove from the fire and drain, and put mushrooms in jars. Add to the liquor and spice an equal quantity of white wine and vinegar; add a few bay leaves; let boil a few minutes. Pour it over the mushrooms and seal at once.

[235]

SOUTHERN YELLOW PICKLES

Take six pounds of sugar, one ginger, one horseradish, five tamarisk, eight ounces mustard, two pepper and one of mace, with three gallons of vinegar. Quarter your cabbage (*10 to 12 heads*), scald in strong brine, let lie one day, then place it in the sun till *crisp* dry. Put it in vinegar to soak out the salt. Then pack it in a stone pot, putting between the layers the pulverized and mixed spices, shred horseradish, tamarisk and sugar. *Cover* with the best cider vinegar. See daily, for a week, that it *stays* covered. (May possiby be improved by a few turnings-off [*of the vinegar*] and scaldings.) Cover *close*: keep pot *in the sun* for awhile; always in a dry place. Peaches, cucumbers, onions, *et ceteras*, may be added, if prepared in brine and then in vinegar. Should not be used in under a year:—will improve for many years.

GREEN PICKLE

Cucumbers, snap-beans, gherkins (*small cucumbers*), green fox grapes and (*green*) tomatoes are principally used for this pickle. Put your materials in brine that will bear an egg. Let them remain so for a fortnight, or as long as you choose, for they remain for six months, or even a year, thus without injury if you only see to it that they are well covered with grape leaves, weighted down upon them and submerged in brine. When you are ready to pickle, take them out and soak them in weak vinegar for several days, then scald them in strong spiced vinegar. Put (which will be sufficient for a peck of pickles) four ounces long pepper, one ounce of cloves, four ounces of mustard seed (half white, half black), one ounce of mace, two ounces of celery seed, six red pepper pods, a handful of horseradish; sweetening to your taste. Three pounds (*of sugar*) would not be too much for most modern tastes.

SWEET PICKLE

Eight pounds of fruit, four pounds best brown sugar, one quart of vinegar, one cup of mixed whole spices—stick cinnamon, cassia buds (*cardamom can be substituted*), allspice and cloves; less of the latter than the former. Tie the spices in a bag, and boil with the vinegar and sugar. Skim well; then add the fruit. Cook ten minutes, or till scalded and tender. Skim out the fruit, and put into stone (*or glass*) jars. Boil the syrup five minutes longer, and pour over the fruit. The next morning pour off the syrup and boil down again, and do this for three mornings. Keep the bag of spices in the syrup. (*Makes 6–8 quarts.*)

RIPE CUCUMBER OR WATERMELON RIND: Cut the pared rind into slices. Boil one ounce of alum in one gallon of water, pour it on the rinds, and let them stand several hours on the back of the stove (*or, covered, in the hot sun*). Take out into cold water, and when cold, boil them half an hour in the sweet pickle.

RIPE MUSKMELON OR CANTALOUPE: Pare and cut into thick slices. Pour the boiling syrup over them. Proceed as above.

EAST INDIA PICKLE

Take radish pods, green peppers long and round, green (*unripe*) grapes, capers, nasturtiums (*buds or seed pods*), walnuts, butternuts, peaches, apricots, cherries and button onions; pour over them a hot brine that will bear an egg and let them stand four days, stirring every day. Then make a pickle very warm with spices, and after it has been boiled, pour it over them boiling hot; mustard seed must be added, and then it must be covered close from the air. This will keep, if well prepared, two years.

Ground spices can be substituted for whole spices if you tie them up in a muslin bag.

PICKLED MANGOES

Mangoes were melons or peppers or fruits stuffed with a pickling mixture, a nineteenth-century favorite.

Young musk or nutmeg melons	Whole pepper-corns, 1 dozen
English mustard-seed, two handfuls, mixed with	½ tablespoonful of ground mustard to a pint of the mixture
Scraped horse-radish, one handful	1 teaspoonful sugar to the same quantity
Mace and nutmeg pounded, 1 tablespoonful	1 teaspoonful best salad oil to the same
Chopped garlic, 2 tablespoonfuls	1 teaspoonful celery seed
A little ginger	

Cut a slit in the side of the melon; insert your finger and extract all the seeds. If you cannot get them out in this way, cut a slender piece out, reserving it to replace,—but the slit is better. Lay the mangoes in strong brine for three days. Drain off the brine and freshen in pure water twenty-four hours. Green as you would cucumbers (*p. 30*) and lay in cold water until cold and firm. Fill with the stuffing, sew up the slit, or tie it up with pack thread; pack in a deep stone jar, and pour scalding vinegar over them. Repeat this process three times more at intervals of two days, then tie up and set away in a cool, dry place.

They will not be "ripe" in under four months, but are very fine when they are. They will keep several years.

FRENCH PICKLE—DELICIOUS

One colander of sliced green tomatoes, one quart of sliced onions, one colander of cucumbers, pared and sliced, two good handfuls of salt; let all stand twenty-four hours, then drain through a sieve; one-half ounce of celery seed, one-half ounce of allspice, one teaspoonful of black pepper, one tablespoonful of turmeric, one pound of brown sugar, two tablespoonfuls of mustard, one gallon of vinegar.

MUSTARD PICKLE

Two gallons of vinegar, two large cupfuls of (*dry*) mustard, two tablespoonfuls of salad oil, a little salt and a tablespoonful of turmeric powder. Mix together and let it stand a week; then take three hundred small cucumbers (*gherkin size*), six cauliflowers, three quarts of little onions, one quart of nasturtium seeds, six heads of celery, and soak them overnight in strong brine. Steam all but the cucumbers until tender; cook those in a little vinegar until tender. Put all in the mustard and let it stand a week; then put into a preserving kettle, add two cupfuls of brown sugar, and half a cupful of cornstarch. Boil well; skim out the ingredients; add a little red pepper; let the vinegar boil a short time, then pour over the ingredients in cans or jars. (*Makes 20–25 quarts.*)

See July (*p. 211*), *September* (*p. 282, and October* (*p. 320*) *for other pickles.*

AUGUST VEGETABLES

STRING BEANS

Select only those that are tender, cut off the ends, and wash them well, take a handful and lay them even, and cut them very fine with a sharp knife. Put them in when the water boils, and if very tender, they will require but half an hour. Season as peas.

"Most people spoil garden things by over-boiling them. All things that are green should have a little crispness, for if they are over-boiled, they neither have any sweetness or beauty."
Hannah Glasse, *The Art of Cookery*, 1812

FRENCH BEANS À LA MAÎTRE D'HÔTEL

Prepare your beans as for boiling; put into a stewpan a piece of butter, shred parsley, and green onions; when the butter is melted, add the french beans, turn them a few times over the fire, shake in some flour; and moisten with a little good stock well seasoned; boil until the sauce is consumed, then put in the yolks of three eggs beat up with some milk, and add a little vinegar.

Sprinkle buttered green beans with fresh-snipped dill just before taking them from the fire.

TO DRESS BEANS AND BACON

When you dress beans and bacon, boil the (*unsliced*) bacon by itself, and the beans by themselves, for the bacon will spoil the color of the beans. Always throw some salt into the water, and some parsley, nicely picked. When the beans are enough (which you will know by their being tender) throw them into a cullender to drain. Take up the bacon and skin it; throw some raspings of bread over the top, and if you have an iron (*salamander or poker*), make it red hot and hold it over to brown the top of the beans. If

[239]

you have not one, hold it to the fire to brown; put the bacon in the middle of the dish, and the beans all around, close up to the bacon, and send them to table, with parsley and butter in a bason.

RUSSIAN SALAD

All vegetables for this should be cooked, but not until tender, drained and dried on a napkin. To one cup of whole string beans use one-half cup of parsnip and carrot cut in pretty shapes, one-half cup of shredded lettuce, a little sliced beet and a little cold potatoes. Over this pour a French Dressing (*which, in the nineteenth century, means oil and vinegar*).

LIMA BEANS

Cover the beans with freshly-boiled soft water, and boil thirty minutes; drain and add salt, pepper and butter, or a half-cup of boiling cream.

A sprig of mint (*or a slice of onion*) may be boiled with the beans, and removed before serving.

LIMA BEANS

They may be kept through the winter by gathering them on a day before they are in the least hard, and packing them in their pods in a keg. Throw salt in the bottom, then a layer of pods, then salt, then pods, until it is full. Press down with a heavy weight, cover the keg closely, and keep in a cool dry place. When used, soak them in their pods overnight in cold water; the next day shell them, and soak until ready to boil.

BEAN ROLL

Cook lima beans in boiling water until tender; press through a sieve; add salt and pepper, and a tablespoonful of butter to each pint of pulp. Stir in two eggs well beaten, and sufficient bread-crumbs—about half a cupful—to make the mixture thick enough to (*form into a*) roll. Wrap in greased paper, and at serving-time bake for twenty minutes in a quick oven. Serve plain or with tomato sauce (*p. 281*). This takes the place of meat.

SUCCOTASH

Cut the corn from the cobs. Break up the cobs and throw them into the water to cook with the lima beans (do not salt the water). Use just enough water to cook the beans, and keep the pot covered. When they are just tender add the corn, cook three or four minutes, remove the cobs; then thicken the succotash slightly with butter rubbed in flour and a little cream if desired. Season with salt and white pepper, and serve hot.

STEWED PEPPERS

Green or red peppers; three tablespoonfuls of butter; boiling water to cover; one-half teaspoonful of salt; dash of paprika. Cut the peppers in halves, remove the seeds and stem, cut each half into five or six pieces lengthwise. Put the butter into a sauce-pan, and when hot, add the peppers. Shake over the fire for fifteen minutes; then add enough water to cover the peppers. Season with salt and paprika, and cook slowly for twenty minutes. Serve hot as a garnish, plain boiled rice.

STUFFED PEPPERS

Fry for one minute only six medium-sized green peppers in very hot fat; drain and skin them properly, and cut a round piece off the bottom to use as a cover. Remove the insides, and fill them up with a good sausage force-meat; put on the round cover previously cut off, and lay them on an oiled baking-dish. Moisten the peppers lightly with sweet (*olive*) oil, and place them in a slow oven to cook for fifteen minutes; then arrange them on a hot dish. (*Serves 6.*)

FORCEMEAT: Cut up a pound of fresh (*cooked*) pork into small pieces, season with a pinch of salt, a saltspoonful of pepper, half a saltspoonful of grated nutmeg, and the same quantity of powdered thyme, and chop all up very fine. A quarter of a pound of lean raw meat can be added if desired.

PEPPERS STUFFED WITH OYSTERS

Six green peppers; one pint of oysters; one small onion; one heaping tablespoon of butter; bread-crumbs; salt and pepper. Cut off the tops of the peppers and remove the seeds; boil ten minutes and drain. Chop the onion, and mix this, the bread-crumbs, and butter, with the oysters. Season with salt and pepper, and stuff into the peppers. Cover with bread-crumbs and bake in a quick oven for twenty minutes. (*Serves 6.*)

PEPPERS STUFFED WITH CAULIFLOWER

Parboil the peppers ten minutes, stuff with creamed cauliflower, sprinkle with buttered crumbs, bake.

STUFFED GREEN PEPPER

Cut the tops off the bell pepper and remove the seed. Take two of the long green peppers, one small onion, one large tomato peeled, and chop all together very fine. Add stale bread crumbs sufficient to fill five peppers, a teaspoonful of salt, and sweet-oil enough to moisten the whole. Fill the peppers and replace the tops. (*A cup of cooked corn, cut from the cob, and half a pimiento, chopped, can be added for color.*) To be prepared on the day they are to be used. (*Serve cold to 5.*)

PEPPER SAUCE

Take two dozen peppers, and cut them up fine, with double the quantity of cabbage; one root of horse-radish grated; one handful of salt, one full tablespoonful of mustard seed; one tablespoonful of allspice; one dessertspoonful of cloves; two tablespoonfuls of sugar, and a little mace. Boil the spice and sugar in two quarts of the best cider vinegar, which as soon as removed from the fire, and while yet boiling, pour over the other ingredients. When cold, put it in jars, cover close, and keep in a cool place.

Peppers can be chopped and frozen in small quantities for winter use in soups and salads.

[242]

STEWED OKRA WITH RICE

1 quart of okra	1 onion
½ lb. of ham	1 tablespoon of powdered dry
1 red pepper	sassafras leaves (p. 260)
1 pint of white stock	1 pint of tomatoes
1 cup of rice	

Wash the okra, and cut in thin slices. Cut the ham into dice and fry it until brown. Peel and cut the tomatoes, put them into a porcelain-lined or granite kettle with the okra, ham, stock, the pepper cut in small pieces, and an onion cut in slices; cover the kettle and *simmer* gently for a half-hour. While this cooks, wash and boil the rice. When the okra is done, add the salt, pepper and sassafras leaves (called filée), let it boil up once, and serve with the rice around the dish. (*Serves 8.*)

OKRA SOUP

"Soup" was sometimes the whole dinner, boiled in one pot, then served in courses.

1 chicken	1 green and 1 red pepper
1 pound of veal	1 carrot
2 pounds of beef	1 onion
½ a peck of okra	1 tablespoon of butter
1 pint of green corn	3 even tablespoons of salt
1 pint of lima beans	3–4 sprigs of parsley
4 quarts of water	3–4 sprigs of celery
6 good-sized tomatoes	

Cut the chicken and put it in the kettle with the butter and tomatoes, which must be peeled and sliced; add the veal and beef, cut in small pieces, and the okra sliced, the green corn cut from the ear, the beans, celery, parsley, and salt, with one quart of water. Boil three or four hours; add the remainder of the water, let it boil half an hour, then strain it (*add the sassafras*), and serve, reserving the okra, corn, etc., to be eaten as a vegetable in the second course; or remove simply the meat with part of the vegetables, leaving a tolerably thick soup. This is especially good the second day. (*Serves 6–8.*)

TO KEEP OCHRAS

Take ochras when they first come in season, slice them thin; with a long needle run a strong thread through the slices, and hang them up in your store-room in festoons. In winter, use for soups; boil till quite dissolved.

SUMMER SQUASH

They are good when yellow and tender, but when the skin becomes hard they are out of season. Cut off the top and lower part, and wash and boil with other vegetables or alone as long as potatoes, or if large and not very tender, longer. Have a cloth strainer ready in a pan and put them into it when done; if the seeds are large, take them out; if not, let them remain; press the squash by winding up the ends of the strainer and using a beetle (*masher*) to extract all the water; then lay it in a pan, add salt and butter, mash well, and it will be a nice dish indeed. Cooked in any other way, they will be watery and insipid (*but try slicing them thin and frying them in butter anyway*).

VEGETABLE MARROW (*SUMMER SQUASH*)

Choose eight young small ones, with smooth skin, and put them to boil (*whole*) in two quarts of water, in which you have put one ounce of salt, the same of butter; try with a needle if tender, then dish them tastefully on mashed potatoes in a dish, put half a pint of melted butter (*p. 107*) in a pan. When near boiling, add the yolk of an egg, two pats of butter, a little sugar and the juice of half a lemon mixed together, sauce over, and serve. (*Serves 8.*)

Cucumbers may be dressed the same way.

GOURD (*SUMMER SQUASH*) SOUP

should be made of full-grown Gourds, but not those with hard skins; slice three or four, and put them in a stew-pan, with two or three Onions and a good bit of Butter; set them over a slow fire till quite tender (be careful not to let them burn), then add two ounces of crusts of Bread and two quarts of good Consomme, season with salt and Cayenne pepper, boil ten minutes or a quarter of an hour, skim off all the fat and pass it through a tammis (*or blend it*), then make it quite hot, and serve with fried bread (*croutons*). (*Serves 8–10.*)

VEGETABLE SOUP

Take three or four young carrots, three young turnips, and one leek; scrape the carrots and peel the turnips, and cut them in thin slices; cut each slice of turnip in four; put them in two quarts of broth, seasoned with salt and pepper to taste; cover it, and let them boil for fifteen minutes, then add a head of white lettuce cut small, and a bunch of parsley broken up; cover it and let it boil for fifteen minutes longer, and it is done. (*Serves 8.*)

EGG PLANT

Boil them whole in plenty of water until tender, then take them up, drain them after having taken off the skins, cut them up and mash them in a deep dish or pan; mix with them some grated bread, powdered marjoram, and a large piece of butter and a few pounded cloves. Grate a layer of bread (*crumbs*) over the top and brown it in an oven. Send it to table in the same dish.

BAKED EGGPLANT

Cut in halves a nice smooth eggplant, scoop out the center, leaving with the skin about one-third of an inch, chop the inside of the eggplant very fine, two ripe tomatoes, one onion, some bread crumbs, a little parsley, and green pepper—onion and pepper to be chopped separately very fine, salt, butter, and very little pepper; mix very smooth, put in the shell, butter on top and bake (*at 350°*) half a hour. (*Serves 4–6.*)

Eggplant can be stuffed with any duck stuffing. See p. 293.

"Egg-plant is sometimes eaten at dinner, but generally at breakfast. Cucumber also makes a nice breakfast dish."
Miss Eliza Leslie, *Directions for Cookery*, 1870

[245]

FRIED EGG PLANT

Cut the plant around in slices half an inch thick; sprinkle with pepper and salt and press with a light weight for an hour or two; drain on a napkin; dip each slice in beaten egg, then in cracker dust; fry in butter until a light brown. (*Serves 4.*)

EGG PLANT FRITTERS

Select a large egg plant, leave it unpared and with the stem on; boil it in a porcelain kettle, in slightly salted water, until so tender that it can barely be taken out without breaking; remove the skin, put the pulp in a colander and press the water from it; mash it very fine, add salt and pepper to the taste, also two ounces of butter rubbed with three even tablespoons of flour; add a well-beaten egg and mix thoroughly. Have ready some hot butter and lard in a frying-pan; drop in the egg plant by spoonfuls and fry on both sides. (*Serves 6.*)

TO FREEZE CORN

Prices for sweet corn drop drastically toward the end of August, so now is the time to buy in bulk—from farmers, if possible—for freezing and canning.

Drop the husked ears, three or four at a time, into boiling water. Scald for no more than 2 minutes. Let the ears cool, then cut the corn from the cob with a sharp knife and freeze immediately without seasoning. A tube cake pan, with a tube hole just big enough to hold the end of the ear steady while the kernels fall into the pan as you cut them, is very useful.

MACON SWEET POTATO PIE

Sweet potatoes can be harvested in late August, but are generally scarce in the stores until September.

Boil sweet potatoes tender (*without peeling them; it will take longer than for white potatoes*), line your dish with a rich paste, slice in the (*peeled*) potatoes very thin, season highly with butter, sugar and cloves, pour a little brandy over the top, cover with a rich paste, and bake about as long as for an apple pie.

SUGARED SWEET POTATOES

Boil sweet potatoes until they are soft; slice them as usual for frying, but before putting them in the frying pan, roll in sugar, then fry (*in butter*). Parsnips may be cooked the same way.

SWEET POTATO CAKES

Grate boiled sweet potato and mix with an equal quantity of flour, four ounces of butter; add salt and milk; cut out (*like cookies*) and bake in a hot oven; slice and butter for tea.

SWEET POTATO PUDDING

Boil one quart of sweet potatoes very tender, rub them while hot through a colander, add six eggs (*whites and yolks beaten separately, whites folded in last*), twelve ounces of powdered sugar, ten ounces of butter, nutmeg and lemon. Line a dish with paste. When baked, sprinkle the top of the pudding over with sugar and cover it with bits of citron. (*Glaze it under the broiler.*)

For a sweet potato soufflé to serve as a vegetable with pork, substitute 2 tablespoons brown sugar and 1 teaspoon salt for the powdered sugar, omit both citron and glaze.

MELONS

"*A silver spoon is a neat and pleasant article with which to eat small ripe melons.*"

Marion Harland, *Breakfast, Dinner and Supper*, 1897

It is almost sacrilege to do anything more with small, ripe melons, than to eat them with a silver spoon, perhaps with some lime juice squeezed over them, or with a scoop of sherbet or some strawberries or blueberries inside. If you must, they may be sliced up with prosciutto as an hors d'oeuvre.

MUSHROOMS

These are good every way when fresh; for a dish, take about fifty buttons, cut the root off, wash and rub the skin off with a cloth, cut them in slices, tail and all, put them in a stewpan with two ounces of butter, a small teaspoonful of salt, two pinches of pepper, and the juice of half a lemon, put them on the fire, simmer till tender, and dish them up on a nice crisp toast; should you require any sauce, add, when nearly done, half a spoonful of flour, a gill of broth, milk or cream; stew a few minutes longer, pour over toast and serve.

"A little red wine may be added to mushrooms, but the flavor of the mushrooms is too delicious to require aid from any thing."
Mrs. Webster, *The Improved Housewife*, 1854

MUSHROOMS

The following recipes deal with wild mushrooms. Their flavors and colors are various and delicious—but do not touch them *unless you are completely familiar with them. Many of them have deadly look-alikes.*

FAIRY-RING (MARASMUS OREADES): If they are dry when gathered, soak them in water for a little while, and then sauté or stew them. Put a tablespoonful of flour into a saucepan; when it bubbles add a tablespoonful of flour and cook a few minutes; then add a cupful of water or milk, stir until smooth, and add a pint of the "fairies." Simmer fifteen minutes, season with salt and pepper, serve over buttered toast.

AGARICUS CAMPESTRIS: Cut off the stem near the cup, peel them and lay them with the gills up upon a dish and sprinkle them with salt. After a little time they will be quite moist; then strew them in a sauce, or broil them in butter.

AGARICUS PROCERUS: Remove the scurf spots and broil in plenty of butter. Serve on toast or with meat.

AGARICUS RUSSULA: Scrutinize carefully for worms (tiny holes in the stem). The noxious russulas closely resemble the succulent ones, so care is required to discriminate them; wash well, peel and broil as directed for *campestris*. Lay them under a broiled steak, so they will absorb the juices of the meat.

COPRINUS COMATUS and COPRINUS ATRAMENTARIUS: They should be gathered at the white or pink stage. Fry them in butter or stew with butter and a little milk or cream. They are very juicy.

THE BOLETI: Any of this class which have any tinge of red on the under surface should be rejected. Slice them and sauté in butter, or dip them in fritter batter (*p. 73*), or egg and crumb them, and fry in smoking-hot fat. These mushrooms should be carefully examined for insects, as they are quickly attacked.

PUFF BALLS: All are edible when gathered at the white stage. Cut them in slices half an inch thick. Either sauté them in butter or dip them in beaten egg and fry in hot fat or cook on a griddle. Season with salt and pepper.

CLAVARIA: Separate the branches, and stew in white sauce; or sauté them in butter, seasoning with lemon juice, salt and pepper.

TO DRY MUSHROOMS: Place them in a saucepan, and cook with gentle heat until the moisture they give is evaporated; then place them on a hot shelf until they are thoroughly dry. Pound them to powder in a mortar, and place the powder in well-closed jars.

MUSHROOM FORCE-MEAT BALLS

Peel mushrooms and fry in batter; when cold, mince them and add an equal quantity of bread crumbs, salt, yolk of one egg, and sufficient milk to make of right consistency; make into small balls and poach for soup, or fry in boiling fat and serve for a garnish.

> *"It is always safe to use canned mushrooms, which are convenient and cheap, but tough and indigestible, and we caution those who eat them to masticate diligently."*
> Mrs. Rorer, *The Philadelphia Cook Book*, 1886

TO POT MUSHROOMS

Choose large buttons, or those in which the inside is not yet the least brown; peel and wipe out the fur of the larger ones, and to every two quarts put one-half drachm (*$\frac{1}{16}$ ounce*) of pounded mace, two drachms (*¼ ounce*) white pepper, and six or eight cloves in powder. Set them over the fire, shake and let the liquor dry up into them. Then put to them two ounces of butter and stew them until they are fit for eating; pour the butter from them, and let them become cold. Pack them close into a pot, making the surface as even as possible; add some butter lukewarm, and then lay a bit of white paper over them, and pour clarified suet (*or lard*) upon it to exclude the air.

The liquor you pour off the mushrooms is a excellent peppery sauce for steak. The potted mushrooms will keep under refrigeration for nearly six months and taste fresh when you use them. Heated in the butter, they are delicious with steak or with eggs.

MUSHROOM CATSUP

This is expensive to make unless you happen to catch the mushrooms on sale, or unless you are very sure of your wild mushrooms. It is a frequent ingredient of old recipes, however, and one batch will last a long time—and it does give a flavor not quite like anything else. Mushroom catsup, called "mushroom sauce," is still available in gourmet shops. Or, if you must, soy sauce may be substituted.

Two quarts of mushrooms; one-quarter pound of salt. Lay in an earthenware pan, in alternate layers of mushrooms and salt; let them lie six hours, then break into bits. Set in a cool place three days, stirring thoroughly every morning. Measure the juice when you have strained it, and to every quart allow half an ounce of allspice, the same quantity of ginger, half a teaspoon of powdered mace, a teaspoonful of cayenne. Put into a stone jar (*or a double boiler*) cover closely, set in a saucepan of boiled water over the fire, and boil five hours hard. Take it off, empty into a porcelain kettle, and boil slowly half an hour longer. Let it stand all night in a cool place, until settled and clear. Pour off carefully from the sediment and bottle, filling the flasks to the mouth. Dip the corks in melted rosin, and tie up with bladders (*or use screw-top bottles, and dip the top in melted paraffin to seal it*). The bottles should be very small (*empty spice bottles work well*), as it soon spoils when exposed to the air. (*Makes about 2 cups.*)

The leftover salty mushrooms can be rinsed well and put sparingly into stew for a little extra flavoring.

Mushroom catsup can also be made with whole black pepper as the only spice. A tablespoonful of brandy per pint is added as a preservative.

WALNUT CATSUP

This, like mushroom catsup, is an old ingredient that cannot really be substituted for. Worcestershire sauce, however, will serve roughly the same purpose in a recipe.

Take 300 young walnuts (they are generally in a fit state early in August) (*test by piercing the hulls with a darning needle; the woody part of the shell should not have formed yet, allowing the needle to go all the way through*); pound them small, add, as you pound, one pound of salt; then put them into a quart of vinegar for four days, press all well through a hair bag, add to each quart of the liquor extracted one drachm (*⅛ ounce*) of cloves, one drachm of cayenne, half a pound of anchovies, and one clove of garlic, and boil all together for three-quarters of an hour; skim it till clear, then add half a pint of port wine to each quart, simmer a few minutes longer, let it stand till cold, then pour the ketchup quite clear; or you can add the mace and cloves to it as you bottle it off.

Another: Take a peck of green walnuts, put them in a tub, bruise and mash them, and throw two or three pounds of salt and water enough to cover them. Let them stand six days, straining and mixing them until they become soft and pulpy. Drain out the juice by letting the tub stand on one side a little with the shells in the elevated part. As often as it needs, turn out the liquor and continue as long as there is any, which will be five or six quarts. Then boil it as long as scum rises (*skim*), then add one-quarter pound of ginger and alspice; two ounces of pepper and cloves, and let it boil slowly one-half hour. The slices should be powdered, and a quantity of them should go into each bottle. Cork them tight, put them in a cool dry place one year before it is used.

WALNUT VINEGAR

Put green walnut shells into a brine of salt and water strong enough to float an egg; let them lie covered in this ten or twelve days; take them out, lay them in the sun for a week; put them into a jar and pour boiling vinegar on them; in about a week or ten days pour off the vinegar, make it boiling hot, and pour it over them again. In a month it will be fit for use and will be found excellent to eat with cold meat, and particularly useful in making sauce.

AUGUST FRUITS

Peach-pickers go to work about the second week in August, in the Northeast, and by the end of the third week, prices are usually as low as they will get, although some late varieties are not picked until September.

PEACH PIE

Peel, stone and slice the peaches. Line a pie-plate with a good crust, and lay in your fruit, sprinkling sugar liberally over them in proportion to their sweetness. Very ripe peaches require comparatively little. Pour in a very little water (*with a little tapioca, to thicken the juice*), and bake with an upper crust, or with cross-bars of paste across the top.

Brush the top crust with milk and sprinkle sugar on it. Bake at 375° until the crust is golden, about 45 minutes.

PEACH MERINGUE

Put pared, halved peaches in a pudding dish. Make a soft custard of the yolks of four eggs, a quart of milk and a teacup of sugar; when cold, pour over the peaches. Beat the whites to a stiff froth, add five tablespoonfuls of white sugar (*spread the meringue over the peaches and custard*), and set in the oven to brown. (*Serve cold.*)

PEACH WATER ICE

Put into an enamelled pan half a pint of water, a pound of loaf sugar, the white of an egg beaten to a stiff froth, and one peach kernel, and reduce it over the fire to a syrup; remove the scum, and take it off to cool. Take out the peach kernel, and add to the syrup a pint of pure peach juice, pressed from very ripe fruit (*or a bit more of the whole fruit, puréed in the blender*). Freeze it as usual (*p. 35; makes 1 quart*).

PEACH FRITTERS

Take half a pound of flour and pour over it boiling water sufficient to make it of a consistency to beat smooth, to which add while warm a piece of butter the size of a walnut. When cool, whisk six eggs until thick and light, which add by degrees, with three gills and a half of milk. Then stir in a pound and a quarter of flour, half at a time, with a little salt. Beat all well together. Then pare and slice (just before wanted) some fine ripe peaches. Take out as much batter as will make a sufficient number of fritters for the pan at a time, and stir in lightly as many slices of peach as you think are required to make them nice. By putting the peaches into all the batter, it would by standing a short time become much too thin. Have in a frying pan some boiling lard, put in the batter, allowing a tablespoonful for each fritter. Do not let them touch and fry them a light brown on both sides. Send them to table hot, and eat with butter and sugar, or molasses if preferred. (*Serves 10–12.*)

PEACH PUDDING

One pint of cream; two tablespoonfuls of caster (*superfine*) sugar; half a can (*1 pint*) of peaches, half an ounce of (*unflavored*) gelatin. Dissolve the gelatin in a little warm water. Whip the cream stiffly and add the caster sugar. Chop the peaches into small pieces. Mix all together and pour into a wet mould. Place where it is cold to harden. Turn out when required. (*Serves 4–6.*)

ANOTHER: Take one quart of peaches, pare and stone them, put on to stew in half a cupful of white wine and half a cupful of sugar, add about a dozen blanched almonds when the peaches are tender and the wine has cooked syrupy, pour them in a pudding pan, and pour over them the following: Beat the yolks of nine eggs with one and a half cupfuls of sugar until light, add the grated rind of one-half lemon, half of the stiffly beaten whites of the eggs. Pour over the peaches, and bake in a moderate oven until light brown. Then cover with the remaining whites of eggs beaten with six tablespoonfuls of sugar. Brown lightly again. Serve cold with whipped or sweet cream. (*Serves 8–10.*)

PEACH-LEAF CUSTARD

Take two handsful of peach-leaves, let them come to a boil in a quart of milk, strain and let it cool, beat twenty yolks of eggs, add two quarts of cream and loaf sugar (*to taste*), mix well together, and stir them until they come to the boil. But do not let them boil, take them off, and let it cool, stirring all the time; put in wine-glasses around a "Floating Island." For a dessert for dinner.

Floating island: Put four quarts of cream or milk (*or peach-leaf custard*) in your glass (*bowl*); sweeten and add rosewater and grated lemon peel to your taste, beat the whites of twenty eggs until stiff, color it with quince or currant jelly, beating all the time until it will stand alone, then put it with a tablespoon on top of the milk. To be eaten immediately. (*Serves 15–18. For most purposes, this recipe can be halved or quartered.*)

"Peach leaves steeped in brandy make an excellent seasoning for custards and puddings."
                                Mrs. Ellet, *The Practical Housekeeper*, 1857

PEACHES IN BRANDY

Take the finest white peaches you can get, not over-ripe, rub off the lint with a flannel cloth, cut them down the seam, and cover them with white brandy, let them stand (*covered*) for a week, then make a syrup of a pound of sugar for each pound of peaches, take the fruit from the brandy to the syrup, and boil them until they are clear; then take them out, give the syrup another boil, then put in to the brandy, and then pour it over the fruit; cover close. (This will keep a long time.)

TO PRESERVE PEACHES

Nineteenth-century housewives were canning before the principles of canning were fully understood. Bacteria had barely been discovered in 1850, and the importance of killing them while preserving food could hardly have come to most housewives' attention. So canning was done by trial and error and its practice was full of arcane rituals. One should never, for instance, can

[254]

on a humid day. Sugar, as a preservative, was generously used, so some of the old preserves—a name that covers canned fruit for dessert as well as jams— are a bit sweet for our tastes. The general rule is: ¾ pound of sugar to 1 pound of fruit—or to taste.

Soak your peaches in weak salt water (*drain*), then put their weight of sugar (*or a little less*) to them, and put them over a slow fire until they are tender; take out the peaches and boil the syrup (*to reduce it*); when cold, put them together; put (*in*) brandy and cut oranges (*and bottle*).

PEACH MARMALADE

Peel ripe peaches, stone them, cut them small; weigh three-quarters of a pound of sugar to each pound of cut fruit, and a teacup of water for each pound of sugar; set it over the fire; when it boils, skim it clear, then put in the peaches, let them boil quite fast, mash them fine, and let them boil until the whole is a jellied mass, and thick; then put it in small jars or tumblers; when cold, secure it as for jelly.

Peach marmalade is good with slivers of lemon rind cooked with it, with a chopped-up ripe pineapple, or with a few cloves and a stick of cinnamon.

PEACH BUTTER

Peel and stew your peaches in as little water as possible. When they are done, mash smooth and add 8 or 10 pounds of sugar per bushel of peaches; stir till dissolved.

PEACH LEATHER

To six pounds of ripe peaches, pared and quartered, allow three pounds of the best brown sugar. Mix them together, and put them in a preserving-kettle, with barely enough water to keep them from burning. Pound and mash them with a wooden beetle. Then boil and skim them for three hours or more, stirring them nearly all the time. When done, spread them thinly on large dishes, and set them in the sun for three or four days. (*Bring them in at night.*) Finish the drying by loosening the leather from the dishes, and setting them in the oven after the bread is taken out, letting them remain until the oven is cold. Roll up the leather and put it away in a box.

Apple leather may be made in the same manner.

[255]

Part II: *Recipes*

TO DRY PEACHES

Take ripe, but not soft peaches, pare them and take out the stones, and cut them in halves or quarters, or smaller; spread them out on flat dishes or boards, and set them where the sun will shine all day on them; take them in at dusk or sunset; they should not be put out when the weather is damp or cloudy.

Peaches dry nicely in an oven after baking is done. Turn them while they are drying, that they may dry quickly and perfectly, else they become musty. Keep them in a muslin bag, tied closely and hung up.

CANDIED FRUITS

Make a rich sirup with one pound of granulated sugar to a gill of water. Heat over boiling water until the sugar is dissolved. Pare and halve fine, ripe but solid peaches. Put a single layer of them in the sirup, in a shallow vessel; cook slowly until clear; drain them from the sirup, and put to dry in a moderately heated oven. When fairly dry, they may be eaten at once; or, after drying twenty-four hours, they may be packed for future use. Plums, cherries, and pears may be candied in the same manner.

GREEN GRAPE PIE

When green (*unripe*) and tender, grapes make a good pie. Stew and strain the grapes, unless very small, to separate the seeds, before making them into pies, and sweeten them to your taste. They need no spice. If made into a pie without stewing, put to each layer of grapes a spoonful of water, after a thick layer of sugar.

CRAB-APPLE JELLY

Boil one peck of crab-apples in as much water as will cover them, until soft, then put them into a jelly bag and strain two or three times, until the syrup is very clear; then to each pint of syrup add one pound of sugar; put the sugar in the oven and let it heat thoroughly while the syrup is heating.

[256]

When it boils, pour in the sugar gradually, and boil for fifteen or twenty minutes.

SPICED CRAB-APPLES

Wash small crab-apples well and drop them whole into a syrup made of half their weight in sugar, vinegar to cover, whole cinnamon, cloves and black pepper, and a sliced nutmeg. Stew until tender, then skim them out and put them in sterilized hot jars; reduce the syrup a little and pour it over them. Seal. Like all pickles, they are better kept a month or more before using.

To color them for garnishing holiday dishes, peel them and use food coloring, beet, or spinach juice, or colored decorators' sugar. Apple rings may be spiced in the same way.

ELDERBERRIES

TO PREPARE ELDERBERRIES FOR PIE

Elderberries will be ripe toward the end of August. It takes a skilled eye and a quick hand to beat the birds to them at their peak.

To twelve pounds of berries, add one quart vinegar; boil three hours, then add four pounds of sugar and boil slowly one hour. Will keep several months.

Bake like any fruit pie; serve with sweet or whipped cream.

Strip elderberries from their stems with the tines of a fork. It is simpler and less messy than dealing with them with your fingers.

ELDERBERRY SIRUP

Take berries perfectly ripe; wash and strain them; put a pint of molasses to a pint of the juice; boil it twenty minutes, stirring constantly; when cold, add to each quart, a pint of French brandy. Bottle and cork it tight. It is an excellent remedy for a tight cough.

ELDERBERRY CATSUP

1 quart elderberries	A pinch of ginger
1 quart of vinegar	2 tablespoonfuls white sugar
6 anchovies, soaked and pulled	1 teaspoonful salt
to pieces	1 tablespoonful whole peppers
½ teaspoonful mace	

Scald the vinegar and pour over the berries, which must be picked from the stalks and put into a large stone jar. Cover with a pane of glass, and set in the hot sun two days. Strain off the liquor, and boil up with other ingredients, stirring often, one hour, keeping covered unless while stirring. Let it cool; strain and bottle.

This is used for flavoring brown gravies, soups, and ragouts, and, stirred into browned butter, makes a good piquant sauce for broiled or baked fish.

GOOD ELDERBERRY WINE

Strip the berries clean from the stalks, and put them into a tub; pour boiling water on them, in the proportion of two gallons to three of the berries, press them down into the liquor, and cover them closely. Let them remain in this state until the following day, when the juice must be strained from the fruit; then squeeze from the berries the juice remaining in them, and mix it with what was poured off at first. To every gallon of this mixture, add three pounds of sugar, one ounce of cloves and one ounce of ginger; boil twenty minutes, keeping it thoroughly skimmed. While still hot, put into a cask, or large bottles; fill entirely, and set the wine immediately with a large spoonful of new yeast put into the bung-hole, and stirred round in the liquor. (*See p. 37 for wine-making directions. Keep the cask topped up to replace what will froth out of the bung-hole.*)

FIG MARMALADE

Three pounds of figs, two oranges, two lemons, two pounds of sugar. Use pulp of the oranges, pulp and rind of lemon; chop figs and all together; cook twenty minutes.

NASTURTIUMS

NASTURTIUM-SEED

This is a common substitute for capers in sauces. Capers are themselves the pickled buds of the caper plant, found near the Mediterranean, and perhaps not readily available in the 1800s.

Take the green seed after the flower has dried off. Lay in salt and water two days, in cold water one day (*drain*); pack in bottles and cover with scalding vinegar, seasoned with mace and white pepper-corns, and sweeten slightly with white sugar. Cork, and set away four weeks before you use them.

NASTURTIAN SAUCE

This is by many considered superior to caper sauce and is eaten with boiled mutton. It is made with the green seeds of nasturtians pickled simply in cold vinegar.

Cut about six ounces of butter into small bits, and put them into a small saucepan. Mix with a wineglass of water, sufficient flour to make a thick batter, pour it on the butter, and hold it over hot coals, shaking it quickly round till the butter melts. Let it just boil up, and then take it from the fire. Thicken it with the pickled nasturtian; send to table in a boat.

NASTURTIUM SANDWICHES

Use two-thirds blossoms and one-third leaves. Lay on thin slices of buttered bread, white or brown, cover with another slice, and cut into oblong forms. Pile log-cabin fashion on a dainty doily.

MEAD

Those who keep bees will begin to have plentiful honey about the middle of August, as the bees begin to get ready for winter. Store-bought honey is expensive, often treated to prevent sugaring, and sometimes thinned—so if you want to make mead, it is best to know a beekeeper.

To every gallon of water put five pounds of strained honey (the water must be hot when you add the honey), and let it boil half an hour or longer, skimming it well. Then put in some hops tied in a thin bag (allowing an ounce to each gallon), and let it boil half an hour longer. Strain it into a tub (*let it cool, then add wine yeast*) and let it stand four days (*covered with a towel*). Then put it into a cask, adding for each gallon a jill of brandy and a sliced lemon. If a large cask, do not bottle it till it has stood a year. (*This will be rather sweet. The following recipe is drier.*)

ANOTHER: Boil honey—three or four (*2 or 3*) pounds to a gallon of water—for an hour, skimming carefully, draining the skimming and returning to what has run through. When nearly cool, strain in a teacup of yeast for nine gallons (*and the juice of 4 lemons or limes per gallon*) and let it ferment. (*See p. 37 for wine-making directions.*) Put it in a cool place and bottle in a year.

Currants and raspberry juice, spices and aromatic herbs are often added to mead; the last toward the end of fermentation in a muslin bag weighed down with a piece of flint. Six quarts of red currants and two of black will do for twenty-five pounds of honey.

SASSAFRAS POWDER (*FILÉ*)

Gather sassafras leaves in August, dry them in the shade, powder them, sift and bottle. (*Use them for Sassafras gombo, p. 271, or for Okra and rice, p. 243.*)

FROGS

A WHITE FRICASSEE OF FROGS

Frogs are rarely to be found in the market. The best Florida frogs can occasionally be had frozen, but as the swamps are being filled in, frogs are on their way out. The following recipes are for those few people who can still catch fat August bullfrogs.

Cut off the Hinder Legs, strip them of the Skin, and cut off the Feet, and boil them tender in a little Veal Broth, with whole Pepper and a little Salt, with a Bunch of Sweet-Herbs and some Lemon-Peel. Stew them with a Shallot, till the Flesh is a little tender; strain off the Liquor, and thicken it with Cream and Butter; Serve them hot with Mushrooms pickled (*p. 235*), tossed up with the Sauce. They make a good Dish, and their Bones being of a very fine Texture, are better to be eaten than those of Larks.

GUMBO WITH FROGS

Brown in half an ounce of butter, in a saucepan, one chopped onion with about one ounce of raw ham cut into dice shape, half a green pepper cut in small dice, and half a tablespoonful of salt and a teaspoonful of pepper. Moisten with one quart of white broth or consomme, add one tablespoonful of raw rice, six sliced gumbos (*okras*), and one sliced tomato. Let all cook thoroughly for about twenty minutes; and five minutes before serving, add a quarter of a pound of raw frogs' legs cut up into small pieces. (*Serves 2–3.*)

FROGS À L'ESPAGNOLE: The same, adding one green pepper and two tomatoes, and omitting the gumbo.

$\begin{bmatrix} 12 \end{bmatrix}$

SEPTEMBER

Chicken; oysters; tomatoes; carrots; celery; pears; grapes

CHICKEN

"No sort of animal food is so delicate and delicious as that of fowls and birds; and none so generally healthful. Seldom does it disagree with those in health. The feeble in constitution, and such as are debilitated by sickness, find the flesh of fowl a nutritious and most agreeable diet."

Mrs. Webster, *The Improved Housewife,* 1854

Chicken was once a year-round affair, when the chickens took care of reproducing themselves. The use of the incubator instead of the hen for hatching eggs and certain other modern interferences—such as the way the egg-sitting instinct has been bred out of Leghorns, the best white-egg producers, during the last 25 years—has made it more seasonal. Chicks are usually timed hatched in February so that they are laying in late July or August. For eating, 4- to 10-month-old chickens are best. Since September is nearly dead-center of that time-span, chicken prices tend to drop then. Here, therefore, is chicken:

BRAISED CHICKEN

Two chickens weighing about five pounds, six ounces of bacon, six ounces of celery, one pound of turnip, two onions, one and a half pints of water, one and a half teaspoonfuls of summer savory, one and a half teaspoonfuls of black pepper, one-third teaspoonful of cayenne pepper, three teaspoonfuls of salt.

Put the bacon in an iron frying-pan and let it fry slowly until much of the fat has come from it. Have the chickens rubbed on the inside with one teaspoonful of salt and half a teaspoonful of summer savory mixed; truss them nicely, then lay them in the hot fat, and turn often until they are a fine rich brown; then place them in an iron kettle with the sliced vegetables, summer savory, etc., and (*less than a cup of*) water; cover closely, and cook slowly till tender. (*This was done in what we now call a Dutch oven, an iron kettle on legs with a rimmed cover—still available—on which hot coals were placed while it stood in the fireplace. We get the same effect by cooking it outside in the approved manner, or by using a very tightly covered pot in the oven at 375°.*) Lay the chicken on a platter, with the strips of bacon over the legs and wings; skim the fat from the gravy and thicken it with two tablespoonfuls of flour rubbed smooth in two tablespoonfuls of water. (*Add a little hot juice to this before you pour it into the gravy, to prevent lumping.*) The gravy can be strained or not, as preferred. (*Serves 6–8.*)

> "*Fowls are sometimes stuffed with boiled celery, cut into pieces an inch long; or with macaroni which has been boiled and seasoned with salt and pepper.*"
>
> *Mrs. Lincoln's Boston Cook Book, 1896*

FRIED CHICKEN WITH OYSTERS

Take a nice tender chicken, open it down the back, and after cleaning it well, pound all the bones quite flat (*this was a curious nineteenth-century habit, to smash the bird with the flat of a cleaver, thereby achieving a nice nonangular shape*); then wash and wipe it dry on a clean towel; after which, season with salt and pepper and fry slowly in sweet lard until well done, and a fine brown on both sides, then put it on a dish, and place it where it will keep warm. Should any brown particles remain in the pan, remove them, and pour in one gill of hot water, and dredge in one teaspoonful of flour, stirring it well all the time. Have ready about twenty-five large oysters, which remove from their liquor, and put into the pan with the gravy; then let it simmer until the oysters are sufficiently cooked, observing to stir them all the time. When done, pour them over the chicken, and send to table hot. (*Serves 4.*)

FRIED FOWL

"Fowl," in modern supermarket parlance, is chicken that is too old and tough for anything but soup. But as the nineteenth century used it, fowl and chicken are usually interchangeable.

When you have cut the pieces at every joint, put them into a basin with a little salt, pepper, a spoonful of oil, and two of vinegar, and a little chopped eschalot, stir them well in it, and let remain for half an hour; have ready a quart of batter (*p. 73*), and take a fork and dip each piece one after the other into it, and then let it drop into the frying-pan, in which is sufficient hot fat to cover them; fry a nice color, and serve in a pyramid, with fried parsley over, or any sauce you like.

BROILED FOWL À LA TARTARE

"Tartare" means cold, not raw.

Make half a pint of sauce as follows: two spoonfuls of chili vinegar, two of Harvey's sauce, two of catsup, one of shopped eschalot, ten of plain melted butter; put into a stewpan and boil for twenty minutes. Ornament an oval dish by placing on the border cut gherkins, (*pickled*) beet-root, olives; place the sauce on it, and lay the fowl very hot over it; thus the fowl is hot and the sauce cold, but together very good. (*Serves 4.*)

FOWLS, (*EAST*) INDIAN WAY

Prepare and cook the fowls, or re-warm some that may be left, cut the remains of a tongue into pieces one inch long, and one-half inch in thickness, cut three times the quantity of plain boiled macaroni the same way, with a few mushrooms, and add the whites of four eggs to it, with some broth and half a pint of white sauce; when boiling, add a quarter of a pound of grated Parmesan, and half that of Gruyère, shake the stewpan so that the contents are well mixed, add a little salt and cayenne, put the fowl on a dish, sauce over, and serve.

"To make a fowl tender, give it a tablespoonful of vinegar half an hour before killing."

Elisabeth S. Miller, *In the Kitchen*, 1875

CAPON À L'ESTRAGON

Capons are de-sexed roosters, fatter, larger, and more tender than their more capable brothers. Fat roasting chickens may be substituted.

I have been told many fanciful epicures idolize this dish. The bird should be trussed for boiling; rub the breast with half a lemon, tie over some thin slices of bacon, cover the bottom of a small stewpan with thin slices of the same, and a few trimmings of either beef, veal or lamb, two onions, a little carrot, turnip and celery, two bay-leaves, one sprig of thyme, a glass of sherry, two quarts of water; season lightly with salt and pepper, and nutmeg. Simmer about an hour and a quarter, keeping continually a little fire on the lid (*or, bake it in a 350° oven; remove the capon*), and pass (*the gravy*) through a tammy (*or strain it, or blend it*) into a small saucepan, add a drop of coloring to give it a nice brown color, boil a few minutes longer, and take about forty tarragon leaves; wash, and put in the boiling gravy, with a tablespoonful of good French (*wine*) vinegar, and pour it upon the capon when you serve it. All kinds of fowls and chickens are continually cooked in this manner in France. They are also served with rice. (*One capon serves 5–6.*)

CAPONS, WITH QUENELLES AND TONGUE

When you are either roasting or braising, you make about twenty quenelles with a tablespoon, out of the forcemeat of veal (*p. 124*). Proceed (with the capon) and cook the same as above; when done, make a roll of mashed potatoes, which put around the dish you intend to serve it in, have ready cut from a cold tongue as many pieces of the shape of the quenelles, warm them gently in a little gravy, then put the quenelles on the border, with a piece of tongue between each; put the fowl in the centre, have ready a quart of new white sauce, which pour over the fowl and quenelles. Glaze the tongue and serve very hot. I have found this dish at first rather complicated but now my cook can do it without my assistance; it looks and eats well, but is only adapted for a dinner of importance.

[265]

THE SAME, WITH CUCUMBERS: Cut about four nice fresh cucumbers into lengths of two inches, peel and divide them down the middle, take the seedy part out, trim the corners, put about thirty of them into a stewpan, with two ounces of butter, a spoonful of eschalot, and the same of sugar; lay on a very slow fire for half an hour, or till tender; lay them on a border of mashed potatoes, with quenelles as above, and place the tongue between; in another stewpan you have put a little butter and the trimmings of the cucumbers, then add a quart of white sauce, boil and pass through a tammy (*or blend*), adding a little sugar or other seasoning if required, and finish with half a gill of good cream sauce over all except the tongue, which glaze.

DUMPOKHT, THE DISH MENTIONED IN THE ARABIAN NIGHTS AS THE KID STUFFED WITH PISTACHIO NUTS

Clean and truss a fowl or rabbit (*if you should happen to lack a kid*) as for roasting; then stuff it with sultana raisins, pistachio-nuts, and boiled rice in equal parts. Rub fine one ounce of coriander-seed, freed from the husks, four onions, a dozen peppercorns, six cloves, and a teaspoonful of pounded ginger. Set twelve ounces of butter in a stewpan over the fire, rub the pounded ingredients over the fowl or rabbit, and let it fry until perfectly well browned and tender. Have boiled in a quart of white broth (*p. 131*) twelve ounces of rice, two ounces of sultana raisins, two ounces of pistachio nuts and two of almonds, the latter blanched and cut into thin slices. When the rice is nearly tender, strain off the broth and add the rice to the fried fowl; stir the whole well, that the butter may completely saturate the rice, and keep it near the fire to swell till wanted. In serving, surround the fowl with the rice.

Chestnuts may be substituted for pistachio-nuts. (*Serves 4.*)

LEMON CREAM SAUCE FOR STEWED CHICKEN

One-quarter pound of butter, half an ounce of flour, one pint of sweet cream, half a teaspoonful of salt, one lemon, ten white peppercorns.

Let the cream simmer over boiling water with the yellow rind of the lemon cut in strips, and the peppercorns, until it is flavored; rub the flour with the butter, which may be softened with a little of the hot cream; strain the cream, stir in the flour and salt, and let it cook until it is thick as a boiled custard. Arrange the chicken on a platter, pour this dressing over it, garnish with parsley, and serve.

WHITE FRICASSEE OF CHICKEN

Cut up the fowls (*cut up in nineteenth-century fashion, a chicken emerges in 10 pieces: 2 thighs, 2 drumsticks, 2 wings, the breast divided in half along the breastbone and the back divided crosswise*), soak them in milk and water for two hours; then put them in a stewpan with butter rolled in flour, add salt and pepper, and half a pint of milk, with an egg beaten in it; let them stew gently for an hour.

FRICASSEED CHICKEN, BROWN

Clean, wash and cut up a pair of young chickens. Lay in clear water for half an hour. If they are old, you cannot brown them well. Put them in a saucepan with enough cold water to cover them well, and set over the fire to heat slowly. Meanwhile, cut half a pound of salt pork into strips, and fry crisp. Take them out, chop fine, and put into the pot with the chicken. Fry in the fat left in the frying-pan one large onion or two or three small ones, cut into slices. Let them brown well, and add them also to the chicken, with a quarter teaspoonful of allspice and cloves. Stew all together slowly for an hour or more, until the meat is very tender; you can test this with a fork. Take out the pieces of fowl and put in a hot dish, covering closely until the gravy is ready. Add to this a great spoonful (*2 tablespoonfuls*) of walnut or other dark catsup (*Worcestershire will do*), and nearly three tablespoonfuls of browned flour, a little chopped parsley, and a glass of brown sherry. Boil up once; strain through a cullender, to remove the bits of pork and onion; return to the pot, with the chicken; let it come to a final boil, and serve, pouring the gravy over the pieces of fowl. (*Serves 6.*)

CHICKEN CURRY WITH COCOANUT

Cut the chicken as for a fricassee, put it in a saucepan with half a pint of cold water, cover closely, and let it simmer until tender. Grate a cocoanut, and pour over it one and a half gills of tepid water (*canned coconut may be treated as fresh coconut, by allowing for its extra sweetness*); let it stand half an hour. When the chicken is tender, take it out, and add to the gravy three tablespoonfuls of flour rubbed smooth with one and a half ounces of butter and a tablespoonful of curry; let it stew a few minutes; pour in, through a strainer, the water from the cocoanut; add the chicken, let it boil once, then serve. Toasted slices of cocoanut are also a great improvement to the curry. (*Serves 4.*)

"Curry should always be eaten with a spoon. Only globe-trotters use forks."

Eighteen Colonial Recipes, 1845

VIRGINIA CHICKEN PUDDING

Beat ten eggs perfectly light, add to them a quart of rich milk, four ounces of drawn butter (*p. 107*), pepper and salt; stir in sufficient flour to make a thin batter; then take four young chickens, clean them neatly, cut off the legs, wings, etc. Put them all in a sauce-pan, with salt and butter and pepper, and a bundle of thyme and parsley; boil them till nearly done, then take out the chicken, and put it in the batter, and pour the batter in a deep dish and bake it. White gravy for sauce. (*Serves 10–12.*)

CHICKENS BAKED IN RICE

Joint a chicken as for fricassee; with pepper and salt season it well; place it in a pudding dish (*casserole*) lined with slices of bacon or ham; add an onion finely minced, and a pint of veal gravy; pile up the dish full of boiled rice well pressed; cover it with a paste of flour and water (*to be discarded, not eaten; a tight lid will do*), and bake in a slow oven one hour. If veal gravy be wanting, substitute water (*or, better, chicken bouillon*), with additional seasoning and ham. (*Serves 3–4.*)

CHICKEN CROQUETTES

Two tablespoonfuls of butter, four tablespoonfuls of flour, one pint of cream or white stock, one-half teaspoonful of salt, one-half teaspoonful of celery salt, one-half saltspoonful of cayenne, one tablespoonful of grated onion.

Melt the butter, add flour and let cook; add cream and other ingredients. The croquettes can be made wholly of chicken, or a combination of chicken, veal, oysters, sweet-bread and crab. The meat is chopped, then thoroughly combine all the ingredients. Make into shapes about two and a half inches long, round, and flat at each end. Roll, first in sifted bread crumbs, then in beaten egg; again in bread crumbs, and fry in boiling fat. Serve with tomato sauce (*p. 281*).

CHICKEN TERRAPIN

Chop one cold roast chicken and one par-boiled sweetbread moderately fine. Make one cup of rich cream sauce, with one cup of hot cream, a quarter of a cup of butter and two tablespoonfuls of flour. Then put in the chicken and sweetbread. Salt and pepper to taste. Let it heat over hot water fifteen minutes. Just before serving, add the yolks of two eggs, well-beaten, and one wineglass of sherry wine. (*Serve over toast, or rice, to 6.*)

CHICKEN CHARTREUSE

A chartreuse is a fancy dish disguised as a plain dish. The name is attributed to the monks of Chartreuse who are supposed to have invented it to dodge fast days.

Chop very fine nine ounces, or a heaping cupful, of cold cooked chicken; add the inside of two sausages, or two ounces of lean cooked ham, chopped fine, three tablespoonfuls of powdered bread crumbs, one tablespoonful of capers, or one tablespoonful of chopped parsley, two tablespoonfuls of lemon juice or vinegar, a speck of cayenne, two eggs well-beaten, and enough hot soup stock (*bouillon will not do as a substitute, since you want the jellying properties of stock; if you have none, use canned madrilene*) to make it quite moist. Add salt and pepper to taste, the amount depending upon the seasoning in the sausage. The sausage may be omitted, and a larger amount of chicken used. Butter a small (*1 quart or less*) mould, and pack the meat in closely to within an inch of the top to allow for swelling. Put it on a trivet in the kettle (*pour water around it, two-thirds of the way up the mold*) and steam for three hours. If no uncooked meat be used, one hour will be sufficient. Cool it in the mould; when ready to serve, dip the mould quickly into warm water and loosen the meat around the edges with a thin knife and remove the mould.

CHICKEN PÂTÉ

Put half an ounce of isinglass (*or 1 envelope of unflavored gelatine*) to soak. Cut a chicken as for a fricassee, cover with water, and let it simmer until the meat slips easily from the bones. Have ready some hard-boiled eggs. Cut the chicken in thin slices; return the bones to the water in the kettle to enrich the jelly. Wet a plain mould, and line it with thin slices of lemon and egg, then fill it, seasoning with salt, pepper, and a little mace or nutmeg, with layers of chicken and egg, adding now and then small bits of boiled ham, bacon or pork, and slices of lemon. Season with gravy, add the isinglass (*or gelatine*) and when dissolved, pour over the chicken; cover with a crust or tin cover; bake in a moderate oven three-quarters of an hour. To be served cold the following day. Three or four eggs and one lemon may be used for this quantity. Sliced mushrooms are an improvement to the paté, and also thin slices of boiled red beets.

SYDNEY SMITH'S RECEIPT FOR (*CHICKEN*) SALAD DRESS-ING

Sydney Smith was a noted English clergyman and humorist. His receipt is reproduced in almost every nineteenth-century cookbook that exists. Like Shakespeare, he seems to have believed in giving shaky brains (women's and boy actors') verse to help them remember things.

> Two boiled potatoes, strained through a kitchen sieve
> Softness and smoothness to the salad give;
> Of mordant mustard take a single spoon—
> Distrust the condiment that bites too soon;
> Yet deem it not, thou man of taste, a fault,
> To add a double quantity of salt.
> Four times the spoon with oil of Lucca crown,
> And twice with vinegar procured from town;
> True taste requires it, and your poet begs,
> The pounded yellow of two well-boiled eggs.
> Let onions' atoms lurk within the bowl,
> And scarce suspected, animate the whole;
> And lastly, in the flavored compound toss
> A magic spoonful of anchovy sauce.
> Oh, great and glorious! Oh, herbaceous meat!
> 'Twould tempt the dying Anchorite to eat.
> Back to the world he'd turn his weary soul,
> And plunge his fingers in the salad bowl.

The mustard is dry, not made; oil of Lucca is olive oil; the bowl may be rubbed with garlic instead of onion, and Worcestershire or Harvey's may—

with but a little loss—be substituted for anchovy sauce (the thing is catching!).

COCK-A-LEEKIE, A SPECIAL FAVORITE OF JAMES I

Stew a large fowl, a marrowbone, and two or three pounds of beef with four to six quarts of water and the white ends of two or three leeks, cut in pieces. Just before serving, add half a pound of prunes, which dish with the soup and fowl; but not the meat or marrowbone, which, when put to boil, must be divided (*cut up*) and left uncovered.

OR: Put seven pound of the upper end of a leg of beef and an old fowl in a pot with water enough to cover it; the white parts of two or three dozen leeks, half-boiled and sliced, and one pound of prunes. Stew until the meat be tender, skimming it well, and if you choose, the fowl may be disjointed and sent up with the soup (*they may be puréed in the blender with a little broth*); but no other seasoning is usually employed than salt and allspice, with a small quantity of mace. (*Serves 6–8.*)

SASSAFRAS GOMBO

Take a quart or a pint of oysters, according to the quantity of stock required; parboil them in their liquor, to which, if undiluted, add a cupful of water while over the fire. This being done, take them off the fire, and set them aside. Slice and cut up a good-sized onion, having ready also a teaspoonful of finely chopped parsley or celery. Cut up in not large pieces a chicken or half of one, according to the stock desired, and four or five ounces of ham in small pieces. You now have all the materials for your stock, which is made as follows: First fry your onions in hot lard; when softened and turning brown, skin them out of the lard, taking care to leave no particles, which, charring, would impart a bitter flavor to the stock. Then throw into the hot lard your chicken and ham, which, when done brown, sprinkle gradually with a cupful of hot water, throwing in the chopped parsley or celery; cover the vessel, and give a simmer of five minutes on a slow fire. At this point may be added, if acceptable, half a pod of cayenne pepper, or a sufficient quantity of the ground to give pungency; a dash of mushroom catsup (*p. 250*), and one of Worcestershire sauce may be added. No cold water is to be used in making stock. Continue every five minutes to add a cupful of hot water, keeping up the simmering, but never boiling, until you have your due quantity of stock for the number of plates which you may have to serve. The last addition of liquid, to complete, is to be made from the liquor of the oysters, which, with them, is thrown in to simmer a few minutes. Thus far, we have a rich composite stew, which is now to be converted into gombo by the following process; have ready about a heaped tablespoonful of sassafras leaves (*dried*), finely powdered (*p. 260*). Draw your stock from the fire and by sprinkling the sassafras over the liquid, rapidly beating it at the same time, thoroughly incorporate the powder with the stock and, *Io pæan!* The gombo is done.

N.B. Never attempt to add the sassafras while the vessel is on the fire. The result of so doing would be to precipitate the powder to the bottom, and literally, send your gombo to pot. The gombo may be served as a thickened soup to be eaten with rice or bread, as may be preferred. The rice, however, is an element of the ritual of gombo.

ASPIC JELLY

1 *fowl*	1 *carrot*
1 *shin of beef*	1 *stalk of celery*
1 *knuckle of veal*	1 *turnip*
1 *cloves*	½ *package unflavored gelatin*
1 *bay leaf*	1 *cupful sherry or Madeira*
2 *onions*	

Put the chicken, beef and veal in a pot. Cover them well with cold water, and let it simmer for five or six hours, with the pot covered closely. An hour before removing from the fire, add the carrot cut into dice, the cloves and bay leaf. Fry in butter the onions and celery cut into pieces, to a dark brown, and add them to the stock at the same time. Remove from the fire, strain, and add one-half package (2 *envelopes*) of gelatin which has been soaked for an hour in one cupful of water, and one cupful of sherry or Madeira. Stir until the gelatin is dissolved. Set away until the next day. There should be two quarts of jelly. If it is not solid enough to stand, more gelatine may be added at the time of clearing. Boiling down the aspic will not make it more firm.

To CLARIFY: Remove all grease from the top of the jelly, and wipe it off with a cloth wet in hot water, so every particle of grease will be removed. Stir into the cold jelly the beaten white and shells of three eggs. Put it on the fire, and continue to stir until it boils. Let it boil for five minutes; then strain it through a double cloth. If not perfectly clear, strain again. Let the jelly drain through the cloth without pressure.

See October (p. 296) for rabbit and game-bird recipes adaptable for chicken.

CHICKEN LIVERS WITH MADEIRA

Put a tablespoonful of butter in the chaffing-dish; add the livers cut into pieces; cook them directly over the flame, turning them occasionally, and dredge them while cooking with a tablespoonful of flour. It will take about five minutes to cook them; add a cupful of stock and a few drops of mushroom ketchup or Worcestershire. Then place the pan in the double-pan containing water already hot; add to the livers half a cupful of Madeira and a few stoned (*ripe*) olives; season with salt, pepper and paprika after the wine is in; cover and let it simmer a few minutes. Serve with croutons.

OYSTERS

Oysters are again in season after the summer dearth, but we have far fewer of them, and they are enormously more expensive than they were in the nineteenth century. All oysters brought to market now are farmed—and within the last twenty years the wholesale price has gone from $12.00 a barrel (which holds 3 bushels) to more than $20.00 a bushel, partly because of an explosive increase in starfish, the oyster's natural enemy, responding to an ecological imbalance. Because oysters are farmed, the price as long as they are in season does not fluctuate much.

Oysters were one of the most common delicacies a hundred years ago, and the seacoasts apparently had no monopoly on them. Scalloped oysters were a traditional Thanksgiving dish in Ohio. Charles Brown, a corporal in the Union Army in 1862, wrote to his family in Rochester, New York, to thank them for the barrel of oysters they had sent—which arrived in good condition a month later. The secret was in the shipping: seawater or salted water changed daily, with a couple of handfuls of cornmeal scattered through it, over oysters laid deep-shell down.

Oysters were also pickled and preserved. We can buy them now canned (canned oysters are good for flavoring, but don't stand up to cooking very well), or freshly shelled in most fish markets, or fresh from the sea in some seaside towns. If you are desperate, they can be frozen to keep them a week or so, but it is not recommended. When you can buy them, gobble them up as quickly as possible. Here are recipes—but nothing can really equal a raw, fresh oyster, with a little sauce or pepper vinegar (p. 445).

Part II: Recipes

"Everybody seems to know every thing that can be said about oysters—that they are in season in all the months that contain the letter R, that they are a luxury which all must learn to enjoy, though all shrink from the first attempt to swallow a fellow-creature alive; that they are decidedly wholesome; and that they harmonize with brown bread and butter. It is well known that oysters, combined with a milk diet, are most beneficial where a tendency to consumption exists. Of course, they should be eaten with moderation, and are most wholesome raw, with a little pepper only."

The Cuisine, by An Eminent French Caterer, 1872

OYSTERS À L'ALEXANDRE DUMAS

Place in a sauce-bowl a heaped teaspoonful of salt, three-quarters of a teaspoonful of very finely crushed white pepper, one medium-sized, fine, sound, well-peeled and very finely chopped shallot, one heaped teaspoonful of very finely chopped chives, and half a teaspoonful of parsley, also very finely chopped up. Mix together lightly, then pour in a light teaspoonful of olive oil, six drops of Tabasco sauce, one saltspoonful of Worcestershire sauce, and lastly, one light gill, or five and a half tablespoonfuls, of good vinegar. Mix it thoroughly with a spoon; send to the table and with a teaspoon pour a little sauce over each oyster just before eating it.

OYSTERS ROASTED

Wash the shells perfectly clean, wipe them dry, and lay them on a gridiron, the largest side to the fire; set it over a bright bed of coals; when the shells open wide and the oyster looks white, they are done; fold a napkin on a large dish or tray, lay the oysters in their shells, taking care not to lose the juice. Serve hot, with cold butter and rolls or crackers.

DEVILED OYSTERS

Time, three or four minutes. Open a sufficient number of oysters for a dish, leaving them in their deep shells, and their liquor; add a little lemon juice, pepper, salt and cayenne; put a small piece of butter in each and place the shell carefully on a gridiron over a clear bright fire, to broil a few minutes. Serve them on a napkin with bread and butter.

SMOTHERED OYSTERS, MARYLAND FASHION

Drain all the juice from a quart of oysters. Melt in a frying-pan a piece of butter the size of an egg, with as much cayenne pepper as can be taken upon the point of a penknife, and a saltspoonful of salt. Put in the oysters and cover closely. They are done as soon as the edges ruffle. Serve on thin pieces of buttered toast for breakfast or supper. A glass of sherry is often added.

SCALLOPED OYSTERS

Sprinkle the bottom of a pudding dish or granite baking-pan, with cracker meal (*or crumbled soda crackers*). Put over this a layer of oysters. Sprinkle salt, pepper, butter, chopped parsley and another layer of cracker meal. Then add another layer of oysters, and so on until the pan has been almost filled, but leaving a margin. Then beat the yolks of two eggs light, mix with one cup of milk, and pour into the pan over the whole. Sprinkle the top with cracker crumbs and bake in the oven from thirty to forty-five minutes.

OYSTER SALAD

Directions for dressing one gallon of oysters: heat the oysters until they plump or curd; mix together the well-beaten yolks of twelve raw eggs, half a cupful of made mustard, one teacupful of white sugar. These ingredients must be made hot, and be ready to pour over the oysters as soon as these are ladled out of the kettle. As soon before the time of serving as is practicable, chop up as much bleached celery as will fill a quart measure; add to it the dressed oysters, mixing lightly with a wooden fork and spoon, and placing it in a salad bowl, ready for serving.

PIGS IN BLANKETS

Pigs in blankets are now little wieners in pastry, not oysters.
Select large plump oysters, roll each in a thin slice of fresh bacon, skewer with a wooden toothpick; place them in a pan singly with a little butter, pepper and salt; let them remain in the oven until thoroughly heated, not baked, and serve just as they are, using the sticks as a handle. When once tasted, pigs in blankets will prove a toothsome morsel never to be forgotten.

OYSTER POTATO BALLS

This is a very palatable dish for suppers, and its production being so simple, it requires only to be pointed out to become popular. Beard a dozen (more or less, according to the number you provide for) small plump oysters, cover them singly with a plain mashed potato paste (*p. 78*), roll them in flour, or beat-up egg and bread-crumbs, into balls, and (*deep*) fry them in butter or dripping. Put into each ball when you make it up a teaspoonful of the oyster liquid.

OYSTER SOUP (*OR STEW*)

Take the oysters out of the liquor; to every quart of liquor add a pint of water or of milk; then set it on the fire with the oysters. Mix a large spoonful of flour with a little water, and stir it into the liquor as soon as it boils. Season with pepper, salt, and a little butternut or walnut vinegar, or common vinegar; add a small piece of butter, and, as soon as it boils up again, pour it on buttered toast, cut in small pieces.

ANOTHER: Take of water and milk, each three pints, set it on the fire to boil; roll half a pound of crackers or soda biscuits (*into rough crumbs*), and add to it, with one pint of oysters; let it boil until the flavor of the oyster is given to the soup, and the crackers are well swelled, then add salt and pepper to taste, and three pints more of oysters, and a quarter of a pound of butter; put some crackers in the tureen, and pour the soup over. A sprinkle of cayenne pepper is by some considered an improvement. (*Serves 16–20.*)

OYSTER LOAF

Cut a round piece, five inches across, from the top of a nicely baked round loaf of bread, remove the crumb, leaving the crust half an inch thick; make a rich oyster stew, and put it in the loaf in layers sprinkled with bread crumbs; place the cover over the top, cover the loaf with beaten yolk of an egg and put it in the oven to glaze. Make a wreath of curled parsley on a platter, with the stems turned in, and place the loaf on them, concealing all but the leaves. Serve very hot. (*Serves 4–6.*)

OYSTER PATTIES

Stew some large oysters with a little nutmeg, a few cloves, some yolk of eggs boiled hard and grated, a little butter and as much of the oyster liquid as will cover them; when stewed a few minutes, take them out of the pans to cool. Have shells of puff paste previously baked in small patty pans, and lay two or three oysters in each (*with a small lump of butter*).

PICKLED OYSTERS

Scald the oysters in their own liquor, with a little water added, till they are plump. Skim them out, and drop into a bowl of cold water; rinse well and put them in glass jars.

Scald an equal quantity of the liquor and vinegar with whole peppercorns, mace and salt, and when perfectly cold fill the jars up with it. These will keep two or three weeks.

OYSTER SAUCE (*FOR TURKEY OR LOBSTER*)

is made of half a pint of oysters boiled in a pan, thickened with a lump of butter rolled in flour. Only let it boil once. Serve this by itself, for every person does not like oyster sauce. (*Makes 1 cup.*)

TOMATOES

September is the month to do something about tomatoes. In July, they are still green, and everybody, sick of wooden-tasting cold-storage tomatoes, is impatient for them to ripen. In August, they are ripe, a novelty, sliced red and raw and delicious on the plate at every meal. By September, let's face it, tomatoes are almost old hat. They are flooding in—as plentiful and as cheap as they'll ever be during the year—faster than they can be eaten. After the commercial pickers are through, farmers often offer the remains to do-it-yourself pickers. It is time to can, and preserve, and freeze, and generally to fiddle with tomatoes.

TO DRESS TOMATOES

The most simple method of cooking them is to boil them like vegetables, in boiling water and salt, for a quarter of an hour; then drain, peel, mash them smooth, with a due proportion of salt and pepper; add a minced eschalot; or roast them in a Dutch oven (*or under a broiler*), turning them frequently for ten minutes or a quarter of an hour. They must then be served whole.

Ripe tomatoes are easily skinned for cooking or preserving: dip them in rapidly boiling water, count ten slowly, take them out and strip the skins off them.

FORCED TOMATOES

Open the top and extract the seeds (*leaving a fair-sized hole*) from half a dozen tomatoes; fill up the middle with sausage meat; put them into a stewpan with as much bouillon as will cover them, a clove of garlic, two teaspoons of salt, and half a teaspoon of cayenne. Stew gently (*uncovered*) for a quarter of an hour in good gravy; then take out the garlic, add a teaspoon of lemon juice, and serve in the gravy. (*Serves 6.*)

DEVILED TOMATOES

Cut four large tomatoes in (*thick*) slices, and lay aside. Rub yolks of two hard-boiled eggs with one tablespoonful of vinegar, one tablespoonful of melted butter, one teaspoonful of sugar, pinch salt, mustard and cayenne. Put whole on stove, and when boiling, stir this into beaten yolk of a raw egg. Let come again to a boil. Broil the slices of tomato, lay on a dish, and pour dressing over. Serve hot. (*Serves 4–6.*)

JUMBLE-I

It is a favorite dish in the south. Take a teacup of bacon cut into dice, one large onion sliced, fry together until brown; then add one can (*a home-canned can holds 1 quart*) of tomatoes and a cup of (*uncooked*) rice; salt, pepper and a little water; cover it and cook slowly until the rice is done. The oftener you warm over, the better it gets. (*Serves 4–6.*)

A VEGETARIAN SUPPER DISH

Break two ounces of macaroni into short lengths, throw in boiling water and boil rapidly for twenty minutes. Rub the hard-boiled yolks of two eggs to a paste; add gradually four or five tablespoonfuls of cream. Rub together a tablespoonful of butter and one of flour; add the egg and half a cupful of milk; stir over hot water until you have a thick golden sauce; add half a teaspoonful of salt and a dash of pepper. Chop the macaroni fine and add it to the sauce. Cut a slice from the stem ends of good solid tomatoes, scoop out the centres, stand the tomatoes in a baking pan, fill the centres with the macaroni, dust with breadcrumbs, and bake in a moderate oven for thirty minutes, until the tomatoes are perfectly soft but not broken.

Serve on slices of toast, either plain or with cream sauce. (*Grated*) cheese may be added to the macaroni, which will give greater food value. (*Serves 4–6.*)

EGYPTIAN TOMATOES

Peel and scoop the centres of five or six solid tomatoes; put on ice until perfectly cold. When ready to serve, arrange the tomatoes on lettuce leaves and fill the centres with finely-chopped cress that has been seasoned with grated onion, half a teaspoonful of celery seed, a dash of salt and pepper. Pour over a little french dressing (*oil and vinegar, sometimes flavored with mustard*) and serve at once. (*Serves 6.*)

TOMATO SALAD

Pare the tomatoes; remove the centre, thus forming a cup; fill with pieces of celery and a cream mayonnaise (*p. 190*) seasoned with salt, pepper, and a dust of sugar.

Raw tomatoes are good dipped in tarragon or chervil vinegar just after peeling them, while they are still warm.

Part II: *Recipes*

SIMPLE TOMATO JUICE

Peel the best, ripest tomatoes. Purée them in the blender; put through a food mill to get the seeds out; add salt and pepper; bring to a boil, pour into glass jars, and process 30 minutes under boiling water to can. For a blended juice, purée celery, carrots, parsley, onions, etc., with the tomatoes.

TOMATO PIE

Take ripe tomatoes, skin and slice them. Sprinkle over a little salt and let them stand a few minutes, pour off the juice and add sugar, one-half cup cream (*beaten with*) one egg, nutmeg, and cover with a rich paste, and bake in a moderate oven one-half hour. This makes an excellent and much approved pie.

TOMATO ASPIC

Soak a half box (*2 envelopes*) of gelatine in a half-pint of water for an hour. Bring to a boil the liquor in a quart can of tomatoes; add to it a teaspoonful of onion juice, two teaspoons of sugar, a teaspoon of minced parsley, and a bay leaf with pepper and salt to taste. Simmer twenty minutes, add soaked gelatine, stir until it dissolves, strain through flannel into mold. (*Makes 3½ cups.*)

TOMATO SOUP

Slice two onions and fry them in butter until brown; remove them and fry two dozen tomatoes just sufficiently to heat them through, then put them into a stewpan with their gravy and the onions, add a head of celery and a carrot sliced; stew gently one-half hour. Add three pints of gravy (*or beef stock*), stew one hour and a half; pulp the whole of the vegetables through a sieve (*or food mill*), season with white pepper, salt and cayenne. Serve with sippets of toasted bread cut in slices. (*Serves 10.*)

CREAM OF TOMATO SOUP: Scald one quart of either fresh or canned tomatoes for about ten minutes; then stir in a fourth of a teaspoonful of dry soda; when the foaming ceases, put in one quart cold sweet milk, into which has been stirred two tablespoonfuls of flour; add salt and red pepper, and let the soup boil for ten minutes longer, constantly stirring it; strain through a sieve or colander into tureen, upon a piece of butter as large or larger than an egg; stir until the butter is dissolved; serve at once. (*Serves 6.*)

QUICK COLD TOMATO SOUP: *Put 1 quart of stewed tomatoes, 1 cup of cream or sour cream, 2 teaspoonfuls of dill, white pepper, and a little salt into the blender, half at a time; purée and serve. Or, substitute 6 ice-cubes—½ cup—of beef stock for half the cream. Serves 6.*

SPAGHETTI SAUCE

It saves space to make tomatoes into sauce to can or freeze. Sauté chopped onions in olive oil, add a little chopped celery, peppers, parsley, garlic, carrots, or any of the usual accoutrements of spaghetti sauce—but be careful not to overpower the tomato. Flavor with basil, orégano, bay, thyme, and marjoram. Add the peeled tomatoes and simmer in a large uncovered pot until reduced to the right consistency. It usually takes 6–8 hours, but can be hurried if you cheat and add canned tomato paste. Do not add salt or meat: both reduce the length of time the sauce can be kept frozen, and both can be added later. Stir the sauce occasionally as it cooks, more often as it gets thicker. When it is done, cool and freeze in one-meal-size packages, or can. This can also be used to flavor stews or fricassees, or for any purpose for which you might use store-bought tomato paste.

TOMATO SAUCE

Cut in two, twelve perfectly ripe red tomatoes; press the seeds and watery part out; then put them into a saucepan, with a quarter of a spoonful of cayenne, and a quarter of a pint of gravy (*stock*); cover and set by the side of the fire to stew gently for an hour; when the fruit should be melted, press it through a sieve (*or food mill*) and simmer the sauce over the fire for a few minutes, add half a teaspoonful of salt. Serve in a tureen (*with meat, fish, or vegetables*).

TOMATOES PRESERVED

In Asia Minor they are preserved for use during the winter in the follow-ing manner: cut them in two, and sprinkle on them considerable salt to remain over night. Next day pass through a colander (*or food mill*). Set the part strained through to dry in the sun, in shallow dishes, in a depth of an inch or less. Dry it to more consistence than jelly, and put it in covered jars for use. If it is not sufficiently dry to keep, add more salt and expose it again to the sun. A tablespoonful will season a soup of stewed meat.

TOMATO KETCHUP

To a gallon of skinned tomatoes, put four spoonfuls of salt, four of black pepper, three of (*dry*) mustard, half a spoonful of allspice, and eight pods of red pepper. All the ingredients should be made fine (*chopped*) and simmered slowly in a pewter (*enamel*) basin, in sufficient sharp vinegar to have two quarts of ketchup after simmering three or four hours and straining it through a wire sieve. (*Vinegar may be added little by little, as necessary.*) Those who like it may add two spoonfuls of the juice of garlic, after the simmering is over, and the ingredients somewhat cooled. (*Save old catsup bottles and store home-made catsup in them.*) May be used in a week. (*Can be stored almost indefinitely.*)

TOMATO CHUTNEY

Two pounds (*chopped*) apples, mangoes or ripe tomatoes; one-half pound green ginger; two pounds raisins; one-half pound salt (*or less*); one-half pound garlic (*8 cloves*); one pound almonds; three pounds (*brown*) sugar; five teaspoons chilies (*or Tabasco sauce*); two tablespoonfuls vinegar. All to be finely mixed. Cook over a slow fire to proper consistency, or let stand in the sun.

This is a very hot chutney, authentically Indian. I add 2 pounds of chopped green tomatoes and ½ pound of sliced red onions, which I salt and let stand overnight, then drain. The almonds are added last, to keep their crunchy texture. Makes 8 pints.

PRESERVED TOMATOES (*A SWEET RELISH*)

Take of small, ripe tomatoes one peck, stick them full of holes (*with a fork*), make of eight pounds of sugar (*and 2 cups of water*) a syrup, and put them in it, with eight lemons sliced, and two ounces of race (*green*) ginger chopped fine, boil slowly three hours; take the tomatoes out, and boil the liquor to a syrup. (*Put the tomatoes in jars and pour the hot syrup over them; seal.*)

PICKLED TOMATOES

They should not be very ripe. Mix in a stone jar an ounce of mustard, half an ounce of cloves, half an ounce of (*whole*) pepper, with half a jar (*fill the jar half full*) of vinegar. Lay in the tomatoes with a dozen of onions and cover it close for a month. They will then be fit for use. If the jar is kept well covered, they will keep a year. The onions may be omitted if you choose, and more spice substituted.

GRANDMOTHER WEAVER'S TOMATO PRESERVES (*JAM*)

Simmer the peel of one lemon and one orange, cut in slivers, in a syrup made of two pounds of sugar and their juice until the peel is nearly tender. Add twelve large yellow tomatoes (red will do), peeled and chopped, the chopped pulp of the orange and lemon, three or four sticks of cinnamon and several cloves. Boil, stirring occasionally, about thirty minutes, or until moderately thick. Put in jars; when cool, seal with parafin.

TOMATA HONEY

Tomatoes frequently ended in "a" in the early nineteenth century.

To each pound of tomatas, allow the grated peel of a lemon and six fresh peach-leaves. Boil them slowly till they are all to pieces; then squeeze, and strain them through a bag. To each pint of liquor allow a pound of loaf sugar and the juice of one lemon. Boil them together half an hour, or till they become a thick jelly. Then put it into glasses, and lay double tissue paper closely over the top. It will be scarcely distinguishable from real honey. (*The pulp, with spices added, should be usable as tomato paste.*)

[283]

AUTUMN SOUP

Take six pounds of lean (*meat*), cut up in one quart of water to one gallon, add the hock of a ham, boil and skim it, and put in two quarts ochras, cut in small slices, an onion sliced, two quarts ripe tomatoes cut up, one quart lima beans; simmer four hours slowly; add the green (*sweet*) corn grated off eight ears, season the soup and boil until the meat is in rags and the soup thoroughly done. (*Serves 18–20.*)

CARROTS

STEWED CARROTS

One and a quarter pounds of carrots, two ounces of butter, two gills of cream, two teaspoonfuls of salt, one pinch of cayenne pepper, the yolks of two eggs.

Divide the carrots lengthwise unless quite small, and boil until perfectly tender (*about 20 minutes*); take them from the water, slice them very thin in a saucepan, add the butter, stir the salt and pepper in the cream, and pour it over the carrots; let them stew fifteen minutes, then put them in a vegetable-dish, and leave the saucepan with the cream on the stove; when it boils, stir in the well-beaten yolks, and pour over the carrots. (*Serves 6.*)

CARROTS WITH CURRY

Stew young carrots and cut them in quarters lengthwise; to half a gill of the water in which they were stewed add one gill of cream, and an ounce of butter rubbed with half a tablespoonful of flour, a little salt, and a teaspoonful of curry powder; let it simmer in a saucepan until thickened; slide in the carrots, cover for a few moments, then serve hot.

CARROTS, SWEET AND SOUR

Peel carrots and cut in one-inch pieces. Put on to boil in cold salt water, and cook until tender. Drain off water. Brown one-half cupful sugar in skillet with one tablespoonful of flour, and one-half cupful vinegar and rub smooth. Add one-half cupful soup stock, and put carrots in. Let whole boil up together.

CARROT PUDDING

Mix in a bowl half a pound of flour, half a pound of chopped (*ground*) suet, three-quarters of a pound of grated carrot, one-quarter of a pound of raisins stoned, one-quarter of a pound of currants, and a quarter of a pound of sugar, brown or sifted white; place these in a mould or dish, beat up two whole eggs, and the yolks of four in a gill of milk, grate a little nutmeg in it, and add it to the former; bake or steam forty-five minutes.

ANOTHER: A coffeecup of boiled and strained carrots, five eggs, two ounces of sugar, two of butter, cinnamon and rosewater (*or a little orange juice; blend the well-beaten eggs with the carrots and other ingredients*); bake in a deep dish (*in a 375° oven for 45 minutes*) without paste.

COMMON CARROT SOUP

The most easy method of making this favorite English soup is to boil some highly colored carrots quite tender in water slightly salted, then to pound or mash them to a smooth paste, and to mix with them boiling gravy (*or purée in blender with the gravy*) or a strong beef broth in the proportion of two quarts to one and a half pounds of carrots; then to pass the whole through a strainer, to season it with salt and cayenne, to heat it in a clean stewpan and to serve it immediately.

CELERY

Celery, which is ready in late September and early October, can be eaten other ways than crisp and raw. It can be stewed like onions, dutched like lettuce—or dipped in batter and deep-fried.

CELERY VINEGAR

Cut up a bunch of fresh celery into small bits, or pour ¼ pound of celery seed into a jar; scald 1 teaspoonful salt, 1 tablespoonful white sugar and 1 quart best vinegar, and pour over the celery stalks or seed; let it cool, and put away in one large jar tightly corked. In a fortnight, strain and bottle in small flasks, corking tightly.

CELERY SALT

Save the root of the celery plant; dry and grate it, mixing it with one-third as much salt. Keep in a bottle well corked. It is delicious for soups, oysters, gravies and hashes.

PEARS

Bartlett pears are usually ready in late August, sometimes earlier. The hard winter pears, best for canning or baking, need just a nip of frost. Seckels, ready in late September, are best for canning whole, spiced with cinnamon and red candy hearts for decorating Thanksgiving and Christmas meats, or boiled in light ginger-flavored syrup for winter desserts.

COMPOTE OF PEARS

Compotes of fruits of all kinds are used either for *entremets*, garnished with biscuits or pastry, or for dessert. They are usually served in deep glass dishes, known in the dessert services as *compotiers*.

Make a syrup of ten ounces of sugar, half a pint of water, and two cloves; when boiled thick, take out the cloves, and add a glass of port wine; put one pound of good baking pears on the fire for a few minutes in boiling water till you can draw off the skin; core them, and put into the syrup; boil gently for twenty minutes; or the pears be large, half an hour, till they are tender; then turn out with the syrup. (*Serves 4.*)

BAKED PEARS

Hard pears, or windfalls, are delicious pared, cored and cut in quarters. Fill a deep pudding dish with them; for two quarts add one cup of sugar and one cup of water. Bake closely covered, in a very moderate oven for several hours. (*Try mixing the pears with a few crab-apples or quinces. Test for done-ness with a cake tester; when nearly tender, remove the cover and sprinkle some sugar over the top to brown. A little butter added, or brown sugar instead of white, makes a richer dish.*) When done, and still hot, they may be sealed in Mason's jars, and will keep indefinitely. (*But to make sure, process them 20 minutes in a boiling water bath.*)

PEAR MARMALADE

Pare, divide and core large pears, boil them in as much water as will cover them till they are tender, then take them out, and put into the same water the parings and cores of the pears; boil till half reduced, and strain. Use the strained liquor, in making a syrup of three-quarters of a pound of sugar, and a pint for every pound of pears. When this syrup is boiled till it jellies on the spoon (*p. 28*), put in the pears and boil up, stirring them for a few minutes until the marmalade is smooth and ready for the pots.

PEAR CHIPS

Wipe 8 pounds of pears, remove stem, core and cut into small pieces. Add 4 pounds of sugar and ¼ pound of Canton (*crystallized*) ginger and allow to stand overnight. In the morning add 4 lemons cut in small pieces, rejecting the seeds, and cook slowly 3 hours. Put in a stone jar. (*Or drain and dry in a cool oven, to eat as candy. Makes 4 pints.*)

GRAPES

GRAPE JELLY

Select grapes that are not too ripe—Isabella or Concord—and after washing and removing from their stems, boil them twenty minutes and strain. Then add a pound of granulated sugar to a pound of the juice and boil it for five minutes longer until the sugar is thoroughly dissolved. Then put it into jelly glasses, and invariably it will "jell," unless the grapes are too ripe.

See pp. 28–29 for jelly-making processes. Grapes are high in pectin and do not need added pectin. Wild-grape jelly needs more sugar. Occasionally crystals form in grape jelly. It is tartaric acid and harmless.

GRAPE SHERBET

Sweeten one quart of grape juice to taste; add one cupful of sugar to two cupfuls of orange juice and stir until the sugar is dissolved. Add to the grape juice, turn into the freezer and freeze. When nearly frozen, remove the dasher and beat in with a spoon the white of an egg beaten light with two teaspoonfuls of powdered sugar. Beat well, pack and stand away to ripen (*p. 36*).

TO PRESERVE GRAPES IN BRANDY FOR WINTER DESSERT

Take some fine close bunches of grapes, prick each twice with a fine needle, and lay them carefully in jars, cover the grapes thickly over with pounded sugar candy (*rock candy*), and then fill up the jars with good brandy. Tie the jars tightly over with a bladder (*or paraffin, or plastic*) and set them in a cool place.

TO PRESERVE GRAPES

Take a cask or barrel inaccessible to the external air, and put into it a layer of bran dried in an oven, or of ashes well-dried and sifted. Upon this place a layer of grapes, well cleaned and gathered in the afternoon of a dry day, before they are perfectly ripe. Proceed thus with alternate layers of bran and grapes until the barrel is full, taking care that the grapes do not touch each other, and to let the last layer be of bran; then close the barrel so that the air may not be able to penetrate, which is the essential point. Grapes thus packed will keep nine or even twelve months. To restore them to freshness, cut the end of the stalk of each bunch of grapes and put that of white grapes into white wine and that of black grapes into red wine, as you would put flowers into water to revive or keep them fresh.

WHITE GRAPE SALAD

Take two cups of white grapes, cut in half and take out the seeds. Add one cup English walnuts, and mix the following mayonnaise: yolks of three eggs, three-eighths cup of butter, one and one-half tablespoon sugar, one-half teaspoon (*dry*) mustard, one-half teaspoon salt, beat until light, then add one-half cup of vinegar and cook until thick. Add a little cayenne pepper and thin with cream. (*Serves 4–6.*)

[13]

OCTOBER

Goose; duck; rabbit; squirrel; game birds; apples; cider; quinces; potatoes; green tomatoes; cabbage; cauliflower; earth vegetables; leeks and onions; pumpkins; nuts

October usually marks the beginning of the various game hunting seasons. I include these recipes out of a fondness for game rather than any fondness for hunters—most of those I have seen at close range seem just as happy to shoot cats, or windows, or each other, as they do game. (Personally I prefer old-style poachers, those who still hunt for food and not out of some misguided search for masculinity.) Nothing is quite so special as meat brought in properly from the woods, prepared with care and eaten with reverent relish.

Modern cookbooks don't go in much for game. It is not readily available, for one thing—though rabbits and pheasants can be bought frozen these days, and Rock Cornish game hen can be substituted in recipes for game birds. But these old recipes are too good to be lost.

Goose, that rather maligned bird, and domestic duck just seem to fit naturally with pheasant and quail and hare.

GOOSE

ROAST GOOSE

Peel and cut in rather small dice six middle-size onions, put in a pan, with two ounces of butter, half a teaspoonful of salt, a quarter ditto of pepper, a little grated nutmeg and sugar, six leaves of fresh sage chopped fine, put on fire, stir with wooden spoon till in pulp. Then have the goose ready trussed and stuff it whilst hot, tie the skin of the neck to the back, pass the spit through, and roast before a moderate fire; baste (with butter, then with dripping), give a nice yellow color (*when the leg will pull away from the body, it is done*), remove it from the spit, take off the string, and serve with half a pint of good brown gravy under, and apple-sauce in a boat. (*One goose serves 6 comfortably.*)

THE SAME WITH ANOTHER STUFFING: I have tried it with the liver chopped and mixed with the onions; I also at times add two cold potatoes cut in dice and a spoonful of boiled rice; it removes the richness of the fat, and renders it more palatable and digestive; and I also sometimes add twenty chestnuts cut into dice.

GOOSE ROASTED

Having the goose ready the day previous to using take three cloves of garlic, which cut in four pieces each and place inside the goose, and (*next day*) stuff it as follows: take four apples, four onions, four leaves of sage not broken, four leaves of lemon-thyme not broken, and boil in a stew-pan with sufficient water to cover them; when done, pulp them through a sieve, removing the sage and thyme, then add sufficient pulp of mealy (*mashed*) potatoes to cause it to be sufficiently dry without sticking to the hand, add pepper and salt, and stuff the bird, having previously removed the garlic, tie the neck and rump, and spit it, paper (*cover*) the breast, which remove after it has been at the fire twenty minutes; when done, serve plain with a thickened gravy.

> "*How to chuse a tame goose: If the bill be yellowish, and she has but few hairs, she is young; but if full of hairs, and the bill and foot red, she is old: if new, limber-footed; if stale, dry-footed.*"
> Hannah Glasse, *The Art of Cookery*, 1812

Part II: Recipes

PRESERVED GOOSE FOR THE FARM OR COUNTRY HOUSE

In case you have more geese in condition and season than what you consume, kill and cut them up into pieces, so that there should be as little flesh left on the carcase as possible, and bone the leg; rub into each piece with your fingers some salt, in which you have mixed a little saltpetre, put them into an earthen pan, with some thyme, bay-leaf, spice, a clove or chopped garlic, rub them for a couple of days, after which dip each piece in water and dry on a cloth; when you have chopped fine and melted all the fat you could get from the goose, and scraped a quarter of a pound of fat bacon and melted with it, pass through a sieve into a stew-pan, lay the pieces on it, and bake very gently in a slow oven until a stiff piece of straw will go through it, then lay it in a sieve, when nearly cold put it in a bowl or round preserving jar, and press a smaller one on top so that it forms one solid mass, pour the fat over, when cold cover with a piece of bladder (*plastic*), keep it in a cold place, and it will be good for months together; and is excellent for breakfast, luncheon or supper, having previously extracted the fat. Last winter (*1856*) I kept some for three months, quite sweet. Ducks may be served in the same way.

GOOSE PIE

An old goose is as nearly good for nothing as it is possible for anything which was once valuable, and is not now absolutely spoiled, to be. The best use to put it to is to make it into a pie, in the following manner. Put on the ancient early in the morning, in cold water enough to cover it, unsalted, having cut it to pieces at every joint. Warm it up gradually, and let it stew—not boil hard —for five hours. Should the water need replenishing, let it be done from the boiling kettle. Parboil a beef's tongue (corned), cut into slices nearly half an inch thick, also slice six hard-boiled eggs. Line a deep pudding-dish with a good paste, lay in the pieces of goose, the giblets chopped, the sliced tongue and egg, in consecutive layers; season with pepper, salt, and bits of butter, and proceed in this order until the dish is full. If the goose be large, cut the meat from the bones after stewing and leave out the latter entirely. Intersperse with strips of paste, and fill up with the gravy in which the goose was stewed,

[292]

thicken with flour. Cover with a thick paste, and when it is done, brush over the top with the beaten white of egg. In cold weather this pie will keep a week, and is very good.

DUCK

TO ROAST DUCKS

Put into a pair of ducks, an onion chopped fine, and a few sage leaves, pepper and salt; spit, and dust them with flour and baste them with lard. Roast half an hour, with a very hot fire. The quicker roasted, the better they will baste. Dust them with flour and baste them, just before taking from the spit. Prepare a gravy of the gizzards and pinions, a large mace blade, a few peppercorns; a teaspoonful of lemon pickle (*p. 404*), and a spoonful of catsup; strain and turn it on the ducks. Send onion sauce in a boat. (*Serves 4.*)

ONION SAUCE: Peel four white onions, boil tender, press the water from them and mince fine. Have ready one teacupful of hot milk in a saucepan, stir in the onions, then three tablespoonfuls of butter and salt and pepper. Boil up once. If you want to have it particularly fine, make nice melted or drawn butter (*p. 107*); beat the mashed onions into it; add a teacupful of cream or new milk, season, boil up once and serve.

STUFFING FOR ROAST GOOSE OR DUCK

Boil three large onions half an hour; press them, and mince finely with one tablespoonful of sage and four tablespoonfuls of bread crumbs; add one teaspoonful of salt, one of moist (*brown or raw*) sugar, one of mustard, half a teaspoonful each of pepper and mace, and a dessertspoonful of vinegar. This is, we think, an improvement on the common onion-and-sage dressing.

APPLE STUFFING: Take half a pound of the pulp of tart apples that have been baked or scalded; add two ounces of bread crumbs, some powdered sage, a finely shred onion; season well with cayenne.

Serve duck with watercress and apple salad, with orange salad, or with celery and small squares of fried hominy.

TO ROAST WILD DUCKS

Time: twenty-five to thirty-five minutes. Wild ducks; butter; flour; cayenne pepper; one lemon; one glass of port wine. When the ducks are trussed, spit them, and put them down to roast before a brisk fire, keeping the spit in rapid motion. Baste them plentifully with butter, dredge them lightly with flour, and send them up nicely frothed and browned, with a good gravy in the dish. Before serving it, the breast should have a few incisions made across it with a knife, and a piece of fresh butter put on it; then cut a lemon across, on one half put a little salt, on the other a very small quantity of cayenne pepper; put the lemon together and squeeze the juice over the ducks, then add a glass of warmed port wine, and your ducks will be ready to carve.

DUCKS À L'AUBERGISTE (OR TAVERN-KEEPERS' FASHION)

Truss one or two ducks with the legs turned inside, put them into a stewpan, with a quarter of a pound of butter; place them over a slow fire, turning round occasionally until they have taken a nice brown color, add two spoonfuls of flour, mix well with them, add a quart of water, with half a tablespoonful of salt and sugar, let simmer gently until the ducks are done (but adding 40 button onions well peeled as soon as it starts to boil), keep hot; peel and cut ten turnips in slices, fry them in a frying-pan in butter, drain upon a cloth, put them into the sauce and stew until quite tender; dress the ducks upon your dish, skim the fat from the sauce, which has attained a consistency, add some fresh mushrooms, pour round the ducks and serve. (*One duck serves 2—but not generously.*)

BRAISED DUCKS

Ducks that are tough and unfit to roast are improved by being braised (*p. 19*) with onions, carrots and turnips.

TO STEW A DUCK

Half-roast a large duck. Cut it up, and put it into a stew-pan with a pint of beef-gravy, or dripping of roast-beef. Have ready two boiled onions, one-half a handful of sage leaves (*about 2 tablespoons of fresh leaves, or 1 of dried*) and two leaves of mint, all chopped very fine and seasoned with salt and pepper. Lay these ingredients over the duck. Stew it slowly for a quarter of an hour. Then put in a quart of young green peas. Cover it closely, and simmer it a half hour longer, till the peas are quite soft. Then add a piece of butter rolled in flour; quicken the fire and give it a boil. (*Serves 3.*)

DUCKLINGS WITH TURNIPS: Proceed as for stewed duck and peas, but instead of peas, use about forty pieces of good turnips cut in moderate-sized square pieces, having previously fried them of a light yellow color in a little butter or lard, and drained them upon a sieve.

TO ROAST CANVAS-BACK DUCKS

Truss and put in each a thick crumb of bread soaked in Port wine, and then roast them before a quick fire about fifty or sixty minutes. Squeeze over each an orange or lemon, serving them up hot in their own gravy and eating with currant jelly. Serve up, too, a gravy of the giblets stewed in butter, rolled in flour and a little water.

SALMI OF WILD DUCK

One wild duck, one lemon, one bunch of sweet herbs, cayenne pepper, salt, black pepper, one sherry glassful of port, one pint of well-seasoned gravy, eight olives. Roast the duck and be careful it is not too much dried; cut into neat pieces; put the gravy with all the seasonings, the juice of half the lemon and a pinch of cayenne. Stew for an hour; then strain, thicken with arrowroot, and color brown. Pour over the pieces of duck, which should be laid in a clean stew-pan. Stone the olives and warm up with the duck. Place in a silver entrée dish; garnish with olives and crisp toast sippets. (*Serves 2.*)

TO BOIL A DUCK OR RABBIT

Use a good deal of water and skim it as often as anything rises. Half an hour will boil them. Make a gravy of sweet cream, butter, add flour, a little parsley chopped small, salt and pepper, and stew until done, and lay them in a dish and pour the gravy over them.

RABBIT

Rabbit and hare are not the same thing. Hare is wild, larger and gamier —and, in the Southwest, sometimes dangerous to eat because it is a disease carrier. But it was an esteemed dish in the nineteenth century, so much so that cooks occasionally doctored beef to try to make it taste like hare. Rabbit is either the wild bunny, or, more commonly, the little animal raised in the back yard with the chickens. It is still available in city butcher shops, and recently has appeared in frozen-food cases. A mature rabbit (and watch for that small-print "mature" on the packages of frozen rabbits) is fit only for stews, soups and fricassees, but is delicious then. Chicken makes an approximate substitute in these recipes if you have no rabbits.

TO ROAST RABBITS

After casing (*skinning and gutting*) two rabbits, skewer their heads with their mouths upon their backs, stick their forelegs into their ribs, skewer the hind legs doubled (*this was the approved position in which nineteenth-century rabbits appeared at table*); next make a stuffing for them of the crumbs of half a loaf of bread, a little parsley, sweet marjoram and thyme—all cut fine, salt, pepper and nutmeg, with four ounces of butter, a little good cream, and two eggs; put it into their bodies, and sew them up; dredge and baste them well with lard; roast them about an hour. Serve them up with butter and parsley. Chop the livers, and lay them in lumps around the edge of the dish. (*Serves 4–6.*)

13: OCTOBER

TO ROAST A HARE

Make a pudding thus: Take a quarter of a pound of beef suet, as much crumb of bread, a handful of parsley chopped fine, a little nutmeg grated, some sweet herbs of all sorts, such as basil, marjoram, winter savory, and a little thyme chopped very fine, a little nutmeg grated, some lemon-peel cut fine, pepper and salt, chop the liver fine, and put in with two eggs, mix it up, and put it into the belly, and set or skewer it up; then spit it and lay it to the fire, which must be a good one. A good-sized hare takes an hour, and so on in proportion.

DIFFERENT SORTS OF SAUCE FOR A HARE: Take for sauce, a pint of cream, a half a pound of fresh butter; put them in a sauce-pan, and keep stirring it with a spoon till the butter is melted, and the sauce is thick; then take up the hare, and pour the sauce into the dish.

ANOTHER WAY TO MAKE SAUCE FOR A HARE IS: To make a good gravy, thickened with a little piece of butter rolled in flour, and pour it into your dish. You may leave the butter out, if you do not like it and have some currant jelly warmed in a cup, or red wine and sugar boiled to a syrup, done thus: take a pint of red wine, a quarter of a pound of sugar, and set it over a slow fire to simmer about a quarter of an hour. You may do half the quantity, and put it into your sauce-boat or bason.

TO FRICASSEE A RABBIT

Cut it in pieces, reserve the liver; put a piece of bacon cut in slices into a stewpan and brown it well and lay it aside; put the rabbit into the stewpan with a piece of butter; turn and toss the rabbit until it is quite white. When it is getting brown, dredge a spoonful of flour over it, turning it all the while, and when the flour is dry, put the rabbit on a plate. Then add another piece of butter to the remaining sauce and stir it well together and when brown, add a cupful of water (*or chicken bouillon*); continue stirring and put in the rabbit with plenty of very small onions, the bacon, some mushrooms, a bunch of parsley and some salt and pepper; let it stew gently over a slow fire four hours (*3 hours is plenty*). Add the liver and a glass of port wine (*or Madeira*) one hour before serving, and should there not be sufficient sauce, a little gravy from time to time put in hot. (*Serves 4.*)

[297]

RABBIT SOUP À LA REINE

Wash and soak thoroughly three young rabbits, put them whole into the soup pot, and pour on them seven pints of cold water or clear veal broth; when they have stewed gently about three quarters of an hour, lift them out, and take off the flesh of the backs with a little from the legs, should there not be half a pound of the former; strip off the skin, mince the meat very small and pound it to the smoothest paste (*or blend it with a little of the broth*); cover it from the air and set by. Put back into the soup the bodies of the rabbits, with two mild onions of moderate size, a head of celery, three carrots, a faggot of savory herbs, two blades of mace, half a teaspoonful of peppercorns, and one ounce of salt. Stew the whole softly three hours; strain it off, let it stand to settle, pour it gently from the sediment, put from four to five pints into a clean stewpan and mix it very gradually while hot with the pounded rabbit flesh; if the liquid be not added gradually at first, the meat will gather in lumps. Add as much mace and cayenne as will season the soup pleasantly and pass it through a sieve. Put into a clean stewpan and when it boils, add one and a quarter pints of good cream mixed with one tablespoonful of arrowroot; salt, if needed. (*Serves 10–12.*)

HARE SOUP

Put half a pound of butter into a stewpan, and when melted, add three quarters of a pound of flour, and half a pound of streaky bacon cut in very small pieces; keep stirring over the fire until becoming lightly browned. You have previously cut up a hare into neat smallish pieces; put them into the stewpan and keep stirring round over the fire until they are set; then fill it up with five quarts of water, add two onions, a head of celery, a bunch of parsley, thyme, and bay-leaves, a blade of mace and four cloves; when boiling, season with one ounce of salt and a little pepper, and let it simmer at the corner until the pieces of hare are done, which should be about an hour, if a young hare, but double its time if a very old one; the better plan is to try a piece occasionally. When done, take out the best pieces and the inferior ones pound in a mortar (*or blend with a little broth*), removing the bones; put it back in the soup and pass all through a tammy (*fine sieve*), boil for ten minutes, and serve. The above quantity would be sufficient for two tureens. A glass of wine may be added. Rabbit, pheasant, grouse, partridge and other game soups may be made in the same way. (*Serves 15–20.*)

RABBIT OR HARE PIE

Cut into pieces, season with pepper, salt, nutmeg, and mace; put it into a jug (*a large bean-pot will do, or a small covered casserole*), with half a pound of butter, close it up, set it in a copper (*pan*) of boiling water, and make a forcemeat, with a quarter of a pound of scraped bacon, two onions, a glass of red wine, crumbs of bread, winter savory, the liver cut small, and nutmeg. Season high with pepper and salt; mix it well up with the yolks of three eggs, raise the pie (*line the dish with pastry*), and lay the forcemeat in the bottom of the dish. Then put in the rabbit or hare, with the gravy that came out of it; lay on the lid, and send it to the oven. An hour and a half will bake it. (*Serves 4.*)

JUGGED HARE

One hare, one and a half pounds of beef, half a pound of butter, half a pint of port wine, one onion, one lemon, six cloves, salt, pepper and cayenne to taste. Skin, clean and wash the hare, cut it in pieces, dredge with flour and fry in hot butter. Have ready one and a half pints of gravy made from the beef, and thickened with an even tablespoonful of flour; put this into a jar with the fried hare, an onion stick with the cloves, the lemon peeled and cut in half, and a good seasoning of pepper, salt and cayenne; cover the jar tight and put it up to the neck in a kettle of boiling water; let it stew until the hare is quite tender, keeping the water boiling; when nearly done pour in the wine and add a few fried forcemeat balls. Serve with currant jelly. (*Serves 6.*)

SQUIRREL

BRUNSWICK STEW

2 *squirrels—three if small*	6 *potatoes, parboiled and sliced*
1 *quart of tomatoes, peeled and sliced*	6 *ears green corn, cut from the cob*
1 *pint butter-beans, or Limas*	½ *lb. butter*

½ *lb. salt pork*   1 *tablespoonful salt*
1 *teaspoonful ground pepper*   2 *teaspoonfuls white sugar*
Half a teaspoonful cayenne   1 *onion, minced small*
1 *gallon water*

Put on the water with the salt in it, and boil five minutes. Put in the onion, beans, corn, pork or bacon cut in shreds, potatoes, pepper, and the squirrels, which must first be cut into joints and laid in cold salt and water to draw out the blood. Cover closely and stew two and a half hours very slowly, stirring frequently from the bottom. Then add the tomatoes and sugar, and stew an hour longer. Ten minutes before you take it from the fire, add the butter, cut into bits the size of a walnut, rolled in flour. Give a final boil taste to see that it is seasoned to your liking, and turn into a soup-tureen. It is eaten from soup-plates. Chicken may be substituted for squirrels. (*Serves 4–6.*)

Or, squirrel may be substituted for chicken in many chicken recipes. Its taste is richer—as if chicken were all dark meat.

GAME BIRDS

Most of these are available from fancy butchers.

"How to chuse a pheasant: The cock, when young, has dubbed spurs, when old, sharp small spurs. The hen if young, has smooth legs, and her flesh is of a curious grain: if with egg she will have a soft open vent; and if not, a close one."
Hannah Glasse, The Art of Cookery, 1812

TO ROAST A PHEASANT

Time, from half an hour to an hour, according to the size of the pheasant. After the pheasant is trussed, spit it, and roast it before a clear, quick fire; baste it frequently with butter, sprinkle over it a little salt, and dredge lightly with flour, to froth it nicely. When done, serve it up with a little good brown gravy round it, and the remainder in a tureen, with another of bread sauce. (*Serves 3–4.*)

Bread sauce: Let a sliced onion and six pepper-corns simmer in half a pint of milk over boiling water, until the onion is perfectly soft. Pour it on half a pint of bread crumbs without crust, and leave it covered for an hour; beat it smooth, add mace, cayenne, salt and two ounces of butter, rubbed in a little flour; add enough sweet cream to make it the proper consistency, and boil it a few minutes. It must be thin enough to pour.

TO ROAST A FOWL PHEASANT-FASHION

If you should have but one pheasant, and want two in a dish, take a large full-grown fowl, keep the head on, and truss it as you do a pheasant; lard it with bacon, but do not lard the pheasant, and nobody will know it.

PHEASANT STEWED WITH CABBAGE

The following is an excellent method for dressing a pheasant which should prove to be rather old. Procure a large savoy (*cabbage*), which cut into quarters and well wash in salt and water, after which, boil it five minutes, in plain water, then drain it quite dry, cut off the stalk, season it rather highly with pepper and salt, have ready a middling-size onion and half a pound of streaky bacon, which, with the cabbage, put into a stew-pan, covering the whole with a good broth; let it simmer at the corner of the fire for three quarters of an hour, then thrust the pheasant (previously three parts roasted) into the cabbage, and let them stew nearly three quarters of an hour longer, or till the stock has reduced to a glaze and adheres thickly to the cabbage, when dress the cabbage in a mound upon your dish, with the bacon, cut in slices around, and the pheasant upon the top, half way buried in the cabbage; have a little game sauce, which pour round and serve. (*Try the gravy, p. 302. Serves 4–6.*)

TO ROAST PARTRIDGE, PHEASANT, QUAILS OR GROUSE

Pick and draw the birds immediately after they are brought in. Before you roast them, fill the inside with pieces of a fine ripe orange, leaving out the rind and seed. Or stuff with grated cold ham, mixed with bread-crumb, butter, and a little yolk of egg. Or chop some fine raw oysters, omitting the hard part, and mix them with salt and nutmeg (*and a little buttered bread crumbs*), and add some beaten yolk of egg to bind the other ingredients. Lard them with small slips of the fat or bacon drawn through the flesh with a larding needle. Roast them before a clear fire.

Make a rich gravy of the trimmings of meat or poultry, stewed in a little water, and thicken with a spoonful of browned flour. Strain it, and set it on the fire again, having added half a pint of claret, and the juice of two large oranges. Simmer it a few minutes. Pour some of it into the dish with the game and serve the remainder in a boat.

If you stuff them with force-meat, you may, instead of larding them, brush over with beaten yolk of egg, and then cover them with bread-crumb grated finely and sifted.

TO STEW PARTRIDGES

Truss a brace of partridges like fowl for boiling; pound the livers with twice the quantity of fat bacon and bread-crumbs boiled in milk (*pour boiling milk over the crumbs and when they have absorbed as much as they will, squeeze them gently*); add some mushrooms and chopped parsley, mace, grated lemon peel, salt and pepper; stuff them; tie them at each end, and place them in a stewpan lined with bacon. If you have it, add a quart of good gravy. If not, two onions, water, a few blades of mace, and a bunch of sweet herbs. Stew gently till they are tender; take them out; strain, and thicken the sauce with flour and butter; heat, and pour it on the birds.

PARTRIDGE PIE

Line the bottom of a pie-dish with slices of veal cut moderately thick and rather lightly seasoned with white pepper and salt; have ready picked, drawn and trussed a couple of young partridges, pour one glass of sherry over the veal, and lay in the partridges, breast to breast, laying a piece of fat bacon over each, cover with paste, sticking the feet of the partridges in the top of the pie, and bake rather better than an hour in a moderate oven. (*Serves 4–6.*)

PARTRIDGE OR CHICKEN SAUSAGE

Take partridge or chicken meat free from all skin or bone, four times as much pork suet, and chop it together fine. Flavor it to taste with nutmeg, cloves and black pepper. Stir some milk through it. Add egg yolks and bread crumbs so that you can shape it like sausages, and fry them.

13 : OCTOBER

GROUSE

The Scotch method is to plain roast the grouse, dress it upon toast, and pour plain melted butter over. But they may be dressed in any of the ways directed for pheasant, with the exception of being stewed with cabbage.

GROUSE, ROASTED À LA SAM WARD

Take two fine fat grouse; pick, singe, draw, and dry them well; then truss them nicely. Place them in a roasting-pan, putting inside of each bird a piece of broiled toast four inches long and two wide. Drip in on each toast, with a spoon, a small glassful of good Madeira wine or sherry; season the grouse with a pinch of salt; spread a little butter over. Put them in a brisk oven, and let cook for eighteen minutes, taking care to baste them frequently. Lay them on a hot dish, untruss, strain the gravy over, and decorate with a little water-cress. Serve with a little red currant jelly, separate. (*Serves 3–4.*)

RECEIPT FOR SAUCE FOR WILD FOWLS

Port Wine or Claret, 1 glass
Sauce à la Russe (the older the better), 1 Tablespoonful
Catsup, 1 ditto
Lemon Juice, 1 ditto
Lemon Peel, 1 slice
Shalot (a large), 1 sliced
Cayenne Pepper (the *darkest*, not that like Brick dust), 4 grains
Mace, 1 or 2 blades

To be scalded, strained, and added to the mere gravy that comes from the Bird in roasting. To complete this, the Fowl should be cut up in a Silver Dish which has a lamp under it, while the Sauce is simmering with it.

Part II: *Recipes*

TO ROAST WOODCOCKS OR SNIPES

Pluck them, but do not draw them, put them upon a small spit, dust (*with flour*) and baste them well with butter, toast a few slices of bread, put them under the birds while they are roasting; if the fire be good, they will take about ten minutes roasting; when you draw them upon the toasts on the dish, pour melted butter round them and serve them up.

BRAISED PIGEONS STUFFED WITH PARSLEY

These recipes for pigeons are included in memory of the time, one or two hundred years ago, when flights of passenger pigeons, now extinct, blackened the skies for days. Recipes like these probably had something to do with their extinction—but without the kind of greed that led hunters to shoot thousands in order to pick up the hundred or so fattest birds, we might still have known what they tasted like. Pigeons now are carefully hand-raised in little cages. By making allowances for a larger bird, Rock Cornish game hens may be substituted here—or in any other game-bird recipe.

Allow one pint of loose parsley for each pigeon. Wash, remove the large stems and chop very fine. Adding salt and pepper and two or three tablespoons of water while chopping. Stuff the pigeons with the parsley; add also the heart and a half inch cube of salt pork for each pigeon. Add the water left in the tray to that in the stewpot, enough to braise them, and serve on buttered toast.

PIGEONS WITH PEAS

Cut the pigeons in halves, trimming them neatly. Put a spoonful or two of butter in a saucepan and when hot add the pigeons with one-half dozen cloves and one division of garlic. Keep the pot closely covered, and shake it frequently to stir pigeons. Cook rather slowly about one hour. When you think they are done, uncover the pot and try them. If done, take peas without any water and add them to the pigeons. (*Cook uncovered.*) Have ready on a platter some bread nicely toasted, and when the peas are heated pour the whole in the butter and their own juices. Before serving them add salt if the butter and peas do not make the dish salt enough.

PIGEON PIE

Take four pigeons, and season them with salt and pepper, and put inside each a large piece of butter and the yolk of a hard-boiled egg. Have ready a good paste, allowing a pound of sifted flour to a half pound of butter. Roll it out rather thick and line with it the bottom and sides of a large deep dish. Put in the pigeons and lay on the top some bits of melted butter rolled in flour. Pour in nearly enough of water (*or light wine*) to fill the dish. Cover the pie with a lid of paste rolled out thick. (*Serves 4.*)

See also partridge pie, p. 302.

NEW ZEALAND MODE FOR COOKING BIRDS

Cover the bird in its feathers with a paste made of mud and water, dig a hole in the ground and build a fire in it, when burned down place the bird in the coals, cover, and leave it until baked. When the paste is removed, the feathers fall off, leaving the bird ready to be eaten. The entrails will be found dried in a small ball, which can be easily removed. This mode has been adopted in Louisiana, and is highly appreciated.

APPLES

Apples *are* October, autumn, the embodiment of the harvest. Their winey smell transforms roadside stands and cider mills. They are never so crisp and delicious as they are right after they are picked from the tree. Everything possible ought to be made out of apples in October. Here are a few standard and a few unusual recipes for them.

APPLE SAUCE

Apples should be pared and quartered. If tart, you may stew them in water; if not, in cider. After stewed soft, add a small piece of butter, and sweeten to taste. Another very good way is to boil the apples without paring with a few quinces and molasses, in new cider, till reduced one half. Strain the sauce when cold. Made thus, the sauce will keep good for months.

Do not overcook apple sauce or it turns mealy. Sweetening after it is cooked gives it a better flavor and color and reduces the chances of burning. Try adding a few cloves, some stick cinnamon and, if the apples are sweet, a little lemon juice.

APPLE PIE

Apple pie is not as ancient an institution as one might think. Most of the oldest books don't even mention it, and the late-nineteenth-century authors tend to apologize for including such low-class fare. The pies were usually just fruit and sugar surrounded by pie crust, but here are a couple more interesting ones. The year's first apples make the best pies.

Pare, core and slice ripe, tart winter apples—Pippins, Greenings or Baldwins—line your dish with a good crust, put in a layer of fruit, then sprinkle light-brown sugar thickly over it, scatter half a dozen whole cloves upon this. Lay on more apples, and so on, until the dish is well filled. Cover with crust and bake (*in a 375° oven for about 45 minutes*). Sift powdered sugar over the top before sending to table.

ANOTHER: Line a pie plate with paste and fill it heaping full of tart apples, sliced very thin. Sweeten and spice (*with sugar, honey, or molasses; with cinnamon and nutmeg*) to taste, mixing well into the apples. Put in plenty of butter and moisten well with cream. Bake until the apples are thoroughly done. Use no upper crust. Equal quantities of apple and rhubarb make a good pie.

APPLE MERINGUE PIE

Stew and sweeten ripe juicy apples. Mash smooth, and season with nutmeg. Fill the crust, and bake until just done. Spread over the apple a thick meringue made by whipping to a stiff froth the whites of three eggs for each pie, sweeten with a tablespoonful of powdered sugar for each egg. Flavor this with vanilla; beat until it will stand alone and cover the pie three-quarters of an inch thick. Set back in the oven until the meringue is well set. Eat cold.

APPLE CUSTARD PIE

Make 3 cups stewed apple very sweet, and let it cool. Beat 6 separated eggs light, and mix the yolks well with the apple, seasoning with nutmeg only. Then stir in gradually 1 quart milk, beating as you go on; lastly add the whites; fill your crust and bake (*in a hot oven*) without cover.

AMHERST PUDDING

Take six eggs, six ounces of loaf sugar, six of butter, five apples, one grated nutmeg, one lemon (*rind*) grated, with the juice; two spoonfuls rose water. (*Peel, core, and cook them in a very little water until they are soft. Stir in the sugar, butter, nutmeg, and lemon rind and juice—I prefer to omit the rosewater. Beat the eggs well and add. Bake at 350° until set. Serves 4.*)

CHARTREUSE OF APPLES

Boil half a pound of Carolina rice in a quart of milk, with four ounces of sugar, till tender. Pare seven good-sized apples, and take out the cores without opening them through. Put into each apple a spoonful of raspberry jam, and fill up with cream. Arrange them in a deep dish, and pour the rice round them, but not over them, making the whole smooth; cover the top with (*stiffly*) beaten whites of egg, and sift sugar entirely over it. Bake forty minutes. This is a good and wholesome pudding. (*Serves 7.*)

APPLE PUDDING

Take the peel of lemons, boil them in water till the juice is out; take seven apples, stew them in water, stir in a lump of butter and a little cream, one nutmeg grated, seven eggs (*well-beaten*); sweeten to your taste. (*Bake in a 375° oven until a knife inserted in it comes out clean. Serves 6–8.*)

MOLASSES SAUCE, FOR APPLE PUDDINGS AND DUMPLINGS: One pint of molasses; one tablespoonful of butter; the juice of one lemon, or a large spoonful of vinegar. Boil twenty minutes. It may be thickened with a table-spoonful of cornstarch dissolved in a little water, but is good in any case. Serve hot.

APPLE TAPIOCA PUDDING

Pick over and wash three-quarters of a cup of pearl tapioca. Pour one quart of boiling water over it, and cook in the double boiler till transparent; stir often, and add half a teaspoonful of salt. Core and pare seven apples. Put them in a round baking dish, and fill the cores with sugar and lemon juice. Pour the tapioca over them and bake (*at 375°*) until the apples are soft. Serve hot or cold, with sugar and cream.

A custard can be substituted for the tapioca. Serve with wine or raspberry sauce. Serves 7.

STEAMED APPLE AND INDIAN MEAL PUDDING

Scald two cups of corn meal with boiling water (enough to wet it), add one teaspoonful of salt, one-fourth of a cup of molasses, and two tart apples, cut into eighths and cored, but not pared. Dissolve half a teaspoonful of soda in warm water, and add to the meal. Add more warm water to make a batter thin enough to pour. Pour into a greased pail (*or pudding mold*), place it on a trivet in a kettle of boiling water. Cook three hours. The water must not stop boiling. To be eaten with roast meat (*as a substitute for vegetables*). The next day warm what is left in the meat gravy. (*Serves 6–8.*)

BAKED APPLES

Core and pare sour apples. Put them in a shallow earthen baking dish, fill the cavities with sugar mixed with grated lemon (*or orange*) rind; add water (*or red wine*) to cover the bottom of the dish. Bake in a very quick oven till soft, basting often with the syrup. (*Three or four whole cloves and half a stick of cinnamon in the syrup improves it.*)

QUINCES: may be baked in the same way, adding a little more water, as they require a longer time for baking. When eaten hot, with butter and sugar, they are delicious.

[308]

DUTCH APPLE CAKE

1 pint flour	*1 egg*
½ teaspoon salt	*1 scant cup milk*
½ teaspoon soda	*4 sour apples*
1 teaspoon cream of tartar	*2 tablespoons sugar*
¼ cup butter	

Mix the dry ingredients in the order given; rub in the butter; beat the egg and mix it with the milk; then stir thin into the dry mixture. The dough should be soft enough to spread half an inch thick on a shallow baking pan. Core, pare, and cut four or five apples into eighths; lay them in parallel rows on top of the dough, the sharp edge down, and press enough to make the edge penetrate slightly. Sprinkle the sugar on the apples. Bake in a hot oven twenty or thirty minutes. To be eaten hot with butter as a tea cake, or with lemon sauce as a pudding.

LEMON SAUCE: Boil 2 cups hot water and 1 cup sugar five minutes, and add 3 heaping teaspoonfuls corn starch, wet in a little cold water. Cook eight or ten minutes, and add the grated rind and juice of one lemon and 1 tablespoon butter. Stir until the butter is melted, and serve at once. If the water boils away and the sauce becomes too thick, add more hot water till of the right consistency.

APPLE FROSTING FOR CAKES

White of one egg, one grated sour apple (a Baldwin is good), a scant measuring cup of sugar; beat all together with a large silver fork, about thirty minutes until stiff enough to stand; put in for filling and top frosting.

APPLE JOHNNY CAKE

1 pint white (corn) *meal*	*½ teaspoon cream of tartar*
2 tablespoons sugar	*Milk enough to mix quite soft*
½ teaspoon salt	*3 apples, pared and sliced*
½ teaspoon soda	

Mix in the order given. Bake in a shallow cake pan thirty minutes.

[309]

APPLE FRITTERS

Two eggs, half a pint of milk, two cups of flour, one teaspoon of salt, four apples, lemon juice. Beat the eggs stiff and stir them with the milk. Add gradually to the flour and salt, making a stiff batter. Have ready four apples, cored, pared and chopped. Sprinkle the apples with sugar and squeeze a little lemon juice over them. Mix them with the batter. (*Deep*) fry in boiling lard a tablespoonful at a time and serve hot with sifted sugar over them. (*Makes about 20.*)

APPLE DUMPLINGS

Pare tart mellow apples, take out the cores with a small knife, and fill the holes with sugar. Make good pie crust, roll it out about two-thirds of an inch thick, put it into pieces just large enough to enclose one apple. Lay the apples on them, and close the crust tight over them. Tie them up in small pieces of thick cloth, that has been well floured, put the dumplings in a pot of boiling water, and boil them an hour without any intermission. If allowed to stop boiling, they will be heavy. Serve them up with pudding sauce (*p. 307 or p. 309*), or butter and sugar.

APPLE BREAD

Weigh one pound of fresh juicy apples; peel, core and stew them into a pulp, being careful to use a porcelain kettle or a stone jar, placed in a kettle of boiling water (*the purpose of this is to cook the apples without any water; you can get the same result by baking them in a tightly covered dish*); mix the pulp with two pounds of best flour; put in the same quantity of yeast you would use for common bread (*1 package*) and as much water as will make a fine smooth dough; put it into a pan and place it in a warm place to rise, and let it remain two hours at the least. Form it into rather long shaped loaves, and bake in a quick oven. (*Makes 2–3 loaves.*)

APPLE JELLY

Take the core from fine rich Pippins or tart apples, put enough water to them to cover them. When boiled to a pulp, strain them through thin muslin (*or, for marmalade, omit straining, add thin-sliced lemon peel*); measure the liquor, and to each pint put a pound of white sugar, flavored with lemon, and boil it to a fine jelly; try it by putting some in a saucer to cool. Keep it in tumblers or wide-mouthed jars (*covered with paraffin; see p. 28 for jelly-making details*).

APPLE BUTTER

Take tart cooking apples, such as will make good sauce. To three pecks, after they are peeled and quartered, allow nine pounds of brown sugar and two gallons, or perhaps a little more, of water. (*The butter is richer if cider, first boiled to reduce by half, is substituted for water.*) Put the sugar and water in your kettle, and let it boil; then add the apples. After they begin to cook, stir constantly until the butter is done. Try it by putting a little on a saucer, and if no water appears around it, the marmalade is ready for the cinnamon and nutmeg "to your taste."

SPICED APPLES

Eight pounds (*small*) apples, four pounds sugar, one quart vinegar, stick cinnamon and whole cloves to taste. Boil vinegar, spices and sugar together. When boiling, put in the whole fruit, part at a time, and cook till tender, then skim out. When all the fruit is cooked, boil the syrup down till it is real syrup and pour over the fruit. In cold climates this keeps as long as the family permits. Mangoes may be treated the same way.

TO PRESERVE APPLES

Dry a glazed jar perfectly well, put a few pebbles in the bottom, fill the jar with apples, and cover it with a piece of wood made perfectly to fit, and over that put a little fresh mortar: the pebbles attract the damp in the apples;

the mortar draws the air from the jar, and leaves the apples free from its pressure, which, together with the principles of putrefaction which the air contains, are causes of decay. Apples thus kept have been found quite sound, fair, and juicy, in July.

TO DRY APPLES

Apples may be dried in the same manner as peaches: pare off every particle of the skin, and take out all the core; dry them where no dust may come to them. The best apples for drying are those too sour to use in any other way.

"Preserve apples on shelves made by strips of wood about two inches wide, placed an inch and a half apart, and the apples laid between them, singly in rows without touching, often inspected. Apples may also be preserved in large barrels with dry sand but require to be used immediately when taken out."
Mrs. Ellet, *The Practical Housekeeper*, 1857

FIG AND APPLE BEVERAGE

Have two quarts of water boiling, into which throw six fresh dry figs, previously opened, and two apples, previously cut into six or eight pieces each; let the whole boil together twenty minutes, then pour them together into a basin to cool, then pass through a sieve; drain the figs, which will also be good to eat. (*Serves 8.*)

CIDER

The following recipes are hopeless (and in the case of the first, pointless) if you use cider from the supermarket, either pasteurized or with preservatives added. Cider must be got directly from the mill, straight out of the press, if possible. If you are lucky enough to have your own press, the pulp left from the pressing is good animal feed.

TO KEEP CIDER SWEET

When barreling the cider, put into each barrel or keg a gill of white mustard seed. This will retard it becoming hard or sour.

MULLED CIDER

This is excellent, and to be good must be served as soon as it is prepared. Put one quart of cider on to boil, add to it twenty whole cloves. When it comes to a boil, let it boil three minutes, then add white sugar to make it rather sweet. Beat six eggs, whites and yolks together, until very light. Pour the boiling cider upon the eggs, beating rapidly all the while, then pour the mixture backward and forward, from one pitcher to another, until rather frothy and well mixed. Pour into glasses, grate a little nutmeg on top of each glass and serve right away. (*Wine may be mulled the same way; serves 6–8.*)

TO KEEP CIDER GOOD FOR YEARS

Take the cider when you think it will suit your taste, put it into a kettle, and boil it very little. Make a bag and put into it a quarter of a pound of hops, then put the bag with hops into the kettle with the cider and tie it fast to the handle so that the bag with the hops will not touch the bottom of the kettle; scum off the cider while you have it on the fire, and after it has boiled a short time, take it off the fire, and let it cool down lukewarm; put it into a sweet (*new or well-cleaned*) barrel, and add one pint of good brandy. Bung it up, and it will keep the same as you put it into your barrel for years. (*A quarter of a pound of hops should be enough for 50 gallons.*)

HOW TO MAKE APPLE WINE

To every gallon of cider, immediately as it comes from the press, add two pounds of sugar. Boil it as long as any scum arises (*but no more than 20 minutes*), then strain it through a sieve and let it cool; add some good yeast, mix it well; let it work in the tub two or three weeks, then skim off the head; draw it off close and tun it (*put it in the barrel*); let it stand one year, then rack it off, and add two ounces of isinglass to the barrel; then add half a pint of spirits of wine (*or brandy*) to every eight gallons. (*See pp. 37–41 for general wine-making instructions.*)

TO MAKE CIDER HARD

Add 1 pound of sugar to each gallon of cider straight from the mill (not processed), and a handful of raisins; let it stand, protected from the air and especially from fruit flies, but not tightly covered, about 3 weeks.

CIDER VINEGAR

Should either the apple wine or the hard cider go awry—the most common cause is too much exposure to air and fruit flies or too little sugar—complete the process and turn it into vinegar. Unless you get your cider very inexpensively, or have your own apples, it is usually no saving to make your own vinegar.

Take six quarts of rye meal; stir and mix it well into a barrel (*50 gallons*) of strong hard cider of the best kind; and then add a gallon of whiskey. Cover the cask, leaving the bung loosely in it; set it in the part of your yard that is most exposed to the sun and air; and in the course of four weeks (if the weather is warm and dry), you will have a good vinegar fit for use. When you draw off a gallon or more, replenish the cask with the same quantity of cider and add about a pint of whiskey. You may thus have vinegar constantly at hand for common purposes.

MOLASSES

Take new sweet cider just from the press, made from sweet apples, and boil it down as thick as West India molasses. Four or five barrels will make one of good molasses. It should be boiled in brass and not burned, as that would injure the flavor. It will keep in the cellar. (*It makes a good ice-cream topping.*)

QUINCES

Quinces, quince pie, quince jelly, were once common foods. But American quince bushes have been suffering from a blight, and they are harder to find than they once were.

BAKED QUINCES

Pare and quarter; extract the seeds and stew the fruit in clear water until a (*broom*) straw will pierce them; put into a baking-dish with a half cupful of sugar to every eight quinces; pour over them the liquor in which they were boiled; cover closely, and steam in the oven one hour; take out the quinces, lay them in a covered bowl to keep warm; return the syrup to the saucepan, and boil twenty minutes; pour over the quinces, and set away covered, to cool. Eat cold. (*See p. 308 for another recipe.*)

QUINCE JELLY

Pare and slice the quinces, and add for every five pounds of fruit a cup of water. Put the peelings, cores, and all into a stone jar; set this in a pot of boiling water, and when the fruit is soft and broken, proceed as with other jellies.

QUINCE MARMALADE

Pare, core and slice the quinces, stewing the skins, cores and seed in a vessel by themselves, with just enough water to cover them. When this has been simmered long enough to extract all the flavor, and the parings are broken in pieces, strain off the water through a thick cloth. Put the quinces into the preserve-kettle when this water is almost cold, pouring it over them and boil, stirring and mashing the fruit with a wooden spoon as it becomes soft. The juice of two oranges to every three pounds of the fruit imparts an agreeable flavor. When you have reduced all to a smooth paste, stir in a scant three-quarters of a pound of sugar for every pound of fruit; boil ten minutes more, stirring constantly. Take off, and when cool put into small jars, with brandied papers (*or paraffin*) over them.

QUINCE CHEESE: is marmalade boiled down *very* thick, packed into small pots. It will turn out as firm as cheese, and can be cut in slices for luncheon or tea.

PRESERVED QUINCES

Choose fine yellow quinces. Pare, quarter and core them, saving both skins and cores. Put the quinces over the fire with just enough water to cover them, and simmer until they are soft, but not until they begin to break. Take them out carefully, and spread them upon broad dishes to cool. Add the parings, seeds, and cores, to the water in which the quinces were boiled, and stew, closely covered, for an hour. Strain through a jelly-bag, and to every pint of this liquor allow a pound of sugar. Boil up and skim it, put in the fruit and boil fifteen minutes. Take all from the fire, and pour into a large deep pan. Cover closely and let it stand twenty-four hours. Drain off the syrup and let it come to a boil; put in the quinces carefully and boil another quarter of an hour. Take them up as dry as possible, and again spread out upon dishes, setting these in the hottest sunshine you can find. Boil the syrup until it begins to jelly; fill the jars two-thirds full and cover with the syrup. The preserves should be of a fine red. Cover with brandied tissue-paper (*or paraffin*).

POTATOES

Potatoes are (*usually*) dug just about the time of the first frost. In the country they can be had very inexpensively. In the city prices tend to fall in February and March, when stocks of unsold potatoes likely to spoil begin to worry wholesalers. New potatoes are not good for baking; mealy old potatoes are best for making into bread and pastry (*see January, pp. 49, 68*).

POTATOES À LA MAÎTRE D'HÔTEL

With young potatoes they are excellent. Boil middle-sized young ones cut in slices of a quarter of an inch thick, put in the stewpot half a pint of milk or the same of broth, a little salt, grated nutmeg, pepper and a tablespoonful of fresh chopped parsley, then simmer on the fire; when boiling, add a quarter of a pound of fresh butter, the juice of a lemon; stir well for a few minutes; when each piece is well covered with the sauce, dish up, and high in the center, as they must appear light.

POTATO RISSOLES (*OR CROQUETTES*)

Boil the potatoes floury; mash them, seasoning with salt and a little cayenne; mince parsley very finely and work up in the potatoes; adding eschalot also chopped small; bind with yolk of egg, roll into balls and fry with fresh butter over a clear fire (*or dip the balls in egg, then bread crumbs and deep-fry them*). Meat finely shred, bacon or ham, may be added.

"In some families, it is the custom to brown the mashed potatoes for
a few minutes under the roast meat before it is taken from the spit."
The Cuisine, by An Eminent French Caterer, 1872

POTATO SOUFFLÉ

Steam six good-sized potatoes in their jackets. When done, peel and mash them; add one tablespoonful of butter, a half-pint of hot cream, one teaspoonful of salt, and black pepper to taste. Now beat until smooth and light. Beat the whites of two eggs to a stiff froth, stir them quickly into the potatoes, heap in a baking-dish and put in a quick oven to brown. Serve in the dish in which they were baked. (*Serves 6.*)

Two heaping tablespoonfuls of grated cheese added with the cream is an improvement.

SARATOGA CHIPS

Wash and pare off the skins of two or three or more large potatoes, and when you have done this, go on paring them, cutting them as thin and as evenly as possible in ribbons nearly an inch wide (*this requires deft use of the paring knife, not the potato peeler*); throw them into boiling fat; let them take a nice color, drain them well before the fire, sprinkle with salt, and serve immediately (or they lose their crispness), piled high upon a napkin. They may be sent in with game in the third course. (*In the nineteenth century, this was a very fancy dish.*)

[317]

PUFFED OR SOUFFLÉ POTATOES

Peel the potatoes; cut the sides square, and trim off the corners so as to give an oval shape. With one even slice, cut them one-eighth of an inch thick the length of the potato; they must all be the same size and shape. Soak them in cold water for half an hour; dry them on a napkin, and fry them in fat that is only moderately hot until they are soft but not colored. Remove and place them on a sieve to drain and cool. Then immerse them in hot fat, when they will puff into balls. Toss the basket, and remove any that do not puff. Sprinkle with salt and serve them on a napkin, or as a garnish. Holland potatoes are best for this purpose; it is impossible to get the same results with most of the other varieties.

POTATOES

They are nice and look well grated, minced with the yolk of an egg, made into small cakes and fried in butter for breakfast.

Potatoes, boiled and mashed while hot, are good for use in making bread, cake, puddings, etc. They save flour, and less shortening is necessary.

POTATO DUMPLINGS

Boil three Irish potatoes until done. Peel and run through a potato masher very light, add salt to taste and a little sugar, cinnamon and nutmeg; also add two eggs. Beat all together very light, then add flour enough to make them hold together. Try by dropping a little into soup. If not stiff enough, add more flour. Drop in by tablespoonfuls ten minutes before serving, and let boil.

POTATO SALAD

One pint each cold boiled potatoes and beets cut into small pieces and seasoned with salt and pepper; add a finely chopped raw onion. Take one salt-spoon of salt, half a saltspoon of pepper, three tablespoons of oil, and a very little mustard, all beaten well together, then add vinegar enough to moisten the vegetables; garnish with lettuce or hard-boiled eggs.

[318]

ANOTHER: 2 cups of mashed potato, rubbed through a collander
(*or 2 cups of potatoes cooked until just tender and diced*)
¾ of a cup of chopped cabbage, white and firm
2 tablespoonfuls of cucumber pickle, also chopped
Yolks of 2 hard-boiled eggs, pounded fine

Mix all together. Pour on a dressing made thus:

1 raw-egg, well-beaten	1 teaspoonful of flour
1 saltspoonful of celery-seed	½ cupful of vinegar
1 teaspoonful of white sugar	Salt, mustard, and pepper to
1 tablespoonful of melted butter	taste

Boil the vinegar and pour it upon the beaten egg, sugar, butter and seasoning. Wet the flour with cold vinegar, and beat into this. Cook the mixture, stirring until it thickens, when pour, scalding hot, upon the salad. Toss with a silver fork, and let it get very cold before eating.

POTATO SOUP

3 potatoes	½ teaspoon celery salt
1 pint milk	½ saltspoon white pepper
1 teaspoon chopped onion	¼ saltspoon cayenne
1 stalk celery	½ tablespoon flour
1 teaspoon salt	1 tablespoon butter

Wash and pare the potatoes, and let them soak in cold water half an hour. Put them into boiling water, and cook until very soft. Cook the onion and celery with the milk in a double boiler. When the potatoes are soft, drain off the water and mash them. Add the boiling milk and seasoning (*or purée in a blender*). Put the butter in a small saucepan, and when melted and bubbling, add the flour, and when well mixed, stir into the boiling soup; let it boil five minutes, and serve. This flour thickening keeps the potatoes and milk from separating, and gives a smoothness and consistency quite unlike the granular effect which is often noted. If you like, put one tablespoonful of fine chopped parsley into the soup just before serving. When you wish a richer soup, use a quart of milk, and add two eggs, well-beaten, after you take it from the fire.

TO PRESERVE POTATOES FROM FROST

If you have not a convenient store place for them, dig a trench three or four feet deep, into which they are to be laid as they are taken up, and then covered with the earth taken out of the trench, raised up in the middle like the roof of a house, and covered with straw to carry off the rain. They will be thus preserved from frost and can be taken up when wanted.

GREEN TOMATOES

Just before the first frost, every tomato should be stripped from the garden plants. The large green ones can be wrapped individually in newspaper and packed loosely in a crock or cardboard box. They will ripen gradually and can be used over the next couple of months. The small ones may be pickled.

GREEN TOMATO PICKLE

These can also be made in July, while you are waiting for tomatoes to ripen.

One peck of green tomatoes, twenty-four large cucumbers, twelve large onions. Chop these ingredients very fine, salt well and hang out in the air over night (*in colanders, sieves, cheesecloth bags, or wire baskets*); this will allow all the juice to drain off. The next morning place the chopped ingredients in a kettle and cover with the best cider vinegar and let come to a boil. Put into jars and leave until celery time in the fall (*2 or 3 months*), then take one dozen bunches of celery, chop very fine, and add spices; two pounds of stick cinnamon, two pounds of whole mustard seed, and red pepper to taste, to each pint of this mixture add one pint of sugar and boil all together before putting into jars. (*Makes 12–16 quarts.*)

GREEN TOMATOES, PICKLED

One peck of green tomatoes; six large onions, one cupful of salt, three quarts of vinegar; two pounds of sugar; two tablespoonfuls of cloves, two tablespoonfuls of ginger; two tablespoonfuls of mustard; two tablespoonfuls of cinnamon, half a teaspoonful of cayenne pepper. Slice the tomatoes and onions. Sprinkle them with the salt, and let stand overnight. In the morning, drain, add to the tomatoes two quarts of water and one quart of vinegar. Boil fifteen minutes, then drain again and throw this vinegar away. Take the sugar, two quarts of vinegar and the other ingredients, and boil together with the tomatoes for fifteen minutes. Put in glass jars and cover tightly. (*Makes 6 quarts.*)

TO PICKLE TOMATOES

Cut a peck of green tomatoes in slices and lay in a stone jar; cover with one pint of molasses. Skim when it ferments, and your pickles are made. This is *good*. (*Makes 3–4 quarts.*)

PICKLED GREEN TOMATOES

Puncture the tomatoes with a fork, place them on a dish, and sprinkle with salt. Let them remain for two or three days, then rinse off the salt in clear water; put them in a preserving kettle, cover them with water, which keep scalding hot (*but do not boil*) for one hour; then take them out, let them drain and put them in jars. Boil the vinegar, with some cloves, alspice, and stick cinnamon. When cold, pour over sufficient to cover them.

TOMATO PIE

Pick green tomatoes, pour boiling water over them, and let them remain a few minutes; then strip off the skin, cut the tomatoes in slices, and put them in deep pie plates. Sprinkle a little ginger and some sugar over them in several layers. Lemon juice, and the grated peel, improve the pie. Cover the pies with a thick crust, and bake them slowly about an hour.

THE LAST END OF THE GARDEN

One gallon chopped cabbage, one-half gallon green tomatoes chopped, one-half quart lima beans boiled, one quart small white onions, one-fourth peck yellow wax string beans cut up and boiled, one-hundred small cucumbers not over two inches long, one dozen small sweet peppers, four carrots chopped, two quarts large cucumbers, cut up, one and one-half pounds of brown sugar, one ounce black pepper, whole grains, one dozen ears green corn cut off the cob, one-fourth gallon cider vinegar, three-fourths pound mustard, one pint salt. Scald vinegar; stir the mustard in cold vinegar until of the consistency of cream, then stir in the hot vinegar, add salt, pepper, sugar and the vegetables well mixed and cook twenty minutes. Serve with meat. (*Makes 15–20 quarts.*)

CABBAGE

CABBAGE

All vegetables of this species should be carefully examined and washed, cut in two, and placed in cold water awhile, with a little common salt thrown into it. It is said that this will draw out the worms or insects. They should be boiled an hour or more, and the water pressed out before sent to table. They should be kept in the cellar, or in a hole in the ground.

But good cabbage boiled no more than 20 minutes in a very little salted water, with plenty of butter, is delicious. The stalks, after the leaves are cut off, can be used in soup stock.

RED CABBAGE

Cut up some red cabbage as if for sour krout, pour over it some vinegar and rich soup stock, season it with salt and pepper, boil it slowly for three or four hours. Half an hour before serving, stir in with the cabbage an onion cut fine and fried in butter with some flour to a yellow color, and just before serving pour over a little red wine if you like. (*An apple, chopped, cooked, and added with the onion, is nice.*)

STUFFED CABBAGE

A large head of cabbage; one pint of force meat made out of any tender meat (*chicken, turkey, veal, lamb*) with all the following ingredients, save the yolk of one egg: two-thirds of a gill of chopped suet, half a gill of fine bread crumbs, one small onion, one teaspoonful of salt, one-third of a teaspoonful of pepper, one-third of a teaspoonful of marjoram, two eggs. Take out the stalk and enough of the cabbage from the centre to leave room for the force meat; wash the cavity with the reserved yolk, fill it with the force meat; tie in a cloth, and boil for three hours or more. Serve on a platter with drawn butter (*p. 107*), and garnish with parsley. (*Serves 4–6.*)

RICE À LA RISTORI

Wash well and drain a quarter of a pound of good Italian rice; shred two ounces of bacon into small pieces, and place them in a saucepan with a medium-sized, chopped-up raw cabbage, letting them steam for thirty minutes. Add a pinch of salt, half a pinch of pepper, and a teaspoonful of chopped parsley; put in the rice, and moisten with half a pint of white broth. Cook for fully a quarter of an hour longer, and serve with grated Parmesan cheese sprinkled over it. (*Serves 4–6.*)

BUBBLE AND SQUEEK

An American distortion of an English dish.
Boil a few greens or a savoy cabbage in plain water until tender, which then drain quite dry in the colander or sieve, put it upon a trencher (*wooden dish*) and chop it rather fine with a knife; then for one pound of salt beef you have in slices, put nearly a quarter pound of butter into a fry pan in which sauté the beef gently but not too dry; when done, keep it hot, put the cabbage in the fry pan, season with a little salt and pepper, and when hot through, dress it upon the dish, lay the beef over, and serve. Endive or large cabbage (*head*) lettuces may be used instead of cabbage, but care must be taken to drain off all the water. (*Serves 3–4.*)

SALAD DRESSING FOR COLD SLAW

Slaw was always "cold."
One tablespoon each: mustard, salt, sugar; three eggs, one cup cream, scant cup vinegar; cook till it thickens; stir while cooking.

Part II: Recipes

CABBAGE SOUP

Boil corned beef in a pot of water until half done, then add two small heads of cabbage, cut in quarters; when it is done tender, take out the largest pieces and drain them in a colander, and set it over a pot of hot water to keep it hot; if the meat is tender, take that up also, and add to the soup a cup of pearl barley or rice, a dozen or more potatoes peeled and cut in halves, two or three turnips, and some sliced or grated carrots; if liked, an onion or two may also be added; let it boil until the vegetables are all done; put the meat on a large dish and the cabbage and other vegetables on small dishes, for side dishes. Thicken the soup with a tablespoonful of flour made in a thin paste with water and serve in a tureen, hot. This makes a good family dinner. (*Serves 6.*)

SOUR KROUT

Cut cabbage fine, as if for slaw, then pack down in a cask, first a sprinkling of salt, then a layer of the cabbage, then salt, then cabbage, until it is full, or nearly so. Then press it down closely, pounding it with something heavy to pack it close. Lay over it a round cover with a heavy stone (*to keep the cabbage under the brine*) to ripen. It is not used until it has undergone a fermentation. When prepared for the table, it is (*drained, rinsed*) fried in butter or nice dripping, and is with many a favorite dish.

> "*Some people think sauer kraut is improved by a mixture, between the layers, of caraway, whole pepper and juniper berries, or to have the barrels smoked with juniper.*"
> Mrs. Ellet, *The Practical Housekeeper*, 1857

Sauerkraut may be cooked with caraway, pepper, and juniper berries, too. In the nineteenth century it was spelled with great variety and imagination.

SOURCROUT, BAVARIAN WAY

Well wash one quart of sourcrout, and put it into an earthen pan with a quarter of a bottle of Rhenish wine or any other light wine, and stew it for three hours; and then add some veal gravy, well seasoned, and stew for three hours longer, and serve with sausages, or you may put in a duck or a goose when you add the veal stock, and serve with it. (*Serves 3–4.*)

CAULIFLOWER

CAULIFLOWERS

Separate the green part, and cut the stalks close, let it soak awhile in cold water; tie it in a cloth, and lay it in boiling milk, and water, observing to skim it well. When tender, which will be an hour and a half or two hours (*or rather less*), take it up and drain it well; send it to table with melted butter in a boat. Broccoli is cooked in the same manner.

CAULIFLOWER DRESSED LIKE MACARONI

Boil a cauliflower in milk and water, with a little butter, half an hour, skimming it well; when tender, drain and divide up small; put a quarter pound of butter, half as much grated cheese, half a gill of milk, in a pan to boil up, and put in the sprigs of cauliflower; stew five minutes, then put it into a dish, grate over it as much more of cheese and brown it with a shovel (*or under the broiler; serves 4*).

CAULIFLOWER SAUCE

1 small cauliflower	1 small head of celery
3 tablespoonfuls butter, cut in bits and rolled in flour	Mace, pepper and salt
	1 teacupful milk or cream
1 onion	1 teacupful water

Boil the cauliflower in two waters, changing when about half done, and throwing away the first, reserve a cupful of the last. Take out the cauliflower, drain and mince. Cook in another saucepan the onion and celery, mincing them when tender. Heat the reserved teacupful of water again in a saucepan, add the milk; when warm, put in the cauliflower and onion, the butter and seasoning

—coating the butter thickly with flour; boil until it thickens. This is a delicious sauce for boiled corn beef or mutton.

PICKLED CAULIFLOWER

Select the whitest and closest, when full grown; cut off the stalk and divide the flower into eight or ten pieces, scald them in strong salt and water; let them remain in the brine until the next day. Then rinse and dry them. Lay them carefully in a jar, not to break or crush them, and pour over them hot spiced vinegar. When the vinegar is cold, a few barberries or green grapes, put in the same jar, do not injure them and add much to their beauty on the table. Broccoli and asparagus the same.

EARTH VEGETABLES

All earth vegetables taste better for a bit of frost before they are pulled from the ground. Turnips and parsnips can be left all winter and pulled in the spring, sweet and fresh. Once they are pulled, however, they must be protected from freezing or, like potatoes, they will turn mushy and rot.

TURNIPS

Pare or scrape the outside; if large, cut them in quarters; boil as long as potatoes. When tender, take them in a pan, lay a small plate over them to press out the water; when pressed once, heap them high and press again, repeating it until the water is out. Then add salt and butter and send them to the table hot. Dish them, and lay the pepper in regular spots if you wish them to look well. Turnips should be kept in the cellar, where they will not dry or freeze. Ruta baga is cooked in the same manner.

"Take care not to set turnips in a part of the table where the sun comes, as it will spoil the taste."
Miss Eliza Leslie, *Directions for Cookery*, 1870

GLAZED TURNIPS WITH GRAVY

Pare, and cut pear-shape, twelve equal-sized small white turnips; parboil them for five minutes, and drain them when done. Butter the bottom of a frying-pan capable of holding them one beside the other, and let them get a golden color, adding half a pint of powdered sugar. Moisten with half a pint of white broth, half a pinch of salt, and add a very small stick of cinnamon. Cover with a buttered paper cut in the shape of the frying-pan (*or with a loose lid*) and place it in the oven to cook for twenty minutes. When the turnips are cooked, lift off the paper. Place the turnips on a hot dish, and reduce the gravy to a glaze for six minutes. Arrange them nicely on a dish, pour a half-gill of good broth into the saucepan to loosen the glaze, remove the cinnamon and throw the sauce over the turnips. (*Serves 6–8.*)

PARSNIPS

These were once considered poisonous before they had been frozen.
Pare or scrape and cut in rings; boil till tender, then brown, using half butter and half lard. Serve. They can be boiled and mashed, adding salt and a piece of butter, and served, or, the mashed parsnips can be made into croquettes with the addition of an egg and cooked in boiling fat. The croquettes must, of course, be dipped in egg and bread crumbs before frying.

TO BOIL PARSNIPS

Wash your parsnips well, boil them until they are soft, then take off the skin, beat them in a bowl with a little salt, put to them a little cream and a lump of butter, put them in a tossing pan, and let them boil until they are like a light custard pudding, put them on a plate and send them to table.

PARSNIP FRITTERS

Boil tender, mash smooth and fine, picking out the woody bits. For three large parsnips allow two eggs, one cup rich milk (*or, since the distance from the cow is greater now, ½ cup milk and ½ cup light cream*), one tablespoon butter, one teaspoon salt, three tablespoons flour. Beat the eggs light, stir in the mashed parsnips, beating hard; then the butter and salt, next the milk, lastly the flour. Fry as fritters (*in deep fat*) or as griddle cakes.

SALSIFY

This improves if left in the ground all winter.

This excellent plant grows like a parsnip and is, in flavor, very much like fresh oysters. Scrape them, and cut them round in slips, boil them tender in milk and water, season them well with pepper, butter and salt; make a nice toast, moistened with the gravy laid in the bottom of the dish, and pour the whole over it. You could scarcely detect the difference. There should be but a suitable quantity of the gravy; too much lessens the flavor.

It is sometimes cut up and parboiled, chopped fine and fried in butter, or the roots may be fried whole in batter.

SALSIFY (OR OYSTER-PLANT)

Take twelve middling-sized ones, scrape them until quite white, rub each with lemon and put in cold water; put into a stewpan a quarter of a pound of beef suet, cut in small dice, one onion, a little thyme, a bay-leaf, a tablespoon of salt and four cloves; put on the fire, and stir for five minutes, add two tablespoons of flour, and stir well, then add three pints of water; when just boiling put in your salsify, simmer till tender; they will take nearly an hour; dish on toast, sauce over with maître d'hôtel or onion sauce.

JERUSALEM ARTICHOKES

One of the best and most useful vegetables ever introduced to table, and anything but appreciated as it deserves to be. Choose twelve of the same size, peel them and shape them like a pear, but flat at the bottom, wash them well, boil gently in three pints of water, one ounce of salt, one of butter, and a few sliced onions; when tender, make a border of mashed potatoes on a dish, fix them on it, point upwards, sauce over with either cream sauce or melted butter, and place a fine Brussels sprout between each, which contrast is exceedingly inviting, simple, and pretty. (*Serves 6–8.*)

LEEKS AND ONIONS

A touch of frost won't hurt the leeks in the garden. The onions are better off without it. Scallions, with all the green part, can be substituted for leeks–but the result isn't quite the same.

ONIONS

It is well to boil onions in milk and water, to diminish their strong taste. They require an hour or more (*for large ones*), and when done, press out the water a little, and season them with a little salt, pepper, and a little melted butter. They should be served hot with baked or roasted meats. They should be kept in a dry place.

ONIONS À LA CRÈME

Peel and boil some middle-sized onions in salt and water until quite tender, drain them, and throw them into a stewpan with two ounces of butter rolled in flour; shake them round till the butter is quite dissolved, add a teaspoon each of salt and white pepper, and then stir in by degrees, as much cream as will nearly cover them. Shake the pan round, till it is on the point of boiling; then serve.

TO DRESS SPANISH ONIONS

Take off two skins. Take four large onions, put them in a stewpan sufficiently large so they may not touch each other, put in a small piece of York ham and a quarter pound of salt butter, cover them close, put them on a slow stove or oven, keeping them turned carefully until all sides are done; they will take about two hours: then take them up and glaze them (*with butter and a very little sugar*), thicken the gravy, and season with salt and pepper. (*Serves 4.*)

ONIONS (TO DRY THEM)

Free from the outer skin, dry gradually in a slow oven to a deep brown, flatten it (*when quite dry, put into airtight containers*), and it will keep almost any length of time and is extremely useful for heightening the color and flavor of broths and gravies.

ONION SOUP

Put half a pound of butter into a stewpan and let it boil; have ready ten or twelve onions peeled and cut small, put them into the butter and fry a nice brown; sprinkle in a (*very*) little flour, and shake the pan often; keep it over the fire for some minutes, then pour in three pints of boiling milk, stir it well; cut some pie-crust in slips, throw it in, add salt (*white pepper and mace*) to taste, then let it boil for ten minutes, stirring it frequently, then take it from the fire; beat the yolks of two hard-boiled eggs with a tablespoonful of vinegar; first mix some of the soup with this, then stir it to the remainder. (*If you omit the pie crust, serve with croutons. Serves 6–8.*)

ANOTHER: Onions, peeled and cut into pieces, then shred into a pan and fried in either butter or oil, without any broth, but simply having boiled water poured over them, and some toasted bread seasoned merely with salt and pepper (*and grated cheese*), are considered very refreshing when thus made into a soup, and are much used by the ladies of Europe, after the fatigues of a ball.

LEEK OR ONION SOUP

The liquor in which the leg of mutton has been boiled will do very well for this broth. Mix a spoonful or two of oatmeal, according to the quantity of broth, in cold water, very smooth, the same as if for gruel; add a little of the broth by degrees, until the whole is incorporated; then boil the liquor with any quantity of leeks or onions—both or either—until it becomes the consistency of cream (*puréeing in the blender helps*). Or, omit the oatmeal and substitute flour, stirring the soup very hard for five minutes; and when you are about to take it from the fire, stir in the yolks of two eggs, beat up with a little more broth, and serve it immediately.

ONIONS PICKLED

Peel and soak them in salt and water three days. Then just scald them in milk and water, drain and dry them. Scald the spices with the vinegar, adding a piece of alum, and when cold, pour over them. If kept in bottles, put a few spoonfuls of sweet (*olive*) oil on top. Cover close.

ONION VINEGAR

Mince 6 large onions, strew on 1 tablespoonful salt, and let them stand five or six hours. Scald 1 quart best vinegar in which 1 tablespoonful white sugar has been dissolved, pour over the onions; put in a jar, tie down the cover, and steep a fortnight. Strain and bottle.

Onions can be chopped, measured into useful portions, and stored in the freezer almost indefinitely. If you do not use many, it is better to do this than to let the last ones rot in the bag.

Stock will be clearer, and just as well flavored, if you leave the onions unpeeled.

To extract onion juice, press the cut onion on the grater and move it slightly.

WINTER SQUASH

Winter squash is any variety with a hard skin—acorn, butternut, etc.

This is a very nice vegetable. It is good to use in August, and should be kept in a dry, and in winter, a warm place (*it will keep three or four months without refrigeration, in a dark place*). Pare it, scrape out the seeds, cut it in pieces; boil it in a small quantity of water. When done, which will be in half or three-quarters of an hour, press out the water as dry as possible, mash well and season with salt and butter.

Or, cut it in half, remove the seeds, put butter and nutmeg, or chopped onion, in the cavity, and bake for 1 hour in a moderate oven, in a covered pan.

PUMPKINS

Pie is not the only way to deal with leftover Halloween pumpkins. Bread, puddings, and relishes may be made from it. Pumpkin thickens things in the way that corn meal does, so the batter will look sloshy.

SQUASH OR PUMPKIN PIE

Cut the squash or pumpkin in several pieces, remove the seeds, but leave it unpared; lay it in the steamer (*or in a colander over boiling water, covered*), and when cooked scrape it from the rind and press it through the colander (*or a food mill*). To a quart of this allow one pound of brown sugar, eight eggs, one quart of milk, five ounces of butter, one teaspoonful of salt, two tablespoonfuls of ginger and four tablespoonfuls of cinnamon (*perhaps less of ginger and cinnamon*). Beat the butter with the warm squash, the sugar, salt, spice and the yolks of the eggs; stir in the milk, which should be boiling; then add the whites, beaten to a stiff froth; mix well; pour in paste-lined plates and put them in quite a hot oven (*425°*) that the egg and milk may not separate. In ten minutes reduce the heat (*to 375°*) as fast cooking makes them puffy. (*Bake about 40 minutes. A splash of rum or bourbon added with the milk does not hurt. Makes 4 pies.*)

> "*The American pie is perhaps the most ridiculed of all dishes. It has, however, great popularity and undoubted merits.*"
> Mary Ronald, *The Century Cook Book*, 1896

PUMPKIN PUDDING

Three pounds of pumpkin; six ounces of butter; six eggs; two tablespoonfuls of wine; one tablespoonful of brandy; sugar to taste; one teaspoonful of cinnamon. Cut the pumpkin in slices, pare it, take out the seeds and soft parts; cut it into small pieces, and stew it in a very little water, until it becomes tender; then press it in a colander until quite dry, turn it out in a pan, put the butter in, and a little salt; mash it fine. When cool, whisk the eggs until thick, stir in; then add sugar to taste, with the brandy, wine and spice. This is (*easily*) sufficient for three or four puddings. Line your plates with paste and bake in a quick oven.

[332]

SQUASH BREAD

1 cup squash, stewed and sieved (pumpkin may be substituted)	1 teaspoon salt
	1 tablespoon butter
	½ cup yeast
2 tablespoons sugar	Flour enough to knead it
1½ cups scalded milk	

Mix the sugar and salt with the squash, add the butter melted in the hot milk, and when cool, add the yeast and flour. Knead fifteen minutes. Let it rise till light, knead and shape into loaves or biscuit. When well-risen, bake. (*Makes 2–3 loaves.*)

PRESERVED PUMPKINS (*A RELISH*)

Cut the pumpkin into leaves, etc., according to taste, sprinkle them with white sugar grated, let them lay all night; make a syrup pound for pound (*1 pound sugar to 1 pound pumpkin*), cut some lemons in thin slices, add a little race (*green*) ginger, and boil slowly until done.

ANOTHER WAY: Take ten pounds of pumpkin, ten pounds of sugar, ten oranges; put (*about 1 cupful of*) water in your kettle, then a laying of pumpkin (*peeled and cut into strips*), then a laying of sugar; (*then the limes and oranges, sliced very thin; alternate layers until all is in the kettle*) and put it over a slow fire, and when done, add essence of cloves and cinnamon (*or cook with a few sticks of cinnamon and whole cloves and remove them when done*).

NUTS

Most nuts are harvested around this time. They will be cheaper and more readily available in stores near Thanksgiving.

TO BLANCH ALMONDS

Pour boiling water on them, until their skins are easily removed, then throw them into cold water to whiten them; drain them from the water to pound them, but do not wipe them dry, as the water will prevent their oiling (*as will a few drops of rosewater or vanilla*).

ALMOND PUDDING

Take a pound of almonds after they are cracked and shelled; put them in warm water, take the skins off, then pound them, and wet with rose water; take six eggs, ten ounces of sugar pounded and sifted, and beat it with the eggs well; then put in your almonds with a pint of cream; put them into a basin and stir them well together over a few coals until they are warm; then put it into a thin dish, paste (*pastry*) only round the sides of the dish, and bake it (*at 375°*) three quarters of an hour. (*Serves 6.*)

CHESTNUT PUDDING

Take one pound of chestnuts, roasted and skinned, and rub them through a cullender. Mix with them half a pound of white sugar, a pint of cream or half a pound of butter, a teaspoonful of powdered cinnamon, a grated nutmeg, and a wine-glassful of rose-water (*or 1 tablespoon of vanilla*), and one of wine. Set it away to get cold. Then beat six eggs very light, and add them by degrees to the mixture, alternately with half a pound of mashed potatoes. Bake it three-quarters of an hour (*at 375°*) in a buttered dish. (*This was served as a vegetable with game: Serves 8.*)

To roast the chestnuts, cut a slit in the under side and put them in a hot oven for about 15 minutes, or fry in a little oil until they pop. If the inner skins are stubborn, pour boiling water over them and let stand a few minutes.

CHESTNUT SOUP, À LA JARDINIÈRE

Place one pint of purée in a saucepan, moisten it with a pint of white broth (*p. 131*), and a glassful of Madeira wine. Boil for thirty minutes, then put in a quarter of a carrot, the same of turnip (cut small), a tablespoonful of asparagus tops, six Brussels sprouts, and a piece of cut-up cauliflower the size of an egg. Boil all together for fifteen minutes and serve after seasoning with half a tablespoonful of salt and a teaspoonful of pepper. (*Serves 6–8.*)

PURÉE OF CHESTNUTS: Boil one pound of chestnuts ten minutes; peel and skin them immediately; put them in a saucepan with a quart of white broth, a tablespoonful of salt and two teaspoonfuls of pepper, and a quarter-pound of butter. Let all boil well for thirty minutes; rub through a sieve (*they are too thick to blend*).

PEANUT SOUP

When one does not use meat, an excellent soup can be made using salted peanuts as the base. Grind the peanuts, cover with a pint of water and allow to simmer about two hours. Have a pint of tomatoes, an onion cut up fine, salt, pepper, a pinch of spice, a teaspoonful of sugar, a pint of hot water cooking in another vessel. When ready strain the nut liquid into the other, thicken with flour and serve in half an hour. A cup of peanuts will be required for a quart of soup.

HICKORY NUT PUDDING

One pound chopped bread, one pound seeded raisins chopped, one pound currants, one pound nuts after they are shelled, one-half pound suet, one-half pound sugar, one cup molasses, five eggs, one pint of milk, spice of all kinds; (*pour into a buttered mold and*) steam seven hours. (*Serves 10–15.*)

SAUCE: Three eggs, one cup sugar beaten light; one pint cooked corn-starch (*boiling water thickened with cornstarch*); one-half ball (*¼ pound*) butter; two tablespoonfuls brandy.

HICKORY NUT MACAROONS

One pound of hickory nuts, one pound of sugar, two ounces of cinnamon, five tablespoonfuls of flour, whites of twelve eggs. (*Bake according to directions on p. 427.*)

NUT SALAD

One cup of nuts, two cups celery cut fine, four apples. Mix with the following dressing: (*beaten*) whites of two eggs, one teaspoon each of salt, pepper, and sugar, one cup vinegar and one teaspoon flour; cook and add a little cream. (*Serves 6–8.*)

[14]

NOVEMBER

Beef; stocks, gravies, soups; innards; preserved beef;
mutton; pork; venison; turkey; cranberries; fruitcake;
Thanksgiving dishes

We have it easier than the nineteenth-century woman did. Either she hacked what she wanted from her own butchered cow hanging in the shed, or she bought her meat from the market in huge chunks, a haunch at a time. We've got the friendly supermarket with its Saran Wrap and see-through plastic trays. If at times the cuts seem somewhat anonymous, a little amorphous, well, that's progress.

Before refrigeration the slaughter and preparation of meat animals was strictly a seasonal affair. It would not be done until the weather was cold enough to help preserve the meat. It usually was not done until the summer pasturage was gone and the animal had finished fattening itself for the winter. What could not be eaten immediately was smoked, pickled, salted, or potted— or, if the weather cooperated, frozen. After a good, deep freeze, the meat could be wrapped and packed in bran or oats. That insulation, plus continued cold weather, might keep it good until March.

There are no longer predictable seasonal variations in meat, even in price. Animals are fattened for slaughter, and slaughtered, year-round. If the price or the availability of certain kinds or cuts seems to fluctuate, it does so by fashion or freak, and not out of any necessity springing from the nature of the beasts.

Therefore, I follow the by-gone seasons in listing meat recipes. Lamb appears in April, since spring lambs born in February were usually ready for slaughter in April, and since lamb has some traditional connection with Easter, which sometimes falls in April. Veal, the meat from another baby animal, is also listed in April. But beef, mutton, and pork are naturally November phenomena. So is turkey, along with cranberry sauce and stuffing and all those other Thanksgiving institutions.

Venison is more seasonal now than it was in the nineteenth century, when one could buy it along with beef in the market. Now, the deer season usually begins in mid-November, when the deer have finished mating, and lasts into December. So here are recipes for venison, and for bear.

For authenticity of cut (and for the very best results) a cooperative butcher is essential.

BEEF

ROAST DONE TO A TURN (*OF THE SPIT*)

A roast was roasted in those days. Anything that went into an oven was baked meat, not roast. Cooking done in an open fireplace makes more difference to meat than it does to most other dishes—and the roast was the supreme test of the cook.

Build a fierce hardwood fire so that the coals will extend three inches beyond the end of the meat. Never start roasting over a fresh or old fire. Hickory, oak or apple wood is best, but plan to have the fire ready in time to allow sixteen minutes per pound until eating time.

Rub the roast with unsalted butter or grease, dredge it with flour, place it on the spit across the fire (*in a 300° oven*), about ten or twelve inches above the coals. Turn it, basting it at fifteen-minute intervals with unsalted butter until there are enough drippings in the dripping pan under the spit to use them for basting. When the meat starts to sweat, move it to six or eight inches from the coals (*turn the oven to 325°*), place the meat screen before the fire. When the roast is about half done (a twelve-pound roast is the proper size), stir the coals to start browning the meat. Sprinkle it with salt, marjoram; lower the spit (*raise the oven heat to 400°*) and start basting every five minutes. Half an hour before it is done, dredge the roast very evenly and finely with flour, baste it with melted butter. This "frothing" gives it a smooth, golden-brown glaze.

FOR GRAVY: Stand the roast on end, when you remove the spit; put a funnel in the spit hole and pour half a cup of salted beef broth through the hole to start the juices flowing into the platter.

A GOOD ROAST, BAKED NOWADAYS: *Allow about 15 minutes per pound in an oven set at 325°. You can lard it with slivers of garlic before you roast it, if you like, but do not salt it. Baste with butter melted in a little water. (Some people start the roast at 400°, reduce the heat to 350° after 20 minutes. Allow 10–12 minutes per pound by this method.)*

For pan gravy, put a pitcher of hot salted broth by the carver, let him pour a tablespoonful over each serving.

YORKSHIRE PUDDING

Put six tablespoonfuls of flour into a basin, with six eggs, a pinch of salt, and a quarter of a pint of milk, mix all well together with a wooden spoon, adding the remaining three-quarters of a pint of milk by degrees; you have previously set a shallow tin dish under a piece of roasting beef before the fire; an hour before serving, pour in the batter, leaving it under the meat until quite set and rather brown on top, when turn the pudding over upon the dish you intend serving it upon, and again place it before the fire until the other side is rather browned, when it is ready to serve with the meat. This pudding is also excellent baked under a small piece of beef of about five or six pounds. It is also frequently baked beneath a shoulder of mutton; also baked in an oven with a few spoonfuls of gravy added, if the fire is not large enough. (*If you have a rack high enough to allow the pudding to be made under the roast in the roasting pan, the drippings add a lot of flavor.*)

A MARINADE TO BASTE ROAST MEATS

Chop up some fat bacon with a clove of garlic and a sprig of parsley; add salt, pepper, a spoonful of vinegar and four spoonfuls of oil; beat it up well and baste the meat with it.

SAUCES FOR ROAST BEEF

PIQUANTE SAUCE (BAKED FISH, ROAST AND BROILED MEAT):

2 *cups of brown stock*	1 *teaspoon sugar*
4 *tablespoons butter*	2 *tablespoons chopped pickle*
2 *tablespoons flour*	1 *tablespoon chopped capers*
Dash of cayenne	½ *teaspoon salt*
1 *tablespoon chopped onions*	1 *teaspoon tarragon vinegar*

Place the butter in a sauce-pan, and when it begins to brown add the flour, and stir until it is well brown but do not let it burn. Draw to a cooler place on the range and slowly add the stock, stirring constantly; add salt and cayenne, and let simmer for ten minutes. In another sauce-pan boil the vinegar, onion, and sugar rapidly for five minutes; then add it to the sauce and at the same time add the capers, pickle, and tarragon vinegar. Stir well and let it cook for two minutes to heat the pickle. If the sauce becomes too thick dilute it with a little water.

HORSERADISH SAUCE: Grate two tablespoons of horseradish, pound it in a mortar with a teaspoon of salt, half a teaspoon of mustard, powdered, and half a teaspoon of sugar in powder; mix it gradually with four tablespoonfuls of cream, and then stir in quickly two tablespoonfuls of vinegar.

FILLETS OF BEEF

Cut the inside of a sirloin or rump (*this usually means "cut a fine steak," which was cut thinner than we usually cut them now, but here it means slice the fillet*) in slices half an inch thick; trim them neatly, melt a little butter in a sauté or frying pan; season the fillets; fry them lightly, serve with tomato sauce (*p. 281*), sorrel (*p. 189*), anchovy butter or gherkin sauce.

SAUCES FOR STEAK

TO MAKE ANCHOVY SAUCE: Take a pint of gravy, put in an anchovy, take a quarter of a pound of butter rolled in a little flour, and stir them all together until it boils. You may add a little juice of a lemon, catsup, red wine, and walnut liquor, just as you please. Plain butter melted thick (*p. 107*) with a spoonful of walnut pickle, or catsup, is good sauce, or anchovy. In short, you may put as many things as you fancy into sauce.

GHERKIN SAUCE: Put into a sauce pan a piece of butter rolled in flour, some salt, pepper, and one or two pickled cucumbers or gherkin pickles minced fine. Moisten it with boiling water. Let it stew gently a few minutes and serve it up.

SAUCE ROBERT: Half a pint of beef broth, one and a half ounces of butter, one tablespoonful of flour, one teaspoonful of salt, one-third of a teaspoonful of pepper, one teaspoonful of made mustard, one teaspoonful of vinegar, a small onion chopped fine, juice of half a lemon. Put the butter in a frying-pan and when hot, throw in the onions; stir them until brown, being very careful that they do not burn; sift in the flour, stir and fry a little longer; add the broth, pepper, salt, etc., and simmer for ten minutes. Pour it over nicely broiled beefsteaks.

BEEFSTEAKS À LA FRANÇAIS

Cattle were not raised specifically for meat until nearly 1900. The nineteenth-century housewife could count absolutely on meat as tough as nails. The old recipes take this for granted and specialize in tenderizing methods: spicing, larding, marinading, beating, and long, long cooking. Unless you want to adapt them for better meat—less cooking, less pounding, etc.—many of the following recipes will work best for Commercial or Utility beef, the cheapest grades now generally available.

Take a fine steak, and dip it into cold spring water, let it drain a few minutes, lay it in a dish and pour over it sufficient clarified butter, hot, and cover it; let it remain twelve hours, then remove the butter and roll the steak with the rolling pin a dozen times rather hardly, let it lay in front of the fire ten minutes; turning it once or twice. Put it into a frying pan with (*hot*) water half an inch in depth and let it fry until it browns.

Mince some parsley fine, chop an eschallot as fine as can be, and season them with cayenne, salt and a little white pepper; work them with a lump of butter and when the steak is brown, take it from the pan, rub it well with the mixture on both sides and return it to the pan until done enough; dish it, thicken the gravy in the pan with a little butter rolled in flour if it requires it, and pour it over the steak and serve.

FILLET OF BEEF BRAISED

Take the inside of a sirloin of beef (*a thin sirloin steak*) rolled together so as to bring the fat into the centre. Then strew the bottom of the stewpan with a few slices of ham (*lean bacon*) in which a small quantity of gravy (*½ cup or less of stock or bouillon*) has been put, just to prevent the bottom of the pan from burning; and on this place the meat, covering it with chopped carrots, celery, button onions and a pickled chili together with a sliced gherkin, sweet herbs, salt, mace and a little allspice, and simmer until tender, then brown it before the fire or with a salamander, skim and season the sauce and send the meat, sauce, and vegetables up in the same dish. (*Serves 3–4.*)

"*To make tough beef tender, soak it in vinegar and water (½ cup vinegar to 1 quart water), for about twelve hours.*"
Mrs. Crowen, *The American System of Cookery*, 1870

RUMP STEAK STUFFED

Two pounds rump steak, two ounces suet, three ounces of bread crumbs, six olives, one dessertspoonful of chopped parsley, pepper and salt, two eggs. Peel and chop the olives small; chop the suet; put into a basin with the crumbs, parsley, olives, suet, pepper and salt; mix well with the eggs; spread the mixture on a steak, roll and tie securely; place in a greased paper and roast about three quarters of an hour. (*Serves 4.*)

FRENCH ROLLS: Cut strips of beefsteak to make a roll as long as a knife-blade and larger than a sausage, stuff with a prepared stuffing and sew it up and bake it or fry it in batter. Melt butter for a gravy.

ROLLED BEEF THAT EQUALS HARE

Take the inside of a large sirloin (*a steak cut about ½ inch thick*) soak it in a glass of vinegar mixed with a glass of wine, a teaspoon of Jamaica pepper (*allspice*) and a clove or two, in the finest powder, for forty-eight hours; have ready a very fine stuffing (*p. 390*) and bind it up tight. Roast it on a hanging spit (*a contraption that resembled a milk can cut in half with a hook at the top, which was placed in front of the fire like a reflector oven; to imitate the effect, wrap the steak around the spit of a rotisserie and tie it in place—or bake it at 325° for about 45 minutes*) and baste it with the marinade, unless the outside is all dried up, then baste with butter. (*Serves 3–4.*)

BEEF IN A MARINADE

Cut the inside of a sirloin in slices; put them into a marinade made as follows:—take equal parts of vinegar and water, slice some carrots and onions, add some salt, add a few peppercorns with a clove of garlic. Let all stew together till the goodness be extracted from the vegetables, then strain it and let it stand until cold. Let the meat stand in this pickle for twenty-four hours before it is dressed, then let it stew gently in a good gravy until quite tender. Add a wineglassful of port wine; one table-spoonful of mushroom catsup, one teaspoonful of shallot vinegar, and some butter rolled in flour; place the meat neatly in the dish and pour the sauce over it.

TO STEW BEEF

It should be put down (*a rump roast or chuck roast, generally, whole, not cubed, about 4 pounds in weight*) in a pot with just sufficient cold water to cover the meat, and closely covered. After boiling three or four hours, according to the size of the piece, cut into small pieces not larger than dice, two or three carrots and heads of celery, along with a little sweet herbs and put them into the pot along with a couple of large onions stuck full of cloves, and let it simmer two or three hours, taking care to skim off any grease that may appear on the top. By this time the meat will probably be tender enough; when take out the whole onions, mince them and fry them in butter, to be mixed with the gravy made by the meat, which season with salt and cayenne, or chili-vinegar, to which add some walnut or mushroom ketchup. Thicken the gravy with a little flour and brown it, if necessary, with a spoonful of sugar burnt soft (*p. 437*) which besides imparting its color, adds an agreeable flavor. Such is the most simple mode, but the sauce may be much improved by a glass or two of port wine and a spoonful of curry powder; if the odor of garlic be not objected to, a clove boiled in the stew will be found to give it a fine flavor. Garnish with the vegetables.

A BEEF STEW

Take two or three pounds of the rump of beef, cut away all fat and skin and cut it into pieces two or three inches square, put it in a stewpan and pour upon it one quart of broth, let it boil, sprinkle in a little salt and pepper to taste, when it has simmered (*uncovered*) for two hours shred finely (*grate*) a large lemon (*rind*), add it to the gravy and in twenty minutes pour in a flavoring composed of two table-spoonfuls of Harvey's sauce (*or Worcestershire or A-1*), the juice of the lemon, a spoonful of flour and a little ketchup, add at pleasure two glasses of Madeira or one of sherry or port one quarter hour after the flavoring, and serve. (*This goes exceptionally well with mashed sweet potatoes. Serves 6–9.*)

Beef may be stewed in wine, beer, or tomato juice, adding to each the appropriate herbs and vegetables. After browning the beef in a mixture of butter and bacon fat, and dredging with a couple of tablespoonfuls of flour, add—with wine—bay leaves, thyme, marjoram, parsley, small onions, potatoes, and mushrooms.

With beer, add bay, thyme, parsley, garlic, a couple of juniper berries, a stalk of celery, onions, parsnips, and potatoes.

And with tomato juice, add basil, orégano, bay, garlic, a very small bit of chopped onion, carrots, and potatoes. Add salt and pepper to all versions.

BEEFSTEAK AND OYSTER PIE

Pound the steaks well and put layers of them and of oysters. Stew the liquor and beards of the latter with a bit of lemon peel, mace and a tablespoon of walnut ketchup (*or Worcestershire*). When the pie is baked, boil with three spoonfuls of cream, and one ounce of butter rubbed with flour (or alternatively, a few spoonfuls of beef gravy and port wine), strain it and pour it into the dish; for a small pie one dozen oysters will be sufficient (*top the pie with a good puff-paste crust—see p. 76—or a crust according to the recipe below*); the pie may be baked in a couple of hours. (*A small pie serves 2–3.*)

CRUST FOR MEAT PIES:

1 quart of flour	*1 teaspoonful of soda wet with*
2½ cups milk	*hot water and stirred into the*
2 teaspoonfuls of cream-tartar	*milk*
sifted into the dry flour	*1 teaspoonful salt*
3 tablespoonfuls of lard	

Work up very lightly and quickly (*like biscuit dough*), and do not get too stiff.

BEEF COLLOPS

Take some rump steaks, or tender pieces cut like Scotch collops, only larger (about three inches long), hack them a little with a knife (*or Swiss them by sprinkling with flour and pounding with the edge of a plate*) and flour them; put a little butter in a stewpan and melt it, then put in your collops, and fry them quickly for about two minutes; put in a pint of gravy, a little butter rolled in flour, seasoned with pepper and salt; cut four pickled cucumbers in slices, half a cup of walnuts, and a few capers, a little onion shred very fine; stew them five minutes, then put them into a hot dish and send them to table. You may put half a glass of white wine into it.

CANNELON OF BEEF WITH MUSHROOM SAUCE

Two pounds of lean beef cut from the round (*ground round, in other words*) the grated rind of half a lemon, one tablespoonful of onion juice, two tablespoonfuls of melted butter, a few gratings of nutmeg, a teaspoonful of salt, one-fourth teaspoonful of pepper; chop the meat fine and add the remaining ingredients in the order given. Shape in a roll six inches long, wrap in buttered paper, place on rack in dripping pan, and bake thirty minutes. Baste every five minutes with one-fourth cupful of butter melted in one cupful of boiling water. Serve with brown mushroom sauce. (*Serves 4–6.*)

Brown mushroom sauce: Prepare a pint of mushrooms by cutting off the stalks, peeling the tops, and cutting in quarters; boil twenty minutes in enough stock to just cover them, then add one-fourth of a teaspoonful of nutmeg, cayenne and salt to taste; thicken with browned flour (*p. 438*); boil two or three minutes, beat in a tablespoonful of butter, add a teaspoonful (more if you like) of lemon juice and serve.

SPANISH FRICEO

This dish is made from good beef (the same kind as is used for beefsteak), lean pork or young mutton. The best is beef and pork in equal quantities. Two pounds of meat is enough for six or eight persons. The meat is beaten till soft and then cut in thin slices, cut raw potatoes in thin slices, washing them before they are cut, but not after, and take two soup plates of them.

Mix with the potatoes two saucerfuls of onions cut in slices. Take a pudding dish and put the meat and potatoes in layers. Scatter over each layer some pepper, some Jamaica pepper (*allspice*), and salt; put on every layer of potatoes a piece of butter and at least three-quarters of a tablespoonful of thick sour cream. Close the pudding dish well and put it into boiling water (*halfway up the sides*), and let it boil for one and one-half hours.

GERMAN OYSTER SOUP

1 shin of beef, 1 tin of oysters, large or small (*1 quart or 1 pint*) according to size of family. Boil the shin to a strong soup, skimming off the fat as usual. Add a few pieces of mace and some salt. A little while before dinner, add the liquor from the oysters and after it boils up add one teaspoonful of butter, with enough flour or cornstarch to thicken the soup. Let the oysters be put in last, just long enough to heat thoroughly.

MINCED BEEF WITH CUCUMBERS

Take a fine rump steak undressed (*uncooked*) and with a sharp knife shred it fine (*or get your butcher to run 2 pounds of round steak through the grinder once only*). Put it into a stewpan with a little clarified butter and some salt; stir it over a quick fire for a few minutes, then add half a pint of good beef gravy; let it boil gently until it becomes of a proper thickness (*like fibrous mashed potatoes*). Cut two fine cucumbers in slices the thickness, of a crown piece (*a little more than ⅛ inch*) and put them with an onion sliced in a stewpan with some clarified butter, a little vinegar, a lump of sugar, and fry them of a fine brown color; put them into a stewpan with some plain sauce (*stock or bouillon*); let it simmer gently until sufficiently done; then lay the mince in the dish and pour the cucumber over it; thicken the sauce with a little flour and butter; add the squeeze of a lemon just before serving. (*Serves 4.*)

BOUILLI

This is probably the origin of the British "bully beef." Almost any meat boiled for soup or stock can be served as boiled meat if not overcooked. Take it out of the liquid, slice it thin, serve it hot with horseradish or a sauce.

Boil seven or eight pounds of beef in more water than enough to cover it;

remove the scum as it rises, then put in two carrots, two turnips, two onions, two heads of celery, two or three cloves, a fagot (*about ¼ bunch, tied together*) of parsley and sweet herbs. Let it boil gently four or five hours. Put a carrot, a turnip, an onion and a head of celery in to cook whole and take them out when done and cut in small squares. Take out the meat carefully, skim off the fat, and lay the sliced vegetables into the soup, and add a spoonful of ketchup to heighten the flavor. Pour in a soup tureen. (*Serves 15 or so.*)

SAUCES FOR BOILED BEEF

SHALLOT SAUCE: Take half a pint of water in which meat has been boiled, add a wineglass of vinegar and two or three shallots cut fine, and half a teaspoon of salt; put these into a saucepan over the fire, work a teaspoon of flour into a piece of butter the size of an egg, and stir them into the hot water and let them simmer for fifteen minutes.

ANCHOVY SAUCE: Soak some anchovies in water for two or three hours, then put them in a stewpan with cold water, and set them on coals to simmer until the anchovies are dissolved; then strain the water, add to it a wineglass of red wine and half a pint of melted butter; let it simmer for half of an hour, then serve with boiled fish or meat.

AN OLD-FASHIONED BOILED DINNER

Notwithstanding that this dish has fallen into ill-repute with many people, it *may* be prepared so as to be both palatable and nutritious for those who exercise freely.

Four pounds of corned beef, two or three beets, a small cabbage, two small carrots, one small white French turnip, six or eight potatoes of uniform size, and one small crook-neck squash.

Wash and soak the corned beef in cold water, and put it on to boil in fresh cold water; skim, and simmer, but not long enough for it to fall to pieces. Let it cool in the liquor in which it was boiled. Put it into a flat, shallow dish, cover it with a board, and press it. Remove all the fat from the meat liquor, and save it to clarify for shortening. Save the meat liquor, but do not let it stand in an iron pot or tin pan. Boil the beets the day before, also, and cover them with vinegar. The next day, prepare the vegetables. Wash them all, scrape the carrots, and cut the cabbage into quarters; pare the turnip and squash, and cut into three-quarter inch slices, and pare the potatoes. Put the meat liquor on to boil about two hours before dinner time; when boiling, put in the carrots, afterward the cabbage and turnip, and half an hour before dinner, add the squash and potatoes. When tender, take the vegetables up carefully; drain the water from the cabbage by pressing it in a colander, slice the carrots. Put the cold meat in the centre of a large dish (*or, it may be reheated in some of the liquor*), and serve the carrots, turnip and potatoes around the edge, with the squash, beets and cabbage in separate dishes. This may all be done the same day if the meat be put on to boil very early, removed as soon as tender, the fat taken off, and the vegetables added to the boiling liquor, beginning with those which require the longest time to cook. Whichever way the dish is prepared, boil the beets alone. (*Serves 8–10.*)

The next morning, use whatever remains of the vegetables as a vegetable hash.

VEGETABLE HASH: Equal parts of cabbage, beets and turnips, and as much potato as there is of all the other vegetables, chopped all very fine; add a little salt, and pepper; put a spoonful of drippings in the frying-pan, and when hot, add the hash, and cook slowly until warmed through.

BEEF RISSOLES

Mince and season cold beef, and flavor it with mushroom or walnut ketchup. Make of beef dripping a very thin paste (*a pie crust, substituting dripping for shortening*), roll it out in very thin pieces about four inches square; enclose in each piece some of the mince. (*Wet the edges and fold them over to make a square package; deep*) fry them in dripping of a very light brown. The paste can hardly be rolled out too thin. (Either bacon grease or lard is excellent to fry them).

BEEF À LA MODE

This is one of the standard nineteenth-century dishes. Most recipe books include several versions of it. Eaten cold, generally, but sometimes served hot, it made meat that was probably otherwise nearly inedible tender and tasty.

Choose a piece of thick flank of a fine heifer or ox (*its flanks thicken as an animal grows, so old-time flank steak was probably more substantial than that we buy now; any cheap but lean roast should do*); cut into long strips some fat bacon, but quite free from yellow; dip them into vinegar, and then into a seasoning ready prepared of salt, black pepper, allspice, and a clove, all in a fine powder (*ground*), with parsley, chives, savory and knotted marjoram shred as small as possible and well mixed. With a sharp knife make holes deep enough to let in the larding, then rub the beef over with the seasoning, and bind it up tight with tape (*muslin strips*). Set it in a well-tinned pot over a fire or rather, stove; three or four onions must be fried brown and put to the beef, with two or three carrots, one turnip, a head of celery, and a small quantity of water, let it simmer gently ten or twelve hours (*3 or 4 is enough*), or until extremely tender, turning the meat twice.

ANOTHER: Take a round of beef (*a good round now would be marbled with fat almost exactly as the larding would marble it—and would weigh 20 pounds or more; try this with a cheap bottom round or chuck roast, and decrease the recipe accordingly*); remove the bone (*if it has one*) from the middle and trim away the tougher bits about the edges, with such gristle, etc., as you can reach. Set these aside for soup stock. Bind the beef into a symmetrical shape by passing a strip of stout muslin as wide as the round is high, about it and stitching the ends (*tightly*) together at one side. Have ready at least a pound of fat salt pork, cut into strips as thick as your middle finger, and long enough to reach from top to bottom of the trussed round. Put half a pint of vinegar over the fire in a tin or porcelain saucepan; season with three or four minced shallots or button onions, two teaspoonfuls made (*prepared*) mustard, a teaspoonful nutmeg, one of cloves, half as much allspice, half-spoonful black pepper, with a bunch of sweet herbs minced fine and a tablespoonful brown sugar. Let all simmer for five minutes, then boil up once, and pour while scalding hot, upon the strips of pork, which should be laid in a deep dish. Let all stand together until cold. Remove the pork to a plate, and mix with the liquor left in the dish enough bread-crumbs to make a tolerably stiff force-meat. If the vinegar is very strong, dilute with a little water before moistening the crumbs. With a long, thin-bladed knife, make perpendicular incisions in the meat, not more than half an inch apart; thrust into these the strips of fat pork, so far down that the upper ends are just level with the surface, and work into the cavities with them a little of the force-meat. Proceed thus until the meat is fairly riddled and plugged with the pork. Fill the hole from which the bone was taken with the dressing and bits of pork (*or rub what is left over the top*). Put into a baking pan; half-fill this with boiling water; turn a large pan over it to keep in the steam, and roast slowly (*at 250°*) for five or six hours, allowing half an hour to each pound of meat. Do not remove the cover except to baste (and this should be done often), until fifteen minutes before you draw it from the oven. Set away with the muslin band still about it, and pour the gravy over the meat. When cold, lift from the gravy—which by the way, will be excellent seasoning for your soup-stock—cut the stitches in the muslin girdle, remove carefully and send the meat to table, cold, garnished with parsley and nasturtium blossoms. Carve horizontally, in slices thin as a shaving. Do not offer the outside to anyone; but the second cut will be handsomely marbled with the white pork, which appearance will continue all the way down.

Beef à la mode will keep at least three weeks in the refrigerator, and can be used like cold cuts. The slight vinegar tang may not be to everybody's liking, but if you run across a pot-roast sale and have no freezer, this is an excellent way to take advantage of it.

RAGOUT OF BEEF À LA MODE

Cut cold beef à la mode into pieces about one inch square. To every pint of these squares, allow: 1 tablespoonful of butter, 1 tablespoonful of flour, 1 tablespoonful of Worcestershire sauce, salt and pepper to taste, 1 tablespoonful of mushroom catsup, ½ pint of stock, and 1 tablespoon of sherry (if you use wine). Put the butter in a small stewpan, and stir until a dark brown; then add the flour, mix well, add the stock, and stir continually until it boils; then add the meat, sauce, catsup, salt and pepper, and let it *simmer* gently for fifteen minutes. Take from the fire, add the wine; dish, garnish with potatoes, and serve.

SPICED ROUND

To twelve pounds of beef, take half a pound of brown sugar, one-fourth pound saltpetre, one tablespoonful mace, two tablespoonfuls allspice, and two tablespoonfuls black pepper. Beat all fine and rub over the round; then rub well with one-half pound of salt. Put in a vessel with all the spices and salt in and around the beef. Every few days turn the round in the brine that will be formed by the salt. It will be ready for use in (*three or*) four weeks.

This quantity may be divided into two roasts. Cook just as a fresh roast, except from one-half to one hour more time is required. (*Or, bake it and let it cool in the brine with a little water and suet. Serve cold.*) This is a very old recipe. It was handed down to Mrs. Margaret C. Greenway, who was born in 1800, by her mother, and has been tested by several generations of her descendants

RUTGERS ROLLETJES

Ten pounds of beef, five ounces of salt, three quarters of an ounce of pepper, half an ounce of cloves, tripe. The beef should be sirloin, or from the best cuts, and about one-third fat. Chop it in squares about the size of dice, and mix in the salt, pepper and cloves. Take pieces of tripe about ten inches square, make bags of them, and fill with the beef; sew them up and boil them four hours. Put the bags in a butter firkin filled one-third with vinegar and the rest with the liquor from the pot, having skimmed off the fat, which is kept for frying the rolletjes. Do not use it for a month. It will keep all summer by (*scalding the liquid occasionally and*) adding vinegar. When ready to use, take a very sharp knife, cut it in slices about one-third of an inch thick, and fry with unpared slices of sour apples; serve with a little of the fat from the gravy. This is used principally in Lent, when poultry and fresh meats are scarce, and is considered a capital substitute for fish by the Dutch burgomeisters.

FRITTADELLA, OR TWENTY RECIPES IN ONE

The use of leftovers became a high art, of necessity, since the amounts of meat cooked were so huge. Entrées, or "made dishes" composed of leftovers variously treated, were as acceptable as fresh concoctions, even at formal dinners, and they were normal fare for most lunches.

Put half a pound of bread to soak in a pint of cold water, take the same quantity (*in bulk, not weight*) of any kind of roast or boiled meat, with a little fat, chop it up like sausage meat, then put your bread in a clean cloth, press it to extract all the water, put into a stewpan two ounces of butter, a tablespoonful of chopped onions, fry for two minutes, then add the bread, stir with a wooden spoon until rather dry, then add the meat, season with a teaspoonful of salt, half the same of pepper, a little grated nutmeg, the same of lemon peel, stir continually until very hot; then add two eggs, one at a time, well mix together, and pour into a dish to get cold. Then take a piece as big as a small egg and roll it to that shape, flatten it a little, egg and bread-crumb over, keeping the shape, then put into a fry-pan a quarter of a pound of lard or oil; when hot, but not too much so, put in the pieces, and sauté of a nice yellow color, and serve very hot, plain, on a napkin. These can be made with the remains of any kind of meat, poultry, game, fish, or even vegetables, even shrimps, oysters and lobsters.

A FAMILY FRENCH SALAD FOR THE SUMMER

Cut up a pound of cold beef into thin slices, which put into a salad-bowl with about half a pound of fresh lettuce (*bibb or butter*), cut in pieces similar to the beef, season over with a good teaspoon of salt, half that quantity of pepper, two spoonfuls of vinegar and four of good salad oil, stir all together lightly with a fork and spoon, and when well mixed, it is ready to serve. For a change, cabbage-lettuce (*head lettuce*) may be used, or if in season, a little endive, or a little celery, or a few gherkins; also to vary the seasoning, a little chopped tarragon and chervil, chopped eschalots, or a little scraped garlic, if approved of, but all in proportion, and used with moderation. White haricot beans (*p. 78*) are also excellent with it. (*Serves 3–4.*)

POTATO AND MEAT SALAD

Proceed as in the last, but omitting the lettuce; if any cold potatoes remain from the previous dinner, peel and cut them into pieces the size of a shilling (*quarter*); but four times the thickness; put them into a salad bowl, with the meat, and season as before, but using more oil and vinegar, and adding a teaspoonful of chopped parsley A small quantity of any description pickle might be added to this salad, as also some anchovies, or olives. (*Serves 3–4.*)

RÉCHAUFFÉ OF ROAST BEEF

Some slices of cold roast beef, underdone (*rare*) if possible; one tablespoonful of butter; three tablespoonfuls of red-currant jelly; (*a chopped shallot, if you like*), a wineglassful of sherry or Madeira, salt and cayenne. Put the butter and the currant jelly in the chafing dish; when melted, add the wine, a pinch of cayenne, and the salt. When this sauce is thoroughly hot, add the beef cut up small, in neat, rather thick slices. Heat it through but do not let it boil.

MEAT AND VEGETABLE PIE

Take either cold beef, veal or mutton, mince it fine, and mix it with some bread crumbs; have a dish covered with paste, put some mince at the bottom, then put in a few bearded oysters, next the limbs of chicken, turkey or rabbit boned; then put a layer of peas or spinach, some forcemeat balls, and a few mushrooms, pour in some rich gravy, thicken with cream and flour; strew it over thickly with bread crumbs and at the top, an egg beat well; then bake in the oven.

STOCKS, GRAVIES, SOUPS

Nineteenth-century stocks are careful constructions of odd bits, leftovers, and good meat, used to heighten the flavors of other dishes, or to serve as bases for soup. Bouillon, made from cubes, can always be substituted for stock, but home-made stock is so little bother that it's worth it. Make it from scraps the butcher trims from your meat, plus a few soup bones, in the odd moments while the meal cooks. Freeze it in ice-cube trays to have little bits for gravy as you need it, or can it in quart jars for soup. See pp. 131, 438 for white stock.

BROWN STOCK

Brown 4 pounds of lean beef, cubed; 2 pounds of breast of veal chopped up; some cracked beef bones, and an old chicken, in butter or beef fat. Pour on 6 quarts of cold water when the meat is nicely browned. Skim when it comes to a boil, then simmer, covered, 5 or 6 hours. Add 2 carrots chopped up, 2 small whole unpeeled onions with 2 cloves stuck in each, 1 small turnip or parsnip and 2 stalks of celery, 2 whole cloves of garlic, parsley, thyme, 1 bay leaf, salt and whole pepper to taste. Bring to a boil again, skim, and simmer 2 hours longer, adding a little boiling water if necessary to bring the liquid back up to 6 quarts.

Strain the stock, let the liquid get cold, then take off the fat from the surface. Reheat, clarify (see below) if you want to, then can or freeze it for use when you want. Canned stock will keep about 3 months; frozen, without salt in it, will keep a year. Stock will keep in the refrigerator about 2 weeks if you bring it to a boil every couple of days to prevent fermentation. Makes 6 quarts.

Almost any meat trimmings can be used, as long as there is twice as much lean as there is fat, and as long as the water is added in proportion to the lean meat—less water for less lean.

TO CLARIFY STOCK, IF REQUIRED

If in some cases, by some accident, your stock should not be clear, put it (say three quarts) into a saucepan, place it over a good fire, skim well, and when boiling, have ready the whites of three eggs well separated from their yolks, to which add half a pint of water; whisk well together, then add half a pint of boiling stock gradually, still whisking the eggs; then whisk the boiling stock, pouring the whites of the eggs, etc., in whilst so doing, which continue till nearly boiling again, then take it from the fire, let it remain until the whites of the eggs separate themselves, pass it through a clean cloth into a basin. All clear soups ought not to be too strong of meat and must be of a light brown sherry or straw color. All white and brown thick soups should be rather thin, with just sufficient consistency to adhere lightly to a spoon when hot.

GRAVY

A good nineteenth-century gravy, delicately flavored and hardly thicker than cream, bears more resemblance to stock than it does to the lumpy sludge we sometimes call gravy now. "Gravy" and "stock" are often interchangeable in recipes.

The skirts of beef (*or the shin*) and the kidney make quite as good gravy as any other meat, if prepared in the same manner. The shank bones of mutton (*or lamb*) add greatly to the richness of gravies, but they should first be well soaked and scoured clean. The taste of gravies is improved by tarragon, but it should be sparingly used immediately before serving.

Put the beef, bones and all, with as many quarts of water as there are pounds of beef in a close vessel, and set it where it will warm gradually. Let it boil very slowly for six hours at least, only uncovering the pot once in a great while to see if there is danger of the water sinking too rapidly. Should this be the case, replenish with boiling water, taking care not to put in too much. During the seventh hour, take off the soup and set it away in a cool place, until next morning. Then remove the cake of fat from the surface, take out the meat, which you can use for mince-meat if you wish; set the stock over the fire and throw in a little salt to bring up the scum. When this has been skimmed carefully off, season with pepper, more salt, and sweet herbs if you wish, and put in butter the size of an egg, well-rubbed with flour, until it is thick enough. A glass of brown sherry imparts a flavor that renders it particularly palatable.

RICH BROWN GRAVY SOUP

Take four pounds of beef steak, quite lean, and fry it light brown, with three sliced onions; put into a stewpan four ounces of butter, and when dissolved, shake it around the pan, and lay in the meat and onions with a carrot, a turnip, and a head of celery, sliced, a blade of mace, two teaspoonfuls of salt, and a drachm (*⅛ ounce*) of cayenne. Pour over a quart of clear stock, and stew gently, adding by degrees two quarts of water, and carefully removing the scum as it rises. Let it simmer for six hours, then strain, and when cool clear it of the fat. When heated, add a glass of Madeira or sherry. This is a strong and rich soup. Serve with boiled macaroni cut in pieces in it. (*Serves 8–10.*)

OX-TAIL SOUP

Time, four hours and a half. Two ox-tails; a quarter of a pound of lean ham; a head and a half of celery; two carrots; two turnips; two onions; a bunch of savory herbs (*sage, savory, juniper berries, etc.*); five cloves; a wineglass of catsup, and one of port; with three quarts of water.

Cut up two ox-tails, separating them at the joints; put them into a stewpan with about an ounce and a half of butter, a head of celery, two onions, two turnips, and two carrots cut into slices, and a quarter of a pound of lean ham cut very thin; the peppercorns and savory herbs, and about half a pint of cold water. Stir it over a quick fire for a short time to extract the flavor of the herbs, or until the pan is covered with a glaze, then pour in three quarts of water, skim it well, and simmer slowly for four hours, or until the tails are tender. Take them out, strain the soup, stir in a little flour to thicken it, add a glass of port wine, the catsup, and half a head of celery (preferably boiled and cut into small pieces). Put the pieces of tail into the stewpan with the strained soup. Boil it up a few minutes, and serve. This soup can be served clear, by omitting the flour and adding to it carrots and turnips cut in fancy shapes, with a head of celery in slices. These may be boiled in a little of the soup, and put into a tureen before sending to table. (*Serves 4–6.*)

MOCK TURTLE SOUP

Take a pound and a half of lean veal or tripe (*tripe is best*), cut it into small slices, and fry to a delicate brown. Cut the meat from three cow-heels in tolerably large pieces, then put it with the fried veal or tripe into a pint and a half of weak gravy (*or bouillon*), with three anchovies, a little salt, some cayenne pepper, three blades of mace, nine cloves, the green parts of three leeks, three sprigs of lemon, thyme, some parsley, and lemon peel; chop these last very fine before adding them, let the whole stew gently (*covered*) for three hours; then squeeze the juice of three lemons to it; add three glasses of Madeira wine, and let it stew for one hour more, then skim off the fat and serve. (*Serves 4.*)

HESSIAN SOUP

Cut into slices three pounds of shin of beef, lay it in a stewpan, put in three onions, five carrots, eight potatoes, one and a quarter pints of split peas, three heads of celery, some whole pepper, salt; pour in by degrees seven quarts of water; stew until reduced to half. If the soup alone be required, strain off the vegetables. If not, serve as cooked. (*Serves 10–12.*)

INNARDS

In France and England these parts of the animal are still known as "offal." We now call them "variety meats." But nineteenth-cenutry Americans were both less brutal and more direct.

TO FRY TRIPE

Tripe should always be boiled 20 to 30 minutes before cooking, in court bouillon (p. 164) if you have it, then drained, or it will be tough.

Lay a piece of tripe in salt and water overnight, then dry it with a clean

[356]

cloth, dredge it with flour, have some lard hot in a pan, lay the tripe in, season with pepper, when done on one side and a delicate brown, turn the other; when both sides are done, lay it on a dish, add some vinegar to the gravy and pour it over the tripe; or the vinegar may be omitted, and the gravy added by those who like it.

It may also be dipped in fritter batter (p. 73) and deep-fried.

TRIPE LYONNAISE

Cut tripe in small pieces (*after boiling it*). Fry one tablespoonful of chopped onion in one heaping tablespoonful of butter until yellow. Add the tripe, one tablespoonful of vinegar and one tablespoonful of chopped parsley, salt and pepper to taste. Simmer five minutes, and serve plain or on toast.

STEWED KIDNEY

Because of the cuts government inspectors must make to grade meat, opening the fat that encloses the kidneys (which allows air in and hastens spoilage), beef kidneys should be carefully chosen. Look for bright color, clear white fat.

Slice the kidneys and take the gristle out. Soak all night in salted water. Wash them and dice them. Stew with water just to cover. Add one teaspoonful of walnut catsup (*p. 251, or Worcestershire*), pepper, salt and a chopped onion (in season add one large tomato, skinned and seeded and chopped). While stewing, melt butter the size of a walnut in one gill of water in the fry pan. Dredge in flour and when it is brown, add it to the stew.

BEEF KIDNEY HASH

Cut the kidney in pieces, removing all fat; put in cold water with one teaspoon salt, and soak over night, then put into a kettle with one quart of cold water and a small onion; boil it until tender, changing the water once during the boiling. After the kidney is cooked, chop, but not too fine; put into a kettle; add some of the liquor in which the kidney was boiled, salt, pepper, a little butter, curry, and sprinkle over a little dry flour to make it of a creamy consistency. The hash should not be watery and yet not too thick. (*Serve over toast to 3 or 4.*)

[357]

TO ROAST A BEEF'S HEART

Cut open, to remove the ventricles or pipes, soak in water to free it of blood, and parboil it about ten minutes. Prepare a highly seasoned stuffing and fill it. Tie a string around it to secure it. Roast till tender. Add butter and flour to the gravy, and serve up hot in a covered dish. Garnish with cloves stuck over it, and eat with jelly. They are good boiled tender and fried with butter, cut in thin slices, seasoned with salt and pepper. (*Serves 4.*)

FRESH BEEF TONGUE

Take a green (*unpickled*) tongue, stick it with cloves and boil it gently for three hours; then brush over with the yolk of an egg, dredge it well with bread crumbs, and roast it, basting it well with butter. When dished, serve it with a little brown gravy flavored with a glass of wine, and lay pieces of currant jelly round it. A pickled tongue, well washed, may be dressed in the same way. (*Serves 4.*)

PRESERVED BEEF

With no refrigeration, meat not eaten immediately had to be preserved by salting or smoking. I include recipes for the curing of meat here because they seem to have disappeared from contemporary cookbooks, because—if you have the cow, the space to work in, and the inclination—you can have meat of a richness and flavor that just doesn't exist otherwise, and because these recipes can be adapted perfectly adequately for use with smaller pieces of meat.

FOR CURING BEEF

Let your meat be cold, not frozen. For two hundred pounds use two quarts of molasses, half a pound of saltpetre, half a bushel of salt. Dissolve your saltpetre in warm water, then add your molasses, pack down your beef tight, putting salt in your barrel and between each layer, let a suitable proportion be put between each layer of the above composition (*heat to boiling in water; cool to cold before you put it on the beef*). Cover the beef. Add two ounces of pearlash (*1 ounce baking soda*) to the composition, and some think pepper or cinnamon a great improvement. It will be very sweet, tender and nice either way.

"*Put your refuse pork or beef brine on asparagus beds. While it adds to the growth of the asparagus, it destroys the weeds.*"

Mrs. Webster, *The Improved Housewife*, 1854

DUTCH HUNG BEEF

Rub a lean piece of beef—about twelve pounds—with molasses, and turn it frequently, in three days wipe it dry, salt it with one pound and turn it frequently, in three days wipe it dry, salt it with one pound of salt and one ounce of saltpetre in fine powder, rub in well, turning every day for fourteen days; roll it as tightly as you can in a coarse cloth, lay a heavy weight upon it (*to press out the juice*); hang it to dry in the smoke from wood, reversing it every day; boil in spring water, press while hot, and grate or rice it (*like chipped beef*) to fancy.

JERKED BEEF

Cut the beef into thin slices, dip them into salt or seawater and dry them in the hot sun. (*This is eaten raw.*)

TO CORN BEEF SIMPLY

Rub in plenty of salt, and set it in the cellar for a day or two. If you want to keep it longer, rub in more salt and secure it from the flies.

TO POT BEEF IN IMITATION OF VENISON

Put eight or ten pounds of lean beef in a deep dish; pour over it a pint of red wine and let it lie two days; season it well with mace, pepper, salt and a clove of garlic; then put it into a closely covered pot along with the wine, and another glassful if it be not sufficient, and bake it three hours in a quick (*375°*) oven; when cold, pound it to a paste, pack tightly in a pot and cover with melted clarified butter. Cover closely from the air. (*This will keep 2 months in the refrigerator.*)

TO CURE BEEF TONGUE

Throw a handful of salt over the tongue, seeing that it is sprinkled on both sides, let it remain to drain until the following day. Make a pickle of one tablespoonful of common salt, half that quantity of saltpetre, and the same quantity of coarse sugar as salt, rub this mixture well into the tongue, do so every day for a week; it will then be found necessary to add more salt; one tablespoonful will suffice; in four days the tongue will be cured sufficiently.

Some persons do not rub the pickle into the tongue, but let it absorb it, merely turning it daily, this method will be found to occupy a month or five weeks before it will be cured. When the tongue is to be dried, affix a paper to it with the date; smoke over a wood fire four days, unless wrapped in paper, and then as many weeks as will be required.

To DRESS THEM: Boil the tongue tender; it will take five hours; always dress them as they come out of the pickle. If they have been smoked and hung long they should be softened by lying in water five or six hours. They should be brought to a boil gently and then simmered. When they have been on the fire two hours and the scum removed as it arises, throw in a pinch of sweet herbs.

MUTTON

Mutton—sheep a year or more old—is still available, but not always easy to come by. The flavor is stronger than that of lamb, richer; some people claim it is gamey. But good mutton is as much more interesting than lamb as good beef is more interesting than veal. Legs of Australian or New Zealand lamb, imported frozen, come close to it in taste.

If necessary, lamb may be substituted in any of the recipes below by adjusting the cooking time and checking to make sure the seasonings don't overpower the more delicate taste.

See April (p. 131) for lamb recipes in which mutton may be substituted.

[360]

HAUNCH OF MUTTON

Rub with vinegar and dry thoroughly every day as long as possible. If the weather be muggy, rubbing with sugar will prevent its turning sour; if warm weather, pepper and ground ginger rubbed over it will keep off the flies.

When ready, paper the fat (*in roasting over an open fire, the fatty part of the meat was covered with greased paper or a paste of flour and water to prevent the fat from dripping into the fire, causing it to flame up and scorch the meat*), commence roasting some distance from the fire (*or bake in a 325° oven, 15–20 minutes to the pound; mutton, like good beef, should be somewhat rare*), baste with milk and water first, then when the fat begins dripping, baste with its own dripping; half an hour previous to its being done, remove the paper from the fat, place it closer to the fire, baste well. Serve with currant jelly. A saddle of mutton may be dressed in the same way. (*A haunch will serve 15.*)

Legs and haunches were occasionally decoratively larded—holes punched in the shape of a flower, for instance, from the top to the bottom of the roast, and filled with strips of salt pork. Each horizontal slice would have a pattern of the larding in it.

TO DRESS A LEG OF MUTTON WITH OYSTERS

Parboil some fine well-fed oysters, take off the beards and horny parts; put to them some parsley, minced onion and sweet herbs, boiled and chopped fine, and the yolks of two or three hardboiled eggs. Mix all together and cut five or six holes in the fleshy parts of the leg and put in the mixture; and dress it in either of the following ways:—tie it up in a cloth and let it boil two and a half to three hours according to its size; or braise (*bake, tightly covered, in a 325° oven*), and serve with a pungent brown sauce (*p. 436; a leg serves 8–10*).

ROAST MUTTON À LA VENISON

Next to a haunch of venison or a handsome 12-pound roast of beef, a saddle of mutton was the accepted central attraction of a formal dinner. It was cut across the entire sheep, from the tail—excluding the haunches—up to and including the first two or three short ribs.

A Christmas saddle of mutton is very fine prepared as follows:—wash it well, inside and out, with vinegar. Do not wipe it, but hang it up to dry in a cool cellar (*about the temperature of a butcher's cooler, 40°*). When the vinegar has dried off, throw a clean cloth over it to keep the dust off. On the next day but one, take down the meat and sponge it over again with vinegar, then put it back in its place in the cellar. Repeat this process three times a week for a fortnight, keeping the meat hung in a cold place, covered, except while you are washing it.

When you are ready to cook it, wipe it off with a dry cloth but do not wash it. (*It may be marinated a day or two in wine flavored with ginger and pepper.*) Roast—basting the first hour with butter and water; afterwards with the gravy, and keeping the meat covered with a large tin pan (*or an aluminum-foil tent*) for two hours. A large saddle will require four hours to roast. When it is done, remove it to a dish, and cover it to keep it hot. Skim the gravy, and add half a teacupful of walnut, mushroom or tomato ketchup, a glass of Madeira wine, and a tablespoonful of browned flour. Boil up once and send to table in a sauce boat. Always send round currant or some other tart jelly with roast mutton. If properly cooked, a saddle of mutton, prepared in accordance with these directions, will strongly resemble venison in taste. (*Serves 10–12.*)

> *"When a joint of meat is roasted, pour the drippings into a pan of cold, clean water; heavy particles will sink; melted fat floats and when cold forms a clear cake of fat,"* that may be used for soap or for making candles.
>
> Mrs. Ellet, *The Practical Housekeeper*, 1857

SADDLE OF MUTTON

This excellent and handsome joint, the two loins, usually weighs from ten to twelve pounds. It is fit for cooking after it has hung a few days, if prime mutton, as it is the most tender part. It is the duty of the butcher to raise the skin from it which is then skewered over it again to preserve the juices when roasting; let it roast two hours, or a quarter longer if large.

It may be served with currant jelly or port wine sauce. Stewed lentils (*p. 84*) are often placed around it.

PORT WINE SAUCE: Boil for thirty minutes in a quarter of a pint of water six cloves and two ounces of sugar; then add two glasses of port wine, and simmer five minutes, and strain the liquor into a quarter of a pint of very rich melted butter; stir all for five minutes over the fire; then serve immediately.

WINE SAUCE FOR VENISON OR MUTTON: Warm two gills of the liquor the meat was boiled in, or of the drippings; mix two teaspoonfuls of scorched (*browned*) flour, with a little water, and stir it in when the gravy boils; season it with cloves, salt and pepper; stir in a spoonful of warm jelly; and just before taking from the fire, a gill of wine.

SHOULDER OF MUTTON, PROVINCIAL FASHION

Roast a fine shoulder of mutton; whilst roasting mince ten large onions very fine, put them in a stewpan with two tablespoonfuls of salad oil, pass them ten minutes over a good fire, keeping it stirred, then add a tablespoonful of flour, stir well in, and a pint of milk, seasoned with a little pepper, salt and sugar; when the onions are quite tender and the sauce rather thick, stir in the yolks of two eggs and take it off the fire; when the shoulder is done, spread the onions over the top, egg over, cover with bread crumbs, put in the oven ten minutes and salamander a light brown color, dress upon your dish, put the gravy from it in your stewpan, with a pat of butter, with which you have mixed a little flour, boil up, add a little scraped garlic, pour round the shoulder and serve. (*Serves 6.*)

BOILED MUTTON

The leg is best boiled unless the mutton is young and very tender. Wash it clean and wipe dry. Do not leave the knuckle and shank so long as to be unshapely. Put into a pot with hot water (salted) enough to cover it, and boil until you ascertain, by probing with a fork, that it is tender in the thickest part. Skim off all the scum as it rises. Allow about *twelve* minutes to each pound. Take from the fire, drain perfectly dry, and serve with melted butter, with capers or (*pickled*) nasturtium seed (*p. 259*); or if you have neither of these, some cucumber or gherkin pickle stirred into it. If you wish to use the broth for soup (*see p. 330, Leek or onion soup*), put in very little salt while boiling; if not, salt well and boil the meat in a cloth.

PLAIN SUET DUMPLINGS TO EAT WITH BOILED MUTTON: Sift two pounds of flour into a pan, and add a saltspoonful of salt. Mince very fine one pound of beef suet, and rub it into a stiff dough with a little cold water. Then roll it out an inch thick or rather more. Cut it into dumplings with the edge of a tumbler. Put them into a pot of boiling water, and let them boil an hour and a half. Send them to table hot, with mutton, or with molasses after the meat is removed.

TO RAGOO A LEG OF MUTTON

Take all the skin and fat off. Cut it very thin the right way of the grain, butter your stew-pan, and shake some flour into it; slice half a lemon and half an onion, cut them very small, with a little bundle of sweet herbs and a blade of mace. Put all together with your meat into the pan, stir it a minute or two, and then put in six spoonfuls of gravy, and have ready anchovy minced small; mix in with some butter and flour, stir it all together for six minutes, and then dish it up. (*Serves 6.*)

MUTTON HARICOT

"Haricot" may be a corruption of "haut ragout," a fancy stew.
Take a loin of mutton, cut it into small chops, season it with ground pepper, allspice and salt; let it stand all night; and then fry it. Have a good gravy well seasoned with flour, butter, ketchup and pepper if necessary. Boil turnips and carrots, cut them small, and add to the mutton (*which, after frying, you have*) stewed in the gravy, with the (*whole*) yolks of hard boiled eggs and force-meat balls (*p. 124*). Some green pickles will be an improvement.

"Professional cooks agree that the perfection of frying fat is equal parts of lard and beef dripping."
Ladies' Aid Society, *"Still Another" Cook Book*, 1888

SOYER'S NEW MUTTON CHOP

"Soyer's new mutton chop," a dish that made a moderate sensation in the 1850s, was composed of a couple of double chops, steak-sized, cut from the front end of the saddle.
Trim a middling size saddle of mutton which cut into chops half an inch thick with a saw without at all making use of a knife (the sawing them off jagging the meat and causing them to eat more tender), then trim them into

shape; season well with salt and pepper; place them upon a gridiron (*or under a broiler on a rack*) over a sharp fire, turning them three or four times; they would require ten minutes of cooking; when done, dress them upon a dish, spread some small pieces of butter over each and serve with fried potatoes around. By adding half a tablespoon of good sauce to each chop when serving, and turning two or three times, an excellent entrée is produced. Do try them and let me know your opinion.

BAKED MUTTON CUTLETS

Cut them from the neck, and trim neatly. Lay aside the bits of bone and meat you cut off, to make gravy. Pour a little melted butter over the cutlets and let them lie in it for fifteen minutes, keeping them just warm enough to prevent the butter from hardening (*over the pilot light of the stove, or in a 200° oven with the door open*); then dip each in beaten egg, roll in cracker-crumbs and lay them in your dripping pan (*or roaster*) with a *very* little water at the bottom. Bake quickly, and baste often with butter and water. Put on the bones, etc., in enough cold water to cover them; stew, and season with sweet herbs, pepper and salt, and a spoonful of tomato catsup. Strain when all the substance is extracted from the meat and bones; thicken with browned flour and pour over the cutlets when they are served.

Lentils, a purée of white beans, or stuffed eggplant were traditionally served with mutton chops.

IRISH STEW

Cut up about two pounds of neck of mutton into small cutlets, which put in a proper-sized stewpan with some of the fat of the mutton; season it with half a tablespoonful of salt; a quarter of an ounce of pepper, with the same of sugar, six middle-sized onions, one quart of water; set them to boil, and simmer half an hour; then add six middling-sized potatoes, cut them in halves or in quarters, stir all together, and let it stew gently for about one hour longer; if too fast, remove it (*some of the gravy: stoves were not controllable then*) from the top, but if well done, the potatoes will absorb all of it and eat very delicate. (*Serves 4–6.*)

CHINA CHILO

Mince a pint basin of undressed (*raw*) neck of mutton or leg and some of the fat; put two onions, a small (*head of*) lettuce, a pint of green peas, a teaspoonful of pepper, four spoonfuls of water, and two or three ounces of clarified butter into a stewpan closely covered; simmer two hours, and serve in the middle of a dish of boiled rice; if cayenne is approved, add a little. (*Serves 3–4.*)

ANOTHER WAY: Chop very fine two small young lettuces, two onions, a pint of green peas, and a couple of young cucumbers, or the fourth of a pint of mushrooms; season with one teaspoonful of salt and half a teaspoonful of pepper; mince the meat of a neck of mutton uncooked and mix it with the vegetables in a stewpan; add four tablespoonfuls of water and two ounces of butter, clarified will prove to be the best; let them well amalgamate over a slow fire; keep them stirred for fifteen minutes, then cover down close and simmer *very* slowly for two hours.

MUTTON, VENISON STYLE

This is also excellent for reheating roast beef or steak.

Cut roasted or boiled mutton in thin slices. Put into the chaffing-dish four tablespoonfuls of tomato ketchup, one tablespoonful of tarragon vinegar, four tablespoonfuls of currant jelly and (*a minced shallot cooked in*) a tablespoonful of butter; stir all these ingredients until hot. (*Add a little red wine, if you like.*) Put in sufficient mutton to saturate the sauce thoroughly; add half a teaspoonful of salt and a sprinkling of pepper. It is now ready to serve.

TURESICUS

Mince very fine parts of a cold boiled leg of mutton and mix it with rice (*cooked*), season it very high with black pepper, add salt, and make it into balls the size of a cabbage leaf (two to three inches in diameter). Tie each ball separately in a cabbage leaf; boil it about half an hour and serve immediately; very hot.

KIDNEY BREAD-CRUMBED

Split sheep's kidneys (*lamb kidneys are better*), as many as you may require for your party; cut them open very evenly lengthwise, down to the root, but not to separate them; then have some small iron or wooden skewers, upon which thread the kidneys quite flat, by running the skewer twice through each kidney, that is, under the white part; have ready upon a plate an egg well beaten up, season the kidneys with a little salt and pepper, dip them into the egg, then lightly cover them with breadcrumbs, put them upon the griddle, which place over a moderate fire, broil them about ten minutes, turning when half done, have ready a little maître d'hôtel butter (*p. 108*), put about half an ounce in each kidney, and serve immediately upon a very hot dish. Dressed this way, they may also be served upon toast.

KABABS FOR BREAKFAST

Put thin slices of well-seasoned kidney and bacon, with beef or mutton also if you please, upon skewers. Have ready fine bread crumbs, with a light grating of lemon rind, brush them over with egg and roll them into the crumbs. Hang up the skewers to roast and put a slice of toast under to secure the gravy (*or put them on a rack in the broiler, with the toast under the rack*). If, instead of meat an oyster be put between each slice of bacon and kidney, it will be found very superior.

ROGNON DE MOUTON À LA FRANÇAISE

Take half a dozen fine mutton kidneys, clear them of fat and skin, and cut them into thin slices; powder them immediately with sweet herbs in fine powder, parsley that has been chopped, dried and powdered, cayenne and salt; put into a stewpan two ounces of clarified butter, or fresh if the former is not in reach, put in the slices of kidney, fry them; they must brown very quickly. They must be done on both sides; dredge flour over them, moisten with lemon juice; in five minutes the kidneys will be done; lift them out into a very hot dish around which are laid sippets (*triangles of bread fried or toasted*); pour into the gravy two glasses of champagne, give it a boil, pour it over the kidneys and serve. (*Serves 4–6.*)

[367]

TO MAKE A SCOTCH HAGGIS

Take the stomach of a sheep. The washing and cleaning is of more con-sequence than all, as it will be of a bad color and a bad taste if not well cleansed; when clean, turn it inside out, then let it lie for a day or two in salt and water. Blanch the liver, lights (*lungs*) and heart of the sheep, lay them in cold water, chop all very fine; the liver you had better grate, chop a pound of the suet very fine, dry in the oven a pound of (*cooked*) oatmeal; mix all this well together; season with pepper and salt, a little chopped parsley and a little chopped onion; then sew up in the bag (*the stomach*); before you finish sew-ing it, add a few spoonfuls of a good white stock; put it in a stewpan with a drainer; boil it in water, keeping it well covered all the time, prick it all over with a small larding pin to keep it from bursting; it will take several hours to boil; be careful taking it up, and let your dish be large enough.

Legs of mutton can be cured into hams (pp. 381–384). They need a little less smoking, and are particularly good smoked over a fire of walnut bark or chips. If hung (hoof end down) until completely dry, they can be eaten raw, in thin slices, like jerked beef.

PORK

Pork was a lower-class meat in those days, "an unwholesome meat, and should never be eaten by children, or people with weak digestion, nor, indeed, by any one except in cold weather." (*Mrs. Lincoln's Boston Cook Book*, 1896) Pork raised the temperature of the blood, subjected the partaker to fits of un-certain temperament, and inclined one toward gout. Of course, the common practice of feeding hogs almost entirely on kitchen slops may have had some-thing to do with the health and taste of the meat, and hence the attitude toward it.

ROAST LEG OF PORK

One weighing about seven pounds is enough (*legs run larger now, a difference in the way the meat is cut; a full one would be 12–14 pounds, so a half-leg would be about right.*) even for a large family. If the pig be young, the leg will be even smaller. Score the skin in squares, or parallel lines running from side to side, for the convenience of the carver. If the joint be that of a full-grown hog, rub into the top, after scoring it deeply, a forcemeat of bread-crumbs seasoned with sage and chopped onion, wet with the juice of a lemon or a very little vinegar, pepper and salt to the taste. Rub this in hard until the cracks are filled, with a sharp knife make incisions close to the knuckle-bone and stuff with the forcemeat, tying a string tightly about it afterward, to prevent the escape of the seasoning. Rub over with butter, when the meat is warm throughout; then baste with the fat. Skim all the fat from the drippings that can be removed before making the gravy. Send around tomato or apple sauce, and pickles, with the roast pork.

A shoulder is roasted in the same way.

TO ROAST A SUCKING PIG

A sucking pig, which should be about three weeks old, must be dressed as soon after being killed as practicable. When scalded and prepared for cooking, lay in the belly a stuffing of bread, sage and onions, pepper and salt, with a piece of butter; sew it up, rub the skin of the pig with butter, skewer the legs back, that while roasting the inside as well as outside of the pig may be thoroughly browned; it must be put to a quick fire, but at such a distance as to roast gradually (*325° in the oven*), and a coating of flour should be dredged over it that it may not blister, or, it should not be left a minute; if floured, when the pig is done, scrape the flour off with a wooden or very blunt knife and rub it with a buttered cloth; cut off the head and dividing it, take out the brains, mix them with a little gravy or bread sauce, divide the pig in half from neck to tail, and lay each inside flat on the dish, so that the two edges of the back touch; place each half of the head with the outer side uppermost at each end of the dish and an ear on each side (*this was considered the proper way for a pig to appear at table; we would probably leave him impressively whole, with an apple or an ear of corn in his mouth*); the gravy should be poured in the dish hot and the whole served as hot as possible.

To scald a sucking pig: It is usual to procure the pig from the butcher ready prepared for cooking, but in the event of its being required to scald it after killing, we subjoin the following receipt:

Plunge the pig into cold water the instant it is killed; let it remain five minutes; have ready pounded resin (*under 10 pounds a pig doesn't need it*), and rub well with it over the skin; plunge it into a tub of scalding water, let it remain only half a minute, remove it, and immediately take off the hair; lose no time, if the hair should not come freely from some parts, rub it again with resin and put it into the scalding water, and then remove the hair. When it is all off, wash it well with warm water, and then in cold, changing the water several times that no flavor of the resin may be retained; cut off the feet at the first joint, slit it down the belly and remove the entrails; put aside the liver, heart and lights, with the feet; wash again inside and out the pig, dry it well and keep it from the air by covering it with a cloth.

TO ROAST A (*SUCKLING*) PIG IN THE PHILADELPHIA WAY

Wash and dry it; rub it well, inside and outside, with sage and cayenne pepper. Boil twenty good sized potatoes, mash them while hot, add butter, a little milk and two minced onions and minced sweet herbs with seasoning of salt and pepper and bread crumbs. Stuff the pig and fasten up the opening with skewers. Roast (*or bake*) it for three hours in a pan, with water sufficient to form a gravy, thickened with a little flour and well stirred. Baste the pig, while roasting, with oil or butter to make it brown; and if necessary add a little boiling water to the gravy. The taste of the pig roasted before the fire is preferable to one baked in the oven.

Make a sauce of the feet, tongue, liver and heart.

HASLET SAUCE FOR ROAST PIG: This sauce is made of the feet, tongue, liver and heart of the pig. Scald the tongue, and take off the skin. Clean the feet, liver and heart; put them in a saucepan, with a pint of water, and a little salt. Let them boil until they are tender; then take them up, chop them very fine, and return them to the saucepan, with the water they were boiled in. Pare and mince one onion, a little sweet marjoram and parsley, and add to it. Place the saucepan over the fire. Mix one teaspoonful of flour into one ounce of butter, and stir it into the sauce, then season with cayenne pepper and salt, if more is necessary. Boil all well together. Before it is removed from the fire, add one gill of Madeira wine. Serve hot. This sauce requires to be very highly seasoned. (*Makes 1 pint.*)

TO BARBECUE SHOAT, A SOUTHERN DISH

Shoat means a fat young hog, headless and footless, cut into four quarters, each weighing six pounds. Make several incisions between the ribs of the forequarter, and stuff it with a rich forcemeat; put it in a pan with a pint of water, salt, pepper, two cloves of garlic, a tumbler of good red wine, and one ounce of mushroom catsup; bake it, and thicken the gravy with browned flour and butter. If not sufficiently brown, add a little burnt sugar to the gravy. Garnish with (*forcemeat*) balls.

TO ROAST A LOIN (*OF PORK*)

Take a sharp penknife and cut the skin across, then cut over it in the opposite direction so as to form small squares, or diamonds; rub every part over it with a mixture of salt and pepper, put bits of butter the size of hickory nuts over the skin side, and roast or bake it.

LOIN OR NECK OF PORK, NORMANDY FASHION

Procure a neck or loin, put it in a common earthen dish, having previously scored the rind, rub over with a little oil, place about twenty potatoes, cut in halves or in quarters, in the dish with the pork, ten onions peeled, and twenty apples, peeled and quartered. Place in a warm (*325°*) oven, for an hour and a half or more, then dress it upon your dish with the apples, onions and potatoes around, and serve.

TENDERLOIN OF PORK WITH FRIED APPLES

Cut the thin membranous skin from the tenderloin (*the filet mignon of the loin, not the smoked tenderloin*), and put the latter in a marinade of claret seasoned with whole spice and a few slices of oranges. Let it stand in this four hours; drain and dry on a cloth, and split in two lengthwise; rub it with butter and broil till well done. Put in the center of a dish a mound of fried apples; arrange the meat around it and serve. The marinade may be boiled down, thickened, and served as a sauce, if a sauce is desired. (*Serves 6.*)

FRIED SOUR APPLES: Wash, and cut them in quarters, then core them; have about half an inch of hot drippings in the frying-pan; put the apples in it and turn them until they are brown all over; just before they are done, sprinkle them with two or three tablespoonfuls of sugar.

PORK WITH OYSTERS

Select a thick tenderloin. Slit down the length of the center, being careful not to cut too deep. This will, by tieing the corners, form a sort of boat. Fill with oysters. Season with butter, salt and pepper. Place in a hot oven and baste occasionally with the same dressing. One-half hour, or longer if the loin is large, will make a savory dish.

PORK STEAKS

Those from the loin are best, but they can be cut from the neck. Remove the skin and trim neatly. Broil over a clear fire, without seasoning, adding salt and pepper, a pinch of sage, another of minced onion and a lump of butter after they are put into the hot dish. Then cover closely and set in the oven for five minutes, until the aroma of the condiments flavors the meat.

FRIED PEACHES

Take peaches not fully ripe, wash them and wipe them, then cut them in slices a quarter of an inch thick, and fry in the pan after pork; serve with the meat. This is a South Carolina dish.

"Sauces to serve with roast pork or pig: mashed potatoes; boiled onions, turnips mashed, pickled beets, mangoes or cucumbers, or dressed celery and cranberry sauce, stewed apples or currant jelly."
Mrs. Crowen, *The American System of Cookery,* 1870

PORK CUTLETS

Perhaps few things of a simple nature, and served in a plain way, are better than a hot pork chop, cut about half an inch thick, trimmed neatly and broiled upon the gridiron.

OR: Fry in salad oil; serve with sauce Robert (*p. 437*) or gherkin sauce (*p. 341*). The gherkins being shred fine into some good thick brown gravy.

OR: Marinate the cutlets four hours in oil with an onion in slices, parsley, bay-leaf, pepper and salt; fry them in the marinade; serve with tomato sauce.

OR: Cut them from a small delicate loin of pork, trim them neatly, fry them a light brown; put into a small stewpan a little vinegar and eschalot chopped very finely, two tablespoonfuls of tomato sauce and sufficient brown gravy to make it tasty. Stew the cutlets in the sauce five minutes, and send them to table handsomely dished.

SPARE-RIB

Spare-rib should be basted with a very little butter and a little flour, and then sprinkled with a little dried sage (*and roasted over the fire*). Applesauce and potatoes for roasted pork.

ROAST SPARE-RIB

When first put down to the fire, cover with a greased paper (*or foil under it, if cooking over an open fire; over it, otherwise; sparerib as cut in the nineteenth century was thicker than ours*), until it is half-done. Remove it then and dredge with flour. A few minutes later, baste once with butter, and afterward, every little while, with its own gravy. This is necessary, the spare-rib being a very dry piece. Just before you take it up, strew over the surface thickly with fine bread-crumbs seasoned with powdered sage, pepper and salt, and a small onion minced into almost invisible bits. Let it cook five minutes and baste once more with butter. Skim the gravy, add half a cupful of hot water, thicken with browned flour, squeeze in the juice of a lemon, strain, and pour over the meat in the dish. Send tomato catsup around with it, or if you prefer, put a liberal spoonful in the gravy, after it is strained.

TO ROAST A VERY FINE HAM

The day before you intend to cook it, take the ham out of the water (*in which it was soaked to remove the saltiness of the cure: most hams no longer need soaking*), and having removed the skin, trim it nicely, and pour over it a bottle of inferior white wine; let it steep until next morning, frequently during the day washing the wine over it; put it in a cradle-spit (*or use a rotisserie*) in time to allow at least six hours (*2 to 3 hours: our hams are smaller*) for slowly roasting it; baste with hot water continually. When done, dredge it with fine bread raspings (*crumbs*) and brown it before the fire.

HAM GRAVY: Take the wine in which the ham was steeped, and add to it the essence or juice which flowed from the meat when taken from the spit; squeeze in the juice of two lemons; put it into a saucepan, and boil and skim it; send it to the table in a boat. Cover the shank of the ham (which should have been sawed short) with bunches of double parsley and ornament it with any garnish you may think proper.

BAKED HAM

Soak for twelve hours (*if home-cured*). Trim away the rusty parts from the underside and edges, wipe very dry, cover the bottom with a paste made of flour and hot water (*rolled out like pie crust, to keep the outside from cooking too quickly*) and lay it upside down in the dripping pan, with water enough to keep it from burning. Bake (*in a reflector oven; both paste and water are unnecessary in a regular oven, set at 325°*) five hours, or allow fully 25 minutes to a pound. Baste now and then, to prevent the crust from cracking and scaling off. When done, peel off this and the skin and glaze. Cut paper frills for around the knuckle and garnish with parsley and sliced red beet—pickled.

A HAM

(If not too old) put in soak (*in cider or wine*) for an hour, taken out and wiped, crust (*pastry*) made sufficient to cover it all over, and baked in a moderately heated oven, cuts fuller of gravy, and of a finer flavor, than a boiled one.

BOILED HAM

A small ham is good boiled in cider fifteen minutes to the pound, then left to cool in the liquor, skinned and dried.

BARBECUED HAM

If your ham is raw (*fresh*), soak; then lay upon it a quarter of a teaspoonful of made mustard. Pour about them some vinegar, allowing half a teaspoonful to each slice. Fry quickly and turn them often. When done to a fine brown, transfer to a hot dish; add to the gravy in the pan half a glass of wine and a very small teaspoonful of white sugar. Boil up and pour over the meat. Underdone ham is nice barbecued.

HAM DUMPLINGS

Chop some cold ham, the fat and lean in equal proportions. Season it with pepper and minced sage. Make a crust, allowing half a pound of chopped suet, or half a pound of butter to a pound of flour. Roll it out (*½ inch*) thick and divide it into equal portions. Put some minced ham into each, and close up the crust. Have ready a pot of boiling water (*or stock*) and put in the dumplings. Boil them about three quarters of an hour.

SHRIVELLED HAM

Shave the ham very thin. Shake it in a hot pan with butter until it shrivels.

A PORK STEW

Take pieces of fresh pork, sweet-bread, liver, heart, tongue and skirts. Boil in just enough water to cook them tender. Before they are done, season them with salt and considerable pepper, and let them fry after the water is out to a fine brown. It is an excellent dish.

PORK AND PEAS PUDDING

Soak the pork, which should not be a fat piece (*a lean pork butt is good*), overnight in cold water; and in another pan a quart of dried split peas. In the morning put on the peas to boil slowly until tender. Drain and rub through a cullender (*or mash*); season with salt and pepper, and mix with them two tablespoonsful of butter and two beaten eggs. Beat all well together. Have ready a floured pudding cloth (*p. 27*), and put the pudding into it. Tie it up, leaving room for swelling; put on in warm, not hot water, with the pork, and boil them together an hour. Lay the pork in the centre of the dish, turn out the pudding, slice, and arrange about the meat. (*Serves 4–6.*)

The pot liquor is excellent for soup; add an onion, a carrot, a tomato, a parsnip, and more split peas, and cook until they are tender, then purée them in the blender.

STEWED PORK

Take some lean slices from the leg. Cut into dice an inch square, put into a pot with enough cold water to cover them, and stew gently for three quarters of an hour, closely covered. Meanwhile, parboil half a dozen Irish potatoes, cut in thick slices, in another vessel. When the pork has stewed the allotted time, drain off the water from these and add them to the meat. Season with pepper, salt, a minced shallot, a spoonful of pungent catsup and a bunch of aromatic herbs. Cover again and stew twenty minutes longer, or until the meat is tender throughout. If your meat be not too fat, this stew will be very good, especially on a cold day. (*Serves 6.*)

CHESHIRE PORK-PIE

Cut two or three pounds of lean fresh pork into strips as long and wide as your middle finger. Line a buttered dish with puff-paste (*p. 76*); put in a layer of pork seasoned with salt, pepper, nutmeg or mace; next a layer of juicy apples, sliced and covered with about an ounce of white sugar; then more pork, and so on until you are ready for the paste cover, when pour in half a pint of sweet cider or wine, and stick bits of butter all over the top. Cover with a thick lid of puff-paste, cut a slit in the top, brush over with beaten egg, and bake an hour and a half. (*Serves 4–6.*)

Yorkshire pie is made the same way, with the omission of the apples and sugar and nutmeg, and the addition of sage to the seasoning.

BACON AND CABBAGE

Boil some fine streaked part of bacon (*unsliced*) with a little stock and the ends of eight or ten sausages, boil in the same stock some white cabbages for two hours; add salt and spice, and serve very hot; place your sausages and cabbages around your dish, and the bacon in the middle.

PIGS' KIDNEYS

Cut them open lengthwise, season well with pepper and salt, egg over (*brush with a pastry brush dipped in one egg beaten with one tablespoonful of water*), dip into breadcrumbs with which you have mixed some chopped parsley and eschalot, run a skewer through to keep them open and broil for a quarter of an hour over a good fire; when done, place them upon a dish, have ready an ounce of butter with which you have mixed the juice of a lemon, a little salt and pepper and a teaspoonful of French or common mustard; place a piece upon each of the kidneys, place in the oven for one minute and serve.

STEWED SAUSAGE MEAT WITH CHESTNUTS

Take twenty or thirty sound chestnuts, roast them over a slow fire and when sufficiently roasted to remove the husk, take them off, peel them, removing the inner skin as well as the husk, and put them aside sufficiently near the fire not to cool too readily. Cut into diamonds half a dozen thin slices of sausage meat, and fry them brown in a little fresh butter. When they are a good color, take them out and pour three parts of the butter in which they have been fried into a small well-tinned or earthen vessel. Thicken it while heating with a spoonful of flour, and pour in gradually a pint of good gravy, with a glass of old brown sherry or two of Madeira. Put in a fagot of herbs and season to palate, a little cayenne may accompany the common pepper. As soon as it boils, lay the sausage cakes round the saucepan close to the sides, leaving the center clear, and in this space put the chestnuts. Let them stew slowly three quarters of an hour; then dish them, arranging the sausage and chestnuts in the same manner as in the saucepan; pour the gravy over them, reserving the fagot of herbs first, and serve. (*Serves 4–6.*)

PARSNIPS WITH SAUSAGE

Take cold boiled parsnips and slice them an eighth of an inch thick. Fry in lard and drain. Arrange around fried sausage rounds.

TO TRY LARD AND TALLOW

"Every housekeeper knows how unfit for really nice cooking is the pressed lard sold in stores as the 'best and cheapest.' "
Mrs. Ellet, The Practical Housekeeper, 1857

Lard tries easier the day the pork is butchered. It need not then be washed except where stained. Cut it into pieces; put it in an iron pot with a very little water to prevent burning; boil it slowly over a moderate fire, stirring it occasionally to prevent burning, till the scraps are quite brown (*but the fat is not*); strain it through a coarse cloth, spread over a cullender, into your lard tub, what you want for your nicest without squeezing the strainer, then squeeze the scraps as dry as possible. Use the last strained first, as it will not keep so long as the first. Keep your lard covered in a cool dry place. Some salt the lard while trying, others do not. The scraps are nice for eating. Tallow is tried the same way. It should lie where perfectly cool and dry several days, and be stirred before trying. The leaves (*still available and downright cheap in butcher shops*) make the nicest lard.

Coffee cans are ideal for storing it.

"Suet and lard keep better in tin than in earthen. Suet keeps good a year, if chopped, packed in a stone jar and covered with molasses."
Marion Harland, Common Sense, 1883

"While lard is melting, you may put in a sprig of rosemary."
Mrs. Ellet, The Practical Housekeeper, 1857

TO MAKE SAUSAGE

6 *lbs. lean fresh pork*	6 *teaspoonfuls salt*
3 *lbs. fat fresh pork*	2 *teaspoonfuls powdered mace*
12 *teaspoonfuls powdered sage*	2 *teaspoonfuls powdered cloves*
6 *teaspoonfuls black pepper*	1 *grated nutmeg*

Grind the meat, lean and fat, in a sausage-mill, or chop it very fine. The mill is better and the grinding does not occupy one-tenth of the time that chopping does. One can be bought for three or four dollars (*it is still nearly the same price*) and will well repay the purchaser. Mix the seasoning in with your hands, (*fry a little and*) taste to be sure all is right, and pack down in stone jars, pouring melted lard on top. Another good way of preserving them is, to make long narrow bags of stout muslin, large enough to contain, each, enough sausage for a family dish. Fill these with the meat, dip in melted lard, and hang from the beams of your cellar.

If you wish to pack in the intestines of the hog, they should be carefully prepared as follows: empty them, cut them in lengths, and lay for two days in salt and water. Turn them inside out and lay in soak one day longer. Scrape them, rinse well in soda and water, wipe and blow into one end, having tied up the other with a bit of twine. If they are whole and clear, stuff with the meat; tie up and hang in the storeroom or cellar.

To fry them, some dip in egg and pounded cracker—others roll in flour before cooking. Their own fat will cook them. The fire should be very brisk.

SAUSAGE #2

2 *lbs. lean pork*	1 *teaspoonful cayenne*
2 *lbs. lean veal*	5 *teaspoonfuls salt*
2 *lbs. beef suet*	3 *teaspoonfuls sweet marjoram*
Peel of half a lemon (grated)	*and thyme, mixed*
One grated nutmeg	2 *teaspoonfuls sage*
1 *teaspoonful black pepper*	*Juice of a lemon*

This is very fine. Stuff in cases.

Chop suet with a little flour to keep it from sticking. Sausages may always be smoked.

"If you like to know what you are eating, have your sausage prepared at home or by someone whom you can trust."
                            Mrs. Lincoln's Boston Cook Book, 1896

THE UNIVERSITY RECEIPT

To two pounds of lean pork, young, white and delicate, put three-quarters of a pound of minced beef suet; the pork must first be chopped very fine; add three dessertspoonfuls of bread which has been dipped in port wine, dried and grated fine; work it together with the yolks of three eggs smoothly beaten; season it with pepper and salt and dried sage; a little cayenne may be introduced and a *very small* piece of garlic. Work the whole well together in a mortar until it forms a paste; it may then be put into wide skins or pressed down into jars for future use. It is cut into square pieces, dredged with flour, fried in fresh butter and sent to table on toast.

SPANISH OR PORTUGUESE SAUSAGE

are made from the fat and lean of the back and loins of a well-fed two-year-old hog, finely minced or pounded together and strongly seasoned with cloves of garlic and green or red capsicums (*pepper*) or chilies; but as these cannot always be conveniently procured in this country, cayenne pepper may be substituted. The whole should be covered with any sort of strong, dry wine, until absorbed by the ingredients, which will occupy perhaps a few days, according to the quantity. Fill the largest skins you can get with the meat, fat and lean alternately, occasionally adding some of the wine. Tie up in links, and hang them in a room where they will not get damp or become too dry, and they will keep twelve months.

They are sometimes fried, and eaten either alone or as a relish with poultry, but more frequently put into stews.

BLACK PUDDINGS

Stir three quarts of sheep's blood with one spoonful of salt till cold, boil one quart of grits in sufficient water to swell them, drain, and add them to the blood with one pound of suet, a little pounded nutmeg, some mace, cloves, and allspice; one pound of the hog's fat cut small, some parsley finely minced, sage, sweet herbs, a pint of bread crumbs, salt and pepper; mix these ingredients well together, put them into well-cleaned skins, tie them in links, and prick the skins, that while boiling they may not burst. Let them boil twenty minutes, and cover them with clean straw (*or shredded newspaper*) until they are cold.

SCRAPPLE

Boil a pig's head two hours in four quarts of water with a little sage, salt and pepper, cut the flesh from the bones, mince it fine and return it to the liquor; add enough sifted cornmeal to thicken; simmer two hours, and when it should be the consistence of soft mush, not too thick to pour. Put it in pans; when cold and stiff it is sliced, and fried for breakfast.

"At the South, where, in spite of the warm climate, the consumption of pork is double that of the North, the full-grown hog is seldom represented by any of his parts at the table, fresh or pickled, unless it be during the killing-time, when fresh spare-ribs, chine, and steak, with other succulent bits, are welcome upon the choicest bills of fare. The rest of the animal—ham, shoulders and middlings—is consigned to the packing barrel, and ultimately to the smoke-house. . . . Few stomachs, save those of out-door laborers, can digest the fresh meat of a two, or three, or even one year old hog. This is the truthful, but, to unaccustomed ears, offensive name for him at the South and West, where his qualities and habits are best known."

Marion Harland, *Common Sense*, 1883

TO PICKLE PORK

Hams, shoulders, chines and "middlings" are the parts of the hog which are usually pickled. This should be done as soon as may be after the meat is fairly cold. When you can pack down pork within 24 hours after butchering, it is best to do so, unless the cold be severe enough to preserve it longer.

For 80 pounds of meat, pulverize and mix one pint of fine salt with four pounds of sugar or one quart of best molasses and three ounces of saltpetre. Rub the meat *well* all over, and lay upon boards on the cellar-floor for 24 hours. Then, put a few clean stones in the bottom of a barrel; lay sticks across these, that the meat may not soak in the liquor that drains from it. Pack the meat in layers, strewing between these two quarts of salt. Let it lie in the cask for fifteen or sixteen days, every day during this time tipping the cask to drain off the liquor, or drawing it through a bunghole near the bottom. Pour this back in cupfuls over the meat. If you do not mean to smoke the meat, take it out at the end of the fortnight, rub each piece well over with dry salt, and return to the barrel. If the liquor does not cover it, make fresh brine in the proportion of two pounds of salt, a quarter of an ounce of saltpetre, and a quart of water, and pour in when you have boiled it half an hour and let it cool. Lay a round piece of board upon the upper layer and keep this down with stones. Examine from time to time, to make sure the meat is keeping well. Should it seem likely to taint, throw away the pickle, rub each piece over with dry salt, and pack anew. Pork pickled this way will keep two years.

A steady cool temperature is important for the meat to keep well.

TO CURE HAMS

Having pickled your hams (*p. 381*) with the rest of your pork, take them after the lapse of sixteen days from the packing barrel, with the shoulders and jowls. At the South they empty the cask, and consign the "whole hog" to the smokehouse. Wash off the pickle, and while wet, dip in bran. Some use sawdust, but it is not so good. Others use neither, only wipe the meat dry and smoke. The object in dipping in bran or sawdust is to form a crust which prevents the evaporation of the juices. Be sure that it is well covered with the bran, then hang in the smoke, the hock end downward. Keep up a good smoke, by having the fire partially smothered with hickory chips and sawdust, for four weeks, taking care the house does not become hot. Take down the meat, brush off the bran, examine closely, and if you suspect insects, lay it in the hot sun for a day or two. The various ways of keeping hams are too numerous to mention here. Some pack in wood ashes, others, in dry oats; others, in bran. But the best authorities discard packing altogether . . . an admirable housewife covers with brown paper, then with coarse muslin stitched tightly and fitted closely, then whitewashes. But for the paper the lime would be apt to eat away the grease. Still another covers with muslin, and coats with a mixture of bees-wax and rosin. There is no doubt that the covers are an excellent precaution provided always that the insects have not already deposited their eggs in the meat. The bran coating tends to prevent this.

SCHNELLER'S DRY CURE FOR HAMS

For a fresh ham weighing approximately fourteen to sixteen pounds, take a quarter-pound of saltpetre to three pounds of regular salt and one pound sugar. Add some ground pepper and mix well.

Rub the ham all over extremely well, making sure the mixture is worked thoroughly onto all the surfaces of the ham. Sprinkle a liberal amount on the bottom of a container large enough, and place the ham on it. Sprinkle more of the leftover mixture liberally on top. A weight of about eight or ten pounds will aid removal of moisture from the ham.

The ham should be turned and rubbed with the mixture once a week for five to six weeks. If a ham be boned, it will cut the curing time to half, and probably ensure a better cure, as many hams are not cured properly near the center bone, giving the ham a bad and sour taste. If a ham with the bone in is desired, you may purchase a special needle to inject a small amount of the brine solution into the thickest part of the ham and bone joints, especially the H bone.

After the cure, the ham should be soaked first in warm water. The process on this dry-cured ham should be about ten or twelve hours, changing the water once or twice. If the ham is deboned, roll and tie as tightly as possible after the soak process. Hang it to dry for 24 hours and then smoke it.

The smokehouse can be a room about four feet square without windows and with a fairly tightly fitting door. Build a small fire on the concrete floor out of hickory, apple, sassafras or other fruit wood, and some sawdust. If you cover it with a metal plate held up on bricks the heat and smoke will distribute better. Hang the hams as near the ceiling as possible. The first day of smoking, the fire should be quite hot for about two hours—not enough to cook it, but to set the cure and color the meat golden brown. After that, each day smoke it lightly for awhile to perfect the cure and to help it last a long time with only minor refrigeration. This should go on for about four weeks. The same process may be used for bacon. Allow twelve to fourteen days for a good slab to lie in the cure-salt mixture. For loins of pork, allow fourteen to eighteen days, depending on the thickness.

This curing and smoking process makes a ham that you cannot believe— zesty, hearty and above all containing no chemicals, which most meat packers use to effect an instant cure, to tenderize and flavor—and to hold or retain the large amounts of water used in their injection method of vein pumping with pickling brine for added cheap weight.

TO CURE VIRGINIA HAMS

Rub salt, saltpetre, red and black pepper all over the ham, particularly around the bone. Repeat this for several days. Rub black molasses on meat side; cover with salt and every other day rub in thoroughly. Continue rubbing in this preparation every day and turning the hams for about 3 weeks; and then smoke for three weeks. Smoking makes the greatest difference in taste, the smoked hams being much sweeter and firmer. Sack by March 1st.

"The fly may in some measure be prevented by dusting on the parts most likely to be attacked, pepper and ginger mixed, after wiping, which should never be omitted; but a more easy and effectual way is

to exclude the fly by using a wire meat safe. In summer, meat should be wiped every day, or sprinkled with pepper to keep off the fly. In summer two days is long enough (to keep) *lamb and veal, and from three to four for beef and mutton; in cold weather these latter may be kept for more than double that time, without risk of being tainted."*

Mrs. Ellet, *The Practical Housekeeper*, 1857

WESTPHALIA HAMS

Prepare the hams in the usual manner by rubbing them with common salt and draining them; take one ounce of saltpetre, half a pound of coarse sugar and the same quantity of salt; rub it well into the ham, and in three days pour a pint of vinegar over it. A fine foreign flavor may also be given to hams by pouring old strong beer over them and burning juniper wood while they are drying; molasses, juniper berries and highly-flavored herbs, such as basil, sage, bay-leaves and thyme mingled together, and the hams well rubbed with it, using only a sufficient quantity of salt to assist in the cure, will afford an agreeable variety.

"Bear meat is best roasted. It may be treated the same as pork, cooking twenty minutes to every pound."

Mrs. Rorer, *The Philadelphia Cook Book*, 1886

VENISON

Venison, properly treated (gutted instantly, skinned as soon as possible, aged in a refrigerator for four or five days—and not hung outside with its skin on), is one of the richest, sweetest meats it is possible to find. It rarely gets the respect it deserves now. In restaurants, imported venison (it is illegal to sell domestic venison) is always overcooked and tough or overspiced and tasteless. And those hunters who know what to do with the deer they have brought down are in the minority. Nevertheless, here is venison—as it should be.

"Venison is said to be the most easily digested of any sort of meat. It is good for those who have weak and slow digestive powers."

Mrs. Webster, *The Improved Housewife*, 1854

[384]

HAUNCH OF VENISON

If the outside be hard, wash off with lukewarm water; then rub all over with fresh butter or lard. Let the fire be steady and strong (*or the oven be set at 325°*). Pour a few ladlefuls of butter and water over the meat. If the haunch be large, it will take at least five hours to roast. (*Allow 15–20 minutes to the pound*). About half an hour before you take it up, test with a skewer to see if it is done. If this passes easily to the bone through the thickest part, set it down to a more moderate fire and baste every few minutes with claret and melted butter. For gravy, put into a saucepan a pound or two of scraps of raw venison left from trimming the haunch, a quart of water, a pinch of cloves, a few blades of mace, half a nutmeg, cayenne and salt to taste. Stew slowly to one half the original quantity. Skim, strain and return to the saucepan when you have rinsed it out with hot water. Add three tablespoons of currant jelly, a glass of claret, two tablespoons of butter and thicken it with browned flour; send to table in a tureen. Send around currant jelly with venison *always*. (*A large haunch will serve 15, easily.*)

The neck (*allow 15 minutes to the pound*) is roasted precisely as is the haunch. The shoulder is also a roasting piece.

DRIED PEACH SAUCE

Soak a quart of dried peaches in water four hours. Wash them, rubbing them against one another by stirring around with a wooden spoon. Drain, and put into a saucepan with just enough water to cover them. Stew until they break into pieces. Rub to a soft smooth pulp, sweeten to taste with white sugar. Send to table cold, with roast game or other meats.

A SHOULDER OF VENISON

Extract the bones through the underside. Make a stuffing of several slices of fat mutton, minced fine and seasoned smartly with cayenne, salt, allspice and wine, and fill the holes from which the bones were taken. Bind firmly in shape with broad (*muslin*) tape. Put in a large saucepan with a pint of gravy made from the refuse bits of venison; add a glass of Madeira or port wine and a little black pepper. Cover tightly and stew very slowly three or four hours, according to the size. It should be very tender. Remove the tapes with care;

dish, and when you have strained the gravy, pour over the meat. This is a most savory dish. (*Serves 8–10.*)

"To tenderize game, cut it into slices, rub with a carbonate of soda in small quantities. Wash off the next morning and cook."
Marion Harland, *Common Sense*, 1883

VENISON STEAKS

These are taken from the neck or haunch. Have your griddle well-buttered, and fire clear and hot (*cook over charcoal, under the broiler, or in a very hot frying pan*). Lay the steaks on the bars and broil rapidly, turning often not to lose a drop of juice. They will take three or four minutes longer than fine beef steaks. Have ready in a hot chafing dish, a piece of butter the size of an egg for every pound of venison, a pinch of salt, a little pepper, a tablespoon of currant-jelly for every pound, and a glass of wine for every four pounds. This should be liquid, and warmed by the boiling water under the dish by the time the steaks are done to a turn. If you have no chafing dish, heat in a saucepan. Lay each steak in the mixture and turn over twice. Cover closely and let all heat together, with fresh hot water underneath—unless your lamp is burning —for five minutes before serving. If you serve in an ordinary dish, cover and set in the oven for the same time.

ANOTHER: Wash two steaks, season with salt, black and red pepper mixed, and fry a light brown on both sides. When done, place them upon a dish, and dredge into the pan one dessertspoonful of browned flour, to which add gradually one cupful of boiling water (*or even better, a cup of venison stock made with trimmings along the general lines of beef stock, but seasoned more highly, with juniper berries and peppercorns*); stir well, and season to taste. As soon as it comes to a boil, flavor nicely with either sherry or Madeira; then pour it over the steaks while hot. Garnish the top of each with currant jelly and send to table on a well-heated dish. (*Serves 4–8, depending on size of steaks.*)

VENISON PASTY

Almost any part of the deer can be used for the purpose but the neck and shoulders are generally preferred. Cut the raw venison from the bones and set aside those with the skin, fat and refuse bits, for gravy. Put them into a sauce-

[386]

pan with a shallot, pepper, salt, nutmeg and sweet herbs, cover well with cold water, and set on to boil. Meanwhile, cut the better and fairer pieces of meat into squares an inch long and cook in another saucepan until three-quarters done. Line a deep dish with good puff-paste. That for the lid should be made after the receipt appended to this. Put in the squares of venison, season with pepper, salt and butter and put in half a cupful of the liquor in which the meat was stewed, to keep it from burning at the bottom. Cover with a lid of prepared pastry an inch thick. Cut a round hole (*as thick as your thumb*) in the lid and make for it a cylinder of buttered paper. Bake steadily (*at 350°*), covering the top with a sheet of clean paper so soon as it is firm, to prevent it from browning too fast. While it is cooking prepare the gravy. When all the substance has been extracted from the bones, etc., strain the liquor back into the saucepan; let it come to a boil, and when you have skimmed carefully, add a glass of port wine, a tablespoonful of butter, the juice of a lemon and some browned flour to thicken. Boil up once, remove the paper plug from the hole in the pastry, and pour in through a small funnel as much gravy as the pie will hold. Do this very quickly; brush the crust over with beaten egg and put back in the oven until it is a delicate brown, or rather, a golden russet. The pie should only be drawn to the door of the oven for these operations, and everything should be in readiness before it is taken out, that the crust may be light and flakey. Bake two or three hours, guiding yourself by the size of the pie. If you have more gravy than you need, serve in a tureen.

CRUST FOR VENISON PASTY: Dry and sift 1½ lbs. of flour and cut up 6 ounces of butter in it with a knife or chopper until the whole is fine and yellow; salt, and work up rapidly with ice water, lastly adding 3 egg yolks beaten very light. Work out rapidly, handling as little as possible, roll out three times very thin, basting 6 ounces of melted butter (*roll out, spread with butter, fold up, and roll out again*), then into a lid nearly an inch thick, reserving a thinner one for ornaments. Having covered in your pie, cut from the second sheet with a cake-cutter, leaves, flowers, stars, or any figures you like, to adorn the top of your crust. Bake the handsomest one upon a tin plate by itself, and brush it over with egg when you glaze the pie. After the pastry is baked, cover the hole in the center with this.

VENISON HAMS

These are eaten raw, and will not keep long as other smoked meats. Mix together in equal proportions, salt and brown sugar, and rub them hard into the hams with your hand. Pack them in a cask, sprinkling dry salt between them, and let them lie eight days, rubbing them over every day with dry salt and sugar. Next mix equal parts of fine salt, molasses, and a teaspoonful of saltpetre to every two hams. Take the hams out of the pickle, go over them with a brush dipped in cider vinegar, then in the new mixture. Empty the cask, wash it out with cold water, and repack the hams, dripping from the sticky bath, scattering fine salt over each. Let them lie eight days longer in this. Wash off the pickle first with tepid water, until the salt crystals are removed; then sponge with vinegar, powder them with bran while still wet, and smoke for a fortnight, or if large, three weeks. Wrap in brown paper that has no unpleasant odor, stitch a muslin cover around this, and whitewash, unless you mean to use at once. Chip or shave for the table.

Venison sausage can be made like pork sausage. Add a little lemon juice. See pp. 378–380.

VENISON POTTED

Put the venison into a pan and pour red wine over it, and cover it with one pound of butter, put a paste (*or tight lid*) over the pan, set it in the oven to bake. When done, take the meat out of the gravy, beat it well with butter that has arisen to the top, add more if necessary, season with salt, pepper and mace pounded; put into pots, set them in the oven for a few minutes, take them out; when cold, cover with clarified butter.

VENISON SOUP

Take four pounds of freshly killed venison cut off from the bones and one pound of ham in small slices. Add an onion minced, and black pepper to your taste. Put only as much water as will cover it, and stew it gently for an hour, keeping the pot closely covered. Then skim it well, and pour in one quart of boiling water. Add a head of celery cut into small pieces, and three blades of mace. Boil it gently two and a half hours; then put in a quarter of a pound of butter, divided into small pieces, and rolled in flour, and add half a pint of port or Madeira wine. Let it boil one quarter of an hour longer and send it to table with the meat in it.

TURKEY

There is a vast difference between turkeys and geese that have been frozen and those that have not. Fresh ones are in every way superior. The meat deftly picks up the nuances of whatever you stuff it with—so a light hand with the sausage or the oysters is indicated—and unless you insist on roasting it to a frazzle in a hot oven, it cannot help but be juicier and more tender than the frozen birds. The frozen ones have this advantage (I am excepting those pathetic pre-basted things which may be juicy but are also hopelessly tasteless and full of chemicals): you can get as wild as you like with the stuffing without overpowering the meat.

ROAST TURKEY

After drawing the turkey, rinse out in several waters, and in the next to last mix a teaspoonful of soda. The inside of a fowl, especially if purchased in a market, is sometimes very sour, and imparts an unpleasant taste to the stuffing. Then prepare a dressing of breadcrumbs mixed with butter, pepper, salt, thyme or sweet marjoram. You may, if you like, add the beaten yolks of two eggs. A little chopped sausage is esteemed an improvement. Or, mince a dozen oysters (*or more, since our turkeys are larger*) and stir into the dressing. The effect upon the turkey meat, particularly that of the breast, is very pleasant.

Stuff the craw with this, and tie a string tightly about the neck to prevent the escape of the stuffing. Then fill the body of the turkey and sew it up with strong thread. In roasting, if your fire is brisk, allow ten minutes to the pound (*at 400°*). Dredge with flour before roasting (*if you are roasting on an open fire*) and baste often. Roast to a fine brown.

Strew the chopped giblets in just enough water to cover them, and when the turkey is lifted from the pan, add these, with the water in which they were boiled, to the drippings; thicken with a spoonful of browned flour, wet with cold water to prevent lumping. Boil up once, and pour into the gravy boat. Serve with cranberry sauce. Some lay fried oysters in the dish around the turkey.

ROAST TURKEY WITH CHESTNUTS

Truss a turkey for roasting. Boil half of one hundred chestnuts till tender; remove the shell; chop them very fine. Take the marrow of two marrow bones, cut into pieces, stuff the turkey with the marrow and chestnuts (*turkeys averaged about 10 pounds: for larger birds, double the recipe*). Put it down to a good fire and baste it constantly while roasting. When done, take it up, pour over it a little chestnut sauce (*mashed chestnuts added to a cream sauce or to the turkey gravy*), and serve it with brown gravy separately.

ANOTHER CHESTNUT STUFFING FOR CHICKEN OR TURKEY: Shell one quart of large chestnuts (*p. 334*); pour on boiling water, and remove the inner brown skin. Boil in salted water or stock until soft. Mash fine. Take half of the stuffing and mix with it one cup of fine cracker crumbs; season with one teaspoon of salt, one saltspoon of pepper, and one teaspoon of chopped parsley. Moisten with one-third of a cup of melted butter. Professional cooks sometimes add a little apple sauce flavored with wine, lemon and sugar, with a chestnut stuffing.

STUFFING FOR HARE OR TURKEY

Take half a pound of beef suet chopped very fine, some parsley, a little thyme, pepper, salt and spices, the same quantity of bread crumbs as of suet, an egg or two, and mix it whole with a little milk. It would not be amiss to put in a very small bit of butter and to pound the whole in a mortar for a short time. This stuffing may be used with baked pike. If the taste of shallot is not objected to, it will be found to add to the flavor of the stuffing. If you do not like to put it into the mortar, take the rolling pin and mix it with it on the table, which is a better method.

TO ROAST A TURKEY THE GENTEEL WAY

First cut it down the back, and with a sharp penknife bone it, then make your forcemeat (*stuffing*) thus: take a large fowl or a pound of veal, as much grated bread, half a pound of suet cut and beat very fine, a little beaten mace, two cloves, half a nutmeg grated, a large teaspoonful of lemon-peel, and the yolks of two eggs; mix all together, with a little pepper and salt, fill up the places where the bones came out, and fill the body, that it may look just as it did before. Sew it up the back, and roast it. You may have oyster-sauce (*p. 277 or p. 393*), or celery sauce, with it.

WHITE CELERY SAUCE: 2 large heads of celery; 1 teacupful of broth in which the fowl is boiled; 1 teacupful cream or milk; salt and nutmeg. Boil the celery tender in salted water; drain, and cut into bits half an inch long. Thicken the gravy from the fowl—a teacupful—with the flour; add the butter, salt, and nutmeg, then the milk. Stir and beat until it is smooth; put in the celery; heat almost to boiling, stirring all the while; serve in a tureen, or, if you prefer, pour it over the boiled meat or fowls.

TURKEY GALANTINE

Select a young hen turkey. Bone it; spread the boned meat on the table, skin side down. Equalize the meat as well as possible by paring it off at the thick parts and laying it on the thin parts. Leave the legs and wings drawn inside; lay a few lardoons of salt pork on the meat lengthwise. Make a force-meat of another fowl, or of veal, or of both chicken and veal. Chop it to a very fine mince, and pound it in a mortar to make it almost a paste. Season it with salt and pepper, savory, marjoram, thyme and sage—about a half teaspoonful of each of the herbs—one teaspoonful of onion juice, a half cupful of cold boiled tongue cut into dice, some truffles cut into large pieces. Moisten it with stock and mix thoroughly. It will take three or four pounds of meat, according to the size of the turkey, to make a sufficient stuffing. Spread the forcemeat on the boned turkey, having the tongue, truffles, and a few pieces of both white and dark meat of the turkey well interspersed through it. Roll up the turkey, making it as even as possible, and sew it together; then roll it in a piece of cheesecloth and tie it securely at both ends and around the roll in several places.

Place the galantine and the bones of the bird in a kettle with an onion, carrot, celery, bouquet of herbs, and a tablespoonful of salt. Cover it with boiling water and let it simmer three or four hours; then remove it from the fire; let the galantine remain in the water for an hour; then take it out, cut the strings which bind it in the middle, draw the cloth so it will be tight and smooth, and place it under a weight until perfectly cold. A baking-pan holding two flat-irons will answer the purpose. Remove the cloth carefully, set the galantine in the oven a moment to melt the fat, and wipe it off with a cloth; trim it smooth; then brush it over with a glaze or rub it over with beaten egg and sprinkle with crumbs and brown it in the oven; or cover it with chaud-froid

[391]

sauce and ornament it with truffles. When perfectly set, it is brushed over lightly with a little liquid jelly (*gelatine or aspic*).

A galantine is always used cold. Garnish with aspic, made from the water in which it was boiled, strained and cleared. Use a box of gelatine to one and a half quarts of liquid.

CHAUD-FROID SAUCE: Put two tablespoonfuls of butter into a saucepan; when it bubbles add two tablespoonfuls of flour. Let it cook well, but not brown; stir all the time. Add two cupfuls of chicken or veal stock, and stir until it is well thickened. Season with salt and pepper. Then add a half-box of gelatine which has been soaked in a half-cupful of cold water. Stir until the gelatine has dissolved. Strain the sauce, and let it just begin to stiffen before using it. Put a little on ice to see if it is of the right firmness. If it is too stiff, add a little more stock; if not firm enough, add a little more gelatine. It needs to be only firm enough to hold its place without running.

A yellow color can be given it by adding the yolks of three eggs just before removing it from the fire. A brown chaud-froid, which is used for game and dark meats, is made by browning the roux, diluting it with beef-stock. To make a galantine perfectly smooth, fill any irregularity of the surface with a little of the sauce which has been placed on ice to set.

This can be used for cold chicken, game, fish, or almost any other cold meat.

TURKEY WITH SAUSAGE MEAT

At the messes of European regiments in India, it is no uncommon thing to bone a turkey and a fowl and put one inside the other, filling the interstices with sausage meat. A turkey thus prepared takes a long time roasting. When carved, the slices should be cut quite through; and epicures aver that it is one of the finest dishes to come to table.

BOILED TURKEY

It was the habit, in trussing turkey for boiling, to cut the ribs on either side of the backbone from the inside, then to pound the breast almost down with the flat of a cleaver before tying it up. Turkeys were not as hefty nor as fat as they are now: it may have been necessary to keep the breast meat juicy. Sausage or chunks of bacon, surrounding the turkey on its platter, were traditional.

Chop about two dozen oysters and mix with them a dressing compounded as for roast turkey, only with more butter. Stuff the turkey as for roasting and baste about it a thin cloth, fitted closely to every part. The inside of the cloth should be dredged in flour to prevent the fowl from sticking to it. Allow fifteen minutes to the pound and boil slowly.

Serve with oyster sauce made by adding to a cupful of the liquor in which the turkey was boiled, eight oysters chopped fine. Season with minced parsley, stir in a spoonful of rice or wheat (*white*) flour wet with milk, a tablespoonful of butter. Add a cupful of hot milk. Boil up once and pour into an oyster tureen. Send celery around with it.

Turkey dressed this way is also good roasted: "I often reflect to myself, why should this innocent and well-brought up bird have its remains condemned to this watery, bubbling inquisition, especially when alive it has the greatest horror of this temperate fluid." (Alexis Soyer, *The Modern Housewife*, 1850)

TURKEY SCALLOP

Cut the meat from the bones of a cold boiled or roasted turkey left from yesterday's dinner. Remove the bits of skin and gristle and chop the rest up fine. Put in the bottom of a buttered dish a layer of cracker or bread crumbs; moisten slightly with milk, that they may not absorb all the gravy to be poured in afterward; then spread a layer of the minced turkey, with bits of the stuffing, salt, pepper and small pieces of butter. Another layer of cracker, wet with milk, and so on until the dish is nearly full. Before putting on the topmost layer, pour in the gravy left from the turkey, diluted—should there not be enough—with hot water and seasoned with Worcestershire sauce or catsup, and butter. Have ready a crust of cracker crumbs soaked in milk, seasoned with salt and beaten up light with two eggs. It should be just thick enough to spread smoothly over the top of the scallop. Stick bits of butter plentifully upon it and bake. Turn a deep plate over the dish until the contents begin to bubble at the sides, showing that the whole is thoroughly cooked; then remove the plate and brown. A large pudding-dish full of the mixture will be cooked in three-quarters of an hour. Cold chicken may be prepared in the same way.

The minced turkey, dressing or cracker crumbs may be wet with gravy, two eggs beaten into it, and the forcemeat thus made rolled into oblong shapes, dipped in egg and pounded cracker and (*deep*) fried like croquettes, for a side dish to "make out" a dinner of ham or cold meat.

BROWN TURKEY SOUP

Use for this soup the carcass of a cold roast turkey; cut all the scraps of meat from it, and mince them fine; mince also any bits of heart, liver or gizzard which may be available; put two tablespoonfuls of butter in the soup-kettle, and set it on the fire to get smoking hot; peel and slice an onion, and when the butter is hot add the onion to it, together with the minced turkey-meat and any cold stuffing on hand, and let all the ingredients brown together; when they are brown, stir among them two heaping tablespoonsful of flour and let that brown; then pour in four quarts of boiling water, add two teaspoonfuls of salt and a level saltspoonful of pepper. Stir the soup thoroughly, put in the carcass of the turkey without breaking it, cover the soup-kettle, and let the soup cook slowly for at least two hours; then remove the carcass of the turkey, and serve the soup hot, with all the other ingredients in it. A glass of wine poured into the tureen containing the soup is a great addition to it when the flavor of wine is liked. (*Serves 10–15.*)

CRANBERRIES

If you have a freezer space, put in a couple boxes of cranberries. They seem to vanish from the markets on the stroke of New Year's midnight. Other goods that are hard to find except at Thanksgiving or Christmas time: currants, dates, crystallized ginger.

CRANBERRY SAUCE

Wash and pick a quart of ripe cranberries, and put into a saucepan with a teacup of water (*or orange juice*). Stew slowly, stirring often until they are thick as marmalade. They require at least an hour and a half to cook (*or 15–20 minutes, until they pop, for a crisper texture*). When you take them from the fire, sweeten abundantly with white sugar. If sweetened while cooking, the color will be bad. Put them into a mould and set aside to get cold.

OR: And this is a nicer plan—strain the pulp through a cullender or sieve, or coarse mosquito-net (*or food mill*) into a mould wet with cold water.

[394]

When firm, turn into a glass dish or salver. Be sure it is sweet enough. Eat with roast turkey, game, and roast duck.

Cranberry sauce can be canned or frozen. A sliced orange, rind and all, may be cooked with the berries.

CRANBERRY PIE

Pick a quart of cranberries free from imperfections, put a pint of water to them, and put them in a stewpan over a moderate fire; put a pound of clean brown sugar to them and stew them gently until they are all soft, then mash them with a silver spoon, and turn them into a dish to become cold, then make them into pies or tarts and bake. Many persons put flour into cranberry pies; it is a great mistake, as it completely spoils the color.

CRANBERRY TART

One-half pound of cranberries, six tablespoonfuls of sugar, four apples, one half pound of prunes. Wash the cranberries, and pick them from the stalks, peel, core and slice the apples; stone and wash the prunes; put all these with the sugar into a saucepan, and stew them until soft, or about half an hour. Put the mixture into a pie dish and allow to cool. Cover with a short crust (*no bottom crust*), and bake for about half an hour.

CRANBERRY PUDDING

One cup molasses, into which stir one teaspoonful of soda, one cup warm water, one and a half pints of cranberries whole, flour enough to make a soft batter (like gingerbread); steam two hours. (*See p. 27; serves 4–6.*)

FOAMY SAUCE FOR SAME: One half cup butter, beaten to a cream with the same amount of sugar, four tablespoonfuls of cream; set the dish into boiling water just long enough to dissolve the sugar, flavor (*and whip light*).

CRANBERRY SHORTCAKE

Follow the same recipe for strawberry shortcake (*p. 192*); then use cranberry sauce, made with a cup and a half of water to a quart of cranberries and sweetened with a cup of sugar. Serve with whipped cream.

CRANBERRY SNOW

Whip stiff the white of one egg, and add alternately and gradually three tablespoonfuls of sugar and a cup of cranberry sauce. Continue to whip until it has reached at least a pint and a half in quantity, for it swells surprisingly. Finely chopped nuts may be added if desired. (*Serves 4–6.*)

CRANBERRY FRAPPE

Boil four cups of cranberries in three cups of water until soft, then rub them through a sieve (*or purée in a blender*), boil two cups of sugar and one cup of water until it spins a fine thread, then pour slowly over the beaten whites of two eggs. Beat it a few minutes and add the cranberry pulp, one and one-half cups of orange juice and the juice of one lemon. Freeze as ice cream and serve in sherbet cups with turkey or use as a separate course. (*Makes 1 gallon.*)

CRANBERRY SURPRISE

Crumble three lady fingers into a baking dish, cover with a thin layer of cranberry preserves or jelly, dot with small lumps of butter and add a sprinkling of cinnamon. Beat three eggs very light, add two cups of milk. Pour over the fruit and cake, bake as a custard and serve with whipped cream. (*Serves 4.*)

CRANBERRY TEA

Wash ripe cranberries, mash fine, pour boiling water on them and then strain off the water and sweeten it and grate on nutmeg.

INDIAN PUDDING

Scald three pints of milk and stir in it seven (*large*) spoonfuls of Indian (*corn*) meal whilst boiling; set it to cool; stone and put in one to two pounds of raisins, salt and spice to taste. Then beat seven eggs well, and if only milk-warm (*lukewarm*), put them in (*to the milk/meal mixture*) with one to four pounds of (*melted*) butter, and sugar to taste. Stir well together, bake half an hour at a good heat (*375°*).

ANOTHER: Into one quart of boiling milk stir slowly seven tablespoonfuls of Indian meal; then remove from the stove and add one egg, beaten, half a teaspoonful of ginger, two-thirds of a cupful of molasses and a little salt. Bake one hour.

FRUITCAKE

All fruitcakes are the better for keeping, with the air shut out, sprinkled with brandy or rum if they seem to need moisture. Cakes made now will be ready for Christmas and will keep, if sprinkled from time to time, until next Christmas.

FRUIT CAKE

Two pounds of flour (or less)
Two pounds of currants
One and a quarter pounds of butter
One and a quarter pound of sugar

Sixteen eggs
Half an ounce of nutmeg
Three-fourths of a pint of wine, the same of brandy

Soak the currants in the brandy overnight. Cream the butter and sugar; add the eggs one at a time, with a little flour if the batter shows a tendency to curdle; beat well; add enough flour to make a fairly stiff batter, and the wine; stir in the currants and brandy. Bake in a 375° oven with a shallow pan of water in the bottom, until a cake tester or broom straw comes out clean when inserted in the center of the cake. Makes 2 very large cakes, or a number of small cakes.

WASHINGTON CAKE

3 *cups sugar* (or 2 cups   4 *cups flour*
    molasses)   2 *teaspoons cream-tartar*
2 *cups butter*   1 *teaspoon soda*
5 *eggs*   (½ cup brandy)
1 *cup milk*

Mix as usual and stir in, at the last:—

Half a pound of currants well washed and dredged in flour.
A quarter of a pound of raisins seeded and chopped fine, then floured.
A handful of citron sliced fine.
Cinnamon and nutmeg to taste.

Fruitcake takes longer to bake than plain, and the heat must be kept steady. (*Makes 2 large cakes.*)

FRUIT-BREAD PUDDING

1 *quart milk*   ¼ *lb currants, washed and*
5 *eggs*   *picked over*
2 *tablespoonfuls melted butter*   *Handful of shred citron*
2 *heaping tablespoonfuls sugar*   1 *teaspoon soda, dissolved in*
¼ *lb raisins, seeded and*   *hot water*
    chopped   2 *scant cups fine bread crumbs*

Beat the yolks light with the sugar, add the breadcrumbs when they have been well soaked in the milk, and stir until smooth. Next put in the fruit well dredged with flour, the soda, and finally the whites, whipped to a stiff froth. This will require longer and steadier baking than if the fruit were not in. Cover it if it threatens to harden too soon on top. Send to table hot in the dish in which it was baked, or turn out very carefully upon a hot plate. Eat warm, with pudding sauce.

HARD SAUCE, FOR FRUIT-CAKES AND PUDDINGS: Stir to a cream one cup of butter and three cups of powdered sugar. When light, beat in three-fourths of a teacup of wine (*or brandy*), the juice of a lemon, and two teaspoonfuls nutmeg. Beat long and hard until several shades lighter in color than at first, and creamy in consistency. Smooth into shape with a broad knife dipped in cold water, and stamp with a wooden mould first scalded and then dipped in cold water. Set upon the ice until the pudding is served.

See p. 96 for soft sauce, p. 99 for wine sauce.

THANKSGIVING DISHES

THANKSGIVING TEA CAKE

This is a sweet, biscuit-like cake.

One teacup of butter, one teacup of white sugar, two eggs, two coffee-cups of flour, and one teaspoon of essence of lemon. Beat them together till light and creamy (cake cannot be beaten too much), then put it into a small basin (*cake pan*) lined with buttered paper and bake in a quick oven. Citron cut in slips and added to this is an improvement.

MINCE MEAT FOR PIES

2 pounds fresh beef, boiled, and when cold, chopped fine.
1 pound beef suet, cleared of strings and minced to powder.
5 pounds apples, pared and chopped.
2 pounds raisins, seeded and chopped.
1 pound sultana raisins, washed and picked over.
2 pounds currants, washed and carefully picked over.
¾ pound citron, cut up fine.
2 tablespoonfuls cinnamon.
1 teaspoonful nutmeg.
2 tablespoonfuls mace.
1 tablespoonful cloves.
1 tablespoonful allspice.
1 tablespoonful fine salt.
2½ lbs brown sugar.
1 quart brown sherry.
1 pint best brandy.

Mince-meat made by this receipt will keep all winter in a cool place. Keep in stone jars, tied over with double covers. Add a little more liquor (if it should dry out) when you make up a batch of pies. Let the mixture stand at least twenty-four hours before it is used, after it is made. (*Half the recipe makes abundant mincemeat, unless you are planning six or eight family re-unions.*)

THE HON. PAUL RICHARDS' RECEIPT TO MAKE EXCELLENT MINCE PIES, 1735

Take a Neat's (*calf's*) Tongue, boil it and blanch it, add to a Pound of Tongues, two Pounds and a half of Sewet, two Pounds and a half of Currants, after they are washed and cleaned, one Pound of Raisins, stoned and chop'd very fine, a Quarter of an ounce of Mace, a Quarter of an ounce of Cloves, A Quarter of an ounce of Nutmegs, a Quarter of an ounce of Cinnamon, a Pound of dried powdered (*granulated*) Sugar. Squeeze in the juice of three good Lemons, one Orange, six spoonfuls of rosewater or Orange flower water, half a pint of Madeira Wine. Chop the Sewet fine and pick out the skins—put it down close in a Pott after mixing it (*all the ingredients*) well and keep it from the Air, use a little salt (*sprinkled over the top*).

N.B. Mrs. Richards allways added six Pippins (*small, tart apples*), chopt fine, and did not put in any sugar.

[15]

DECEMBER

*Citrus fruits; cakes; icings; raisin, nut, and citron
cakes; cookies; candy; Christmas dishes; beverages*

CITRUS FRUITS

In December, the citrus crops come in, and even in Northern cities prices
for oranges, lemons and limes, tangerines, and grapefruit go down.

SUPERIOR LEMON PIE

Boil six fine fresh lemons in a large quantity of water, until a straw will
penetrate the skin, then take them out with a skimmer, chop them fine, taking
care to take out all the pips; when perfectly fine, dredge over them two teaspoons of flour. To one pound of refined sugar, put a pint of water (*use the
water the lemons were boiled in for a stronger lemon flavor*), and set it to boil;
when it is a nice syrup, stir into it the chopped lemon; continue to stir until it
thickens, and becomes clear, then set it by in an earthen or china dish to cool;
cover a pieplate with a rich paste, put in the prepared lemon as thick (*deep*) as

[401]

you may like, cover with a nice puff paste (*p. 76*) and bake. Lemons prepared in this way are nice for many other uses.

LEMON CREAM

One pint of water; peel of three large lemons; juice of four lemons; six ounces of fine loaf sugar; white of six eggs.

Pare into a pint of water the peel of three large lemons; let it stand four or five hours; then take them out, and put to the water the juice of four lemons and six ounces of fine loaf sugar. Beat the white of six eggs (*to soft peaks*) and mix all together, strain it through a lawn (*very fine*) sieve, set it over a slow fire, stir it one way until as thick as good cream, then take it off the fire, and stir it until cold, and put it in a glass dish.

Orange cream may be made in the same way, adding the yolks of three eggs. (*Serves 4–6.*)

LEMON PUDDING

Beat half a pound of fresh butter to a cream, with half a pound of powdered sugar; then add to it eight eggs, well beaten, with the juice and grated peel of a large lemon; stir it well together; line a dish with puff paste; fill it with the pudding, and bake in a moderate oven.

LEMON CAKE

Take ten eggs, one pound of sugar, one pound of flour, the juice of one lemon and the gratings (*of the rind*) of three. Beat the eggs and sugar well together, put the flour in by degrees, beat till very light, then add the lemon. Dust a little sugar over it before you put it (*in a large tube pan*) in to bake in a slow oven.

"If your gown has become stained with lemon juice or rind, apply ammonia to the spot and it will restore the cloth to its natural color. To remove mildew stains, use lemon juice."

The Caloric Book of Recipes, 1907

GRANDMOTHER DON'S LEMON CAKE

One and a quarter cups of sugar; half a cup of butter; one cup sweet milk; two and a half cups of flour; three teaspoonfuls of baking powder; three egg whites beaten; extract. (*Bake in a moderate oven in two layers.*)

LEMON FILLING: One lemon grated; one cup grated apple; one cup of sugar; yolks of three eggs.

CORNSTARCH FILLING: Half a cup of sugar; one tablespoonful of cornstarch; two egg yolks; two-thirds of a cup of milk; extract. (*Cook as a custard.*)

"Cut lemon and orange peel, when fresh, into a bottle kept full of brandy. This brandy gives a delicious flavor to pies, cakes, etc. . . . Coarse nets suspended in the storeroom are very useful in preserving lemons and oranges."

Mrs. Ellet, *The Practical Housekeeper*, 1857

LEMONADE ICE

With a quart of rich lemonade, mix the well-beaten yolk of six fresh eggs, and freeze it. (*Makes about 1½ quarts.*)

LEMON CHEESECAKES

Take two large lemons, and rub the rind with one pound of loaf sugar (*sugar cubes*), so that all the yellow part is removed; place the sugar in a basin, squeeze the juice of the lemons over. Then add the yolks of six eggs, and beat it all well up, and put by in a jar for use. It will keep for years. Any flavor, such as vanilla, or cinnamon, may be added if liked, when required for use.

Having made a paste (*pie crust*) and lined the (*muffin*) tins, mix one tablespoonful of the mixture with a teacup of good milk, and place a little in each tartlet.

LEMON DROP BISCUITS (*COOKIES*)

Mix together half a pound of powdered sugar and half a pound of fine flour with the finely grated rind of a large lemon; add to it three ounces of dissolved butter, then the beaten yolks of three eggs, and lastly, three ounces of currants, and the white of the eggs in froth. Drop the biscuits on wafer paper and bake for twenty minutes in a slow oven.

LEMON DROPS (*CANDY*)

Take the juice of six fresh lemons strained fine, and mix it with a pound of treble-refined (*confectioner's*) sugar beaten and sifted through a lawn sieve, beat them together an hour (*whip at high speed in the mixer*), it will make them white and bright, then drop them upon writing paper, and dry them before the fire, or in the sun. They are a pretty ornament for a dessert.

LEMON SIRUP

Pare off the yellow part of the rind of fresh lemons, squeeze out the juice, strain it, and to a pint of it put a pound and three quarters of sugar. Dissolve the sugar by a gentle heat, skim it till it clears, then, adding the rinds, simmer gently eight or ten minutes, and strain it through a flannel bag. When cool, bottle it and seal the corks (*with paraffin, or can it*). It is nice to flavor pies and puddings (*or over ice cream*). Orange sirup may be made in the same way, with a little less sugar.

LEMON PICKLE

Grate the yellow rind from twenty-five fresh lemons; quarter them, leaving them united at the blossom (*lower*) end; sprinkle salt over them, and place them in the sun daily till dry; then brush off the salt; put them in a pot with pounded (*ground*) mace and nutmeg, an ounce of each, a handful of scraped dried horseradish, twenty cloves of garlic and a pint of mustard seed. Turn on a gallon of strong vinegar; cover the pot close; let it stand three months; strain it; and when clear, bottle it.

Where the pickle is called for to flavor other recipes, a little grated rind, spices, and a judicious touch of vinegar can be substituted.

[404]

LIME PICKLES, INDIAN RECEIPT

Three ounces red chilis, four ounces garlic, four ounces turmeric, four ounces mustard, three ounces green ginger.

Cut limes in quarters without separating at the bottom. Salt and keep them in the sun six to eight days. Then have the above ingredients rather coarsely pounded, mix well with vinegar and make a paste. Stuff the limes and keep in a jar for a month. Very hot, and much liked by old Anglo-Indians.

JAUNE-MANGE

Put two ounces of isinglass (*or 2 envelopes of unflavored gelatine*) into a pint of water, and boil it until it has dissolved. (*If using gelatine, dissolve it in cold water, pour the boiling ingredients on it, but do not cook.*) Then strain it into a porcelain skillet, and add to it half a pint of white wine; the grated peel and juice of two deep-colored oranges; half a pound of loaf sugar; and the yolks only of eight eggs that have been well beaten. Mix the whole thoroughly; place it on hot coals and simmer it, stirring all the time till it boils hard. Then take it off directly, strain it (*onto the gelatine*), and put it into moulds to congeal. (*Serves 8.*)

ORANGE PUDDING

Pare and cut fine six oranges, strew over them one cup sugar; beat the yolks of six eggs with four tablespoonfuls cornstarch, and strain it in one quart of boiling milk. Put the whole over the oranges while hot; beat the whites of the eggs with two tablespoonfuls sugar and pour over the pudding. Brown in the oven; serve cold. (*Serves 6–8.*)

ORANGE SALAD

Remove the peel and inner white skin from the oranges; cut them up across in (*vertical*) slices; lay them on a dish covered with powdered sugar, and pour over them sherry, Madeira or brandy. (*Let steep an hour or so. Serve with duck, or for dessert.*)

Part II: Recipes

"When lemons or oranges are used for the juice, chop down the peel, put them in small pots and tie them down for use."

Mrs. Ellet, *The Practical Housekeeper*, 1857

Peel freezes and will keep indefinitely.

ORANGE SHERBET (*A DRINK*)

Squeeze the juice from oranges, pour boiling water on the peel, and cover it closely; boil water and sugar to a syrup; skim it clear; when all are cold, mix the syrup, juice and peel infusion with as much water as may be necessary for a rich taste; strain it through a jelly bag, and set the vessel containing it on ice. Or make it in the same manner as lemonade, using one lemon to half a dozen oranges.

ORANGE WATER ICE

Take ten or twelve fine oranges, take off the peels and divide them in quarters, and after taking out the pips pound them with the grated rinds of two of the oranges; then put them into a coarse cloth and press out all the juice, and put it to a pint of water in which is dissolved half a pound of sugar. Freeze as directed for ice cream. (*Cut the oranges in half and take out the pulp carefully. Use the hulls for cups to serve the ice in.*)

ORANGE MARMALADE

Take three dozen Seville oranges, grate the rind of eight, peel the remainder, and throw the rinds in cold water; wash them well and boil until tender; divide the oranges, and scrape out all the pulp, but be careful not to have any of the seeds among it; cut the rinds in thin strips and add them to the pulp and that which is grated. Weigh it and to every pound of fruit add one and a quarter pounds of sugar. Boil it quickly for twenty minutes. (*Makes 8–12 cups of jam.*)

CANDIED ORANGE PEEL

Boil the rind of thick-skinned oranges in several waters, until all the bitterness is extracted. Then boil until tender in clarified sugar (*sugar heated slowly till it is liquid, and skimmed*); when perfectly clear and transparent it is done.

CAKES

Everybody knew how to bake a cake in the nineteenth century. Nearly halfway through the twentieth, baking a cake was my own first cooking lesson for the oven of my grandmother's coal range. The advent of the packaged mix has cut heavily into the practice of the art—but the process (p. 23) is hardly more complicated than adding the water and the milk and the eggs to the packages. I have left out most of the common everyday cakes, the ones we are too familiar with. Simnels (cakes made with fine white flour), marble cakes, pound and angel cakes, fruitcakes, jelly cakes are worth spending the extra time on. Some of these recipes are for enormous amounts, and can easily be halved or quartered. Rule of thumb: 2 cups of flour usually will make a 2-layer cake.

SPONGE CAKE

This recipe dates from the early eighteenth century. It appears in nearly the same form in many modern cookbooks.

Time, three-quarters of an hour to an hour; five eggs; half a pound of sifted loaf sugar; the weight of two eggs and a half (in their shells) of flour (*about 1 cup*); one lemon.

Take half a pound of sifted loaf sugar; break five eggs over it, and beat all together for full half an hour (*until very light, or beat the eggs separately and fold the whites in last*) with a steel fork. Previously take the weight of two eggs and a half in flour. After you have beaten the eggs and sugar together, grate into them the peel of a lemon, and add the juice, if approved. Stir the flour into this mixture and pour it into a tin. Put it instantly into a cool oven (*325°, about 1 hour, less for layered*). Flavor this cake with extract of lemon and vanilla.

"*To improve sponge cake: grate fresh orange peel over the loaf before icing.*"

Elisabeth S. Miller, *In the Kitchen*, 1875

GINGER POUND CAKE

More of a sponge cake than a pound cake.

Half a pound of butter; half a pound of sugar; six eggs; one pound and three quarters of flour; one tablespoonful of cinnamon; two tablespoonfuls of ginger, four teacups (*3 cups*) of molasses, one tablespoonful of saleratus. Stir in the butter and sugar to a cream, beat the eggs very light and add to it, after which put in the spice, molasses and flour, in rotation, stirring the mixture all the time. Beat the whole well, before adding the saleratus, and but little afterwards. Paper the pans (*or grease and flour*) before you put in the mixture, and bake in a very moderate (*at 325°*) oven. (*Makes 2 cakes.*)

CINNAMON CAKE

Take half a pound of dried flour, half a pound of fresh butter, half a pound of sifted sugar, the whites of eight eggs beaten to a snow froth, and sufficient pounded and sifted (*ground*) cinnamon to flavor the cake rather strongly, and to give it a pinkish color; mix all well together very lightly, put it in a buttered mold (*sponge cake pan*), and bake it in a rather quick oven (*375°*) for about half an hour.

A GOOD TIPSY CAKE

Take a stale sponge cake, of the size and form suitable to the custard dish; pierce it over with the point of a larding pin (*or the prongs of a cooking fork*), and by degrees pour over it as much sweet wine and brandy as the cake will absorb; use a ladle or spoon and take up the liquor that flows into the dish to pour over again; then stick it full of blanched almonds split into thin spikes, and pour round it a good rich custard (*p. 94*). Serve as soon as possible.

QUEEN CAKE

One pound butter; one pound of sugar; one pound of flour; ten eggs; one nutmeg grated; two tablespoonfuls of wine. Beat the butter and sugar until very light, to which add the wine and spice, with one fourth of the flour. Whisk the eggs until thick, and add half at a time, with the remainder of the flour. After beating all well together, let the batter remain a short time in a cool place. Then fill your pans rather more than half full, and bake in a quick oven. (*Makes 2 cakes.*)

A DELICATE CAKE

Time: about one hour. Beat seven ounces of butter to a cream, and stir a pound of powdered sugar and a pound of sifted flour into it; then add the whites of eight eggs, beaten to a strong froth, half a small nutmeg grated and a little lemon extract. Beat all well together, and put it into a (*large*) tin lined with buttered paper. Five or six ounces of pounded almonds may be added to this cake, according to your tastes.

MARBLE CAKE

Light: two cups sugar, one cup butter, one half cup sour cream, three and a half cups flour, whites of seven eggs, one teaspoon soda, two teaspoons cream tartar.

Dark: two cups brown sugar, one cup butter, one half cup sour cream, one cup molasses, three cups flour, one half teaspoon of soda, cinnamon, cloves and alspice to taste; yolks of seven eggs. (*Makes 2 large cakes.*)

GRANDMOTHER DON'S SWEET MILK CHOCOLATE CAKE

Half a cup of grated (*unsweetened*) chocolate; one egg yolk; half a cup of sweet milk. Cook until thick. When cool, add one cup of sugar; butter the size of an egg; half a cup of sweet milk; one and a half cups of flour; one level teaspoon of soda; pinch of baking powder; pinch of salt. Bake it in two layers.

CHOCOLATE CREAM CAKE

Powdered chocolate did not become available until after the turn of the century. Most of the cakes with "chocolate" in their names were frosted, not baked, with chocolate.

One and a half cups of sugar; half a cup of butter; two cups of flour; one cup of milk; the whites of four eggs; one teaspoonful of cream of tartar; half a teaspoonful of carbonate of soda. Mix, bake in one tin, and ice as follows: two cups of sugar; half a cup of water. Boil until clear and syrupy—about five minutes hard boiling. Beat well until light and hardening. When the cake is cold, pour this over. Let it harden, which it will quickly do, and then melt two ounces of unsweetened chocolate with a tiny piece of butter the size of a walnut, and pour a thin coating of this over the white icing. Leave a few hours to harden.

CREAM CAKE

Three eggs; one cup of flour; one cup of white sugar; one tablespoon of milk; two of melted butter; one teaspoon of cream-tartar; half a teaspoon of soda. Bake (*in layers*). When cold, cut open; put in cream.

CREAM: Take two eggs, one half a cup of white sugar, one pint of milk, one-third of a cup of flour; stir sugar, eggs, and flour together, and the whole in the boiling milk. Boil five minutes (*stirring constantly*); when cool, flavor with extracts.

"In making cakes, if you wish them to be pleasing to the eye as well as the palate, use double-refined sugar; although clean brown (raw) sugar makes an equally good cake.
Mrs. Crowen, *Every Lady's Cook Book*, 1854

ALICE VAN GRIETHUYSEN'S LAYER TOGA CAKE

Yolks 3 eggs	*1 teaspoon (heaping) soda*
1 cup sugar	*1 teaspoon (heaping) cinnamon*
½ cup butter	*1 teaspoon (heaping) cloves*
1 cup sour cream	*2½ cups flour*
½ cup molasses	

[410]

Bake at 350°.
Frosting: White of eggs with one cup sugar.

COFFEE CAKE

A cake made, naturally, with coffee.

One cupful of sugar, two cupfuls of flour, one-half cupful of butter, one-half cupful of molasses, one-half cupful of cold coffee, one cupful of seeded raisins, two eggs, one teaspoonful of cinnamon, one teaspoonful of mace, one teaspoonful of cloves, one teaspoonful of soda dissolved in the coffee. Mix together, adding the flour last. (*Bake in a 9-inch square pan.*)

ANOTHER: Two and a half pounds of flour, nine ounces of brown sugar, fourteen ounces of butter, one pint of molasses, one pint of strong coffee, two and a half pounds of stoned raisins, one pound of citron, two teaspoonfuls of mace, two of cinnamon and two of nutmeg, one teaspoonful of cloves and one of allspice, two teaspoonfuls of soda dissolved in a little of the coffee. Rub the butter and sugar together, add molasses, coffee and flour alternately, leaving a pint of flour in which to rub the fruit, then the soda, and lastly, the fruit. (*Makes 4–5 loaves.*)

BANANA CAKE

One cup butter, two cups sugar, one cup water or sweet milk, three eggs, four cups flour, three teaspoonfuls baking powder. Bake in layers.

FILLING: Whites of two eggs, one and one-half cups of sugar (*beat the whites stiff, then beat in the sugar gradually*). Spread this on the layers and cover with bananas cut thin, and frost.

COMMON CUP CAKE

The name refers to the measurements, not the form.

One cup of butter; two cups of sugar; four cups of flour; four eggs; one cup of sour milk; one teaspoon of saleratus in water; one teaspoon of essence of lemon; and half a nutmeg (*½ teaspoon*). Beat the mixture well, butter a couple of quart basins (*or 4 layer pans*) and divide the mixture between them. Bake it in a quick oven for three quarters of an hour.

BUTTERCUP CAKE

Three-quarters cup butter, one and one-half cups sugar, yolks of seven eggs, and one whole egg, beaten with the butter and sugar all at once; one-half cup milk, two cups flour, two teaspoons baking powder sifted with the flour four times. Add flour and milk alternately, a little at a time. Bake in gem pans (*muffin tins*), three-fourths full.

FROSTING: Unbeaten yolks of two eggs, one cup powdered sugar; stir in two teaspoons at a time; one-half teaspoon lemon juice. Frost the bottom of the buttercups, and put on the top of each a slice of candied apricot or orange.

POUND CAKE

The name refers to the way the ingredients are measured.

1 *lb. flour*	1 *glass brandy*
1 *lb.* (10) *eggs*	1 *nutmeg*
1 *lb. sugar*	1 *teaspoonful mace*
¾ *lb. butter*	

Cream half the flour with the butter, and add brandy and spice. Beat the yolks until light, add the sugar, then the beaten whites and the rest of the flour alternately. When this is thoroughly mixed, put all together and beat steadily for half an hour. (*Bake in 4 layers.*)

If properly made and baked this is a splendid cake.

COCOA-NUT POUND CAKE

One pound of sugar; half a pound of butter; one teacup of milk; one teaspoonful of saleratus; one tablespoon of essence of lemon and four eggs (*and enough flour to make a batter*). Beat the whole well together until it is light and creamy; then grate the white meat of a cocoa-nut and stir it lightly in (*to use prepared coconut, decrease the sugar to ¾ pound—1½ cups—and use about 1½ cups of coconut*); line a tin basin or square tin pan with well-buttered paper, and put in a quick (*375°*) oven, and cut it in square pieces when done. Icing is a great improvement.

PLAIN LOAF (*YEAST*) CAKE

Mix a pint of lukewarm milk with two quarts of sifted flour and two spoonfuls yeast (*2 packages; cake sometimes seems to have been considered a fancy form of bread and raised cakes are not uncommon*), and set it where it will rise quick. When perfectly light, work in, with the hand, four well-beaten eggs, a teaspoonful of salt, two of cinnamon, and a wineglassful of wine or brandy; work in a pound of sugar and three fourths of a pound of butter, rubbed to a froth (*creamed*), adding another quart of sifted flour, and beating the whole smartly with the hand, ten or fifteen minutes. Set it where it will rise again. When perfectly light, put it into cakepans well buttered, and let them stand fifteen or twenty minutes. Many add a pound and a half of raisins just before putting into the pans, if liked. (*Bake in a moderate oven about 45 minutes. Makes 3–4 loaves.*)

NUMBER CAKE

One teacupful of butter, two teacupsful of sugar, three teacupsful of flour, four eggs, nutmeg and brandy (*to flavor it; milk to make it a batter and 2 teaspoons baking powder*).

Cream the butter and sugar. Add the eggs one by one and beat until light. Add the flour alternately with brandy and enough milk to wet it. Bake in a 350° oven in a square pan until a cake tester (or broom straw) inserted in the center comes out clean.

TO MAKE A SIMNEL

One pound of flour, one quarter pound of butter, one quarter pound of sugar, one pound of currants, two ounces of candied lemon, one quarter ounce of carbonate of soda (*2 teaspoons*) mixed with an egg, and a little milk; to be put in a tin mould (*cake pan*) and baked until enough (*in a 350° oven*).

Part II: *Recipes*

A MADEIRA CAKE

The name refers to the island, not the wine.

Time, one hour. Beat the yolks of four eggs, and whisk the whites to a solid froth; then beat into the whites six ounces of sifted sugar, and when quite mixed, add the yolks, six ounces of flour, four ounces of liquified (*melted*) butter, warm but not hot, and the grated outer rind of one large lemon. Continually beat up as you add the ingredients; and for ten minutes after all are mixed; then pour into a buttered mould (*a small loaf pan; sprinkle the surface with sugar*) and bake in a moderate oven (*350°, for 1 hour*).

"Keep an apple in your cake box and it will keep cake fresh for a long time."

The Caloric Book of Recipes, 1907

JELLY CAKE

Make a cake with a little less flour than usual. Beat it well and have rather a thin batter. Lay your griddle in the oven of a stove and place on it a cake ring well buttered (*a spring-form pan serves well for this cake*); have the griddle well buttered and lay in two and a half tablespoons of the cake batter; bake about five minutes (*in a quick oven*) and turn; proceed thus until it is all baked, when cool, spread them with jelly or marmalade and put two together; fill a plate, and cut in triangular pieces. It is best when fresh.

JELLY FRUIT CAKE

Two cups of sugar, one cup of milk, three eggs, three cups of flour, two-thirds cup of butter, one teaspoon cream-tartar, one-half teaspoon soda. Take two pans (*rimmed baking sheets*) and put one-half the above mixture for the plain cake, and into the other (*half*) put one tablespoon molasses, one large cup chopped raisins, one-fourth pound sliced citron, one teaspoon cinnamon, one-half teaspoon allspice, one-half nutmeg, one-fourth pound flour (*pour it into the second pan*); bake each in a thin cake. Spread with jelly, lay one on the other, and roll; or bake each half in two thin round layers, spread jelly between the layers and stack them, alternating colors.

[414]

GENTLEMEN'S FAVORITE

½ cup of butter, 2 cups of sugar, beaten to a cream; 7 eggs, beaten separately; 2 tablespoons of water, 2 cups of flour, 2 teaspoons of baking powder. Bake in jelly-cake pans in a quick oven.

JELLY: 1 egg, a cup of sugar, 3 grated apples and 1 lemon. Stir until it boils and becomes thick. Let cool before putting on the cake. (*Fill and roll the cake while it is still warm; dust with powdered sugar.*)

NAPLES BISCUITS

Beat eight eggs; add to them one pound of flour, one pound of powdered (*granulated*) sugar, and one teaspoonful of essence of lemon. Bake in a quick oven (*in thin layers, in square pans*). When cold cut it in slices three-quarters of an inch thick; spread each with some jelly, and replace them, according to their original form; have ready an icing, and cover it, both the top and sides, and dry it in a warm room. (*Naples biscuits were popular, and the name was applied to several kinds of cake. One common recipe for Naples biscuits turns out Savoy cakes, or what we now call ladyfingers.*)

ICINGS

TO MAKE ICING FOR CAKES

Beat the white of two small eggs to a high froth; then add to them a quarter of a pound of white sugar ground fine like flour (*confectioners*); flavor with lemon extract or vanilla; beat it until it is light and very white, but not quite so stiff as kiss mixture (*meringue*); the longer it is beaten, the more firm it will become. No more sugar must be added to make it so. Beat the frosting until it may be spread smoothly on the cake.

ANOTHER: One cup of sugar, four tablespoonfuls of boiling water, the white of one egg, a quarter of a teaspoonful of cream of tartar. Boil the sugar and water together until the syrup will "string" when lifted out on a spoon.

Have ready the stiffly beaten white of the egg, and with it the cream of tartar. Pour the syrup slowly on the egg, beating all the time. Beat until it will go on the cake (*without running*). Flavor with a few drops of essence of vanilla (*or lemon juice or orange juice*), or whatever is preferred.

CHOCOLATE ICING (SIMPLE)

Mix together ¼ cake chocolate, 1 tablespoon corn-starch and ½ cup sweet milk; boil it two minutes (after it has fairly come to a boil), flavor with 1 teaspoonful vanilla, and then sweeten to taste with powdered sugar, taking care to make it sweet enough.

A SPLENDID ICING

(Takes lots of beating)

1 *lb. best XXXX* (powdered sugar)	3 *egg whites*
1 *ounce corn starch*	2 *teaspoons lemon*

Put sugar and cornstarch through a sieve, add egg whites and lemon juice. Beat until so firm that when spoon is withdrawn icing will not settle back but stay in shape.

TUTTI FRUTTI FROSTING

One-half teacup of water, three cups of sugar, whites of two eggs; boil the sugar and water together until very thick and waxy; beat the whites of eggs to a stiff froth and pour the sirup over them, beating all till cool. Then add one-half pound of almonds, chopped finely, one small half-teacup of large white raisins and a little citron, sliced thin. Very nice for a sponge cake.

PEAR-FIG FILLING

3 *lbs. pears, ground or chopped*   1 *lb. figs or raisins ground*
2 *lbs. granulated sugar*   *Juice of 1 lemon*

Cook slowly until thick. (*Makes enough for numerous cakes; may be canned or frozen to keep it.*)

SOFT MOLASSES GINGERBREAD

Mix with a pint of molasses, a teacup of melted butter, a pint of flour, two well-beaten eggs, and a spoonful of ginger. The peel of a fresh lemon cut in small strips is an improvement. Dissolve in a tumbler of milk and stir in two spoonfuls of saleratus; add flour to make it of the consistency of unbaked pound cake. Bake about half an hour in (*2 greased*) deep pans.

RAISIN, NUT, AND CITRON CAKES

The variety of cakes containing raisins, or currants, or citron, or nuts is enormous. The reason is simple: they last longer. In fact, any that contains wine or brandy actually improves with age. Some of the lighter ones were frosted, but it was not generally customary. See June (p. 182) for wedding cakes, which always had fruit in them, and November (p. 397) for more traditional fruitcakes and for hard and brandy sauces to go with them.

MRS. MADISON'S WHIM

Two pounds of flour; two pounds of sugar, two pounds of butter, beaten to a cream; twelve eggs, the yolks beaten with the sugar and the whites to a stiff froth; two wineglasses (*or a little more*) of rose-water or brandy, in which lemon rinds have been steeped; two nutmegs grated; and one teaspoonful of saleratus, dissolved in hot water. Beat it well together; then add two pounds of raisins stoned and chopped (*or 12 ounces of raisins, 4 of citron, and 4 of slivered almonds*). Bake in a quick oven. This cake is good for two months' keeping. (*Makes several cakes.*)

SIX MONTHS CAKE

4 eggs	1 teaspoonful soda
1 lb. of raisins	Spice (cinnamon, nutmeg,
2 cups sugar	cloves, allspice, ginger) to
1 cup molasses	taste
1½ cups butter	Flour to make a batter
1 cup milk	

A nice loaf of cake which can be kept for six months or longer.

"*If raisins and currants are rolled in flour before putting into a cake, they will not sink to the bottom.*"

The Caloric Book of Recipes, 1907

HARRISON CAKE

Two cups molasses, heated, with one half cup butter and lard and one cup sugar; one teaspoon cloves; two teaspoons saleratus; one cup sour cream, if you have it; if not, one cup sour milk and a little more butter; flour to thicken as gingerbread; raisins. (*Makes several cakes.*)

DATE CAKE

One cup sugar, half cup butter, three-fourths cup sour milk; one teaspoon soda, one teaspoon all kinds spices, half pound dates, flour enough to make stiff.

GINGER PLUM CAKE

Take one pound and a half of raisins and cut them in two. Wash and dry half a pound of currants. Sift into a pan two pounds of flour. Put into another pan a pound of brown sugar, and cut up in it a pound of fresh butter. Stir the butter and sugar to a cream, and add to it two tablespoons of the best ginger; one tablespoon of powdered cloves; and one of cinnamon. Then beat six eggs very light, and add them gradually to the butter and sugar, in turn with the flour and a quart of molasses. Lastly, stir in a teaspoon of pearlash (*baking soda*) dissolved in a little vinegar, and add by degrees the fruit; which must be well dredged in flour. Stir all very hard; put the mixture in a buttered pan, and bake it in a moderate oven. (*Makes several cakes.*)

RICH PLUM CAKE

Mix two quarts of flour with one pound of sifted sugar; three pounds of currants, one half pound of raisins stoned and chopped; one quarter ounce of mace and cloves, a grated nutmeg; the peel of a lemon cut fine (*grated*); melt two pounds of butter in a pint and a quarter of cream, but not hot; the white and yolks of twelve eggs beaten apart; and half a pint (*2 packages plus 1 cup warm water*) of good yeast. Beat them together a full hour. Put in plenty of citron and lemon. Then butter your pans (*pour in the batter, let it rise an hour or two*) and bake.

MOLASSES PIE

This is the genuine New England dainty, dear to the hearts of children. Mix one-half a pint of the best molasses with a tablespoon of flour, and add the juice of a large lemon, and the rind and pulp chopped fine. Bake with an under and upper crust.

CHESS PIE

4 eggs; 2 cups sugar; 1 cup cream; ⅔ cup butter; two tablespoons flour. Flavor with nutmeg or lemon and bake in a rich crust. This makes two pies.

COOKIES

"Of cakes and biscuits composed chiefly of sugar, butter, flour and eggs, the varieties are innumerable, and though these rich dainties are banished from the diet of the dyspeptic or the abstemious, as unwholesome and unnecessary, they may be usually eaten and enjoyed with perfect safety, when carefully prepared, and taken in moderation, especially the lighter biscuits of sugar and egg. No one but a school-boy would eat a whole slice of rich plum cake; and what cannot a school-boy digest?"

The Cuisine, by An Eminent French Caterer, 1872

COOKIES

One cup of cream; one half cup of butter; one and one half cups sugar; one teaspoon pearlash (*baking soda*); two eggs, (*flour until the dough is*) wet as soft as you can roll, and bake quick. Caraway seed if you please. (*Makes about 50 cookies.*)

TO MAKE SMALL SEED CAKES (*AN EIGHTEENTH-CENTURY RECIPE*)

Take one pound of sugar and as much of flour, a pound of butter washed in rose water (*add ½ teaspoon rosewater to butter*), drean out the rose water. Four eggs and a few drops of oyl of sinnamont and a good handful of carraway seeds; bruse them a little. Mix all well together, then drop them in lumps as large as nutmegs (*half the size of walnuts*) upon buttered paper, bake them in an oven as for makroons (*300°, for about 30 minutes*), then dry them on a dish until crisp. (*Makes about 100 cookies.*)

SEED BISCUITS

Mix one pound of powdered sugar with three pounds of flour, and one ounce of caraway seeds; rub into this one pound of butter, then knead it into a paste with three quarters of a pint of boiling milk; roll the paste very thin, cut it into biscuits, prick it, and bake in a slow oven ten minutes. (*Makes about 275.*)

WINE CAKES

Mix eight ounces of flour with half a pound of finely-powdered sugar, beat four ounces of butter with two tablespoons of wine (*port, sherry, or Madeira*), make the flour and sugar into a paste with it, and four eggs, beaten light; add carroway seeds, and roll the paste as thin as paper; cut the cakes with the top of a tumbler, brush the tops over with beaten white of an egg, grate sugar over and bake ten or twelve minutes in a quick oven. Take from the tins when cold. (*Makes about 50.*)

SCOTCH CAKES

Take two pounds of flour; mix with it one pound of powdered sugar, and half a pound of caraway seeds; melt half a pound of butter and with it mix the sugar to a paste; work it well; add to it a teaspoon of essence of lemon; roll it out to about half an inch thickness; cut it in square cakes; lay them on buttered paper; crimp the edges of each cake with your finger; stick them with a fork, and bake in a quick oven. They should be of a pale brown when done. (*Makes about 150.*)

SCOTCH SHORT-BREAD

Chop 2 lbs flour (*or rice flour*) and 1 lb best butter together, having made the latter quite soft by setting it near the fire. Knead in ½ lb powdered sugar, roll into a sheet half an inch thick, and cut in shapes with a cake-cutter. Bake upon buttered paper in a shallow tin (*a rimmed baking sheet, at 400°*) until crisp and of a delicate yellowish brown.

SAND TARTS

One pound flour, ten ounces butter, one pound sugar, and two eggs, leaving out the white of one. Cream the butter and sugar together, add eggs and flour, and roll out very thin; cut in diamonds, brush over with the white of egg, sprinkle with cinnamon and sugar, and lay on each pieces of blanched almond. (*Bake 10–12 minutes at 400°. Makes 100.*)

CITRON CAKES

Time: fifteen to twenty minutes.

Beat half a pound of butter to a cream, take six new-laid eggs, beat the whites to stiff froth, and the yolks with half a pound of white powdered sugar and rather more than half a pound of sifted flour. Beat these well together, add a glass of brandy, and a quarter of a pound of citron cut in thin slips. Bake it in small heart-shaped tins, or in any form you please, rubbing the tin over with melted butter, and bake in a quick oven. (*Makes 25–30.*)

KRINGLES

Beat the yolks of eight eggs with the whites of two; add to them four ounces of butter just warmed (*room temperature*), and with it work one pound of flour and four ounces of sugar, rolled fine to a stiff paste; sprinkle flour over the cake board and roll them half an inch thick, then cut them in small cakes; bake in a quick oven. (*Makes 75.*)

TRIFLES

One egg to a tablespoonful of sugar, and as much flour as will make a stiff dough; roll it very thin, then cut them in small round or square cakes; drop two or three at a time in boiling lard. When they rise to the surface and turn over, they are done. Take them out with a skimmer, and lay them on a sieve to drain; heap jelly or jam on the centre of each when served. (*Makes 10–12.*)

SAVOY CAKES, OR LADIES' FINGERS

Beat well and separately, the yolks and whites of eight eggs; mix them, and stir in, gradually, a pound of powdered white sugar; after beating the whole well together eight or ten minutes, add the grated rind of a fresh lemon and half the juice, a pound of sifted flour, and two spoonfuls of coriander seed (*optional*). Drop this mixture by the spoonful on buttered baking plates, several inches apart; sift white sugar over them, and bake immediately in a quick oven. (*Makes about 75.*)

OR: With a paper funnel or a thin pipe made for the purpose, lay it out upon the papers into biscuits three inches in length and the thickness of your little finger; sift sugar over, shaking off all that does not adhere to them; place them upon baking sheets, and bake in rather a warm oven of a brownish yellow color; when done and cold, detach them from the paper by wetting it at the back, place them a short time to dry, and they are ready for use.

JUMBLES

These came in many forms, were as well known as sugar cookies are now.

Sift three pounds of flour into a large pan. Cut up a pound and a half of butter into a pound of powdered sugar, and stir them to a cream. Beat five eggs till very light, and then pour them all at once into a pan of flour; next add the butter and sugar, with a large tablespoon of mixed mace and cinnamon, two grated nutmegs (*2 teaspoonfuls*), and a teaspoonful of essence of lemon or a wineglass of rose water. When all the ingredients are in, stir the mixture very hard with a broad knife. Having floured your hands and spread some flour on a pasteboard, make the dough into long rolls (all of equal size), and form them into rings by joining the two ends very nicely. Lay them on buttered tins, and bake them in a quick oven for five or ten minutes. Grate sugar over them.

CHOCOLATE CAKES

One pound of flour; one pound of sugar; one pound of butter; eight eggs; two tablespoons of brandy; a pinch of salt.

Mix the above ingredients well together with a wooden spoon, putting the butter (melted before the fire) in last. Spread a baking sheet with butter, put over it the mixture half an inch thick, and bake it. Cut the cake into oblong pieces, and glaze them thickly with (*melted milk*) chocolate. (*Makes 24–30.*)

VERY RICH COOKIES

Half a pound of butter
One pint and a half of sifted
    flour
One pint of light-brown sugar
One gill of thick sour cream
Two teaspoonfuls of caraway
    seed

One teaspoonful of soda, dis-
    solved in a teaspoonful of
    boiling water
One egg

Soften the butter, stir in the sugar, cream, egg, soda, caraway seeds and flour; roll, cut, lay in a pan, and bake in a quick oven. (*Makes 40.*)

OLY KOEKS, AN OLD DUTCH RECEIPT FROM KINGSTON, NEW YORK

Two pounds of flour
Half a pound of butter
Six eggs

Some mace and yeast
One pint of milk

(*Mix, and let it rise for a couple of hours in a warm place.*) Take up the dough with a spoon (*shape it, put on greased cookie sheets*), two raisins in each. (*Bake in a 375° oven. Makes 150.*)

SUPERIOR GINGER BREAD

1¼ lbs butter
1½ lbs sugar
9 eggs, yolks and whites beaten
    separately
1 wineglass wine

1 wineglass brandy
2 tablespoons ginger and
1 nutmeg, grated, mixed with
2 lbs flour

Mix as for cake in the order given, and spread very thin with a knife on tin sheets. Bake, and cut into squares while warm. This will keep six months. (*Makes 100–150.*)

AUNT ROSE'S SUGAR COOKIES

2 *cups sugar*
1 *cup butter* (*or lard*)
1 *cup sour cream*

1 *teaspoon saleratus*
1 *or* 2 *eggs*
(*flour enough to roll*)

(*Makes about 50.*)

HERMITS

One cup sugar, one half cup butter, one egg, one half cup sour milk, one tablespoon all kinds spices, one half teaspoon soda, one cup chopped raisins; mix soft with flour to roll. Bake in a quick oven. (*Makes 40.*)

CURD CAKES

Beat four eggs light, and stir them into a quart of boiling milk; sweeten it very sweet, and let it cool; then stir in one large coffeecup of flour; one teaspoon of essence of lemon, and two more well-beaten eggs, beat it well; make some sweet butter hot in a thick-bottomed fry-pan, drop the mixture in, in small cakes, some little distance apart; fry them to a fine brown, then take them out on a sieve to drain. (*Makes about 80.*)

HONEY CAKES

Three pounds and a half of flour; one pound and a half of honey; half a pound of sugar; half a pound of butter; half a nutmeg (*½ teaspoon*), and a spoonful of ginger; one spoonful of saleratus. Roll it thin, and cut it in small cakes. Bake in a hot oven. (*Makes 300.*)

LOVE CAKES

To a pound of powdered sugar, add six well-beaten eggs, put as much flour as will make a stiff paste; flavor with essence of lemon. Roll it about half an inch thick, and with a tin cutter the size of the top of a wineglass, cut it in small cakes; strew some sugar and flour over a baking tin, and lay the cakes on it; bake them in a quick oven for ten or twelve minutes; when cold, ice the tops with plain white frosting (*p. 415*), and set them in a warm place to dry; finish by putting a bit of jelly, the size of a large nutmeg, in the center of each. The edge may be finished with ornamental frosting. (*Makes 50–60.*)

KISSES

Beat the whites of four small eggs to a high firm froth; then stir into it half a pound of ground or finely-powdered sugar; flavor it with essence of lemon or rose. Continue to beat until very light; this being done, lay the mixture in heaps on letter paper in the size and shape of half an egg, and at least the distance of an inch apart. Then place the paper containing them on a piece of wood, half an inch thick, and put them into a hot oven; watch them and as soon as they begin to look yellowish, take them out, take the paper from the wood to a table, and let them cool for three or four minutes. Then slip a thin-bladed knife under one very carefully, turn it into your left hand, then take another from the paper in the same manner, and join the two together by the sides that were next to the paper; then lay the kiss thus made on a dish; so continue until all is used; handle them gently while making. These are delicious eating, the outside being hard and the inside a rich creamy moisture, and they present a beautiful appearance. By placing the paper on a baking tin instead of on the board, the bottom will be dried as well as the top, and thereby finish the kisses without joining the two together; those made in this manner are not as delicious as the others; they however look very well—the upper surface may be made smoother by dipping a spoon handle in water and passing carefully over it before baking.

CREAM PUFFS

These are cookies made, not filled, with cream.

Two ounces of finely pounded sweet almonds, the same of clarified butter and sifted sugar, two spoonfuls of flour, the yolks of two eggs, half a pint of cream, and a very little orange jelly; beat all well together; butter the (*muffin*) pans, fill them only half full, bake for half an hour in a slow oven. (*Makes 10–12.*)

CREAM PUFFS

The more usual ones.

One cupful of hot water, one-half cupful of butter, one cupful of flour, three eggs.

Put the water and butter into a small pan and let it boil, then stir in one cupful of flour. Take from the fire, and when nearly cold, stir in three eggs, one at a time, without beating. Drop tablespoonfuls of the dough into a large dripping pan (*or baking sheet*). Have the pan hot, but do not grease it. (*Bake in a hot oven.*) The quantity will make one dozen puffs.

CREAM: Scald one pint of milk in a double boiler. Add three table-spoonfuls of cornstarch dissolved in a little cold milk, then stir in four table-spoonfuls of sugar and two (*well-beaten*) eggs. Flavor with vanilla (or lemon or orange or chocolate). Cut the puffs open and fill with the cream (*or, if you have a pastry bag, fill with the cream, insert the nozzle into the puffs and squirt them full*).

MACAROONS

Time: fifteen or twenty minutes. Blanch eight ounces of fine almonds, and pound them in a mortar to a smooth paste with two tablespoonfuls of rose or orange-flower water; whisk up the whites of eight eggs to a solid froth, and add to it one pound of finely-sifted sugar, then beat in by degrees the almond paste, (*a little nutmeg, and 1 teaspoon of arrowroot*) till thoroughly mixed. Have ready confectioner's wafer-paper (*waxed paper*), and drop the mixture onto it in small rounds. Bake in a moderate oven till lightly colored.

CANDY

ALMOND TAFFY

Boil a syrup of a pound of sugar to half a pint of water to caramel height (*soft-ball stage*), throwing in an ounce of blanched almonds split into strips, and an ounce of butter. When the candy hardens at once in (*cold*) water (*hard ball*) turn it out on a buttered tin, and cut up in thin squares.

MOLASSES CANDY

Take two quarts of West India molasses, one pound of brown sugar and the juice of two large lemons; mix and boil the molasses and sugar three hours over a moderate fire (when done it will cease to boil and be crisp when cold). While boiling, stir it frequently. After boiling two hours and a half, stir in the lemon juice. It will be improved by grating in the yellow part of the rind so finely as not to be visible when boiled. If the lemon is put in too soon, all the taste will be boiled out. When it is quite done, butter a square tin pan and turn the mixture in to cool. If you prefer the candy with ground nuts (*as a brittle*) roast a quart of them, shell and blanch them, and stir them in gradually a few minutes before you take it from the fire. Almonds may be blanched, cut in pieces, and stirred in raw, just when the sugar and molasses have done boiling.

If you wish to make it yellow, take some out of the tin pan while it is yet warm and pull it out into a thick string, between the (*well-buttered*) thumb and forefinger of both hands. Extend your arms widely as you pull the candy backwards and forwards. By repeating this a long time, it will gradually become of a yellow color and of a spongy consistency. When it is quite yellow, roll it into sticks, twist two sticks together, and cut them off smoothly at both ends. Or you may varigate it by twisting together a stick that is quite yellow and one that remains brown.

ANOTHER: Put a pint of common molasses over a slow fire; let it boil; stir it to prevent its running over the top of the kettle. When it has boiled for some time, try it by taking some in a saucer; when cold, if it is brittle and hard, it is done. Flavor with essence of lemon, and stir shelled pea-nuts (ground-nuts), or almonds, into it, and pour it into a buttered basin, or square tin pans, to cool. (*When cold, break it into pieces.*)

CHOCOLATE CARAMELS

Two cups of sugar　　　　　　　*Two ounces of unsweetened*
Half a cup of molasses　　　　　　　*chocolate*
Half a cup of milk　　　　　　　*One teaspoonful of essence of*
One ounce of butter　　　　　　　*vanilla*

Boil all these ingredients together for fifteen minutes, stirring constantly. Then try a few drops in cold water. If it hardens, the caramels are done, and may be taken from the fire; if not, continue boiling for a short time longer.

When cooked sufficiently, remove from the fire and beat steadily until beginning to cool. When almost cold, add the vanilla and pour out into a buttered tin to the depth of half an inch. Before the caramels are quite hard, mark into squares with a knife.

VANILLA CARAMELS

Boil all together two cups of sugar, one cup of milk and a quarter of a teaspoonful of cream of tartar for twenty minutes. Add one teaspoonful of essence of vanilla after removing from the fire. Turn them out into a tin very lightly buttered. Before they harden, mark into neat squares with a knife.

MAPLE CREAM CHOCOLATES

Half a pound of maple sugar, quarter of a pound of Baker's chocolate, half a gill of hot water. Crack the sugar in small bits, put it in a saucepan with the water on the range, but do not let it boil until thoroughly dissolved, when it must boil quite fast for five minutes; while the sugar is boiling, crack the chocolate and put it in a bowl over a boiling teakettle; when the sugar is boiled, take from the fire, put it in a rather cool plate, and beat until so stiff that it may be made into balls; flour the hands very slightly. Take a bit about the size of a common marble, roll it perfectly round in the palm of the hand, and proceed in this way, putting them in a buttered plate; when hard, drop them one at a time in the chocolate; have a fork in each hand, turn the little balls until covered with the chocolate; then place them on buttered paper to cool and harden. (*This may be made with maple syrup instead of sugar, but it should be pure maple syrup, not adulterated with corn syrup.*)

BLACK WALNUT CANDY

Four pounds of brown sugar; one pound of butter; one quart of kernels.

Put the sugar in a saucepan with half a pint of boiling water. Boil hard for twenty minutes; add the butter and boil for five minutes, then add the nuts and stir until it boils; take it off for a minute, and pour into buttered saucers (*to make shapes like pralines*).

PEANUT CANDY

One cup molasses, one half cup butter, two cups sugar, one fourth cup vinegar, one quart raw peanuts blanched. Boil slowly twenty minutes, stirring constantly. Test by dropping into cold water; when it becomes hard and brittle remove at once. Pour into shallow buttered pans; when partly cool, mark in squares and break when cold.

TO MAKE PEPPERMINT DROPS

Two pounds of loaf sugar grated fine, four whites of eggs beaten stiff, four drops of the oil of peppermint; drop them on paper, and dry them in a warm oven.

FRUIT CANDIED

When fruit is preserved, take it from the syrup, dry it in the oven, then dip it in sugar boiled to candy weight and dry it again.

FILLED DATES

Get one pound best dates and remove the stone from each one. Blanch one-quarter pound almonds. Put an almond inside of each date. Roll the date in sugar and serve.

CHRISTMAS DISHES

SUCCOTASH FOR FOREFATHERS' DAY

In New England, December 22 was Forefathers' Day, and the traditional dish was an elaborate succotash.

Soak about a quart of any dried white bean and a half that quantity of dried white corn overnight. In the morning, take six or eight pounds of corned beef and one pound of salt pork, fat and lean; put them to simmer in a large amount of water for about three hours. Then take out some of the pot liquor and pour it over the beans and corn separately, and put them on to cook. Add a four to six pound chicken to the corned beef. One hour later add one large white turnip and eight or ten potatoes to the meat and cook them until tender. Season with pepper and, if necessary, salt.

Mash the beans to a pulp, then add to them the corn with enough pot liquor to make it a thick soupy texture. Serve the beef and chicken in one dish, the potatoes and turnips in another and the succotash in a third. This keeps several days, and it is better re-heated. (*Serves 10–12.*)

A CHRISTMAS GOOSE PIE

These pies are always made with a standing crust. Put into a sauce-pan one pound of butter cut up and a pint and a half of water; stir it while it is melting, and let it come to a boil. Then skim off whatever milk or impurity may rise to the top. Have ready four pounds of flour sifted into a pan. Make a hole in it, and pour in the melted butter while hot. Mix it with a spoon to a stiff paste, adding the beaten yolks of three or four eggs, and then knead it very well with your hands, on the pasteboard, keeping it dredged with flour till it ceases to be sticky. Then set away to cool.

Split a large goose, and a fowl, down the back, loosen the flesh all over with a sharp knife and take out all the bones. Parboil a smoked tongue; peel it and cut off the root. Mix together a powdered nutmeg, a quarter of an ounce of powdered mace, a teaspoonful of pepper and a teaspoonful of salt, and season with them the fowl and goose.

Roll out the paste near an inch thick, and divide it into three pieces. Cut out two of them of an oval form for the top and bottom; and the other into a long straight piece for the sides or walls of the pie. (*A tin form for a standing pie, available in specialty stores, makes this whole thing much simpler.*) Brush the paste all over with beaten white of egg, and when you have the crust properly fixed (the bottom must be a little larger, to turn up around the edges), so as to be baked standing alone without a dish. Put in first, the goose, then the fowl, and then the tongue (*one inside the other*). Fill up what space is left with pieces of pigeons, or of partridge, quails, or any game that is convenient. You may add some bits of ham or some force-meat balls. Lastly, cover the other ingredients with half a pound of butter, and put on the top crust. The lid must be placed not quite at the top edge of the wall, but an inch and a half below it. Close it very well, and ornament the sides and top with festoons and leaves cut out of paste. Glaze the whole with beaten yolk of egg, and bind the pie round with a double fold of white paper. Set in a regular oven and bake four hours.

This is one way of making the celebrated goose pies that it is customary in England to send as gifts at Christmas. They may be carefully covered up from the air, they will be good for two or three weeks; the standing crust assisting to preserve them.

PRACTICAL HOUSEWIFE'S CHRISTMAS HAM

All hams have been pickled, but it is not easy to get those that have been smoked in a smokehouse rather than processed by the meat packer. If you can manage, the difference in flavor is hard to believe. Hams from the supermarket do not need soaking—but try this recipe boiled in beer.

Soak the ham, be the weight whatever it may, half the usual time in water; remove, wash well with cold water, place in a pan large enough and deep enough to contain it, cover with beer or good ale, and let it remain the required time. Boil as usual until the skin can be readily removed; then place the ham in a tin or earthen dish and cover with a common flour and water paste or surround it with batter (*p. 73*). Bake in a moderately heated oven until done, remove the paste or batter (*serve the batter separately like Yorkshire pudding*). Cover with bread raspings (*toasted crumbs*) and serve hot.

Where the vegetables are plentiful, it is desirable to boil ham with three heads of celery, a couple of turnips, half a dozen small onions and a large bunch of sweet marjoram, thyme, etc., put in after the pot has been skimmed.

RICH PLUM PUDDING

One pound of raisins
Half a pound of sultanas or
  currants
Half a pound of sugar
Half a pound of flour
Half a pound of bread crumbs
The juice of one lemon and
  peel grated
One orange peel grated
A pinch of salt
Three-fourths of a pound of suet

One-fourth of a pound of mixed
  candied peel
A small nutmeg grated
A teaspoonful of ground cinnamon
A teaspoonful of pudding spice
  (allspice)
A teaspoon of ginger
Six bitter almonds pounded (or
  1 teaspoon of almond extract)

Mix (the day before the pudding is boiled) with six eggs, and a glass of brandy or curaçao and sufficient Marsala or good homemade wine to make it rather moist, and allow the ingredients to swell well. Boil eight hours if made in one (*covered tin*) mould, six hours if divided into two moulds (*with the water ¾ of the way up the sides; try English stout for the liquor*).

A BOILED PLUM PUDDING

Grate the crumb of a 12¢ loaf of bread (*4 cups*), and boil a quart of rich milk with a small bunch of peach leaves in it (*or add almond extract later*), then strain it and set it out to cool. Pick, wash and dry a pound of currants, and stone and cut in half a pound of raisins; strew over them three large tablespoons of flour. Roll fine a pound of brown sugar, and mince as fine as possible three-quarters of a pound of beef suet. Prepare two beaten (*grated*) nutmegs and a large tablespoonful of powdered mace and cinnamon (*mixed*); also the grated rind and juice of two large lemons or oranges. Beat ten eggs very light, and when it is cold, stir them gradually into the milk, alternately with the suet and bread. Add by degrees the sugar, fruit and spice, with a large glass of brandy and one of white wine. Mix the whole very well and stir it hard. Then put it into a thick cloth that has been scalded and floured; leave room for it to swell, and tie it very well. Put the pudding into a large pot of boiling water, and boil steadily for six hours, replenishing occasionally from a boiling kettle. Turn the pudding frequently in the pot. Prepare half a pound of citron cut in slips and half a pound of almonds blanched and split in half. Stick the almonds and citron all over the outside as soon as you take it out of the cloth. Send it to table hot and eat it with wine sauce.

PLUM PUDDING SAUCE: Boil in a quarter of a pint of water for twenty minutes the thin rind of half a lemon, and a quarter of a Seville orange as thin as possible, with two ounces of sugar; strain the liquor into a quarter of a pint of rich melted butter and stir it over the fire, and half a glass each of brandy, rum and sherry, and a tablespoon of curaçao may be added or not; simmer the whole, mixing it well for five minutes; then serve immediately.

ANOTHER: Take the yolks of three eggs, add a gill of cream and three tablespoonfuls of white sugar, set it over the fire, stir it until it is thick, then add a glass of brandy to it, stirring it all the time.

See also pp. 96, 99, 398.

BEVERAGES

WHIP SYLLABUB

Take one quart of thick cream, one gill of wine, the juice of two lemons, half a pound of loaf-sugar; pour it into a broad pan, then beat it well, and as the froth rises to the top, take it off and put it in a glass.

SYLLABUB

In a pitcher holding one and a half pints, dissolve three-fourths of a gill of sugar in half a gill of wine; take it to the cow and milk until the froth reaches the top of the pitcher.

PUNCH

Pour three pints of boiling water over one and a quarter pounds of loaf sugar; add to this one pint of lemon juice, the juice of six oranges, three pints of rum and one pint of brandy. When ready to serve, put a block of ice in a large punch bowl, pour the punch over it and then add a quart of champagne.

MULLED WINE

One pint of wine; one pint of water; four eggs. Mix the wine and water together, and set it on the fire to boil. Beat the eggs well, and as soon as the wine boils, stir them in rapidly; add a few grains of allspice; and sweeten to your taste. This is sometimes poured over toast, or toast served with it. It is considered very nourishing.

WHITE WINE FILLIP

Take one bottle of sherry or Madeira, or champagne, or any other good white wine, a gill of Noyeau or Maraschino, the juice of half a lemon; add to it a quart of calf's foot jelly (*p. 128*) well sweetened and boiling hot, and serve immediately.

[434]

PORT WINE NEGUS

Take one quart of new port wine, of a fruity character, one tablespoon of spirit of cloves, one teacupful of sugar, one lemon sliced, half a nutmeg grated, pour over these two quarts of boiling water.

NEW YEAR'S EGG NOG

Allow one egg and one tablespoon of sugar to each person. A good proportion is 32 eggs, half a pint of brandy, half a pint of sherry, two and a half quarts of cream, whipped, 32 tablespoonfuls of powdered sugar, a little nutmeg; beat the yolks of the eggs and sugar to a light cream. Add the brandy and sherry drop by drop so as not to curdle. Add nutmeg if desired. Beat the cream very stiff and very cold and add it to the yolks. Beat the whites of the eggs very stiff and blend the last thing of all.

⌈ 16 ⌉

Staples

This is a catch-all section for those recipes with no season, the basic sauces and stocks, the vinegars, those home brews that formed the nineteenth-century "ordinary" and the recipes for soap and candles without which it was impossible to conduct a proper nineteenth-century household.

BROWN SAUCE AND VARIATIONS

1 *pint hot stock* (p. 353)
2 *tablespoons minced onion*
2 *tablespoons butter*
2 *heaping tablespoons flour*
½ *teaspoon salt*

½ *saltspoon pepper*
1 *tablespoon lemon juice*
caramel (see below) *enough to color*

Mince the onion and fry it in the butter five minutes. Be careful not to burn it. When the butter is brown, add the dry flour and stir well. Add the hot stock, a little at a time, and stir rapidly as it thickens, until perfectly smooth. Add the salt and pepper, using more if necessary. Simmer five minutes and strain. (*Basic sauces can be canned or frozen until they are needed.*)

PIQUANTE SAUCE (for beef): One cup brown sauce, one tablespoon each of chopped pickles and capers.

POIVRADE: One cup brown sauce, one teaspoon mixed herbs, thyme, parsley, bay-leaf and cloves. Simmer ten minutes, add two tablespoons of claret, and strain. (*Season with 1 dozen crushed peppercorns a few minutes before straining. If you happen to have been peeling mushrooms, add the skins during the cooking.*)

ROBERT: One cup brown sauce, one teaspoon sugar, one teaspoon made mustard, and one tablespoon of vinegar. (*See also p. 341.*)

OLIVE (FOR ROAST DUCK): Soak twelve (ripe) olives in hot water enough to cover them thirty minutes, to extract the salt. Pare them round and round, in one piece, which should retain the original shape after the stone's removed. Add to one cup brown sauce and simmer ten minutes.

CUMBERLAND: One cup brown sauce, one teaspoon made mustard, two tablespoons of currant jelly and two tablespoons wine.

FLEMISH: Cut one cupful of the red part of carrot into quarter-inch dice, and cook in boiling salted water till tender. Make one cup of brown sauce, add the cooked carrot, half a tablespoonful of chopped parsley, one tablespoon each of chopped pickle and grated horseradish.

À L'ITALIENNE: Fry one tablespoon of chopped shallots in one tablespoon of salad oil till yellow. Add one bay leaf, a sprig of parsley, a tablespoon of chopped mushrooms, fry five minutes. Remove the bay leaf, add two tablespoons of flour, mix well, and add one cup of stock. When smooth, add two tablespoons of mushroom catsup (*p. 250*) and one teaspoon of essence of anchovy (*or 1 pounded anchovy*). Serve without straining.

CARAMEL FOR COLORING

Heat sugar over the fire, stirring frequently, until it melts and turns brown; turn the heat down and keep cooking until it is almost black. Then, very carefully because the sugar is very hot, add half the quantity of boiling water. Stir until it is well mixed, then let cool slightly and bottle for use. All the sweetness will have burned out of the sugar and it can be used as a neutral-flavored coloring.

BROWN COLORING FOR MADE DISHES

Take four ounces of sugar beat fine; put into an iron frying pan, or earthen pipkin; set it over a clear fire and when the sugar is melted, it will be frosty; put it higher from the fire till it is a fine brown; keep it stirring all the time, fill the pan up with red wine, take care it doesn't boil over, add a little salt and lemon; put a little cloves and mace, a shallot or two, boil it gently for ten minutes; pour it in a bason till it is cold, then bottle it for use.

[437]

WHITE STOCK AND SAUCE

Cut and chop a knuckle of veal, weighing about four pounds, into dice; also half a pound of lean bacon; butter the bottom of a large stewpan, with a quarter of a pound of butter, add two onions, a small carrot, a turnip, three cloves, half a blade of mace, a bouquet of a bay-leaf, a sprig of thyme, and six of parsley, add a gill of water, place over a sharp fire, stirring round occasionally, until the bottom of the stewpan is covered with whitish glaze, when fill up with three quarts of water, add a good teaspoonful of salt, and let simmer at a corner of the fire an hour and a half, keeping well skimmed, when pass it through a hair sieve into a basin. In another stewpan put a quarter of a pound of butter, with which mix six ounces of flour, stirring over the fire about three minutes, take off, keep stirring until partly cold, when add the stock all at once, continuing stirring and boiling for a quarter of an hour; add half a pint of boiling milk, stir a few minutes longer, add a little chopped mushrooms if handy, pass through a hair sieve (*or blend*) into a basin, until required for use, stirring it round occasionally, until cold.

See p. 131 for another stock.

GLAZE

is stock reduced to less than one-quarter. It should have a gluey consistency and is useful for browning meats.

WHITE SAUCE

Make a white roux of equal amounts of flour and clarified butter, cooking it no more than 5 minutes, or not long enough to color it. Stir into it enough milk, cream, or white stock to make it the consistency you want—but it should not be thick. Then continue as required by your sauce recipe.

TO BROWN FLOUR

Spread upon a tin plate, set upon the stove, or in a *very* hot oven, and stir continually after it begins to color, until it is browned all through. Keep it always on hand. Make it at odd minutes, and put away in a glass jar, covered closely. Shake up every few days to keep it light and prevent lumping. (*Use to thicken brown gravies and soups. You will need a little more than white flour, since heating it destroys some of its thickening properties.*)

VELOUTÉ

Melt one ounce of good butter in a saucepan, adding two tablespoons of flour, and stir well, not letting it get brown. Moisten with a pint and a half of good veal or chicken stock, the stronger the better. Throw in a garnished bouquet (*parsley, thyme, 1 bay leaf, and 2 cloves, tied around a stalk of celery— or, if dried, tied up in muslin bag*), half a cupful of mushroom catsup (*p. 250*), if at hand, six whole peppers, half a pinch of salt, and a very little nutmeg. Boil for twenty minutes, stirring continually with a wooden spoon; then remove to the side of the fire, skim thoroughly, and let it continue simmering slowly for one hour. Then rub through a fine sieve (*or remove the bouquet and peppers and blend*). This sauce will make the foundation for any kind of good white sauce.

SAUCE ESPAGNOLE, ONE GALLON

Stew in a saucepan two ounces of fat, two carrots, one onion, one sprig of thyme, one bay-leaf, six whole peppercorns, three cloves, and, if handy, a ham bone cut into pieces. Add two sprigs of celery and half a bunch of parsley roots (*not generally available now unless you grow your own; substitute parsley and a little more celery*); cook for fifteen minutes. This is the *mirepoix*.

Mix one pint of *mirepoix* with two ounces of good fat (chicken is preferable). Mix in four ounces of flour and moisten with one gallon of white broth (*stock*). Stir well, and then add, if handy, some baked veal and ham bones. Boil for three hours, and then remove the fat very carefully; rub the sauce through a fine sieve (*or blend everything but the bones*).

MADEIRA SAUCE

Add one small glassful of mushroom catsup to one pint of good Espagnole sauce; also a small glassful of Madeira wine, a bouquet (*parsley, thyme, bay leaf, 2 cloves, and a stalk of celery tied up together or in a muslin bag*) and a scant teaspoonful of pepper. Remove the fat carefully and cook thirty minutes, leaving the sauce in a rather liquid state; then strain and use. (*Add mushrooms, if you like.*)

CHAMPAGNE SAUCE

Place two cloves, six whole peppers, one bay-leaf, half a tablespoonful of powdered sugar in a saucepan with a good glassful of champagne; place it on the fire and reduce for five minutes. Then moisten with three-quarters of a pint of Espagnole sauce, and cook for fifteen minutes longer; strain through a Chinese (*cone-shaped*) strainer and serve.

See Index for other sauces.

ROSEWATER

If you don't happen to have a still, rose brandy (p. 195), or rose butter, or store-bought rose extract can be substituted. Rosewater can occasionally be found in pharmacies. If none of that is possible, substitute vanilla.

On a dry day, gather fragrant, full-blown roses; pick off the leaves; to each peck put a quart of water; put the whole in a cold still, and set the still on a moderate fire, as the slower they are distilled, the better will be the rosewater. Bottle the water immediately after it is distilled.

OIL MAYONNAISE

One egg yolk, oil and one tablespoonful of lemon juice. Beat the yolk, add the oil a few drops at a time, beating continuously (*or dribble it through the hole in the lid of a blender*). The longer it is beaten, the thicker it gets. Thin with lemon juice. Add oil till the right quantity is obtained. Everything must be cold.

MUSTARD SAUCE

Two teaspoons of dry mustard, one teaspoon of butter, one teaspoon of salt, one teaspoon of sugar, one teaspoon of flour, two tablespoons of vinegar, or less of lemon juice. Mix thoroughly; add half a cup of boiling water, and stir over the fire until it thickens, like a custard.

FRENCH MUSTARD

To mustard ground, add tarragon vinegar and oil, with salt and garlic. Tarragon vinegar is made by covering the leaves with vinegar and steeping them in it (*for about two weeks, then strain the leaves out*).

SOY SAUCE

This is American, not Chinese, soy—hence no soy beans.
One pound of salt, two pounds of sugar fried half an hour over a slow fire, then add three pints of boiling water, half a pint of essence of anchovy, a dozen cloves and some sweet herbs. Boil till the salt dissolves, then strain and bottle it.

IMITATION WORCESTERSHIRE SAUCE

Real Worcestershire contains tamarinds.

3 teaspoonfuls cayenne pepper	3 shallots minced fine
2 tablespoonfuls walnut or tomato catsup (strained through muslin)	3 anchovies chopped into bits
	1 quart of vinegar
	½ teaspoonful powdered cloves

Mix and rub through a sieve (*or blend*). Put in a stone jar, set in a pot of boiling water, and heat until the liquid is so hot you cannot bear your finger in it. Strain, and let it stand in the jar, closely covered, two days, then bottle for use.

SCOTCH SAUCE

Take fifteen anchovies, chop them fine, and steep them in vinegar for a week, keeping the vessel closely covered. Then put them in a pint of claret or port wine. Scrape fine a large stick of horseradish, and chop two onions, a handful of parsley, a teaspoonful of the leaves of lemon-thyme, and two large peach-leaves. Add a nutmeg, six or eight blades of mace (*3 or 4 teaspoonfuls*), nine cloves and a teaspoonful of black pepper, all slightly pounded in a mortar. Put all these ingredients into a silver or block tin saucepan, or into an earthen pipkin, and add a few grains of cochineal to color it (*red*). Pour in a large half-pint of the best vinegar, and simmer it slowly till the bones of the anchovy are entirely dissolved.

Strain the liquor through a sieve (*or blend*), and when quite cold, put it away for use in small bottles, the corks dipped in melted rosin (*or paraffin*). Fill each bottle quite full, as it will keep the better for leaving no vacancy.

This sauce will give a fine flavor to melted butter.

CAMP KETCHUP

It was the custom, when traveling, to carry your own seasonings with you. Hence, perhaps, the name.

Take two quarts of strong old beer and one of white wine, add one-quarter pound of anchovies, three ounces of shalots peeled, one-half ounce of mace, the same of nutmeg; three large races (*roots*) of ginger cut in slices; put all together over a moderate fire until one-third wasted. The next day bottle it with the spice and the shalots. It will keep for many years.

A GOOD STORE SAUCE

2 *tablespoonfuls horse-radish* (grated)
1 *tablespoonful allspice*
A grated nutmeg
3 *large pickled onions* (p. 331) *minced fine*
2 *dozen whole black peppers*

A pinch of cayenne
1 *tablespoonful salt*
1 *tablespoonful white sugar*
1 *quart vinegar from walnut or butternut pickle* (p. 194)

Mix all the spices well together; crush in a stone jar with a billet of wood; pour the vinegar upon these, and let it stand two weeks. Put on in a porcelain kettle and heat to boiling; strain and set aside until next day to cool and settle. Bottle and cork very tightly. It is an excellent seasoning for any kind of gravy, sauce, or stew.

As the name implies, this can be stored for a long time.

CURRY POWDER

6 oz. of pale-colored turmeric	5 oz. black pepper
13 oz. coriander seed	3 oz. cummin seed
2 oz. fenugreek seed (or carda-	1 oz. cayenne pepper
mon seed)	

Ground fine and well mixed.
Curry powder is best fresh. Mix it only as you need it.

ESSENCE OF CAYENNE

Put half an ounce of cayenne pepper into half a pint of brandy or wine; let it steep for a fortnight, and then pour off the clear liquor. It is extremely convenient for the extempore seasoning.

ESSENCE OF GINGER

Three ounces of fresh grated Ginger, and an ounce (*1 lemon*) of thin cut lemon peel into a quart of Brandy or Proof Spirit; let it stand for ten days shaking it up every day.

It is nice for flavoring many kinds of sweetmeats; and a little mixed with water serves all the purposes of ginger tea.

TO MAKE ENGLISH SHERRY

Put to thirty pounds of good moist (*brown*) sugar ten gallons of water. Boil it half an hour, skimming it well, and then let it stand till quite cold. Add eight quarts of ale from the ale vat while fermenting, stir it well together, let it remain in the tub till the next day; then put it into the barrel with six pounds of raisins, one quart of brandy, one pound of brown sugar-candy, and two ounces of isinglass. Let it remain three weeks before the barrel is closed, and it must stand twelve months before it is put into bottles. (*See pp. 37–41 for the details of wine making.*)

GINGER POP

Five and one-half gallons water, one-quarter of a pound of ginger-root bruised, one-half ounce tartaric acid, two and a half pounds of white sugar, one gill yeast, one teaspoonful lemon oil, the whites of three eggs well-beaten.

Boil the root thirty minutes in one gallon water, strain off and put the oil in while the water is hot (*sour salt or the rind of 2 lemons can be used as a substitute*), then add the other materials (*the yeast last, when the liquid is lukewarm*). Make at night, and in the morning, skim and bottle, keeping back the sediment.

GINGER BEER

To three gallons of water put three pounds of sugar, and four ounces of race ginger (*ginger root*), washed in many waters to cleanse it; boil them together for one hour, and strain it through a sieve; when lukewarm, put it in a cask, with three lemons cut in slices, and two gills of beer yeast; shake it well, and stop the cask very tight; let it stand a week to ferment, and if not clear enough to bottle, it must remain until it becomes so (*but not more than 2 weeks*); it will be fit to drink in ten days after bottling. (*Siphon it into soda bottles. Caps and a capper can be obtained in some hardware stores, and in wine supply stores.*)

COMMON BEER

Allow at the rate of two gallons of water to a handful of hops, a little fresh spruce or sweet fern, and a quart of bran; boil it two or three hours; strain it through a sieve; stir in, while hot, a teacup of molasses to each gallon of liquor; let it stand till lukewarm; turn it into a clean barrel; add a pint of good yeast to the barrel; shake it well together, and it may be used the next day (*but would be much better at the end of the week*).

SPRUCE BEER

Put into a large kettle, ten gallons of water, a quarter of a pound of hops and a teacup of ginger. Boil them together till all of the hops sink to the bottom, then dip out a bucket full of the liquor and stir into it six quarts of molasses, and three ounces and a half of the essence of spruce. When all is dissolved, mix it with the liquor in the kettle; strain it through a hair sieve into a cask; and stir well into it half a pint of good strong yeast. Let it ferment a day or two; then bung the cask, and you may bottle it the next day. It will be fit to use in a week.

For the essence of spruce, you may substitute two pounds of the outer sprigs of the spruce fir, boiled ten minutes in the liquor.

VINEGAR

Sour beer may be converted into good vinegar by putting into it a pint of molasses and water (*per gallon*), and in two or three days after, half a pint of vinegar; in ten days it will be first-rate.

GARLICK VINEGAR

Garlick is ready for this purpose from Midsummer to Michael-mass. Peel and chop two ounces of Garlick, pour on them a quart of white-wine Vinegar, stop the jar close, and let it steep ten days, shaking it well every day; then pour off the clear liquor into small bottles.

PEPPER VINEGAR

6 *pods red peppers broken up*	2 *tablespoonfuls white sugar*
3 *dozen black pepper-corns*	1 *quart of best vinegar*

Scald the vinegar in which the sugar has been dissolved; pour over the pepper, put into a jar, and steep a fortnight. Strain and bottle.

This is eaten with boiled fish and raw oysters, and is useful in the preparation of salads.

TO MAKE SUGAR, OR HONEY VINEGAR

Dissolve one pint of sugar with seven of water, moderately warm; put it in a cask; stir in a pint of yeast to every eight gallons; stop it close, and keep it in a warm place till sufficiently sour; or to a quart of clear honey, add eight of warm water, mixing it well. After the acetous fermentation, a white vinegar will be formed, in many respects better than common vinegar. (*A little vine-*

gar added at the beginning, to head the fermentation in the right direction, helps.)

To strengthen vinegar, freeze it for a few hours and remove the ice.

FINE HOMEMADE CANDLES

Take ten ounces of fresh mutton fat or suet, one-quarter pound of bleached white wax, one quarter ounce of camphor and two ounces of alum. Cut or break up these articles and then melt them together, skimming them well. (*Make sure the alum is thoroughly dissolved—undissolved alum will form unburnable lumps in the candle. It will form a sediment on the bottom of the pan. The more wax, the less alum is necessary.*) Have ready the wicks, fix them in moulds and pour in the melted liquid, proceeding as in making common mould candles. (*Make sure the wicks are centered by keeping a light tension on them while the candles harden.*) Candles made in this manner are hard and durable and will not run, burning with a clear light. (*Makes 6 candles.*)

Paraffin or candle stubs can be used for the wax, though beeswax is better. Half mutton suet and half beeswax is better still—and an all-beeswax candle is pure luxury. Obtain the suet by rendering the fat cut from lamb chops, etc., or beg it from your butcher, camphor from the drugstore, beeswax from the hardware store or your friendly beekeeper.

YELLOW HARD SOAP

Pour four gallons boiling water on three pounds unslaked lime. Let it stand until perfectly clear, then drain off. Put in six pounds clean fat. Boil until it begins to harden—about two hours—stirring most of the time. While boiling, thin with two gallons of cold water which you have poured on the alkaline mixture after draining off the four gallons. This must also settle clear before it is drawn off. Add it when there is danger of boiling over. Try the thickness by cooling a little on a plate. Put in a handful of salt just before taking from the fire. Wet a tub to prevent sticking; turn in the soap and let it stand until solid. Cut into bars; put on a board and let it dry. This will make about forty pounds of nice soap; much better for washing (*clothes*) than yellow turpentine soap.

"Soap should be cut with a wire or twine, in pieces that will make a long square. When first brought in, keep out of the air two or three

weeks; for if it dry quick it will crack, and when wet, break. Put it on a shelf, leaving a space between, and let it grow hard gradually."
Temperance Cook Book, compiled by a Lady, 1841

TO SWEETEN AND CLARIFY DRIPPINGS

A 1-pound coffee can will hold 2 pounds of grease, drippings from roasts, bacon fat, chicken grease, hamburger fryings—and any other scrap of leftover grease. For frying, or before making soap, mix ½ teaspoon of soda with 1 quart of water, add the drippings, bring to a boil, and skim. Strain the fat through muslin wrung out in hot water, into coffee cans, or let the whole cool until the grease forms a solid cake, then remove it from the pan and scrape the debris from the bottom of the cake. Reheat the grease to evaporate the last of the water from it (water in it will cause it to mold). Do it carefully, stirring constantly. Drops of water exploding into steam can cause the hot grease to splash violently if it is not kept in motion.

WHITE HARD SOAP (*FOR WASHING PEOPLE*)

Put six pounds of clean grease into a dish-pan and melt it. Put a can of Babbitt's (*lye, 1 pound*) into a (*tin*) lard-pail; add to it a quart of cold water, and stir it with a stick or wooden spoon until it is dissolved. It will get hot when the water is added; let it stand until it cools (*to about 80°*). Remove the melted grease from the fire and pour in the lye slowly, stirring all the time. Add two tablespoonfuls of ammonia. Stir the mixture constantly for twenty to thirty minutes, or until the soap begins to set. (*It will be thick as honey. Do not stir longer or it will separate. Pour into cardboard boxes lined with brown paper.*)

Let it stand until perfectly hard; then cut it into square cakes. This makes a very good, white hard soap that will float on water. It is very little trouble to make and will be found quite an economy in a household. Six pounds of grease makes eight and a half pounds of soap.

BAYBERRY SOAP

Dissolve two pounds four ounces of white potash in five quarts of water; mix with it ten pounds of bayberry tallow (*see p. 466*); boil all over a slow fire till it turns to soap; add a teacup of cold water; boil it ten minutes longer;

turn it into tin moulds for a week or ten days to dry, first scenting it with any essential oil that may be preferred. It may be used in three or four weeks, but is best a year old; is excellent for shaving, for chapped hands, and for eruption on the face.

WINDSOR SOAP (*A HAND SOAP*)

To make the celebrated Windsor soap, slice the best white bar soap as thin as possible, and melt it over a slow fire; then take it off when lukewarm; add sufficient oil of caraway to scent it, or any other fragrant oil. Pour it in moulds, and let it remain five or six days in a dry place.

SOFT SOAP

This was used for dish washing instead of detergent and was dipped out of its jar as needed.

10 *lbs grease*	8 *gallons hot water*
6 *lbs washing soda*	

Let it stand for several days until the grease is eaten up. If too thick, add more water. Stir every day. If wood-ashes are used instead of soda, boil the mixture.

Soft soap can also be made by boiling hard soap or soap scraps with water until they are liquid, then adding a little washing soda.

BOILED SUDS

Properly boiled suds are far better than soap for washing (*clothes*), particularly if a washing machine be employed. The suds should be prepared in the following manner: Shred in an earthenware jar the best yellow soap cut in very fine shavings, and pour boiling water to the quantity required. One pound of soap is plenty for one gallon of water. Add to this quantity one-half a pound of the best Scotch (*washing*) soda, and set a jar (covered) on the stove at the back of the kitchen range till the soap is quite dissolved. If this be done on Saturday evening, the soap will be a smooth jelly fit for use on Monday morning.

STARCH

Frozen potatoes will yield more starch, or flour, than fresh ones; it makes nice cakes. Take a coarse tin grater, full of coarse holes, and grate a bushel or two; wash the pulp through a sieve over a tub and pour off the water (*after the starch has settled*). Repeat this, stirring it well when a new water is added, until the water looks clear. It is then fit to use as (*clothes*) starch or (*potato*) flour, after it is dried carefully.

To MAKE STARCH: Allow half a pint of cold water and a quart of boiling water to every two tablespoonfuls of starch. Put the starch into a tolerably large basin; pour over it the cold water, and stir the mixture well with a wooden spoon until it is perfectly free from lumps and quite smooth. Then take the basin to the fire, and whilst the water is actually *boiling* in the kettle, pour it over the starch, stirring it the whole time. If made properly in this manner, the starch will require no further boiling. Take it from the fire, strain it into a clean basin, cover it up to prevent a skin from forming on the top, and when sufficiently cool, that the hand may be borne in it, starch the things. Many persons, to give a shiny and smooth appearance to the linen when ironed, stir round two or three times in the starch a piece of wax candle, which also prevents the iron from sticking.

PART III

The Care of
House and Body

[17]

Remedies

Most old cookbooks included home remedies, of which a surprising number began "Take an ounce of opium. . . ." Below are some—untested, unrecommended—that look as though they still make sense, and some that are just interesting.

Warts: wet them with tobacco juice and rub them with chalk. *Another:* rub them with fresh beef every day until they begin to disappear. This last is simple and effectual.

It is said that half a cranberry bound on a corn, will eradicate it in several nights.

Apply common mud to a bee sting and the pain will disappear.

For a sting: bind on the place a thick plaster of common salt, or saleratus (*baking soda*) moistened—it will soon extract the venom.

Tobacco, wet with spirits, bound on a fresh cut or bruise, will save much pain and soreness.

A styptic, which will stop the bleeding of the largest vessels: Scrape fine two drachms (*¼ ounce*) of castile soap, and dissolve it in two ounces of brandy, or common spirits. Mix well with it one drachm (*⅛ ounce*) of potash, and keep it in a close phial. When applied, warm it, and dip pledgets (*swabs*) of lint.

Bleeding at the chin: A person often cuts himself in shaving; and perhaps just at the moment when he is in a hurry to make his toilet the blood sometimes flows obstinately. Remedy:—a cobweb placed in the cut will speedily staunch the blood; or, if the arms are raised aloft, and kept in that position for a moment or two, the blood will cease to flow.

To stop the flow of blood: Bind the cut with cobwebs and brown sugar, pressed on like lint. Or, if you cannot procure these, with the fine dust of tea.

Scrape raw potatoes and apply to a burn. It will give immediate relief.

Cure for burns: One-third part linseed oil, two-thirds lime water. Shake up well; apply and wrap in soft linen. Unless you can procure this, keep the part covered with wood-soot mixed to a soft paste with lard, or, if you have not these, with common molasses.

For the Heart-ache or the Heart-burn: For the one, keep a conscience void of offense (says a lady, 'the remedy cannot apply where the wife has a drunken husband.'); for the other chew magnesia of chalk, or drink a tumbler of cold milk.

Powder for hiccough: Take a swallow or two of vinegar, or a long draught of cold water. Or, put as much dill seed, finely powdered, as will lie on a shilling (*or a quarter*) into two spoonfuls of syrup of black cherries, and take it presently.

A cure for hiccoughs is to take a long breath and hold it.

Salt and sugar mixed together will sometimes stop coughing.

See Elderberry sirup (p. 257) for a tight cough.

A cold on the lungs can be relieved by dipping a flannel cloth in boiling water, then wring it out and sprinkle with turpentine and lay it on the chest as quickly as possible.

Hot lemonade taken freely on retiring will often break up a cold and help a sore throat.

See Raspberry shrub (p. 205) for fevers.

Blackberry syrup: Take two quarts of ripe blackberries, one pound of loaf sugar, half an ounce of nutmeg, half an ounce of cinnamon, and a quarter of an ounce of cloves, the same of alspice. Boil together for a short time and when cold add one pint of brandy. Strain and bottle. Dose, from a teaspoon to a wine-glass full three or four times a day. This is by some considered a specific in summer complaints.

German cure for consumption: Take a pound of pure honey, and let it boil gently in a stewpan; then, having washed, scraped clean, and finely grated with a sharp grater, two large sticks of fresh horseradish, stir it into the honey as much as you possibly can. It must remain in a boiling state about five minutes, but stirred so as not to burn; after which put it into small earthen pots, or a jar, and keep it covered for use. Two or three tablespoonfuls a day, or more, according to the strength of the patient, and some time persisted in, is said to perform wonders. It is also serviceable in all coughs where the lungs are greatly affected.

Get one shilling's worth of each, liquorice root, lungword and iceland moss, steep a sufficient quantity of each equal parts to make a strong tea, sweeten with rock candy. Take as much as the stomack will barre three or four or five times a day. This will usually remove severe coughs.

Buttermilk poltis: Put it in a bacin on the stove, let it get hot, stir in meal, not thick, spread it on a cloth, lay it on your side and your stomack and throte. It will draw out the eritasion and inflation. Keep it worm, keep your on, keepe worm, heate your feete.

A poltis is good, throw some ashes in some water, settle some of the top to make the poltis, wheate bran is the best to put in, have the ly not strong but slippery, keep your body worm.

The two receipts above must have worked. They were sent in 1850, by Susannah Madison to her granddaughter Eliza, who, although she wasn't very "tuff," managed to live until she was 91.

Boiled flaxseed juice flavored with lemon is excellent to stop coughing.

A gargle of salt water is a good remedy for sore throat.

A teaspoon of flour of sulphur dissolved in hot milk and slowly sipped is very good for sore throat.

A few drops of oil of lavender poured in a glass of hot water and set in a sick room will purify it greatly.

See February (pp. 86–88) for dishes for invalids.

To relieve asthma: soak blotting or tissue paper in *strong* saltpetre water. Dry, and burn at night in your bed-room. I *know* this to be an excellent prescription.

Soda water: take one third of a teaspoon of carbonate of soda, a half that quantity of tartaric acid, loaf sugar to make it pleasant. Dissolve the soda first, and drink while it foams.

Simple mixture for all bowel complaints: take rhubarb, one ounce; saleratus, one teaspoon; pour on them a pint of boiling water. When cold, two teaspoonfuls of essence of peppermint. Dose according to age and urgency of disease; one table-spoon every quarter, half, or one or two hours.

For the dysentery: Bruise one ounce of rhubarb, two drachms (¼ *ounce*) of English saffron, two of cardomom seed, and a large nutmeg; add to them a pint of the best French brandy; set the bottle, loosely corked, in a pot of cold water; heat the water over a moderate fire quite hot, and keep it hot twelve hours, without boiling. It is then fit for use. Take, on going to bed, one spoonful—a teaspoonful for a child.

Raw eggs beaten up and swallowed are an excellent remedy for dysentery. Use one to three a day. Sugar may be added if desired.

For the sick headache: Every other night, for a while, soak the feet on going to bed, in hot water half an hour, adding hot water occasionally during that time, so as to have the water hotter at the time of taking them out than putting them in, to prevent the blood rushing back to the head. Retiring immediately, drink a tumbler of hot ginger tea, and apply a stone jug of hot water to the feet. Some recommend the application of a hops poultice to the head.

Try laying thin slices of potatoes across the forehead when you have a headache.

Applying a cold wet cloth to the back of the neck will aid sleep if loss of sleep is occasioned by too much blood in the head.

Celery, eaten abundantly, is good for neuralgia.

A creak or pains in the back, side, shoulder, etc.: Spread a plaster of hard brown soap on a cloth, wet it over with volatile ointment, and sprinkle it well with cayenne pepper, and it will relieve entirely in a day or two.

Witch hazel extract is a valuable article to keep in the house for sprains and bruises.

The whites of eggs beaten up with salt to the consistency of frosting and applied to a sprain will give you great relief; renew it as it becomes dry.

Volatile liniment: Take and beat one ounce of spirits of ammonia or hartshorn, and as much sweet olive oil until it is thick and looks like cream. This is good for an external application in all swellings or inflammations.

Canker in the mouth: Take half a teaspoon of gunpowder, and dissolve in two spoonfuls of clear water. Roll up a clean cloth like a pipestem; lay one end in the dissolved gunpowder, and the other in a dry saucer; in a few hours the same will contain a liquid as pure as the purest water; sweeten this with loaf sugar or honey and with a soft swab touch the parts affected several times a day, and it very soon destroys the canker.

Healing salve: Take equal parts of rosin, beeswax and sweet oil; melt and mix, stirring until cool. This is a good healing salve for all common sores.

Chapped lips and hands: Take equal parts of beeswax or rosin, mutton tallow or sweet oil, enough to make a soap or ointment; you may add a little rosewater. This occasionally applied will relieve soon.

Honey paste for the hands: Take half a pound of strained honey, half a pound of white wax and half a pound of fresh lard. Cut up the wax very small, put it into a porcelain-lined saucepan, and set it over the fire till it is quite melted. Then add alternately the honey and the lard; stirring them all well together. Let them boil moderately, till they become a thick paste, about the consistency of lip salve. Then remove the saucepan from the fire and stir into the mixture some rose perfume, or carnation, or violet—no other. Transfer the paste, while warm, to gallipots (*little ointment jars*) with covers, and paste a slip of white paper around each.

For keeping the hands white and soft, and preventing them chapping, there is nothing superior to this paste; rubbing on a little of it, after dipping your hands lightly in water.

Soft pomatum: Soak half a pound of fresh lard and a quarter of a pound of beef marrow in water for two or three days; squeezing and pressing it every day and changing the water. Afterwards, drain off the water, and put the lard and marrow into a sieve to dry. Then transfer to a jar, and set the jar into a pot of boiling water. When the mixture is melted, put it into a basin, and beat it with two spoonfuls of brandy. Then drain off the brandy, perfume the pomatum by mixing it with any scented essence that you please, and tie it up in a gallipots. (*Use as hand cream.*)

[18]

Household Hints

To clean mahogany furniture: Take of beeswax two ounces, scrape it fine, put it in a pot or jar, and pour over it enough of the spirits of turpentine to cover it; let it stand a little while (*until the beeswax dissolves*), and it will be ready for use. Apply with a flannel rag, then polish with another flannel rag. Do not put a wax polish on furniture normally polished with oil, and vice versa.

Hot vinegar takes out any stain that may be in mahogany.

To brighten furniture and remove spots; two tablespoons of sweet oil (olive or boiled linseed), one tablespoon of vinegar, half a tablespoonful of turpentine. Use with a bit of flannel. (*Polish immediately with a dry piece of flannel. These two furniture polishes, used year after year, gave the patina so valued by antique collectors.*)

To wash polished furniture; rub with a sponge dipped in warm beer, and dry quickly with a towel.

A hot shovel or a warming pan of coals, held over varnished furniture, will take out white spots. The place should be rubbed while warm, with flannel.

Floor polish: Four ounces of beeswax, 1 quart of turpentine, a piece of resin the size of a hickory-nut. Cut up the beeswax and pound the resin. Melt them together. Take them from the fire and stir in a quart of turpentine. Rub very little on the floor with a piece of flannel; then polish with a dry flannel and a brush.

To separate beeswax from the comb, tie it up in a linen or woolen bag with a pebble or two to keep it from floating; place it in a kettle of cold water and place over the fire; as the wax melts it rises to the surface, while all impurities remain in the bag.

Marble fireplaces should not be washed with suds; it will in time destroy the polish. After the dust is wiped off, rub the spots with a nice oiled cloth, then rub dry with a soft rag.

To remove stains from marble, make a mortar of unslaked lime and very strong lye. Cover the spot thickly with it and leave it on for six weeks. Wash it off perfectly clean, and rub with a brush dipped in a lather of soap and water. Polish with a smooth, hard brush.

To clean stone hearths: To preserve the color of freestone hearths, wash them with water without any soap, rub on them while damp, pulverized freestone, let it remain till dry, and then rub it off. If stained, rub them hard with a piece of freestone (*shale, slate, bluestone, etc.*). To have your hearths look dark, rub them with pure soft soap, or dilute it with water.

To clean carpets, sprinkle the carpet with (*damp*) tea-leaves; sweep well; then use soap and soft warm water for the grease and dirt spots. This freshens up old carpets marvellously. Rub the wet spots dry with a clean cloth.

To clean straw matting, wash with a cloth dipped in clean salt and water; then wipe dry at once. This prevents it from turning yellow.

Straw matting will last longer if given a coat of varnish.

If grease is spilt on the (*wooden*) kitchen floor, pour cold water on it immediately. This will harden it and prevent it from soaking in the floor. Scrape with a knife.

Moisten grease spots in cold water and soda before scrubbing, as it lightens the task.

To clean paint: tea leaves may be saved from the table for a few days and when sufficient are collected, steep, not boil, them for half an hour in a tin pan. Strain the water off through a sieve, and use this tea to wash all varnished paint. It removes spots and gives a fresher, newer appearance than when soap and water are used.

Try soft tissue paper (*or crumpled newspaper*) for cleaning or polishing your mirror.

Dissolve a little washing soda in the water when you wash windows if the glass is very dim with smoke or dirt. Do not let it run on the sash, but wash each pane with old flannel. Polish with chamois skin, or newspapers rubbed soft between the hands.

If a little kerosene is added to the water in which you wash your windows, the effect will be much brighter.

When your kerosene lamps give a bad light, or smoke, or smell, boil the burners half an hour with a tablespoon of soda in the water. Never fill your lamps to the brim, as the oil rises and causes a disagreeable odor.

The best way of cleaning silver is to put a teaspoonful of ammonia into hot soap suds; wash quickly with a soft brush, rinse in clean hot water and dry with a linen towel, then rub with a chamois skin. Do this every day and no powder or cleaning will be necessary, and the silver will last longer besides.

A gold chain may be made to look very bright if dipped in a cup containing one part ammonia and three parts (*soapy*) water.

A piece of camphor kept with your silver will prevent it from tarnishing.

The best thing for cleaning tinware is common soda; dampen a cloth, dip it in soda, rub the tin briskly, after which, wipe dry.

New tins should stand near the fire with boiling water in them, in which has been dissolved a spoonful of soda, for half an hour; then be scoured inside with soft soap; afterward rinsed with hot water. Keep them clean by rubbing with sifted wood ashes.

Copper utensils should be cleaned with brickdust and flannel.

The only thing for scouring copper kettles is salt and vinegar.

Ox olive (*oxylic*) acid for cleaning brass, mix with a little water and rub on.

For cleaning badly tarnished brass: equal parts of flour, salt, and vinegar.

Clean wine and beer bottles by putting in small shot (*or pebbles*) and water and shaking vigorously.

Soak your hair brushes in ammoniated water. This will prevent the bristles from coming out and hardens (*and cleans*) them.

Soak your new brooms in hot strong salt water before using them; it toughens the bristles and the broom will last longer.

Boiling soda water poured down the sink every morning prevents the drain from being clogged with grease.

Baking or washing soda in the rinse water will sweeten sour jars (*or thermos jugs, or refrigerators*).

Save your soap suds for gardens and plants, or to harden cellars and yards when sandy. (*Phosphates, the ingredient in soaps and in modern detergents that makes them dangerous polluting agents in water—where they encourage the growth of microscopic life, thereby using up the free oxygen in water, drowning fish and killing plant life—also make soap suds and detergent suds almost the perfect fertilizers on land. Microscopic life around plant roots swarm with joy, stimulating organic-soil life, and the plants themselves pick up necessary minerals. As long as the concentration is not great enough to soak through to the underground water table, soap suds, coffee grounds, tea leaves, ashes, and the like can be used with abandon.*)

To temper earthen ware when new and before used for baking, put it in cold water to cover and heat it gradually until the water boils. It is less likely to crack. (*Let it remain in until the water has cooled. The same method will work for glass, for bottles which you intend to use for canning, enabling them to stand higher temperatures without breaking. It will not work for crystal.*)

A bit of soap rubbed on the hinges of doors will prevent their creaking.

If a drawer sticks, rub a little fresh lard (*or soap*) on it.

Glass bottles can be cut off below the neck and used for jelly glasses. Tie a cord around the bottle, wet with turpentine or coal oil, and set fire to it. (*Works better if the bottles are very cold. Polish the rough edges with emery paper.*)

Clean your irons on emery paper; it is excellent.

Try a pinch of salt in the water in which you put cut flowers and they will last longer.

When using valuable vases for table decorations, fill one-fourth full of sand to prevent being knocked over.

To prevent onion and cabbage odors when cooking these vegetables, or fish, set a tin cup of vinegar on the stove and let it boil.

Burn an orange peel on the stove for disagreeable odors—the effect is most pleasant.

Save plastic bags. You get them wrapped around food anyway, and they will not decompose, so it is virtuous to use them until they are in shreds. Use them for refrigerator storage instead of aluminum foil or plastic wrap; use them for the freezer; use them to keep home-made bread fresh longer; use them to keep crackers and crumbs in; do not *use them to put garbage in, since it keeps the garbage from returning to the soil. Do not buy them.*

Waterproof composite for boots and shoes: Boiled (*linseed*) oil, half a pint; oil of turpentine, black rosin, and bees' wax, of each one ounce and a half. Melt the wax and rosin, then stir in the oil, remove the pot from the fire, and when it has cooled a little, add the turpentine.

Ironware cement: Stir into the whites of eggs beaten to a froth, enough powdered quick lime to make a consistent paste, and then stir in iron file dust to make a thick paste. Fill the cracks of iron-ware with this cement, and do not use it for some weeks.

Non-returnable soda or beer bottles can be reused if they do not have screw caps. Put up tomato juice or sauces in them, recap using a capping machine available at all wine supply shops and occasionally at antique or junk shops. Bottles made for screw caps will not keep the contents airtight once the original cap is opened, but can be used for vinegars and some catsups.

An excellent stucco which will adhere to woodwork: Take a bushel of the best stone-lime, a pound of yellow oker, and a quarter of a pound of brown umber, all in fine powder. Mix them with a sufficient quantity of hot (but not boiling) water, to a proper thickness; and lay it on with a white-washer's brush, which should be new. If the wall be quite smooth, one or two coats will do; but each must be dry before the next be put on. The month of March is the best season for doing this.

Mason's washes for stucco: Blue—to four pounds of blue vitriol and a pound of the best whiting, put a gallon of water, in an iron or brass pot. Let it boil an hour, stirring it all the time. Then pour it into an earthen pan; and set it by for a day or two till the color is settled. Pour off the water, and mix the color with white-washer's size. Wash the walls three or four times; according as is necessary.

Yellow: Dissolve in soft water over the fire equal quantities separately, of unber, bright oker, and blue-black. Then put into as much white-wash as you think sufficient for the work, some of each, and stir it all together until you have the proper tint. The most beautiful white-wash is made by mixing the lime and size with skimmed milk instead of water.

Superior paint for brick houses: to lime white-wash, add for a fastener sulphate of zinc, and shade with any color you choose, as yellow ochre, Venetian red, etc. It outlasts oil paint.

To make white-wash that will not rub off: Mix up half a pail full of lime and water, ready to put on the wall, then take a quarter of a pint of flour, mix it up with water, then pour on it boiling water in sufficient quantity to thicken it; then pour it, while hot, into the white-wash; stir all well together and it is ready.

A cheap smoke-house: Take a barrel or hogshead, and knock out both heads, and smoke your meat or fish in it. Be careful of your fire. Put a few embers in a suitable vessel, lay on them a few (*corn*) cobs; the cobs may be sprinkled occasionally with water; suspend your meat from sticks laid across the cask, covering it so as to confine the smoke, but not to extinguish the fire.

Cockroaches and beetles may be got rid of by sprinkling borax on the shelves, sinks, etc., which they frequent; ants, by putting almond kernels on the shelves, etc., the ants will leave anything else for these, and you can brush them off into hot water, destroying hundreds at once. Bedbugs will not yield to anything but perfect cleanliness.

To expell ants: a small quantity of green sage, placed in the closet, will cause red ants to disappear.

Cockroaches and rats: Mix well two parts of fine Indian meal with three parts of calcined plaster of paris, made very fine. Pass them, mixed, through a fine sieve, and give it (*in jar lids, placed near their haunts*); placing water near. *Infallible.*

To prevent flies from entering the house, brush the screen doors with kerosene.

Sprinkle the cellar often with chloride of lime and it will be kept free of rats.

In laying up furs for the summer, lay a tallow candle in or near them, and all danger of worms will be obviated.

Scatter a few drops of lavender in your bookcase before shutting it up for the summer and you will find no book mold.

Mock oranges, kept in a bowl, will run roaches. They will not trouble you.

Soap for killing borers in trees: Hard soap rubbed carefully into every place in the tree which seems wounded by them, will destroy effectually these nuisances to gardens and orchards. The rain will dissolve it and force them out of their holes and cause their death.

[463]

How to make trees grow: put two gallons of small potatoes around the roots.

Dying: peach leaves, bark scraped from the bayberry bush, saffron, etc., steeped in water and set with alum will color a bright lemon yellow.

To color food red, use beet-root pounded with water and strained; to color green, take fresh spinach or beet-root leaves, pound them in a marble mortar, and use the juice. To keep it a few days, add a piece of alum the size of a pea to a teacupful, and give it a boil.

Alum or vinegar is good to set the colors of red, green or yellow; salt is good for blue. Before you wash, dip blues in salt and water, use alum after.

A faded dress may be made perfectly white by boiling in cream of tartar water.

Mrs. Shaw's wash: One ounce of alcohol, two ounces of ammonia, one spoonful of salt, ten ounces of water. About one teaspoonful in a basin of water, when washing.

A mixture that will remove grease from the finest fabricks without injuring them may be made from one quart of rain water, two ounces of ammonia, one teaspoonful of saltpetre and one ounce of shaving soap cut up fine. Put a pad of absorbent cotton or blotting paper under the spot in a garment when rubbing it.

Powdered starch applied instantly will take out almost any fruit-juice stain from wash goods, if allowed to remain on the goods for a few hours until the discoloration passes into the starch.

If anything will extract mildew, it is lemon-juice mixed with an equal weight of salt, powdered starch, and soft soap. Rub on thickly and lay upon the grass in the hot sun; renewing the application two or three times a day until the spot fades and comes out. I have also used salt wet with tomato juice, often renewed, laying the article stained upon the grass. Sometimes the stain is taken out, sometimes not.

When laundering lace curtains and a creamy shade is wanted, add clear strong coffee to the starch.

To remove inkstains on clothing, soak the spot in sour milk.

Put a little turpentine in the boiler in which your clothes are boiled; it will whiten them.

If you have a sheer summer dress, one that is limp from wear but otherwise not soiled, sponge it on the wrong side with milk and water, and after it has been ironed it will have a crisp new look.

Never bite thread with the teeth; it damages them.

Glossary

ALUM: an astringent and an emetic that is used in the making of baking powder, pickles, candles, and paper. Still available near spice racks in supermarkets, it will make pickles crisp and green. It can be substituted where the recipe calls for baking ammonia.

BAKING POWDER: 1 part baking soda and 2 parts cream of tartar, plus preservatives. *See* soda.

BAYBERRY TALLOW: the wax of bayberry, used for candles and soap (p. 446). It is extracted like beeswax, by wrapping the berries in a cloth, weighting them down under cold water, heating it, then leaving it to get cold. Remove the wax from the surface of the water.

BEETLE: wooden mallet or large pestle.

BITTER ALMONDS: a relative of sweet almonds, grown in North Africa. No longer used, possibly because they contain traces of prussic acid. Almond extract gives a taste that is probably roughly equivalent, or peach leaves may be substituted.

BLACK ROSIN: the residue of distilled turpentine. Available at some paint stores.

BLOCK TIN: cooking ware similar in shape and weight to copper, made out of tin. Still made and sold in France, and exported to the United States. Available at kitchen specialty stores. Any heavy pot will do as a substitute.

BREADCRUMBS: "dry" means dry, "stale" means soft breadcrumbs.

BROWNED FLOUR: flour that has been scorched in order to color it (p. 438), to produce richer-looking sauces. More browned flour must be used to thicken than white flour, since heating destroys some of its starchiness.

CABBAGE LETTUCE: head lettuce.

CARMELIZED SUGAR: sugar heated until it melts and turns color (p. 437).

CASSIA: the pod of this leguminous plant has cathartic qualities; its oil is aromatic. Cardamom may be substituted.

CAUDLE: "a warm drink for invalids."

CHICORY: a diversified family of salad plants. The tightly furled leaves of the European variety, forced in cellars and in season throughout winter, is usually known as endive. It can be braised, glazed, or wilted as well as used raw in salads. But in old books the curly leaves of the American variety, usually known as chicory, are occasionally called endive also— which can lead to some confusion. The roasted roots are sometimes ground and added to ground coffee in the South, for a brew that approaches espresso flavor.

TO DRESS: primarily, to prepare to serve, putting the food upon the dish to go to the table. But the term is also used generally, to include the entire cooking process. The "dresser," once a kitchen sideboard on which food was dressed, has now moved into the bedroom.

TO EGG OVER: to brush with egg yolk, egg white, or whole egg, beaten up with one tablespoonful of water per egg, in order to protect (pie crusts, to keep them from becoming soggy with the juices of the contents); to glaze (pastries and meats); to cause breadcrumbs to adhere (almost all candidates for deep frying); or to brown (mashed potatoes or meats, which are then put under the broiler).

FORCEMEAT STUFFING: called "meat" because some forcemeats are made with meat. Many are not.

FRENCH DRESSING: this, in the nineteenth century, is oil and vinegar, salt and pepper, with no other flavorings.

TO FROTH: to dust meat with flour, then baste it with butter, just before removing from the fire.

GEM PAN: muffin tin.

GEMS: muffins.

GILL: pronounced "jill." A fourth of a pint, or ½ cup. In English recipes, where it is still used as a measurement, it is 5 ounces, since the English pint is 20 ounces. The American gill was 4 ounces.

GINGER: The root of a tropical plant. It comes in gray and white, the gray being the sharper of the two. "Green," used in recipes, merely means raw, not preserved. Except in pickles, powdered ginger can usually be substituted. Preserved ginger makes a so-so substitute in pickles if green ginger cannot be found; so does dried ginger. Use more ginger and a touch less sugar.

GRAHAM FLOUR: whole-wheat flour.

GRANITE WARE: enameled tin or light iron (or, now, steel), usually a blotchy blue-and-white or black-and-white in color. Its advantage is that it will not react to acid as copper or iron does. Where granite is specifically mentioned, enamel or glass pans may be used.

GRAVY: stock. The juice of anything, not necessarily thickened—and, if thickened, not very thick.

GREEN CORN: Indian or field corn picked while the husks were still green. Over-aged sweet corn is a good substitute.

GRIDIRON: a piece of equipment I have seen only in museums. Either round or square, they look like variously shaped spiderwebs of cast-iron bars, each bar with a groove down its middle to channel the fat of the broiling meat, to keep it from sputtering into the fire and causing flames. The upturned edges, say the old books, were to be kept polished bright, and greased before use. The whole gridiron is usually humped slightly in the middle, perhaps to concentrate the heat under the meat. Our closest equivalent would be the grill on an outdoor barbecue, though skillets with raised bars are still made, for stove-top broiling.

HAIR SIEVE: a strainer with a bottom of hair cloth.

HARTSHORN: liquid ammonia.

HERBS: plants used to flavor food. Sweet herbs are generally basil, thyme, rosemary, bay, marjoram, summer savory, etc., and they are used for stocks, vegetables, stews and, often, meats. Savory herbs—sage, oregano, juniper berries, tumeric, and other more astringent-tasting herbs— are more frequently used for meats. But the whole thing is a matter of taste and judgment. If the herb smells as though it would taste good in whatever you are cooking, chances are that it will.

HULLED CORN: Indian (hard-grained) corn that was soaked in an alkali solution to loosen the hulls, then rubbed to remove them and rinsed with several waters "that there may be no taste of lye." It was then treated like other dried grains or beans.

INDIAN MEAL: corn meal, still available in white and yellow forms.

ISINGLASS: a kind of gelatine prepared from fish. (Not mica, which, when made into sheets to serve as windows, was also called isinglass.) It is still available, but gelatine can easily be substituted.

JAGGING IRON: a wheel with a notched or jagged edge used for decorating. Now known as a pastry wheel and still available.

JAMAICA PEPPER: allspice.

LARD: rendered pork suet, used as a shortening and for frying. I find lard more satisfactory than vegetable shortening or oil for nearly every cooking purpose. It is slower to burn, doesn't splatter as much, seems to soak less into fried foods, and taste much better, with that light, delicate taste vegetable oils only advertise. It smokes less, makes much lighter pastry, costs about the same if you buy it and much less if you render it yourself, has about the same number of calories, and can be reused. Its only drawback, as animal fat, is that it is high in cholesterol.

TO LARD: to insert slivers of suet or fat into holes cut in meat, in order to make it juicier or more tender.

LARDING NEEDLE: a long, very thin cone-shaped needle of tin with the open end shaped something like a set of tweezers. The point makes a hole in the meat, the pincers draw the sliver of salt pork or bacon fat after it. It is not commonly found now except in kitchen specialty shops, partly because meat needs less larding than it once did. But it does a neater, faster job than can be done with a sharp slender knife to make the hole and fingers to poke the fat down it. Lacking a needle, the job is easier if you freeze the fat before larding.

LARDOON: the strip of fat used to lard.

LEMON PICKLE: the liquid from pickled lemons, used for flavorings (p. 404).

LIME: calcium oxide. Quick lime, unslaked lime, burnt lime, and caustic lime are more or less the same thing, a caustic alkali used in compost heaps to speed decomposition, in whitewashes, sometimes in soap making. Slaked lime, for pickles, is lime that has been mixed with water, calcium hydroxide, and is less caustic.

LOAF SUGAR: granulated sugar used to come congealed in loaves, usually conical in shape. To use, it had to be grated, pounded, powdered, or rolled—all terms that occur regularly in old recipes, all meaning roughly the same thing (though "powder" meant more work than "pound").

LYE: originally, the alkaline solution obtained by leaching water through wood ashes, though now the name applies to any strong alkali. Used in soap making, available in hardware stores, and in groceries in some parts of the country.

MACE: the dried outer covering of the nutmeg, slightly milder in flavor. It is rarely available in blades now, though sometimes you can get it in crumbled fragments rather than ground. A blade is a scant ¼ teaspoonful.

MADE DISH: an entrée in the old sense, a dish of meat to which something has been done. A roast, considered meat in its pure state, is not a made dish. A steak, particularly with sauce, is.

Glossary

MEAT SCREEN: a wooden or metal screen to put on the floor about 4 feet in front of the fireplace, about as tall as the fireplace was high, and about 2 feet wider on each end than the fireplace. It concentrated the heat on roasting meat and protected the fire from drafts. Sometimes the meat screen had shelves for warming dishes.

MUFFINS: what we call muffins were "gems" in the nineteenth century. Muffins were about the size and shape of English muffins, baked in muffin rings that looked like large napkin rings, which were generally set on greased baking sheets before the batter was poured in. "Muffin rings were formerly about four inches in diameter, but now, with better taste, they are used much smaller." (Marion Harland, *Breakfast, Dinner and Supper*, 1897)

MUSHROOM CATSUP: the spiced, preserved liquor of mushrooms extracted by salting, then cooking (p. 250). Still occasionally available as "mushroom sauce" in gourmet shops. Half the quantity of Worcestershire or soy sauce may serve as a substitute.

OIL OF TURPENTINE: a turpentine distillate, available in paint and hardware stores. Spirits of turpentine are the volatile oil.

PASTE: pastry.

PEARLASH: purified potash, from which saleratus was obtained by exposing it to carbonic acid gas. No longer used as a leavening agent. Substitute baking soda.

PEASE: dried peas.

PEPPER: all pepper is the fruit of one of a variety of vine-like shrubs native to India, now cultivated almost everywhere. Black pepper is the dried berry; white pepper, the seed with the black hulls removed. Cayenne or red pepper is a ripe fruit, dried and ground. Long pepper is unripe fruiting spikes, ground and used as black pepper is. Pepper loses its pungency when ground, so it is best to buy it whole and use a pepper grinder.

Sweet or green peppers are easily grown—they like a rich soil and sunlight—and can be used in salads, as pickles, stuffed, broiled, or as additions to other dishes. They are in season during the late summer and early fall.

PIE PLANT: an old name for rhubarb.

PIPKIN: a small earthenware pot, often with a handle, for heating sauces.

TO POT MEAT OR VEGETABLES: to preserve them temporarily, usually by cooking them, pounding them to a paste, baking in stone pots and sealing them from the air with clarified butter.

PRESERVING PAN: a flat-bottomed, fairly shallow pan about the size of a skillet, with a large area of surface that allows the contents to reduce rapidly by evaporation. A large frying pan or stewpan can be substituted.

RED TARTAR: unrefined cream of tartar, the reddish crust-like deposit on wine barrels.

RENNET: small portions of the membranes that line the fourth stomach of a calf, salted and preserved, used in making cheeses and puddings because they have the property of causing milk to form smooth curds. The enzyme is now available in tablet form, should you not have a calf's stomach handy.

ROSEWATER: the essence of rose petals concentrated by distilling (p. 440). Rose butter (p. 195) or rose brandy will substitute; rose extract is still available on some supermarket spice racks (use less); and rosewater can be obtained from pharmacists who compound their own drugs, or from some specialty food shops.

ROUX: equal amounts of flour and butter, the flour stirred into the melted butter and cooked until it is the desired color. It is used for thickening and is far superior to flour wet with water, since it almost never produces lumps. Flour rubbed into soft butter, then added to whatever needs thickening, achieves a similar result.

SAGO: a starchy substance derived from the sago palm tree. Not generally available now. Barley may be substituted in most cases.

SALAMANDER: an iron device that was heated red-hot in the fireplace and passed over a dish to brown its top. Sometimes a red-hot poker was used. To "salamander" something meant to brown it. A few minutes under the broiler accomplishes the purpose.

SALERATUS: unrefined soda, once made from the ashes of marine plants. It is refined into sodium carbonate (washing soda) and sodium bicarbonate (baking soda). Dissolving saleratus in hot water (not necessary with baking soda) lessened its caustic properties. Use slightly less baking soda than saleratus. *See* soda.

SALPICON: a mixture of cooked meats, diced, with a sauce and mushrooms or truffles.

SAVORY, WINTER OR SUMMER: an herb usually used with green beans, cucumbers, chicken or light meats, soups or stews. Summer savory is an annual, delicate and tangy in flavor. Planted in the garden among the beans, it seems to help keep bugs away. Winter savory is a perennial of a rougher, sharper flavor, with a bushy appearance if it is kept picked. It does well in poor soil, can be grown in rock gardens.

SIPPETS: bread, usually cut in triangular shapes but sometimes squares, which has been fried or toasted for use as a garnish or crouton.

SODA: a caustic which leavens by releasing carbon dioxide when wet. It also produces toxic substances unless neutralized. Baking powder contains 1 part soda to 2 parts cream of tartar (plus cornstarch or rice flour as a preservative), which when heated combines with the soda to inhibit the toxins. To substitute, use more baking powder than you would have used soda. (One teaspoonful of baking powder per cup of flour is the general rule.) Sour milk, vinegar, and molasses also neutralize soda. Wetting it first, as old recipes usually specify, lessens its rising properties.

SPIDER: cast-iron skillet.

SPOONFUL: a tablespoonful. Sometimes a heaping tablespoonful.

SUET: animal fat before it is rendered into shortening (although some very old recipes use the term to mean shortening). Used in stuffings, sausages, mincemeat, and occasionally in pastry for meat pies. The leaf-fat suet renders up the best shortening. Beef and pork suet are best to render for deep frying; pork and mutton or lamb fat make the best soap and candles.

SWEET-MEAT: anything preserved with sugar, like raisins, currants, mincemeat, sweet pickled fruits or jams.

SWEET OIL: olive oil.

TAMIS, TAMMY: a strainer of hair or worsted (tamis) cloth.

TAPIOCA: a starchy, granular substance prepared from the root of the cassava plant used for making puddings or thickening pies. Available now in quick-cooking or old-fashioned large pearl forms.

TO TRUSS: to tie up for roasting, baking, or broiling. Chickens, ducks, turkeys, and pigs had traditional trussed positions in the nineteenth century, but the main idea is to draw the legs and wings close to the body so they are not overdone and dried out in cooking.

VINEGAR: store-bought vinegar is usually distilled at 5% acidity, the right acidity for making pickles. Cider vinegar is usually best for pickles but white, wine, or herb vinegar can be used according to preference, desired appearance, and taste. The acidity in home-made vinegar is difficult to control, apt to be too strong or, because the chemical process has completed itself (from alcohol to vinegar to water), too weak. Compare carefully with store vinegar before using.

WAITER: attendant at table. Also, a tray.

WINEGLASS: as a measurement, 2 ounces, or ¼ cup. The English wineglass measurement is 5 ounces—which, considering the size of wineglasses, makes more sense. But all the old books agree that a wineglass is ½ gill, and an American gill is 4 ounces.

Bibliography

American Dainties, and How to Prepare Them, by an American Lady. London: L. Upcoll Gill, 1897.

The American Domestic Cookery, formed on Principles of economy for the use of Private Families, by an Experienced Housekeeper. New York: E. Duyckinck, 1823.

The American System of Cookery, comprising every variety of information for ordinary and holiday cookery, by Mrs. T. J. Crowen. New York: W. E. Hilton, 1870.

The Art of Cookery Made Plain and Easy, by Hannah Glasse. Alexandria (Va.): Cottom and Steward, 1812.

Miss Beecher's Domestic Receipt Book, designed as a supplement to her Treatise on Domestic Economy. New York: Harper and Bros., 1846.

Breakfast, Dinner and Supper, and How to Cook Them, by Marion Harland. New York: George J. McLeod and Co., 1897.

The Calendar Club Cook Book. Bridgton, Maine, 1902.

The Caloric Book of Recipes. 1907.

The Century Cook Book, by Mary Ronald. New York: Century Co., 1896.

Common Sense, by Marion Harland. New York: Scribner & Sons, 1883.

The Cook's Oracle, containing Receipts for plain cookery on the most economical plan for private families, the whole being the result of Actual Experiments instituted in the kitchen of a Physician, from the last London Edition, Which is almost entirely re-written, by William Kitchener. Boston: Munroe and Francis, 1822.

The Cuisine, by An Eminent French Caterer. Chicago: R. R. Donnelley, 1872.

Directions for Cookery, in all its Various Branches, by Miss Eliza Leslie. Philadelphia: Henry Carey Baird, 1870.

The Domestic's Companion. New York: G. F. Bunce, 1834.

The Easiest Way in Housekeeping and Cooking, Helen Campbell. Boston: Roberts Bros., 1893.

Edibilia: A Cook Book of Valuable Private Receipts, published by the Ladies of Christ Church, Indianapolis, Ind., 1873.

Eighteen Colonial Recipes.

Every Lady's Cook Book, by Mrs. Thomas J. Crowen. New York: Kiggins and Kellogg, 1854.

Facts for the People, or: Things Worth Knowing, a book of receipts in which everything is of practical use to Everybody. Philadelphia: Laraway and Holstz, 1851.

Fancy Cookery. Muscatine, Iowa.

Food and Cookery for Infants and Invalids, by Catherine Jane Wood. London: Wm. Clowes and Sons, Ltd., 1884.

Mrs. Hale's New Cook Book, by Sarah J. Hale. Philadelphia: T. B. Peterson and Bros., 1857.

Hawaiian Cook Book, by the Ladies Society of Central Union Church. Honolulu: Press Publishing Co. Steam Printers, 1888.

The Home Cook Book, by Ella E. Myers. Philadelphia: Crawford and Co., 1880.

The Housekeeper's Book, comprising advice on the conduct of household affairs in general; and particular directions for the preservation of furniture, bedding, etc.; for the laying in and preserving of provisions, with a complete collection of receipts for economical Domestic Cookery, the whole carefully prepared for the use of American Housekeepers by a Lady. Philadelphia: Wm. Marshall and Co., 1837.

The Improved Housewife, by Mrs. A. L. Webster, alike experienced in the Vicissitudes of life and in Housewifery, whom admonitory years now invite to a more retired and less active life, cheered by affectionate remembrances of patron-friends. Hartford: Ira Webster, 1854.

In the Kitchen, by Elisabeth S. Miller. Boston: Lee and Shepard, 1875.

Ladies' Guide, or, The Skillful Housewife, by Mrs. L. G. Abell. New York: Orange, Judd and Co.,1852.

Ladies' Library Association Common Sense Cook Book. Bradford, Mass., 1891.

Bibliography

The Lakeside Cook Book, by Naomi Donnelley. Chicago: Donnelley, Gassette and Loyd, 1878.

Mrs. Lincoln's Boston Cook Book. Boston: Roberts Bros., 1896.

The Marion Cook Book, by the Royal Oak Presbyterian Missionary Society, Marion, Va., 1909.

Milady's Own Book, by the Fort Sumpter Chapter, Children of the Confederacy, Charleston, S.C., 1905.

Modern Cookery for Private Families, by Mrs. Acton. London: Longman's Green and Co., 1887.

The Modern Housewife, or, Menagere, by Alexis Soyer, edited by an American Housekeeper. New York: D. Appleton and Co., 1850.

The New and the Old in Cookery, by Mrs. L. M. Ludlum. Paterson: Craig, Beckmeyer & Co., *c.* 1891.

The New Family Cook Book, by Jesse Haney. 1891.

The New Process Cook Book, published by the Standard Lighting Co., 1894.

The Old Abingdon (Va.) Cook Book. (date unknown)

On Habits and Manners, by Mrs. M. F. Armstrong. Hampton, Va.: Normal School Press, 1888.

The Philadelphia Cook Book, by Mrs. Sarah Tyson Rorer. Philadelphia: Arnold and Co., 1886.

The Practical Housekeeper, a Cyclopedia of Domestic Economy, edited by Mrs. Ellet. New York: Stringer and Townsend, 1857.

The Principles of Cooking, by Septimus Berdmore. London: Wm. Clowes and Son, Ltd., 1884.

Proved and Tested Cooking Receipts and other Valuable Information, by the ladies of Emmanuel Universalist Church, Rockland, Maine. Courier-Gazette Press, 1893.

Sears' New Family Receipt Book. New York: Robert Sears, 1852.

"Still Another" Cook Book, by the Ladies' Aid Society of First Congregational Church, Oakland, Calif., 1888.

The Table, by Alessandro Filippini. New York: Baker and Taylor Co., 1895.

Temperance Cook Book, being a collection of receipts for cooking from which all intoxicating liquids are excluded. Compiled by a Lady. Philadelphia: Gihon and Kucher, 1841.

Tried Receipts, by the ladies of Grace Church, Say Brook, Conn., 1882.

Tried Receipts. Lakeville, Conn.: Press of Connecticut Western News, 1888.

Twentieth Century Cook Book, by Mrs. C. F. Moritz and Miss Adele Kahn. New York: G. W. Dillingham, 1898.

The Up-To-Date Cook Book, by Charles Wells Moulton, Thought and Work Club, Salem, Mass., 1897.

Bibliography

Widdifield's New Cook Book, or, Practical Receipts for the Housewife, by Hannah Widdifield. Philadelphia: T. B. Peterson and Bros., 1856.

The Young House-keeper, or, Thoughts on Food and Cookery, by William A. Alcott. Boston: George W. Light, 1842.

INDEX

Albany breakfast cakes, 62
Alice van Griethuysen's layer toga cake, 410
Allemande sauce, 168
Alligator pear salad, 190
Almonds
  to blanch, 334
  ice cream, 198
  pudding, 97, 334
  taffy, 427
Ambrosia, 97
Amherst pudding, 307
Anchovy sauce, 341, 347
Apple(s), mostly October
  Amherst pudding, 307
  baked, 308
  baked, ice cream, 198
  bread, 310
  butter, 311
  chartreuse of, 307
  cider
    hard, 314
    to keep good for years, 313
    to keep sweet, 313
    molasses, 314
    mulled, 313
    vinegar, 314
  dried apple cake, 85
  to dry, 312
  dumplings, 310
  Dutch apple cake, 309
  and fig beverage, 312
  fried sour, 371
  fritters, 310

Apple(s) (*continued*)
  frosting, 309
  and Indian meal, steamed, 308
  jelly, 311
  johnny cake, 309
  leather, 255
  mincemeat, 399, 400
  molasses sauce, dumplings, 307
  pie, 306
    -custard pie, 307
    -meringue pie, 306
  to preserve, 311
  pudding, 307
  sauce, 305
  spiced, 311
  stuffing, goose or duck, 293
  tapioca pudding, 308
  and watercress salad, 147
  wine, 313
Apricot ice cream, 199
Artichokes, Jerusalem, 328
Artificial oysters, 222
Asparagus, mostly May, 145
  in ambush, 146
  baked eggs with, 229
  chiffonade, 188
  curry of lamb with, 136
  Hollandaise sauce for, 165
  Soup de l'Asperge, 146
    cream of, 186
  as young peas, 146
Aspic jelly, 272
  tomato, 280
Aunt Mary's papaia pudding, 152

Aunt Rose's sugar cookies, 425
Autumn soup, 189, 284
Avocados, *see* Alligator pear salad

Bacon, mostly November; *see also* Pork
  and cabbage, 376
  and green beans, dressed, 239
  hopping john, 84
Baking, 25
Banana(s), mostly July
  cake, 411
  fried, 211
  fritters, 210
  ice cream, 198
  pudding, 210
Barley broth, Scotch, 83
Barley water, 88
Bass, *see* Fish
Batter bread, 61
Batter for fritters, 73
Bavarian cream, 92
Bayberry soap, 447
Baybury salad, 188
Beans, mostly January and August
  and bacon, 239
  dried, 79
    baked, 79
    black, soup, 82
    Forefather's Day succotash, 430
    haricot, 78, 80
    lentil soup, 83
    limas, 80
    porridge, 81
    red, with burgundy, 80
    winter succotash, 80
  green, 239
    cream of, soup, 186
    French
      à la mâitre d'hôtel, 239
      to pickle with radish pods, 234
  limas, 240; *see also under* Beans—
    dried
    autumn soup, 284
    bean roll, 240
    to preserve, 240
  pickled, 234
  Russian salad, 240
Béarnaise, sauce, 134
Beaten biscuit, 69
Beef, mostly November; *see also* Veal
  à la mode, 348–349

Beef (*continued*)
  ragout of, 350
  bouilli, 346
  brown stock, 353
  bubble and squeek, 323
  cannelon, with mushroom sauce, 345
  collops, 345
  corned beef
    to corn simply, 359
    bean porridge, 81
    bubble and squeek, 323
    cauliflower sauce for, 325
    okra soup, 243
    old-fashioned boiled dinner, 347
  to cure, 458
  Dutch hung beef, 359
  family French salad, 352
  fillets of beef, 340
    braised, 342
  French rolls, 342
  frittadella, 351
  German oyster soup, 346
  gravies, 354
    soup, 355
  heart
    to roast, 358
    with veal stuffing, 127
  Hessian soup, 356
  jerked beef, 359
  kidney
    hash, 357
    stewed, 357
  in a marinade, 343
  marinade for, 339
  meat and vegetable pie, 352
  minced, with cucumbers, 346
  notes on, 21
  olives, 120
  ox-tail soup, 355
  to pot, 359
  potato and meat salad, 352
  roast; *see also* Sauces
    done to a turn, 338
    réchaufé, 352
  rissoles, 348
  rolled beef that equals hare, 342
  Rutgers rolletjes, 351
  salad
    family French, 352
    meat and potato, 352
  sauces, 340, 341, 347; *see also* Sauces
  Spanish friceo, 345

Beef (*continued*)
  spiced round, 350
  steak; *see also* Beef—fillets of beef
    à la Française, 341
    and oyster pie, 344
    rump, stuffed, 342
  stewed beef, 343
  -tea, 86
  tongue, fresh, 358
    to cure, 360
    and quenelles with capon, 265
      the same with cucumbers, 266
  tripe
    to fry, 356
    Lyonnaise, 357
    mock turtle soup, 356
    Rutgers rolletjes, 351
  Yorkshire pudding, 339
Beer
  common, 444
  dandelion, 149
  ginger, 444
  spruce, 444
  vinegar, 445
Beets, mostly July, 219
  beet-root, 219
  French way of dressing, 219
  pickled, 220
  salad, 219
Berries, mostly July
  berry pudding, 201
  blackberry
    jam, 206
    syrup, 454
    wine, 206
  black butter, 202
  blueberry
    cake, 209
    pie, 210
    pudding, 209
    sauce for ice cream, 210
  cherry
    bounce, 203
    cake, 203
    and currant jelly, 203
    ice, 203
    pie, 202
    preserves, 203
    preserved in brandy, 204
    pudding, 202
    shrub, 204
  cranberry

    frappé, 396
    jelly, 208
    pie, 395
    pudding, 395
    sauce, 394
    shortcake, 395
    snow, 396
    surprise, 396
    tart, 395
    tea, 396
  currant
    bread, 208
    cream, pink or red, 208
    green, pie, 194
    jelly, 208
    sauce, 209
    spiced, 209
    and strawberry salad, 192
    water ice, 207
    wine, 209
  elderberry
    catsup, 258
    preserved for pie, 257
    sirup, 257
    wine, 258
  excellent family wine, 201
  gooseberry
    fool, 206
    green, *vol-au-vent*, 206
    pie, 194
    preserved, 207
    sauce, 207
  raspberry
    cream, 208
    ice cream, 198
    jam, 205
    pudding, 205
    sauce for pudding, 205
    shrub, 205
    tart, 204
  sour cream sauce for berries, 201
  strawberries
    cream, 208
    and currant salad, 192
    ice cream, 198
    jam, 193
    in orange juice, 192
    pie, 193
    preserved in wine, 193
    salad, 192
    sauce, for fruit pudding, 194
    shortcake, 192

Beverages; *see also* Wine
  apple and fig, 312
  barley water, 88
  beef-tea, 86
  blackberry syrup, 454
  caudle, for a christening, 89
  cherry bounce, 203
  cherry shrub, 204
  cider
    hard, 314
    to keep good for years, 313
    to keep sweet, 313
    mulled, 313
  cooling drink for feverish thirst, 88
  cranberry tea, 396
  dry plum beverage, 84
  egg nog, New Year's, 435
  elderberry sirup, 257
  ginger pop, 444
  lemon or orange sirup, 404
  molasses posset, 88
  mulled wine, 434
  orange sherbet, 406
  port wine negus, 435
  punch, 434
  raspberry shrub, 205
  syllabub, 434
  tomato juice, 280
  white wine fillip, 434
  wine whey, 33
Beyrout sauce, 170
Bimbo hash, 216
Biscuits, mostly January; *see also* Muffins; Rolls
  beaten, 69
  butter, 68
  buttermilk, 69
  bran or graham, 69
  Miss Yandes' rusk, 70
  rusk, 70
  St. John's round rice bread, 65
  saleratus, 69
  seed, 420
  velvet cakes, 67
Black bean soup, 82
Blackberries, *see* Berries
Black butter, 127, 173
Blackfish, *see* Fish
Black pudding, 380
Black walnut chocolates, 429
Blanc mange, 103
  ornamental froth for, 103

Blanquette of veal, 121
Blueberries, *see* Berries
Blue Island bread, 50
Boiled dinner, 347
Boiled dressing for salad, 190
Boiled suds, 448
Boiling, 21
Bouillabaisse, 180
Bouilli, 346
Bouillon, court, 164; *see also* Stock
Brains, *see* Veal
Braising, 19
Brandied peaches, 254
Brandy, rose, 195
Brandy cream, 92
Brandy sauce, 99, 433
Bread, mostly January; *see also* Biscuits; Muffins; Rolls
  to bake, 14
  quick breads, 58–62
    Albany breakfast cake, 62
    apple johnny cake, 309
    batter, 61
    Carolina corn-cake, 59
    corn, nonpareil, 60
    diet, 59
    graham, 61
    hoe cake, 62
    Indian meal breakfast cake, 62
    johnny cake, 59
    rice, 61
    Sally Lunn, 60, 61
    soft molasses gingerbread, 417
    sour milk brown, 58
    spider corn cake, 60
  yeast breads, 46–56
    apple, 311
    Beaufort rice, 55
    Blue Island, 50
    Boston brown, 54
    brown, 56
    brown or dyspepsia, 55
    croutons, 51
    currant, 208
    family, 51
    for a good baking, 47
    French, 48
    graham, 53
    graham without fine flour, 53
    Italian bread sticks, 63
    kaffee kuchen, 55
    milk, 50

Bread (*continued*)
    potato, 49
    raised brown, 54
    raised with pure potato yeast, 49
    rye, 54
    salt-rising, 52
    squash, 333
    thirded, 51
    wheat and Indian, 52
Breadfruit, 151
    stewed, 152
Bread sauce, pheasant or turkey, 300
Bride's cake, 183
    icings for, 184
Brine for pickles, 31
Brochette of lamb à la Dumas, 135
Broiling, 19
Brook trout, *see* Fish
Brown bread, 54–56, 61
    ice cream, 198
Brown coloring for made dishes, 437
Brown cucumber sauce, 117
Browned flour, 438
Brown sauce and variations, 436
Brown stock, 353
Brown turkey soup, 394
Brunswick stew, 299
Bubble and squeek, 323
Buckwheat cakes, 75
Burnt butter, 165
Burnt cream, 103
Butter, mostly March
    apple, 311
    biscuit, 68
    black, 127, 173
    burnt, 165
    to churn, 106
    to clarify, 106
    drawn, 107
    à la maître d'hôtel, 108
    melted, 107
    peach, 255
    rose, 195
Buttercup cake, 412
Buttermilk biscuit, 69

Cabbage, mostly October, 322
    and bacon, 376
    bubble and squeek, 323
    chartreuse of, 188
    dressing for cold slaw, 323

Cabbage (*continued*)
    old-fashioned boiled dinner, 347
    pheasant (also duck) stewed with, 301
    pickled, 233, 321
    red, 322
    rice à la Ristori, 323
    soup, 324
    sour krout, to make, 324
        Bavarian way, 324
    Southern yellow pickle, 236
    stuffed, 322
    turesicus, 366
Cabinet pudding, 96
Cakes, mostly December; *see also* Icings
    cheesecakes, 108
        lemon, 403
        Mrs. Bratty's, 109
    coffeecakes
        Dutch apple, 309
        kaffee kuchen, 55
    fruitcakes, 397
        apple, dried, 85
        bride's cake, 183
        date, 418
        ginger plum, 418
        Harrison, 418
        Mrs. Madison's whim, 417
        rich plum, 419
        six months', 418
        Washington, 398
        wedding, 182
    jelly, 414
        gentlemen's favorite, 415
        jelly fruit, 414
        Naples biscuit, 415
    layer and loaf
        banana, 411
        blueberry, 209
        buttercup, 412
        cherry, 203
        chocolate cream, 410
        cocoa-nut pound, 412
        coffee, 411
        common cup, 411
        cream, 410
        Grandmother Don's lemon, 403
          sweet milk chocolate, 409
        layer toga, 410
        lemon, 402
        Madeira, 414
        marble, 409

Index

Cakes (*continued*)
    number, 413
    plain loaf, 413
    pound, 412
  to make, 23
  simnel, 413
  sponge cakes
    cinnamon, 408
    delicate, 409
    ginger pound, 408
    queen, 409
    sponge, 407
    tipsy, 408
  Thanksgiving tea, 399
Calf's brains, *see* Veal
Calf's feet jelly, 128
Calf's liver, *see* Veal
Camp ketchup, 442
Candied flowers, 196
  cakes of flowers, 196
Candied fruit, 256, 430
Candles, 446
Candy, mostly December
  almond taffy, 427
  black walnut chocolate, 429
  caramel
    chocolate, 428
    vanilla, 429
  filled dates, 430
  lemon drops, 404
  orange peel, 407
  maple cream chocolate, 429
  molasses, 428
  peach or apple leather, 255
  peanut, 430
  peppermint drops, 430
Cannelon of beef, mushroom sauce, 345
Canning, 32
Canteloupe, 247
  to pickle, 237
  mangoes, 237
Canvasback ducks, *see* Game birds
Caper sauce, for fish, 172
Capons, *see* Chicken
Caramel
  chocolate, 428
  for coloring, 437
  cream, 93
  pudding, 94
  sauce, 93
  vanilla, 429
Caraway buns, 66

Carolina corn-cake, 59
Carp, *see* Fish
Carrots, mostly September
  with curry, 284
  pudding, 285
  stewed, 284
  soup, 285
  sweet and sour, 285
Catfish soup, 180
Catsup
  camp, 442
  cucumber, 215
  elderberry, 258
  mushroom, 250
  tomato, 282
  walnut, 251
Caudle, for a christening, 89
Cauliflower, mostly October, 325
  dressed like macaroni, 325
  peppers stuffed with, 242
  pickled, 326
  sauce, for mutton, corned beef, 325
Cayenne, essence, 443
Celery, mostly September
  batter-fried, 285
  cream soup, 186
  green tomato pickle, with, 320
  nut salad, 336
  salt, 286
  sauce for turkey, 391
  tomato stuffed with, 279
  vinegar, 286
Celia's success, 169
Champagne sauce, 440
Charleston mode of cooking plantains, 211
Charlotte russe, 97
Chartreuse
  of apples, 307
  of chicken, 269
  of spinach or cabbage, 188
Chaud-froid sauce, turkey or meat, 392
Cheese, mostly March
  cakes, 108
  cakes, lemon, 403
  cakes, Mrs. Bratty's, 109
  cottage, to make, 111
  curds and whey, 111
  eggs with, 113
  fondue, Brillat-Savarin, 111
    with Stilton, 112
  macaroni, with, 113

Cheese (*continued*)
  to make, 109
  to pot, 110
  ramakins, 112
  sage, to make, 110
  savory macaroni, 113
  Welsh rarebit, 112
Cherries, *see* Berries
Cheshire pork pie, 376
Chess pie, 419
Chestnuts, mostly October
  pudding, 334
  purée of, 335
  with sausage, 377
  soup, *à la jardinière*, 334
  stuffing, 390
  with turkey, 390
Chicken, mostly September
  aspic jelly, 272
  baked in rice, 268
  braised, 263
  broiled, *à la tartare*, 264
  Brunswick stew, 299
  capon
    à l'estragon, 265
    with quenelles and tongue, 265
      the same with cucumber, 266
  chartreuse of, 269
  chestnut stuffing for, 390
  creole corn, 223
  croquettes, 268
  cock-a-leekie, 271
  cucumber, stuffed with, 217
  curry with cocoanut, 267
  dumpokht, 266
  fricassee
    brown, 267
    white, 267
  fried, 264
    with oysters, 263
  gombo, sassafras, 271
  Indian way, 264
  jelly, 87
  lemon cream for stewed, 266
  livers with Madeira, 273
  mullagatawny soup, 130
  okra soup, 243
  pâté, 269
  pudding, Virginia, 268
  roast, pheasant fashion, 301
  sauce tartare for, 165
  sausage, 302

Chicken (*continued*)
  scallop, 393
  Sydney Smith's receipt, 270
  terrapin, 269
Chicory
  dutched (lettuce), 189
  with gravy, 119
  escalops of veal, *à la chicoree*, 119
  wilted (dandelions), 148
Chiffonade (sorrel or asparagus), 188
China chilo, 366
Chinese rice pudding, 96
Chocolate
  cake, 409, 410
  cakes, 423
  caramels, 428
  cream, 91
  custard, 94
  ice cream, 197
  icing, 416
Chow chow, 214
Chowder
  clam, 162–163
  corn, 222
  fish, 166
Christmas
  goose pie, 431
  ham, 432
  plum pudding, 432, 433
Chutney
  mango, 151
  tamarind, 153
  tomato, 282
Cider, *see* Apple(s)
Cinnamon cake, 408
Citron
  cake, 422
  pudding, 99
Clams, *see* Shellfish
Cock-a-leekie, 271
Cocoanut
  chicken curry with, 267
  ice cream, 198
  pound cake, 412
Cod, *see* Fish
Coffee
  cake, 411
  cream, 92
  ice cream, 198
Colbert sauce, lamb, 135
Cold slaw, 323
Collops of beef, 345

Common beer, 444
Common cup cake, 411
Cookies, mostly December, 420
  Aunt Rose's sugar, 425
  chocolate, 423
  citron, 422
  cream puffs, 426
  curd cakes, 425
  hermits, 425
  hickory nut macaroons, 335
  honey cakes, 425
  jumbles, 423
  kisses, 424
  kringles, 422
  lemon drop biscuits, 404
  love, 425
  macaroons, 425
  to make, 26
  New Year's cake, 46
  oly koeks, 424
  sand tarts, 421
  savoy cakes, 422
  Scotch cakes, 421
  Scotch short-bread, 421
  seed biscuits, 420
  small seed cakes, 420
  superior ginger bread, 424
  sweet potato cakes, 247
  trifles, 422
  very rich cookies, 424
  wine cakes, 421
Cooling drink for feverish thirst, 88
Corn, mostly July, 220
  autumn soup, 284
  chowder, 222
  creamed, 221
  creole, 223
  to dry green, 223
  to freeze, 246
  fried, 220
  green
    baked, 221
    soup, 222
  lamb stew with corn, 136
  oysters, 222
  pudding, 221
  soup, cream of, 186
  succotash, 241
    Forefather's Day, 430
    winter, 80
Corn bread, nonpareil, 60

Corn-cake, Carolina, 59
Corned beef, *see* Beef
Corn pone, 63
  fried, 63
Cottage cheese, to make, 111
Court bouillon, for fish, 164
Crabapple
  jelly, 256
  spiced, 257
Crabs, *see* Shellfish
Crackers
  lemon, 71
  soda, 71
Cranberries, *see* Berries
Cream
  Devonshire, 105
  to preserve, 105
Cream cake, 410
Cream dressing, lobster, 156
Cream, fried, 104
Cream fritters, 73
Cream mayonnaise, 190
Cream puffs, 426, 427
Cream shortcakes, 68
Cream tea cakes, 67
Crème de riz, 129
Croquettes
  chicken, 268
  potato, 317
Crullers, 72
Crumpets, 65
Crust; *see also* Pastry
  for meat pies, 344
  for venison pasty, 387
Cucumber, mostly July; *see also* Pickles
  autumn soup, 189
  Baybury salad, 188
  brown cucumber sauce, 117
  bimbo hash, 216
  capons, with quenelles and, 266
  catsup, 215
  chow chow, 214
  with dill, 218
  fried, 216
    in batter, 216
  Kalamazoo pickles, 214
  lamb or mutton steaks and, 135
  minced beef and, 346
  pickled, 213–215, 236, 238, 320–321
  seven year pickle, 214
  soup, 218

Cucumber (*continued*)
  savory, 218
  spring salad, 147
  stuffed, 217
  unique preserves, 213
  vinegar, 215
  white cucumber sauce, chicken, 217
Cumberland sauce, game, 437
Curd cake, 425
Curds and whey, 111
Currants, *see* Berries
Curry
  carrot, 284
  chicken, 267
  lamb, asparagus tips, 136
  powder, 130, 443
Custard, *see* Pudding(s)
Cutlets; *see also* Lamb; Mutton; Pork;
  Veal
  Soyer's new, 364

Dandelion(s), mostly May, 148
  beer, 149
  salads, 148
  wilted, 148
Date cake, 418
Dates, filled, 430
Delicate cake, 409
Deviled
  clams, 162
  oysters, 274
  tomatoes, 278
Devonshire cream, 105
Diet bread, 59
Dish of snow, 105
Doughnuts, 71–72
Drawn butter, 107
Dressing, salad; *see also* Salads
  boiled, 190
  for cold slaw, 323
  cream mayonnaise, 190
  oil mayonnaise, 440
  salad dressing stock, 190
Dried beans, *see* Beans
Dried fruit, mostly January
  apple cake, 85
  to dry, 256, 312
  peach sauce for game, 385
  plum beverage, 84
  prune jelly, 84
Duck(s), mostly October; *see also*

Duck(s) (*continued*)
  Game birds
  apple stuffing for, 293
  à l'aubergiste, 294
  to boil, 296
  braised, 294
  olive sauce for, 437
  onion sauce for, 293
  orange salad for, 405
  to roast, 293, 294, 295
  salmi of, 295
  sourcrout, Bavarian way, 324
  stewed
    with green peas, 295
    with turnips, 295
Dumplings
  apple, 310
  ham, 375
  plain suet, 363
  potato, 318
Dumpokht (chicken, rabbit, or kid),
  266
Dutch apple cake, 309
Dutched lettuce, 190
Dutch hung beef, 359

East India pickle, 237
Eels, *see* Fish
Eggs, mostly August; *see also* Cakes;
  Puddings
  baked
    with asparagus, 229
    en coquille, 228
  balls, for soup, 231
  with cheese, 113
  gruel, for infants, 90
  omelets, 229
  pickled, 235
  to preserve, 232
    French method, 232
  sauce, for fish, 167
  sour, German style, 229
  stuffed, 231
    Mrs. G's, 230
  toast, 230
Egg nog, New Year's, 435
Eggplant, mostly August, 245
  baked, 245
  fried, 246
  fritters, 246
Egyptian tomatoes, 279

Elderberries, *see* Berries
Endive, *see* Chicory
English sherry, to make, 443
Escalops of veal *à la chicoree*, 119
  with stuffed peppers, 120
Espagnole sauce, 439
Essence of cayenne, 443
Essence of ginger, 443
Excelsior lobster salad, 156

Family bread, 51
Family French salad, 352
Farina, 90
Fig(s)
  and apple beverage, 312
  custard, 95
  marmalade, 258
  -pear filling for cakes, 417
Filled dates, 430
Fillip, white wine, 434
Fish, mostly May; *see also* Shellfish
  baked
    in a crust, 167
    oyster stuffing for, 167
    stuffing for, 167
  bass
    à la Bordelaise, 168
    with white wine, 168
  to boil, 164
    court bouillon for, 164
    sauces for, 165
  bouillabaisse, 180
  brook trout, to fry, 190
  caper sauce for, 172
  carp
    to bake, 179
    to dress a brace, 178
  catfish soup, 180
  chowder, 166
  cod
    cakes, 169
    Celia's success, 169
    salt, stewed, 227
    sauced over with oyster sauce, 168
  eels
    to broil, 176
    fried, 176
  egg sauce for, 167
  to fry, 166
  haddock
    baked, 170

Fish (*continued*)
  stuffed, 167
  halibut
    baked, 170
    St. Laurent, 160
  herring
    broiled, 174
    salad, 174
    to smoke, 175
  lobster sauce for, 157
  mackerel, 173
    to bake, 173
    with black butter, 173
  moultee (Indian), 165
  pike, 178
    to dress, 178
  salmon
    to bake, 139
    to boil, 139
    to broil, 139
    collared, 139
    dried, 140
    à la St. Marcel, 140
    spiced, 140
  salt fish
    mock oyster stew, 227
    soufflé, 227
    stewed cod, 227
  sauce for cold meat, salad, fish, 165
  sauce tartare, 165
  shad
    baked, 114
    planked, 115
    roes, fried, 115
      scalloped, 115
    with sorrel, 114
    spiced, 115
  shrimp sauce for, 159
  small, in a crust, 167
  smelts, 175
  soles
    fillets, with custard or tomato, 171
    aux fines herbes, 171
    a fricassee of, 171
    small, or slips, 171
  sour sauce for, 155
  stock, 181
  sturgeon, 173
  trout
    to bake, 177
    to boil, Isaac Walton's receipt, 177
    to fry, 176

Fish (*continued*)
pickled, 177
turbot, 172
the new French fashion, 172
whitefish baked in custard or tomato,
171
whiting, 175
Five threes sherbet, 200
Flannel cakes, 74
Flemish sauce, beef, 437
Floating island, 254
Foamy sauce, pudding, 395
Fondue
Brillat-Savarin, 111
with Stilton, 112
Forcemeat, 120; *see also* Stuffing(s)
balls for soup, 124
mushroom, 249
veal, 124
Forefather's Day succotash, 430
Fowls, *see* Chicken
Freezing, 35
French beans, *à la mâitre d'hôtel*, 239
French bread, 48
French mustard, 238
French rolls (beef), 342
French rolls (bread), 64
French way of dressing cold beet-root,
219
Fricandeau of veal, 118
Fricassee
brown chicken, 267
chicken, 267
of frog, white, 261
rabbit, 297
of soles, 171
Fried cream, 104
Fried pone, 63
Fried sweet corn, 220
Frittadella, 351
Fritters
apple, 310
banana, 210
batter for, 73
cream, 73
eggplant, 246
parsnip, 327
peach, 253
Frog
à l'Espagnole, 261
with gumbo, 261
a white fricassee, 261

Fruit; *see also names of specific fruits*
ambrosia, 97
cabinet pudding, 96
candied, 256, 430
ice creams, 198–200
macedoine of fruit, 98
sherbets, 198–200
Frying, 20

Galantine of turkey, 391
Game birds, mostly October; *see also*
Duck(s); Goose; Turkey
Canvasback duck, to roast, 295
grouse
to roast, 301, 302
à la Sam Ward, 303
New Zealand mode of cooking, 305
partridge
pie, 302
to roast, 301
sausages, 302
to stew, 302
pheasants
to roast, 300, 301
stewed with cabbage, 301
pigeons
with peas, 304
pies, 305
stuffed with parsley, 304
quail, to roast, 301
snipes, to roast, 304
wild ducks, to roast, 294
woodcocks, to roast, 304
Garlick vinegar, 445
Gelatines, *see* Jellies
Gentlemen's favorite, 415
German oyster soup, 346
Gherkin sauce, 341
Ginger, mock, 213
Ginger, rhubarb, 144
Ginger beer, 444
Ginger bread
soft molasses, 417
superior, 424
Ginger essence, 443
Ginger plum cake, 418
Ginger pop, 444
Ginger pound cake, 408
Glaze, 438
Gombo
with frogs, 261

Gombo (*continued*)
  powder, 260
  sassafras, 271
Goose, mostly October
  apple stuffing for, 293
  Christmas pie, 431
  pie, 292
  preserved, for farm or country, 292
  roast, 291
  sourcrout, Bavarian way, 324
  stuffing for, 291
Gooseberries, *see* Berries
Gourd (squash) soup, 244
Graham
  biscuit, 69
  bread, 53
    without fine flour, 53
  quick bread, 61
Grandmother Don's
  lemon cake, 403
  sweet milk chocolate cake, 409
Grandmother Weaver's tomato preserves, 283
Grape(s), mostly September
  in brandy, 288
  jelly, 208, 288
  pie, 256
  to preserve, 288
  sherbet, 288
  white, salad, 289
Gravies, *see* Stock
Green beans, *see* Beans
Green corn, *see* Corn
Green currant pie, 194
Green grape pie, 256
Green peas, *see* Peas
Green pickle, 236
Green tomato pickle, 233, 238, 282, 320, 321
Green tomato pie, 321
Griddle cakes, 75; *see also* Pancakes
Grouse, *see* Game birds
Guava, mostly May
  jelly, 153
  marmalade, 153
  whip, 153
Gumbo, *see* Gombo

Haddock, *see* Fish
Haggis, to make, 368
Ha-ha (taro), 154

Halibut, *see* Fish
Ham, *see* Pork
Hard sauce, 398
Hard soap, 446, 447
Hare, *see* Rabbit
Haricot beans, 79
Haricot mutton, 364
Hash
  beef kidney, 357
  bimbo, 216
  vegetable, 348
Haslet sauce, roast pig, 370
Hasty pudding, 90
Hermits, 425
Herring, *see* Fish
Hessian soup, 356
Hickory nut
  macaroons, 335
  pudding, 335
Hoe cakes, 62
Hollandaise sauce, 165
Hominy, 81
  browned for breakfast, 81
  cakes, 76
Honey
  tomata, 283
  vinegar, 445
  wine (mead), 259, 260
Honey cakes, 425
Hopping john, 84
Hop yeast, 57
Horseradish, 118
  sauce for roast, 340
Hotch potch, 187
Hot cross buns, 131

Ice cream, Ices, mostly June
  almond, 198
  apricot, 199
  baked apple, 198
  banana, 198
  brown bread, 198
  cherry, 203
  chocolate, 197
  cocoanut, 198
  coffee, 198
    with condensed milk, 198
  cranberry frappé, 396
  currant water ice, 207
  five threes sherbet, 200
  to freeze without a freezer, 200

Ice cream, Ices (*continued*)
  fruit, 198
  grape sherbet, 288
  lemonade ice, 403
  macaroon, 198
  to make, 36
  maple sugar, 100
  Neapolitan, 197
  orange water ice, 406
  peach water ice, 252
  Philadelphia, 197
  pineapple, 198
  pineapple water ice, 199
  pistachio, 198
  raspberry, 198
  roman punch ice, 200
  rum ice, 199
  snow cream, 85
  strawberry, 198
  tutti frutti, 198
  vanilla, 197
  walnut, 198
Icings, mostly December, 415
  almond icing for bride cake, 184
  apple frosting, 309
  chocolate icing, 416
  pear-fig filling, 417
  rhubarb filling, 144
  a splendid icing, 416
  sugar, for bride cake, 184
  tutti frutti, 416
  white, 415
Imitation Worcestershire sauce, 441
Indian muffins, 68
Indian pilau, 133
Indian pudding
  baked, 396
  steamed, with apples, 308
Infants' dishes, mostly February
  caudle, for a christening, 89
  egg gruel, 90
  farina, 90
  graham hasty pudding, 90
    with rice flour, 90
  porridge, 90
Innards, 125–128, 356–358
Invalids' dishes, mostly February
  barley water, 88
  beef-tea, 86
  chicken jelly, 87
  cooling drink for feverish thirst, 88
  lait de poule, 87

Invalids' dishes (*continued*)
  molasses posset, 88
  oyster toast, 88
  panada, 87
  wine whey, 88
Irish stew, 365
Isaac Walton's (trout) receipt, 177
Italian bread sticks, 63
Italienne, sauce *à l'*, 437

Jam, *see* Preserves
Jaune mange, 405
Jellies
  calf's feet, 128
  chicken, for invalids, 87
  gelatines; *see also* Puddings
    aspic, 272
    orange, 405
    prune with almonds, 84
    tomato aspic, 280
    wine, 98
  spreads; *see also* Preserves
    apple, 311
    cherry and currant, 203
    crabapple, 208
    cranberry, 208
    currant, 208
    grape, 208, 288
    guava, 153
    to make, 28
    mint, for roasts, 191
    quince, 315
Jelly cake, 414
  -fruit cake, 414
  gentlemen's favorite, 415
  Naples biscuit, 415
Jerked beef, 359
Jerusalem artichokes, 328
Johnny cake, 59
  apple, 309
Jugged hare, 299
Jumble-i, 278
Jumbles, 423

Kababs for breakfast, 367
Kaffee kuchen, 55
Kalamazoo pickles, 214
Kid
  dumpokht, 266
  to roast, 138

Kidney(s); *see also* Beef; Lamb; Mutton
  beef
    hash, 357
    stewed, 357
  mutton
    breadcrumbed, 367
    à la Française, 367
    kababs for breakfast, 367
  pigs', 377
Kisses, 426
Kringles, 422

Lait de poule, 87
Lamb, mostly April; *see also* Mutton
  brochette, à la Dumas, 135
  chops à la Maintenon, 135
  curry, asparagus tips, 136
  Indian pilau, 133
  leg, à la Bretonne, 133
  mignons, sauce Béarnaise, 134
  mint jelly for, 191
    sauce for, 132
  pie, hot, 137
    with oysters, 137
  saddle, Russian fashion, 132
  steaks and cucumbers, 135
  stew, 136
Lard, to try, 378
Last end of the garden (pickle), 321
Leeks, mostly October
  cock-a-leekie, 271
  soup, 330
    savory cucumber, 218
Lemon(s), mostly December
  cake, 402
  cheesecake, 403
  crackers, 71
  cream, 402
  cream sauce, chicken, 266
  drop biscuits, 404
  drops, 404
  Grandmother Don's cake, 403
  ice, 403
  pickle, 404
  pudding, 403
  sauce for pudding, 309
  sirup, 404
  superior pie, 401
  syrup, for waffles, 75
  turnovers, 73

Lentil soup, 83
Lettuce
  autumn soup, 189
  dutched, 210
  au maigre, 189
  wilted (dandelion), 148
Lima beans, *see* Beans
Lime pickles, 405
Liver, calf's
  larded, 126
  roasted, 125
  sauté, 125
Lobster, *see* Shellfish
Lobster, mock, 122
Love cakes, 425
Luau (taro), 154

Macaroni, 113
  with fowls, Indian way, 264
  savory, 113
  with sweetbreads, 126
  vegetarian supper, 279
Macaroons, 427
  hickory nut, 335
  ice cream, 198
Macedoine of fruits, 98
Mackerel, *see* Fish
Macon sweet potato pie, 246
Madeira cake, 414
Madeira sauce, 439
Mlle. Jenny Lind's soup, 83
Mangoes, mostly May
  chutney, 151
  custard pie, 150
  green, delicious sauce, 151
  meringue, 150
  and potato, 151
Mango pickle, 237
Maple cream chocolates, 429
Maple sugar
  frozen pudding, 100
  sauce for ice cream, 100
  sauce for pudding, 100
  sugaring off, 100
Marble cake, 409
Marbled veal, 123
Marinade
  beef in a, 343
  for roast meat, 339
Marmalade, *see* Preserves
Maryland beaten biscuit, 69

Mayonnaise
  cream, 190
  oil, 440
Mead, 259, 260
Meat gravy, 354
Meat and potato salad, 352
Meat and vegetable pie, 352
Melons, 247
Melted butter, 107
Mignons of lamb, sauce Béarnaise, 134
Milk, mostly March; *see also* Cheese;
    Cream; Ice Cream, Ices
  bread, 50
  curds and whey, 111
  soup, 102
Milkweed tops, 224
Mincemeat, 399
  Richards', 400
Mint jelly, 119
  sauce for roast, 132
Miss Yandes' rusk, 70
Mrs. Bratty's cheesecake, 109
Mrs. Madison's whim, 417
Mock ginger, 213
Mock lobster, 122
Mock oyster stew, 227
Mock pâté de foie gras, 123
Mock turtle soup, 356
Molasses (cider), 314
Molasses candy, 428
Molasses ginger bread, 417
Molasses pie, 419
Molasses posset, 88
Molasses sauce, apple pudding or dump-
    lings, 307
Muffins, mostly January; *see also* Bis-
    cuits; Rolls
  corn meal pone, 63
  cream tea cakes, 67
  crumpets, 65
  Indian muffins, 68
  Laplanders, 66
  raised, 67
  rice cakes, 65
  rye bread cakes, 54
  sweet potato tea cakes, 247
  velvet cakes, 67
Mullagatawny soup, 130
Mulled cider, 313
Mulled wine, 434
Mushrooms, mostly August, 130
  catsup, 250

Mushrooms (*continued*)
  to dry, 249
  forcemeat balls for soup, 249
  pickled, 235
  to pot, 249
  sauce, brown, 345
    white, 117
  stuffing, lamb à la Maintenon, 135
  wild, 248
Muskmelon, *see* Cantaloupe
Mustard
  French, 441
  pickle, 238
  sauce, 440
Mutton, mostly November; *see also*
    Lamb
  boiled, 363
  China chilo, 366
  chops à la Maintenon, 135
    Soyer's new, 364
  with cucumbers, 135
  cutlets baked, 365
  to dress with oysters, 361
  haggis, to make, 368
  ham, 368
  haricot, 364
  haunch
    to roast, 361
    à la venison, 361
  Irish stew, 365
  kidney
    breadcrumbed, 367
    kababs for breakfast, 367
    rognons, 367
  leg
    with oysters, 361
    port wine sauce for, 362
    ragoo, 364
    roasted, 361
    wine sauce for, 363
  to roast à la vension, 361
  saddle, 362
  sauces for, *see* Sauces
  shoulder, Provincial fashion, 363
  Spanish friceo, 345
  suet dumplings, 363
  turisicus, 366
  venison style, 366

Naples biscuit, 415
Nasturtium
  pickled seed, 259

Nasturtium (*continued*)
  sandwich, 259
  sauce, 259
Neopolitan ice cream, 197
New Year's
  cake, 46
  egg nog, 435
New Zealand mode of cooking birds, 305
Nonpareil corn bread, 60
Number cake, 413
Nuts, mostly October; *see also names of specific nuts*
  salad, 336

Oil mayonnaise, 440
Okra, mostly August
  autumn soup, 284
  creole corn, 223
  to keep, 244
  soup, 243
  stewed with rice, 243
Old-fashioned boiled dinner, 347
Olives, veal (or beef), 120
Olive sauce, duck, 437
Oly koeks, 424
Onions, mostly October, 329
  à la crème, 329
  to dress Spanish, 329
  to dry, 330
  pickled, 331
  sauce
    duck, 293
    mutton, 363
  soup, 330
  stuffed with veal, 123
  vinegar, 331
Orange(s), mostly December
  candied peel, 407
  cream, 402
  jaune mange, 405
  juice and strawberries, 192
  marmalade, 406
  pudding, 405
  and rhubarb, preserve, 144
  salad, 405
  sherbet, 406
  sirup, 404
  water ice, 406
Ornamental froth, blanc mange, 103

Ox-tail soup, 355
Oysters, *see* Shellfish
Oysters, corn, 222

Pain perdu, 98
Panada, 87, 124
Pancakes, mostly January; *see also* Waffles
  buckwheat cake, 75
  fine hominy cakes, 76
  flannel cakes, 74
  griddle cakes, 75
  lemon syrup for, 75
  lemon turnovers, 73
Papaia, mostly May
  Aunt Mary's pudding, 152
  meringue, 152
  pie, 152
Parker House rolls, 64
Parsley-stuffed pigeons, 304
Parsnips, mostly October, 327
  to boil, 327
  fritters, 327
  with sausage, 377
  sugared, 247
Partridge, *see* Game birds
Pastry, mostly January
  cream puffs, 425
  crust for meat pie, 344
  crust for venison pasty, 387
  noodles for soup, 78
  plain paste, 77
  potato paste, 78
  puff paste, 76, 77
  tart paste, 78
  vol-au-vent, 143
Pasty, venison, 387
Pâté
  chicken, 269
  mock, de foie gras, 123
  de veau, 122
Peach(es), mostly August
  in brandy, 254
  butter, 255
  candied, 256
  custard, peach-leaf, 254
  dried, sauce for game, 385
  to dry, 256
  fried, with pork, 372
  fritters, 253
  leather, 255

Peach(es) (*continued*)
marmalade, 255
meringue, 252
to pickle, 233, 236
pie, 252
to preserve, 254
pudding, 253
water ice, 252
Peanut
candy, 430
soup, 335
Pear(s), mostly September
baked, 287
chips, 287
compote of, 286
-fig filling for cakes, 417
like mangoes, 151
marmalade, 287
Peas, mostly June, 184
autumn soup, 189
with bacon, 185
cream of, soup, 186
dried
red-eyes, hopping john, 84
and pork, pudding, 375
to dry, 186
with duck, stewed, 295
hotch potch, 187
with pigeon, 304
pudding, 185
soup, 185
timbale, for soup, 186
Pepper(s), mostly August
pickled, 234
with cabbage, 233
sauce, 242
stewed, 241
stuffed, 241, 242
with cauliflower, 242
with oysters, 242
with veal, 120
vinegar, 444
Peppermint drops, 430
Pheasants, *see* Game birds
Philadelphia ice cream, 197
Pickles, for July, August, September,
October; *see also* Catsup; Vinegar
beets, 220
cabbage with peppers, 233
cantaloupe, 236
cauliflower, 236

Pickles (*continued*)
chow chow, 214
cucumber, 213–215, 236, 238, 320,
321
East India, 237
eggs, 235
fish, 115, 140, 177
French, 238
French beans and radish pods, 234
green, 236
green beans, 234
Kalamazoo, 214
last end of the garden, 321
lemon, 404
lime, 405
mackerel, 177
to make, 30
mangoes (cantaloupe), 237
mincemeat, 399, 400
mock ginger (watermelon), 213
mushrooms, 235
mustard, 238
nasturtium, 259
onions, 331
oysters and clams, 163, 277
peaches, 233, 236
peppers, 234
with cabbage, 233
pine-apple, 215
plums, like olives, 233
pork, 381
salmon, spiced, 140, 177
seven year, 214
shad, spiced, 115
Southern yellow, 236
spiced apples, 311
spiced crabapples, 257
sweet, 236
tomatoes
green, 233, 238, 282, 320, 321
ripe, 282, 283
trout, 177
unique preserves, 213
walnuts, 194
watermelon ring, 212, 213, 237
Pies; *see also* Pastry
apple, 306
custard, 307
meringue, 306
blueberry, 210
cherry, 202
chess, 419
cranberry, 395

Pies (*continued*)
  elderberry, 257
  gooseberry *vol-au-vent*, 206
  green currant or gooseberry, 194
  green grape, 256
  green tomato, 321
  lemon, superior, 401
  mango custard, 150
  meat pies
    beefsteak and oyster, 344
    Cheshire pork, 376
    goose, 292; Christmas, 431
    hare or rabbit, 299
    hot lamb, 137
      lamb with oysters, 137
    partridge, 302
    pigeon, 305
    shrimp, 159
    sweetbreads and oyster, 126
    veal, 122
    and vegetable, 353
    vension, 386
  mince, 399, 400
  molasses, 419
  papaia, 152
  peach, 252
  pumpkin or squash, 332
  raspberry, French, 204
  rhubarb, 143
  strawberry, 193
  sweet potato, 246
  tomato, 280
Pigeons, *see* Game birds
Pigs, suckling, *see* Pork
Pigs in blankets, 275
Pigs' kidneys, *see* Pork
Pike, *see* Fish
Pilau, Indian, 133
Pineapple
  ice cream, 198
  pickle, 215
  water ice, 199
Piquante sauce, 436
Pistachio ice cream, 198
Plain loaf cake, 413
Planked shad, 115
Plantains, Charleston mode, 211
Plum ginger cake, 418
  very rich cake, 419
Plums, mostly September
  dry, beverage, 84
  to pickle like olives, 233

Plums (*continued*)
  pudding, 432, 433
    sauce for, 96, 99, 398, 433
Poivrade sauce, 436
Poke, 149
Pone, corn meal, 63
Pork, mostly November
  bacon
    with beans, 239
    cabbage, 376
  Cheshire pork pie, 376
  cutlets, 372
  with fried peaches, 372
  ham
    baked, 374
    barbecued, 374
    boiled, 374
    Christmas, 432
    to cure, 381
    dumplings, 375
    roast, 373
    Schneller's, 382
    shrivelled, 375
    Virginia, 383
    Westphalia, 384
  hominy and pickled pork, 81
  kidneys, pigs', 377
  lard, 378
  leg, to roast, 368
  loin
    Normandy fashion, 371
    and oysters, 372
    to roast, 371
    tenderloin, fried apples, 371
  and peas pudding, 375
  to pickle, 381
  sausage, 378–380
    black pudding, 380
    with parsnips, 377
    pilau, 133
    Spanish or Portuguese, 380
    university receipt, 379
  scrapple, 380
  Spanish friceo, 345
  spare ribs, 373
  steaks, 372
  stew, 375, 376
  suckling pig, 369
    barbecued shoat, 370
    Haslet sauce for, 370
    Philadelphia way, 370
    to scald, 369

Porridge
  bean, 81
  for infants, 90
Port wine negus, 435
Potato(es), mostly October; *see also*
    Sweet potatoes
  biscuit, 68
  bread, 49
    risen with potato yeast, 49
  Celia's success, 169
  dumplings, 318
  à la mâitre d'hôtel, 316
  and mango (or pear), 151
  -oyster balls, 276
  paste, 78
  to preserve from frost, 320
  puffed, 318
  rissoles, 317
  rolls, 66
  salad, 318, 319
    and meat, 352
  Saratoga chips, 317
  soufflé, 317
  soup, 319
Potted
  beef, 359
  cheese, 110
  mushrooms, 249
  shellfish, 157
  venison, 388
Pound cake, 412
Preserves (jam); *see also* Jellies
  apple butter, 311
  blackberry, 206
  black butter, 202
  cherry, 203
  fig marmalade, 258
  guava marmalade, 153
  to make, 29
  orange marmalade, 406
  peach
    butter, 255
    marmalade, 255
  pear chips, 287
  pear marmalade, 287
  pumpkin, 333
  quince, 316
    marmalade, 315
  raspberry, 205
  rhubarb ginger, 144
  rhubarb and orange, 144

Preserves (jam) (*continued*)
  strawberry, 193
  tomata honey, 283
  tomato, 283
Preserving foods; *see also* Pickles, Pre-
    serves
  apples
    to dry, 312
    to preserve, 311
  beef, *see* Beef
  butter, 107
  cream, 105
  to dry corn, 223
  eggs, 232
  elderberries for pie, 257
  elderberry sirup, 257
  fruit, candied, 256
  goose, 292
  gooseberries, 207
  grapes, 288
  ham, *see* Pork
  hare, jugged, 299
  herbs, to dry, 224
  to keep cider sweet, 313
  mincemeat, 399, 400
  mushrooms
    dried, 249
    potted, 249
  mutton, *see* Mutton
  onions, to dry, 330
  orange peel candied, 407
  orange sirup, 404
  peaches, to dry, 256
  peach leather, 255
  pork, *see* Pork
  to pot cheese, 110
  potatoes, from frost, 320
  salmon, to dry, 141
  smoked herring, 175
  strawberries in wine, 193
  tomatoes, 282
  venison potted, 388
Primrose wine, 151
Prune jelly with almonds, 84; *see also*
    Dried fruit
Pudding(s), many in February; *see also*
    Jellies
  almond, 97, 334
  ambrosia, 97
  Amherst, 307
  apple, 307
  banana, 210

Pudding(s) (*continued*)
Bavarian cream, 92
berry, 201
blanc mange, 107
blueberry, 209
brandy, 92
burnt cream, 103
cabinet, 96
caramel, 93, 94
carrot, 284
Charlotte Russe, 97
chartreuse of apple, 307
chestnut, 334
cherry, 202
chicken, 268
Chinese rice, 96
chocolate, 91
citron, 99
coffee, 92
corn, 221
cranberry, 395
   snow, 396
   surprise, 396
curds and whey, 111
custard, 94
   chocolate, 94
   fig, 95
   peach-leaf, 254
dish of snow, 105
floating island, 254
fried cream, 104
fruit-bread, 398
gooseberry fool, 206
hasty, 90
hickory nut, 334
Indian, baked, 396
Indian, steamed with apples, 308
jaune mange, 405
lemon, 402
   cream, 402
macedoine of fruits, 98
to make, 26
orange, 405
pain perdu, 98
papaia, 152
peach, 253
   meringue, 252
peas, 185
   and pork, 375
plum, 432, 433
pumpkin, 332
quaking, 99

Pudding(s) (*continued*)
raspberry, 205
   sauce for, 205
rennet, 95
rice, 95
royal diplomatic, 98
sauces for, *see* Sauces
snow, 85
sweet potato, 247
a trifle, 104
tapioca, 99
   apple, 308
Turkish, 96
velvet cream, 93
wine, 92
Yorkshire, 339
Puff paste, 76, 77
Pumpkin(s), mostly October
bread, 333
pie, 332
to preserve, 333
pudding, 332
Punch, 434

Quaking pudding, 99
Queen cake, 409
Quinces, mostly October
   baked, 308, 315
   cheese, 316
   jelly, 315
   marmalade, 315
   preserved, 316

Rabbit, mostly October
   or duck, to boil, 296
   dumpokht, 266
   to fricassee, 297
   jugged hare, 299
   pie, 299
   to roast, 296, 297
      like kid, 138
   sauces for, 297
   soup
      hare, 298
      à la reine, 298
   stuffing for, 390
Radishes
   pods pickled, 234
   ways of cooking, 191
Ragoo, leg of mutton, 364
Ragout of beef à la mode, 350

Raised brown bread, 54
Raised waffles, 74
Ramakins, 112
Raspberries, *see* Berries
Réchaufé of roast, 352
Red beans with burgundy, 80
Red cabbage, 322
Red-eyed peas, hopping john, 84
Remedies, 86–88
Rennet
  custards, 95
  to make, 128
Rhubarb, mostly May
  dyspepsia cure, 456
  filling for cakes, 144
  ginger, 144
  and orange preserve, 144
  pie, 143
  sweet *vol-au-vent*, 143
  wine, 145
Rice
  Beaufort bread, 55
  bread, 61
  cakes, 65
  chicken baked in, 268
  hopping john, 84
  Indian pilau, 133
  jumble-i, 278
  pudding, 95
    Chinese, 66
    à la Ristori, 323
  St. John's round bread, 65
  stewed with okra, 243
Rich brown gravy soup, 355
Rich plum cake, 419
Rich plum pudding, 432
Rich veal soup, 129
Richards' mincemeat, 400
Rissoles
  beef, 348
  potato, 317
Roasting, 18
Robert sauce, steak, 341, 437
Rock Cornish game hens, *see* Game
  birds
Roe, *see* Fish
Rognons de mouton à la française, 367
Rolls, mostly January; *see also* Biscuits;
  Muffins
  caraway buns, 66
  French, 64
  hot cross buns, 131

Rolls (*continued*)
  Parker House, 64
  potato, 66
  Vienna bread, 63
Roman punch ice, 200
Rose
  brandy, 195
  butter, 195
  water, 540
Royal diplomatic pudding, 98
Rum ice, 199
Rusk, 70
Russian salad, 240
Rutgers rolletjes, 351

Sage cheese, to make, 110
St. John's rice round bread, 65
Salad
  alligator pear, 190
  apple and watercress, 147
  Baybury, 188
  beet, 219
  boiled dressing, 190
  cream mayonnaise, 190
  cucumbers and dill, 218
  dandelion, 148
  dressings, *see* Dressings
  family French (meat), 352
  grape, white, 289
  herring, 174
  lobster, 156
  meat and potato, 352
  nut, 336
  oil mayonnaise, 440
  orange, 405
  oyster, 275
  potato, 318, 319
  Russian, 240
  shrimp, 158
  spring, 147
  stock for dressing, 190
  strawberry, 192
    and currant, 192
  Sydney Smith's receipt (chicken),
    270
  tomato, 279
Sally Lunn, 60, 61
Salmi of wild duck, 295
Salmon, *see* Fish
Salsify, 328
Salt fish, *see* Fish

Salt-rising bread, 52
Sand tarts, 421
Saratoga potato chips, 317
Sassafras
  gombo, 271
  powder, 260
Sauces; *see also* Catsup; Vinegar
  apple, 305
  for beef
    anchovy, 341, 347
    Béarnaise, 134
    brown mushroom, 345
    brown stock and variations, 436
    cauliflower, corned beef, 325
    chaud-froid, 392
    Espagnole, 439
    Flemish, 437
    gherkin, 341
    horseradish, 340
    à l'Italienne, 437
    Madeira, 439
    marinade, 339
    piquante, 340, 436
    poivrade, 436
    Robert, 341, 437
    shalot, 347
    sorrel, 189
    tartare, 165
    tomato, 281
  brown, and variations, 436
  for cakes and puddings
    blueberry, 210
    boiled custard, 94
      chocolate, 94
    brandy, 99, 433
    caramel, 93
    champagne, 440
    cherry, 202
    Devonshire, 105
    foamy, 395
    hard, 398
    for hickory nut pudding, 335
    lemon, 309
    mango, 151
    maple sugar, 100
    molasses, 307
    ornamental froth, 103
    plum pudding, 96, 99, 398, 433
    raspberry, 205
    soft, 96
    sour cream, 201
    strawberry, 194

Sauces (*continued*)
    wine, 96, 99, 398, 433
  cranberry, 394
  for eggs and vegetables
    brown, and variations, 436
    burnt butter, 165
    cream mayonnaise, 190
    Espagnole, 439
    Hollandaise, 165
    mustard, 440
    oil mayonnaise, 440
    tomato, 281
  Espagnole sauce, 439
  for fish
    Allemande, 168
    Beyrout, 170
    black butter, 173
    burnt butter, 165
    caper, 172
    for cold fish, 165
    cream, 155
    cucumber, white, 217
    egg, 167
    elderberry catsup, 258
    Espagnole, 439
    Flemish, 437
    gooseberry, 207
    Hollandaise, 165
    à l'Italienne, 437
    lobster, 157
    for lobster, 157
    Madeira, 439
    mâitre d'hôtel, 108
    oyster, 167, 169, 277
    piquante, 340, 436
    shrimp, 159
    sour, 155
    tartare, 165
    tomato, 281
    white, 438
  French mustard, 441
  for game
    anchovy, 341, 347
    bread, 300
    chaud-froid, 392
    Cumberland, 437
    currant jelly, 208
      sauce, 209
    different sorts, hare, 297
    dried peach, 385
    gooseberry, 207
    onion, 293

[498]

Sauces (*continued*)
  shalot, 347
  for wild fowl, 303
  wine, 363
  mayonnaise
    cream, 190
    oil, 440
  mustard sauce, 440
  for mutton and lamb
    Béarnaise, 134
    cauliflower, 325
    Colbert, 135
    Cumberland, 437
    currant, 209
    Espagnole, 439
    Madeira, 439
    mint, 132
      jelly, 191
    nasturtium, 259
    onion, 363
    piquante, 340, 436
    port wine, 363
    tomato, 281
    wine, 363
  pepper sauce, 242
  for pork
    apple, 305
    celery, 391
    currant jelly, 208
    gherkin, 341
    Haslet, 370
    mustard, 440
    Philadelphia, 370
    Robert, 437
    tomato, 281
  for poultry
    Beyrout, 170
    bread, 300
    celery, 391
    chaud-froid, 392
    chestnut, 391
    cucumber, 217
    Hollandaise, 165
    lemon cream, 266
    olive, for duck, 437
    onion, for duck, 293
    oyster, 167, 169, 277
    tartare, 165
    for wild fowls, 303
  Scotch sauce, 441
  soy sauce, 441
  spaghetti sauce, 281

Sauces (*continued*)
  store sauce, 442
  for veal
    brown cucumber, 117
    horseradish, 118, 340
    Madeira, 439
    piquante, 340, 436
    tomato, 281
    velouté, 439
    white, 438
    white cucumber, 217
    white mushroom, 117
    Worcestershire, imitation, 441
Sausage; *see also* Pork
  chicken or partridge, 302
  oyster, 125
  pilau, 134
  sourcrout Bavarian way, 324
  stuffing for turkey, 389
  with turkey, 392
Sautéing, 21
Savory cucumber soup, 218
Savory macaroni, 113
Savoy cakes, 422
Scalloped oysters (or clams), 275
Scalloped turkey (or chicken), 393
Scallops, *see* Shellfish
Schneller's cure for ham, 382
Scotch cakes, 421
Scotch sauce, 441
Scotch short bread, 421
Scrapple, 380
Seed biscuits, 420
Seven year pickle, 214
Shad, *see* Fish
Shalot sauce, meat, 347
Shellfish, mostly May
  clams
    chowder, 162–163
    deviled, 162
    pickled, 163
    scalloped, 275
    stuffed, 161
  crabs
    to boil, 159
    fricassee of, 160
    hot, 160
    St. Laurent, 160
    soup, 161
  lobster
    to boil, 155
    cream sauce, 155

Shellfish (*continued*)
cutlet, 155
hotch potch, 187
potted, 157
salad, cream dressing, 156
sauce, for fish, 157
à la crème, 157
soup, 156
sour sauce for, 155
oysters
à l'Alexandre Dumas, 274
and beefsteak pie, 344
deviled, 274
and fried chicken, 263
German oyster soup, 346
gombo, sassafras, 271
kababs for breakfast, 367
and lamb pie, 137
and leg of mutton, 361
loaf, 276
mock, 227
omelet, 229
patties, 277
peppers stuffed with, 242
pickled, 163, 277
pigs in blankets, 275
with pork, 372
potato balls, 276
roasted, 274
salad, 275
sauce for
baked fish, 167
cod, 169
lobster, turkey, 277, 393
sausage, 125
scalloped, 275
smothered, 275
soup, 276
stuffing for
baked fish, 167
carp, 178
turkey, 389
and sweetbreads, pie, 126
toast, for invalids, 88
with turkey, 389
scallops, to stew, 163
shrimp
to boil, 158
pie, 159
to pot, 157
salad, 158

Shellfish (*continued*)
sauce for fish, 159
to sauté, 158
Sherbet, *see* Ice cream, Ices
Sherry, to make English, 443
Shoat, to barbecue, 370
Shortcake, cream, 68; *see also specific fruit*
Shrimp, *see* Shellfish
Shrivelled ham, 375
Shrub
cherry, 204
raspberry, 205
Simnel, to make, 413
Sirup; *see also* Shrub
blackberry, 454
elderberry, 257
lemon or orange, 404
Six months' cake, 418
Slips or small soles, 171
Small seed cakes, 420
Smelts, *see* Fish
Snipe, *see* Game birds
Snow cream, 85
Soap
bayberry, 447
hard, 446, 447
soft, 448
Windsor, 448
Soda biscuit, 69
Soft sauce, cake or pudding, 96
Soft soap, 448
Sole, *see* Fish
Sorrel, mostly June
autumn soup, 189
chiffonade, 188
au maigre, 189
sauce for roast, 189
with shad, 114
in soup *de l'asperge*, 146
Soufflé
potato, 317
salt fish, 227
Soup; *see also* Stock
asparagus, 146, 186
autumn, 189, 284
barley broth, 83
beef-tea, 86
black bean, 82
bouillabaisse, 180
bouilli, 346
brown turkey, 394

Soup (*continued*)
  cabbage, 324
  catfish, 180
  celery, 186
  chestnut, 334
  chicken, 87
  chowder
    clam, 162–163
    corn, 222
    fish, 166
  cock-a-leekie, 271
  common carrot, 284
  crab, 161
  cream of asparagus, celery, corn, green pea, spinach, or string bean, 186
  crème de riz, 129
  cucumber, 218
  egg balls for, 231
  forcemeat balls for, 124
  German oyster, 346
  green corn soup, 222
  hare, 298
  Hessian, 356
  hotch potch, 187
  lait de poule, 87
  leek or onion, 330
  lentil, 83
  lobster, 156
  Mlle. Jenny Lind's, 83
  milk, 102
  mock oyster stew, 227
  mock turtle, 356
  mullagatawny, 130
  mushroom forcemeat balls, 249
  noodles for, 78
  okra, 243
  onion, 330
  ox-tail, 355
  oyster, 276
  pea, 185
    cream of, 186
    timbale for, 186
  peanut, 335
  porridge, 81
  potato, 319
  rabbit, 298
  rich brown gravy, 355
  rich veal, 129
  sassafras gombo, 271
  spinach, 186
  tomato, 280, 281

Soup (*continued*)
  turkey, 394
  turtle, 225
  vegetable, 245
  vension, 388
Sour apples, fried, 371
Sour beer vinegar, 445
Sour cream sauce, fruit, 201
Sour dough, 56
Sour eggs, German style, 229
Sourcrout, Bavarian way, 324
Sour krout, to make, 324
Sour milk brown bread, 58
Sour sauce, lobster or fish, 155
Southern yellow pickle, 236
Soyer's new mutton chop, 364
Soyer's stock for all kinds of soup, 130
Soy sauce, 441
Spaghetti sauce, 281
Spanish friceo, 345
Spanish sausage, 380
Spare rib, *see* Pork
Spiced apples, 311
Spiced cherries, currants, gooseberries, 209
Spiced crabapples, 257
Spiced round, 350
Spinach, mostly June
  Baybury salad, 188
  beignets of, 188
  chartreuse of, 188
  with cream, 187
  soup, cream of, 186
Splendid icing, 416
Sponge cake, 407
Spring salad, 147
Spruce beer, 444
Squash, mostly August
  bread, 333
  gourd soup, 244
  pie, 332
  summer, 244
  vegetable marrow, 244
  winter, 331
Squirrel, Brunswick stew, 299; *see also* Chicken
Stew
  beef, 343
  Brunswick, 299
  Irish, 365
  lamb, 136
  mock oyster, 227

Stew (*continued*)
  pork, 375, 376
  veal, 121
Stewing, 21
Stock; *see also* Soup
  brown, 353
  to clarify, 354
  fish, 181
  gravy, 354
  for salad dressings, 190
  Soyer's, 130
  white, 131, 438
Store sauce, 442
Strawberries, *see* Berries
String beans, *see* Beans
Stuffed eggs, 231
  Mrs. G's, 230
Stuffing(s); *see also* Forcemeat
  apple, for goose or duck, 293
  for baked fish, 167, 178
  chestnut, for turkey, 390
  for cucumbers, 217
  for duck, 294
  for game birds, 300, 302, 304
  for goose, 291, 293
  for hare or rabbit, 390
  oyster, 167, 169, 393
  for peppers, 241–242
  for roast pig, 370
  for rump steak, 342
Sturgeon, *see* Fish
Succotash, 80, 241, 430
Suckling pig, *see* Pork
Suet dumplings, 363
Sugar or honey vinegar, 445
Summer squash, 244
Superior lemon pie, 401
Sweetbreads, *see* Veal
Sweet potato(es), mostly August
  cakes, 247
  Macon pie, 246
  pudding, 247
  sugared, 247
Sydney Smith's receipt, 270
Syllabub, 434
Syrup, 75, 454; *see also* Sirup

Tamarind chutney, 153
Tapioca pudding, 99
  and apple, 308
Taro

Taro (*continued*)
  baked, 154
  ha-ha, 154
  fried, 154
  luau, 154
Tartare sauce, fish or chicken, 165
Tart paste, 78
Tea
  beef, 86
  cranberry, 396
Thanksgiving tea cake, 399
Thirded bread, 51
Timbale for soup, 186
Tipsy cake, 408
Toast
  egg, 230
  oyster, 88
Tomatoes, mostly September
  aspic, 280
  baked
    with eggs, 229
    with whitefish, 171
  chutney, 282
  deviled, 278
  to dress, 278
  Egyptian, 279
  forced, 278
  green, pickled, 233, 238, 282, 320, 321
  honey, 283
  juice, 280
  jumble-i, 278
  ketchup, 282
  pickled, 238, 282, 283, 320, 321
  pie, 280, 321
  preserved (jam), 283
  preserved (paste), 282
  preserved (relish), 283
  salad, 279
  sauce, 281
  soup, 280, 281
  spaghetti sauce, 281
  vegetarian supper, 279
Tongue, *see* Beef
Trifle, 104
Trifles, 422
Tripe, *see* Beef
Trout, *see* Fish
Turbot, *see* Fish
Turisicus, 366
Turkey, mostly November
  boiled, 392

Turkey (*continued*)
    oyster sauce for, 393
  bread sauce for, 300
  brown soup, 394
  celery sauce for, 391
  with chestnuts, 390
  galantine, chaud-froid sauce, 391
  to roast, 389
    with chestnuts, 390
    the genteel way, 390
    with sausage, 392
  scallop, 393
  stuffing for, 389–390
  Sydney Smith's receipt for salad, 270
Turkish pudding, 96
Turnips, mostly October, 326
  duck à l'aubergiste, 294
  with duckling, 295
  glazed, with gravy, 326
Turnovers, lemon, 73
Turnpike cakes, 58
Turtle, mostly July
  to dress, 224
  soup, 225
    mock, 356
Tutti frutti ice cream, 199
Tutti frutti icing, 416

Unique preserve, 213

Vanilla
  caramels, 429
  ice cream, 197
Veal, mostly April
  blanquette, 121
  breast of, to roll, 118
  brown cucumber sauce for, 117
  calf's brains, 127
    with black butter, 127
    marinade of, 127
  calf's feet jelly, 128
  calf's liver
    larded, 126
    roasted, 125
    sauté, 125
  crème de riz (soup), 129
  cutlets, 119
    and tomatoes, 119
  escalops
    à la chicoree, 119
    with stuffed peppers, 120

Veal (*continued*)
  forcemeat, 124
  fricandeau of, 118
  horseradish for, 118
  loin or neck, roasted, 117
  marbled, 123
  mock lobster, 122
  mock pâté de foie gras, 123
  mock turtle soup, 356
  mullagatawny soup, 130
  mushroom sauce, white, 117
  olives, 120
  onions stuffed with, 123
  oyster sausage, 125
  pâté de veau, 122
  pie, 122
  rennet, 128
  rich veal soup, 129
  to roast, 116
  savory dish of, 120
  Soyer's stock, 130
  stuffing for beef heart, 127
  sweetbreads and oysters, delicate pie,
    126
  to prepare, 126
  white stock, 131
Vegetable hash, 348
Vegetable marrow, *see* Squash
Vegetable and meat pie, 353
Vegetable soup, 245
Vegetarian supper, 279
Velouté, sauce, 439
Velvet cakes, 67
Velvet cream, 93
Venison, mostly November
  dried peach sauce for, 385
  ham, 387
  haunch of, 385
  pasty, 386
  potted, 388
  sausage, 388
  shoulder, 385
  soup, 388
  steaks, 386
  wine sauce for, 363
Very rich cookies, 424
Vienna bread, 63
Vinegar
  celery, 286
  cider, 314
  cucumber, 215
  garlick, 445

Vinegar (*continued*)
  honey or sugar, 445
  onion, 331
  pepper, 445
  sour beer, 445
  walnut, 251
Virginia chicken pudding, 268
Virginia hams, to cure, 383
Vol-au-vent, 143

Waffles
  of Flatbush, 74
  raised, 74
  syrup for, 75
Walnut(s), mostly October
  candy, 429
  catsup, 251
  ice cream, 198
  pickled, 194
  vinegar, 251
Washington cake, 398
Watercress, mostly May
  and apples, 147
  spring salad, 147
  stewed, 147
Watermelon rind pickle, 212, 237
  mock ginger, 213
Wedding cake, 182
Welsh rarebit, 112
Westphalia ham, 384
Wheat and Indian bread, 52
Whitefish, *see* Fish
White haricot beans, 78, 80
White icing for cakes, 415
White mountain flannel cake, 74

White sauce, 438
White stock, 131, 438
White wine fillip, 434
Whitings, *see* Fish
Wild duck, *see* Game birds
Wilted dandelions, 148
Wine
  apple, 313
  blackberry, 206
  currant, 209
  good elderberry, 258
  English sherry, 443
  excellent family, 202
  to make, 37
  mead, 259, 260
  mulled, 434
  primrose, 151
  rhubarb, 145
  strawberries preserved in, 193
Wine cakes, 421
Wine cream, 92
Wine jelly, 98
Wine negus, 435
Wine sauce
  mutton or venison, 363
  puddings, cakes, 96, 99, 398, 433
Wine whey, 88
Winter squash, 331
Winter succotash, 80
Woodcocks, 304
Worcestershire sauce, imitation, 441

Yeast, 56–58
Yorkshire pudding, 339

1 wineglass = ¼ cup
1 gill = ½ cup
1 teacup = a scant ¾ cup
1 coffee cup = 1 scant cup
1 tumbler = 1 cup
1 pint = 2 cups
1 quart = 4 cups
1 peck = 2 gallons (dry)

1 pinch = what can be picked up between the thumb and first two fingers
½ pinch = what can be picked up between the thumb and one finger
1 saltspoon = ¼ teaspoon
1 teaspoon = 1 teaspoon or 1 kitchen teaspoon
1 dessertspoon = 2 teaspoons or 1 soupspoon
1 spoonful = 1 tablespoon, more or less

"A pint's a pound the world around" for liquids, shortening, chopped meat packed down hard, granulated sugar and salt, mashed potatoes, raw tomatoes.

Butter the size of an egg = ¼ cup or 2 ounces
the size of a walnut = 1 tablespoon
the size of a hazelnut = 1 teaspoon

---

1 pennyweight = 1/20 ounce
1 drachm = ⅛ ounce
1 ounce = 4½ tablespoons of allspice, cinnamon, curry, mustard, paprika
4 tablespoons of cloves, made mustard
3½ tablespoons of nutmeg or pepper
3 tablespoons of sage, cream of tartar, cornstarch
2 tablespoons of salt, or any liquid
1 pound = 2 cups of liquid
4 cups of flour
8 medium-sized eggs with shells
10 eggs without shells
2½ cups of powdered sugar or brown sugar, packed down
4 cups of grated cabbage, cranberries, coffee, chopped celery, cheese
3 cups of corn meal
2 cups of uncooked rice
2¾ cups raisins or dried currants